Klaus Petrus, Markus Wild (eds.)
Animal Minds & Animal Ethics

NB :

ROYAL COLLEGE OF ART
LIBRARY
library@rca.ac.uk
020 7590 4219
This book is due for return on or
before the last date stamped below

-7 MAR 2016

Human-Animal Studies

Klaus Petrus, Markus Wild (eds.)
Animal Minds & Animal Ethics
Connecting Two Separate Fields

[transcript]

Bibliographic information published by the Deutsche Nationalbibliothek
The Deutsche Nationalbibliothek lists this publication in the Deutsche Nationalbibliografie; detailed bibliographic data are available in the Internet at http://dnb.d-nb.de

© 2013 transcript Verlag, Bielefeld

All rights reserved. No part of this book may be reprinted or reproduced or utilized in any form or by any electronic, mechanical, or other means, now known or hereafter invented, including photocopying and recording, or in any information storage or retrieval system, without permission in writing from the publisher.

Cover layout: Kordula Röckenhaus, Bielefeld
Printed by CPI – Clausen & Bosse, Leck
ISBN 978-3-8376-2462-5

Contents

Introduction
Animal Minds and Animal Ethics
Klaus Petrus & Markus Wild | 7

Part One
Animals, Science and the Moral Community

1. Animal Mind
   Science, Philosophy, and Ethics
   Bernard E. Rollin | 15
2. Animal Minds, Cognitive Ethology, and Ethics
   Colin Allen & Marc Bekoff | 37
3. A Form of War
   Animals, Humans, and the Shifting Boundaries of Community
   Justin E.H. Smith | 59
4. Cognition and Community
   Gary Steiner | 83

Part Two
Animal Autonomy and Its Moral Significance

5. Mental Capacities and Animal Ethics
   Hans-Johann Glock | 113
6. The Question of Belief Attribution in Great Apes
   Its Moral Significance and Epistemic Problems
   Robert W. Lurz | 147

7. **Ape Autonomy?**
   Social Norms and Moral Agency in Other Species
   Kristin Andrews | 173
8. **The Nonhuman Roots of Human Morality**
   Evelyn B. Pluhar | 197

Part Three
The Diversity of Animal Ethics

9. **Animal Rights**
   A Non-Consequentialist Approach
   Uriah Kriegel | 231
10. **Taking Sentience Seriously**
    Gary L. Francione | 249
11. **Two Approaches to Animal Ethics and the Case of Great Apes**
    Alessandro Blasimme, Constantine Sandis & Lisa Bortolotti | 269
12. **Personhood, Interaction and Skepticism**
    Elisa Aaltola | 295
13. **Eating and Experimenting on Animals**
    Two Issues in Ethics
    Alice Crary | 321

Contributors | 355

Introduction
Animal Minds and Animal Ethics

Klaus Petrus & Markus Wild

1. BIG ISSUES IN ANIMAL PHILOSOPHY

What may, in very general terms, be called "the animal issue" has drawn wide academic and public attention in the past thirty years. The issues at stake are our (Western) perception of animals, our interaction and involvement with animals, the differences between ourselves and other animals, our moral obligations towards animals, and the practical consequences that a moral standing of animals would have. After the turn of the twenty-first century, animal ethics is very much on the mind of philosophers, ethicists, professionals who use animals, politicians, lawmakers, pet-owners and the general public. A related phenomenon is the explosion of research into the cognitive abilities of animals, as seen in the inspiring work being done on the science of animal cognition and behaviour.

This development has not remained without a direct influence on philosophy, especially regarding not only the philosophy of mind but also moral philosophy. Clearly, the animal issue has engaged philosophers in two related but distinct ways. On the one hand, there has been a growing interest in the question of *animal minds*. Can we attribute mental states to non-human animals? If so, what kinds of mental states? What does the mental life of a non-human animal look like? On the other hand, there also been a growing interest in the question of *animal ethics*. Do we have direct moral obligations towards animals? Do animals have rights? Should states enact strong legal policies with regards to animals? Philosophers working on questions of animal ethics usually draw on research into animal cognition, and subscribe to strong positions regarding animal minds. Philosophers interested in the question of animal minds sometimes draw ethical conclusions from the positions they argue for. In spite of such overlaps, these two areas of research have grown up separately. One reason for this separation stems from the institutional distinction between theoretical and practical philosophy. Philosophers working on ethical questions do not, as a rule, spend a lot of time in the theoretical department, whereas philosophers working on questions of consciousness and mentality are generally not the ones writing about moral issues.

Given this situation, the principal aim of this anthology is to draw links between the philosophy of animal minds and animal ethics. The editors encouraged philosophers working on the philosophy of mind to engage in ethical considerations resulting from their theoretical framework, and they invited philosophers working on animal ethics to elaborate on their views regarding animal minds. The main idea was to build bridges between the fields of animal ethics and the philosophy of animal minds and cognition. Additionally, they encouraged philosophers from both fields to inquire into a third topic, i.e. the question as to whether non-human animals can be considered not only as mindful agents but also as moral or at least as proto-moral—agents. Therefore, besides the contributions on animal ethics and animal minds, this volume includes essays on the topic of *moral behaviour in animals*.

Another observation about current developments in animal ethics and the philosophy of animal minds is the *diversification* of approaches and viewpoints. As some articles in this anthology will show, animal ethics has developed beyond the utility-versus-rights question that dominated the debate into the 1990s, while the philosophy of animal minds has moved out of the naturalistic camp where it was firmly rooted until that decade. In recent years, however, not only have animal ethics and the philosophy of animal minds exhibited a dramatic increase in diversity or breadth of perspectives, the same is also true of research into animal cognition and behaviour.

2. Content of the Volume

2.1 Part One: Animals, Science and the Moral Community

The first part approaches the three big issues mind, ethics and morality—from the perspective of the animal-human-relationship. The most basic relationship for the questions of animal minds and ethics is doubtless natural science. It is the amazing amount of work and progress made in the study of animal cognition that fuels debate on the animal issue. However, scientific relations are neither the only relations between humans and animals, nor even the most deeply rooted. In the course of history, a sense of natural and moral community has been articulated at different times and places. Recent work on animal ethics is merely the culmination of such developments. Of course, the far more salient and dominant aspect in the history of humans and animals is neither a sense of a natural and moral community nor scientific inquiry but utilization, exploitation, ownership, violence and outright extinction.

The four contributions in this part address the following questions: questions: In his article, *Bernard Rollin* examines the interplay between science and ethics. His essay "Animal Mind: Science, Philosophy, and Ethics" illustrates how new findings on animal minds can lead to a gradual change in the attitude of science towards animals. He goes on to show what the impact of this could be on the ethical treatment of animals. Cognitive ethology as an interdisciplinary project is also central to *Colin Allen* and *Marc Bekoff.* Their essay on "Animal Minds, Cognitive Ethology, and Ethics" aims to show that an understanding of cognitive phenomena in animals is essential if such capacities are to form the foundation of scientifically informed ethical reasoning about animals. *Justin E.H. Smith's* "A Form of War: Animals, Humans, and the Shifting Boundaries of Community" shows the long and complex genealogy of the modern conception of moral status, in which humans are supposed to have absolute moral commitment to all other humans while, at the same time, having no properly moral commitments but only indirect ones to the vast majority of other animals. In "Cognition and Community" *Gary Steiner* traces the common notion in Western philosophy that a being's moral status is in some important sense a function of its cognitive abilities. The crux of this way of viewing the comparative moral status of human beings and animals is the idea that the capacities for reason and language are the key to full moral status.

2.2 Part Two: Animal Autonomy and Its Moral Significance

The second part addresses the question of the relationship between animal mentality and animal ethics. Most of the contributors—with the notable exception of Evelyn Pluhar—attack the issue from the perspective of the philosophy of mind. They argue for the core idea that animals are not just convenient subjects for the attribution of mental states and capacities, such as thought, consciousness, agency, mindreading, or empathy but that they possess a mind of their own—an autonomous kind of mind that is not exclusively at the mercy of our interpretative practice. All contributors explicitly address the challenge of moving from animal mental autonomy to animal ethics and animal morals.

Hans-Johann Glock, blending arguments from his numerous articles on animal minds, primarily addresses the first question. In his essay "Mental Concepts and Animal Ethics" he argues that sensation, interests, beliefs and desires, intentional agency and reasoning are applicable to animals for good reasons. Moreover, Glock argues that these mental notions are plausibly connected to various kinds of moral status. Therefore, his contribution relates to the guiding question of animal ethics. The third essay in this section tackles the question concerning mindreading. "The Question of Belief Attribution in Great Apes: Its Moral Significance and Epistemic Problems" by *Robert Lurz*, a leading scholar in the philosophy of animal minds, aims to resolve the longstanding puzzle of how to test belief attribution in apes, and argues that a fundamentally new experimental false-belief test is required—one capable of distinguishing genuine belief-attributing subjects from their perceptual-state attributing and behaviour-reading counterparts. Drawing on her work on the theory of mind in non-human animals, *Kristin Andrews* considers the theory of mind as one capacity that is sometimes thought to be a necessary condition for moral agency. While there is no evidence that great apes have anything like the philosopher's representational concept of belief, there is evidence that great apes have other cognitive capacities that can perform the functions sometimes seen as requirements for moral agency. It is also argued that recognizing social norms drives the development of metacognitive social abilities such as theory of mind. So we should not expect that theory of mind is a necessary condition for moral agency, or so she argues in "Ape Autonomy? Studies in Natural Moral Psychology". In her contribution, "The Non-human Roots of Human Morality," moral philosopher *Evelyn Pluhar* reviews recent empirical findings from cognitive ethology and developmental psychology, and claims that the sentimental roots of a full-blown human morality are present in non-human animals. These roots comprise forms of altruism that transcend kinship and reciprocity as well as forms of empathy that transcend emotional contagion. It is further claimed that non-human animals have a sense of self-awareness and an understanding of agency crucial for pre-moral concern for others. Morality in the demanding sense, however, is the prerequisite of human beings taking a universal point of view.

2.3 Part Three: The Diversity of Animal Ethics

In recent years, the standard utilitarian and deontological approaches to animal ethics have been broadened and amended by alternative moral points of view—the feminist care tradition, virtue ethics, or the capability approach spring to mind. There is, however, more to it, as two pressing questions guide the current debate. Firstly, the very idea of tying moral obligations to mental capacities is criticized by many champions of animal ethics. Why should we look for fancy mental capacities instead of simple sentience? Of course, moral status is still tied to individual animal mentality but an animal does not need to be much of a thinker in order to have a full moral standing. Secondly, the moral individualism of the more traditional forms of animal ethics is challenged. The distinguishing feature of approaches in ethics that count as moral individualism is the claim that a creature calls for specific forms of treatment only insofar as it has individual capacities such as the capacity for suffering or the capacity to direct its own life. However, our moral intuitions do not imply that a human being's moral standing is weakened in the case of "radically cognitively impaired human beings." So, what are the pros and cons of the mental capacity approach, on the one hand, and of the individualistic approach to animal ethics on the other?

In "Animal Rights: A Non-Consequentialist Approach" *Uriah Kriegel* holds an alternative ethical framework—combining Kantian and virtue-ethical elements—against the mainstream consequentialism in discussions of animal rights. The virtuous agent is the one who has the stable disposition to treat all conscious animals as ends instead of mere means. Kriegel is a prominent voice in the contemporary philosophy of consciousness. From this theoretical background, he argues for a principled account of animal consciousness, thereby building a bridge between animal minds (addressing the second question of animal consciousness) and animal ethics. *Gary L. Francione*, is very critical of the idea of adjusting moral standing to mental capacity. In his view, animals do not need any specific cognitive capacities in order to be granted moral status. Instead, he claims that sentience alone is necessary and sufficient for full membership in the moral community. Accordingly, sentient beings should be treated as persons. In contrast, *Lisa Bortolotti, Constantine Sandis* and *Alessandro Blasimme* go into the developments in cognitive ethology and comparative psychology. However, these authors argue that the psychological approach, favoured by Peter Singer, Tom Regan and others, is not exclusive in shaping human attitudes towards non-humans, but that an ethics of care ("vulnerability approach") does so, too. In her article, *Elisa Aaltola* expands on the concept of personhood. Her criticism focuses on the idea that personhood is restricted to human beings because of their mental capacities. In contrast, Aaltola favours an interactive and non-individualistic approach to personhood, according to which it is a dynamic concept that exists outside language, "in the realm of immediacy." Questions of the practical implications of our insights into animal minds are discussed by *Alice Crary* using the example of eating and experimenting on animals. She describes a tenable version of the ethical view of animals that can inform reflection on these issues by addressing some of the very concrete ways in which they arise in the US today.

Acknowledgments

We would like to thank the authors for their readiness to take part in this project. Our special thanks go to Sarah-Jane Conrad and Phil Reynolds. The essays by Bernard E. Rollin and Colin Allen & Marc Bekoff originally appeared in *The Journal of Ethics* in 2007 and are reprinted here with permission. Gary Francione's paper was published originally in the *Journal for Animal Law and Ethics* in 2006 and is reprinted with permission.

Part One
Animals, Science and the Moral Community

1. Animal Mind
Science, Philosophy, and Ethics

Bernard E. Rollin

Given the tendency of 20th century empirically-oriented philosophers and biological and psychological scientists to be agnostic if not downright atheistic about animal mind, it is somewhat surprising to find that their historical ancestors entertained no such reservations. John Locke, for example, responding to Descartes' claim that animals were simply machines, makes patent his belief in their mental lives. Somewhat inconsistently, he allows that they can reason, yet without the ability to abstract. After affirming that perception is indubitably in all animals (Locke 1871, 117), and thus that they have ideas, he asserts that if they have any ideas at all, and are not bare machines, as some Cartesians would have them, we cannot deny they have some reason:

"It seems as evident to me, that they do some of them in certain instances reason, as that they have sense; but it is only in particular ideas, just as they received them from their senses. They are the best of them tied up within those narrow bounds, and have not (as I think) the faculty to enlarge them by any kind of abstraction." (Locke 1871, 127)

In another passage, he mocks those who would assert "that dogs or elephants do not think, when they give all the demonstration of it imaginable, except only telling us that they do so" (Locke 1871, 87).

But it is David Hume who, among empiricists, most unequivocally affirmed the existence of animal thought and mentation. Arguably the greatest skeptic in the history of philosophy, denying the ultimate knowability of mind, body, God, causation, the past or the future, Hume nonetheless extends no doubt to animal mind. In section XIV of the *Treatise*,

"Of the Reason of Animals", he affirms "next to the ridicule of denying an evident truth, is that of taking much pains to defend it; and no truth appears to me more evident, than that beasts are endowed with thought and reason as well as men. The arguments are in this case so obvious, that they never escape the most stupid and ignorant" (Hume 1968, 176ff). (The last sentence is presumably directed at Descartes.)

The certainty of animal thought is affirmed throughout subsequent empiricist British philosophy, with Bentham and Mill drawing moral consequences from animal ability to feel pain and thus of necessity being included in the scope of utilitarian moral concern. (Mill, in fact, was such a thoroughgoing empiricist that he thought mathematics to be inductively based!).

Bentham's famous remark was

"Other animals, which, on account of their interests having been neglected by the insensibility of the ancient jurists, stand degraded into the class of things. [...] The day has been, I grieve it to say in many places it is not yet past, in which the greater part of the species, under the denomination of slaves, have been treated [...] upon the same footing as [...] animals are still. The day may come, when the rest of the animal creation may acquire those rights which never could have been withholden from them but by the hand of tyranny. The French have already discovered that the blackness of skin is no reason why a human being should be abandoned without redress to the caprice of a tormentor. It may come one day to be recognized that the number of legs, the villosity of the skin, or the termination of the *os sacrum*, are reasons equally insufficient for abandoning a sensitive being to the same fate. What else is it that should trace the insuperable line? Is it the faculty of reason, or perhaps, the faculty for discourse?....The question is not, Can they reason? nor, Can they talk? but, Can they suffer? Why should the law refuse its protection to any sensitive being?... The time will come when humanity will extend its mantle over everything which breathes [...]." (Bentham 1948, 310-311)

Mill in turn affirmed that "the reasons for legal intervention in favour of children apply not less strongly to the case of those unfortunate slaves—the animals" (Mill 1852, 546).

Thus we see that from Locke through the Utilitarians there exists the assumption in empiricism of animal mentation, from Hume's claim of animal reason to Bentham and Mills affirmation of animals' ability to feel pain. The scientific culmination of this stance on animal consciousness, however, is reached in the works of Charles Darwin. Darwinian science gave new vitality to ordinary common-sense notions that attributed mental states to animals, but which had been assaulted by Catholics and Cartesians. For Darwin, the guiding assumption in psychology was one of continuity; so the study of mind became comparative, as epitomized by Darwin's marvelously blunt title for his 1872 work, *The Expression of the Emotions in Man and Animals*, a title which brazenly hoists a middle finger to the Cartesian tradition, since Darwin saw emotion as inextricably bound up with subjective feelings. Furthermore, in *The Descent of Man* of the previous year, Darwin had specifically affirmed that "there is no fundamental difference between man and the higher animals in their mental facilities", and that "the lower animals, like man manifestly feel pleasure and pain, happiness, and misery" (Darwin 1971, 448). In the same work, Darwin attributed the entire range of subjective experiences to animals, taking it for granted that one can gather data relevant to our knowledge of such experiences. Evolutionary theory demands that psychology, like anatomy, be comparative, for life is incremental, and mind did not arise *de novo* in man, fully formed like Athena from the head of Zeus.

Darwin was not of course content to speculate about animal consciousness. He explicitly turned over much of his material on animal mentation to a trusted spokesman, George John Romanes, who in turn published two major volumes, *Animal Intelligence* (1882) and *Mental Evolution in Animals* (1884), both of which richly evidence phylogenetic continuity of mentation. In his preface to *Animal Intelligence*, Romanes acknowledges his debt to Darwin, who, in his words, "not only assisted me in the most generous manner with his immense stores of information, as well as with his valuable judgment on sundry points of difficulty, but has also been kind enough to place at my disposal all the notes and clippings on animal intelligence which he has been collecting for the last forty years, together with the original manuscript of his wonderful chapter on 'Instinct.' This chapter, on being recast for the 'Origin of Species', underwent so merciless an amount of compression that the original draft constitutes a rich store of hitherto unpublished material" (Romanes 1978, XI).

While Romanes' work focuses mainly on cognitive ability throughout the phylogenetic scale, he also addresses emotions and other aspects of mental life, all of which, for a Darwinian, ought to evidence some continuity across animal species.

In addition to the careful observations he made, Darwin also pursued a variety of experiments on animal mentation. Darwin placed great emphasis on verifying any data subject to the slightest question. Towards this end, he, for example, contrived some ingenious experiments to test the intelligence of earthworms, a notion which he clearly felt was far beyond the purview of anecdotal information, and which was sufficiently implausible as to require controlled experimentation. These experiments, now virtually forgotten, occupy some thirty-five pages of Darwin's *The Formation of Vegetable Mould Through the Action of Worms with Observations on their Habits,* published in 1886. The question Darwin asked was whether the behaviour of worms in plugging up their burrows could be explained by instinct alone or by "inherited impulse" or chance, or whether something like intelligence was required. In a series of tests, Darwin supplied his worms with a variety of leaves, some indigenous to the country where the worms were found, others from plants growing thousands of miles away, as well as parts of leaves and triangles of paper, and observed how they proceeded to plug their burrows, whether using the narrow or the wide end of the object first. After quantitative evaluation of the results of these tests, Darwin concluded that worms possess rudimentary intelligence, in that they showed plasticity in their behaviour, some rudimentary "notion" of shape, and the ability to learn from experience. Darwin is no romantic anthropomorphist; he clearly distinguishes the intelligence of the worms from the "senseless or purposeless" manner in which even higher animals often behave, as when a beaver cuts up logs and drags them about when there is no water to dam, or a squirrel puts nuts on a wooden floor as if he had buried them in the ground (Darwin 1886, 95).

As Darwin's work quickly became the regnant paradigm in biology and psychology, one would expect that the science of animal mentation would have steadily evolved during the subsequent century and a half as a subset of evolutionary biology. Strangely enough, this is not the case. Despite Darwin's influence, animal mentation disappeared as a legitimate object of study, not only in a Europe influenced by Cartesianism, but in the Anglo-American world as well.

Before we turn to the remarkable story of how this occurred, a story that shakes the foundation of how science believes itself to change, it is worth mentioning that Darwin's work inspired a spurt of concern about the moral status of animals. While Darwin himself did not follow out in the moral realm the logic of attribution of the evolutionary and continuity of consciousness to animals, save for occasional comments like "the love for all living creatures is the most noble attribute of man" (Ryder 1999), a number of his contemporaries did, most notably E.P. Evans in his *Evolutional Ethics and Animal Psychology* (1898) and Henry Salt in *Animal Rights Considered in Relation to Social Progress* (1892). The obvious extension of moral concern to animals as continuous with humans phylogenetically *and* mentally seems to have been forestalled by a self-serving interpretation of Darwin affirming that, since humans were "at the top of the evolutionary pyramid", they were "superior" to lesser beings and thus we didn't need to worry about them morally.

Scientific common sense—my term for the uncritical ideology associated with science for well over 100 years and believed by most scientists—decrees that there are only two ways that established scientific theories or hypothesis can be overturned. The first and most obvious way is through empirical disconfirmation—we gather data or do experiments showing that what was believed is factually falsified. Thus we may believe that "all swans are white" until we find a black swan, or that ulcers cause stress until we found that the primary cause was helicobacter pylori (for simplicity, we are leaving aside the Quinean critique of straight forward verification or falsification). The secondary way of rejecting a theory or hypothesis is by showing that it is conceptually or logically flawed. Thus Einstein demonstrated that Newton's account of absolute space and time was incoherent, for its postulation required of us the ability to measure absolute simultaneity, yet what events we call "simultaneous" depend on the observer measuring them. In a similar way Russell showed Frege's definition of number to generate logically absurdity. This form of disconfirmation is of course much rarer.

From the time of Darwin (and even before, as we have seen), the existence and knowability of animal mentation was taken as axiomatic through the early years of the 20th century. But, after 1920, and even today, it is difficult to find British or American psychologists or classical European ethologists, who would accept that view. (The classic volume, *Instinctive Behavior*, edited by Claire Schiller, chronicles the first interactions of Anglo-American behaviorists with European ethologists of the school of Lorenz and Tinbergen. Though the two schools agreed about little else, they were of one mind in denying consciousness or its knowability in animals.) The obvious question which arises, of course, is whether the assumption of animal mind was empirically disconfirmed, or else found to be conceptually flawed. The surprising answer is—neither. There was no empirical disconfirmation of animal consciousness nor was there any conceptual/logical flaw found in its postulation. In fact, far from being disproved, the knowability of animal consciousness was *disapproved*, disvalued, banished by a valuational revolution cloaked in rhetoric about how to make psychology a "real" science, and all of science allegedly wholly empirical.

In actual fact, there is quite a significant history of science changing in virtue of valuational considerations, rather than by the accepted methods delineated above; it is perhaps surprising that the Scientific Revolution can be so viewed!

To begin with, we must recall that all human cognitive enterprises, of which science is of course a paradigm case, rest on certain foundational presuppositions, what Aristotle called *archai*. As in the transparent case of geometry, all such activities must make certain assumptions in order to function. Again, as in geometry, one cannot prove the assumptions, for it is upon these assumptions that the possibility of proof itself rests. If one could prove the assumptions, it would of necessity be on the basis of other assumptions, which must themselves either be taken for granted or based in other assumptions, etc. *ad infinitum*. That is not of course to suggest that one cannot criticize the assumptions—we have already pointed to examples of logically flawed assumptions in Newton and Frege. But we have also seen that in the case of the assumption that animals possess and evidence mentation and feeling, no such incoherence was discovered.

Are assumptions in science discarded for reasons other than demonstrable logical fallaciousness? Are they adopted for reasons other than to replace fallacious ones or to better account for recalcitrant data? One is compelled to assert that this is indeed the case—they may change for valuational reasons as well. One need look no further than the Scientific Revolution to buttress this claim.

It is well known that the Scientific Revolution inaugurated by Galileo, Descartes, Newton and others, indeed marked a major discontinuity with medieval/Aristotelian science. Aristotelian science was concerned with explaining the world which we find through our senses, which were assumed to be a mainly reliable source of information about that world. And, as the senses tell us, the world is a world of qualitative differences—of things alive and not alive, hot and cold, wet and dry, solid and liquid, good and bad, beautiful and ugly. To be adequate, science must do justice to that world—Aristotle specifically affirms that there thus can be no one master science of everything; each thing must be explained according to its own kind, and each domain of scientific inquiry rests upon assumptions uniquely appropriate to it. A science of inert matter can never serve to explain the behavior of living things—this is a conceptual and methodological necessity based in the patent empirical differences we find in the world. Thus Aristotle definitively rejects the Platonic notion of an underlying reality which required only one language—that of mathematics. The only reason mathematics fits everything, says Aristotle, is that it is so vague and general as to be vacuous, like the "interesting paper" comment which professors at a loss to say anything else scrawl on student essays. For Aristotle, science should tell us what is unique to a domain, not what is common to all domains.

The science of Galileo *et al.* thoroughly rejects the Aristotelian story. It is not that the revolutionaries discovered empirical facts which *falsify* or *disconfirm* the core of Aristotle's account. *Any* empirical facts (i.e. data gathered by the senses) are grist for Aristotle's mill, or are compatible with Aristotle's world view, since they, by definition and of necessity bespeak a world of qualitative differences. What the proponents of revolution must rather do is disvalue certain facts, and ways of looking at the facts which Aristotle holds dear! Aristotle disvalues the quantitative dimensions of the world, the revolutionaries stand him on his head and glorify the quantitative, while trivializing the qualitative. This is not disconfirmation; it is rather a difference in seeing, brought about by a difference in valuing, in much the same way that a son and his parents might look very differently at his potential spouse—he stressing sex appeal and excitement, they stressing reliability and good sense. Looking at the same woman, they thus find very different characteristics in their respective lists of her strengths and faults.

The Scientific Revolutionaries value mathematical unity over sensory diversity; universal intelligibility over fragmented intelligibility; reason over experience; Plato over Aristotle; geometry over natural history; physics over biology. And as Feyerabend (1975) and others have pointed out, they defend their approach at least as much by appeal to value as to fact.

Consider, for example, the classic case of Descartes' defense of the quantitative approach in his *Meditations*. His tack, as every freshman philosophy student knows, is to disvalue the senses as a reliable source of information about reality, striking directly at Aristotle's notion of "what you see is what you get." Descartes' argument essentially proceeds as follows: He provided numerous examples where the senses deceive us. Nothing in sense experience is absolutely certain—we are all familiar with the sorts of mistakes the senses make. Since we can be wrong about any sensory experience, we could conceivably be wrong about every such experience and if we could be wrong about every such experience, we should categorically reject the senses as a source of information. From this basis, Descarte proceeds to deduce what one could not be wrong about, his own existence, and eventually, *a priori*, geometrical knowledge of the world of the sort favored by the New Science.

As soon as one scrutinizes this argument, it is patent that it does not logically compel the abandonment of Aristotelianism, anymore than new data could empirically compel the rejection of Aristotelianism. For Descartes' argument is flawed in many ways. For one thing, by parity of reasoning, one can construct the following argument: Since one *could* be right (as well as wrong) about any type of empirical knowledge, one *could* be right (as well as wrong) about every item of empirical knowledge, therefore one should accept all such knowledge—clearly a fallacious argument isomorphic to Descartes' (Arthur Danto personal communication). Second, as Hume pointed out, we might be wrong in any of our mathematical calculations and proofs (e.g. by misreading a symbol or simply by erring as we do when learning geometry)—thus, even if Descartes is correct about the infallibility of his self-knowledge, that same infallibility does not extend to mathematical physics, both because we can make mathematical errors and, even more important, because we need to apply our mathematical physics to real world situations, and for this we need to rely on sense experience. Descartes' reply is that a benevolent Deity would not deceive us, at least regularly—a response equally appropriate for the Aristotelian against whom Descartes marshalled his arguments in the first place.

Thus Descartes, Galileo, and other figures in the Scientific Revolution neither falsify the Aristotelian approach empirically, nor do they show it to be conceptually flawed at root in ways which could not be turned back on their own positions. Once we realize this, we are in a position to understand that the orthodox notion of how scientific ideas are abandoned will not always stand up. It appears that scientific ideas can change not only because of disconfirming data or because of the discovery of basic logical flaws, but also because of the *rise of new values which usher in new philosophical commitments or new basic assumptions*. Thus, in the case we have been discussing, a variety of new values, ranging from preference for Plato over Aristotle by a group of prominent intellectuals to greater concern about precision in the prediction of projectile movement because of the advent of artillery, to a penchant for reductionism over pluralism, led to a change in basic assumptions about what science should be doing and how it should be doing it. (In the same vein, it has been pointed out that new technology or tools can determine even basic theoretical approaches and assumptions in science, notably in medicine, which situation accords with neither of the classical accounts of scientific change, but does fit better with our valuational account—new technologies are valued sufficiently to subordinate medical approaches and assumptions to their use (Reiser 1978).

It is within this new category that we will attempt to place the abandonment of the common sense/Darwinian approach to animal mentation. It appears that the view that animals have subjective experiences and that these could be studied was given up not because it did not generate fruitful research programs—it surely did, in the hands of people like Darwin and George Romanes. Nor was it given up because it did not explain or allow us to predict animal behavior—it surely did. Nor was it shown to be logically inconsistent or incoherent. Rather, it was abandoned because of some major valuational upheavals and concerns.

What values come into play that worked against the knowability of animal consciousness in the early twentieth century? Most important, perhaps was the marvelous salesmanship of J.B. Watson in selling Behaviorism. (Let us recall that Watson was a major force in developing modern advertising techniques.) Watson sold to scientists, but also sold to the general public—he was one of the rare scientists who loved to talk to reporters about the social utility of the science he advocated. Watson promised nothing less to his peers than creating a new psychology as credible as physics and chemistry!

One has only to examine Watson's own work to see that he was attempting to sell a new philosophical-valuational package. In "Psychology as the behaviorist views it", Watson's (1913) manifesto, he urges psychology to "throw off the yoke of consciousness". Only by so doing can psychology become a "real science". By concerning itself with consciousness, "it failed signally [...] to make its place in the world as an undisputed natural science" like physics and chemistry (Watson 1913, 461). To be a "real science", it must behave like a real science and study what is "observable". Thus he writes "Can image type be experimentally tested and verified? Are recondite thought processes dependent mechanically upon imagery at all? Are psychologists agreed upon what feeling is?" (Watson 1913, 462) Watson assumes, but does not demonstrate, that the answer to all these questions is negative. What is observable is behaviour. What we find in the world are "stimulus and response, habit formations, habit integrations and the like" (Watson 1913, 463). (In fact, of course, these are not directly observable; they are theoretical notions.) "I believe we can write a psychology, define it as Pillsbury [i.e. as the science of behaviour], and never go back upon our definition: never use the terms consciousness, mental states, mind, content, introspectively verifiable, imagery, and the like" (Watson 1913, 463).

Note that Watson does not prove that we *should* do this; he merely affirms that psychology will be more like physics and chemistry if we do and thus advocates it. (The physics Watson admired, of course, is nineteenth-century physics. Twentieth-century physics soon soared beyond mechanism.) To the objection that the abandonment of consciousness is a very heavy price to pay, a violation of what we all know to be part of the furniture of the universe (some would say the best-known part of all the furniture), Watson said little, except that he didn't "care" about consciousness (Watson 1913, 466).

In most of his written work, Watson did not go so far as to say explicitly that there are no such things as consciousness, mental images, and the like; but it is clear that this is his bottom line. Throughout his life, he contended that thoughts, images and the rest were "implicit behavior", small muscular movements in the larynx or other organs which we would be able to detect if we had a more advanced technology. Watson, in essence, paradoxically held that "We don't have thoughts, we only think we do". Subjective mental states are at best dispensable psychic trash, at worse non-existent.

Watson's own deepest mental states are inaccessible to us, of course, not least since he is dead. But he was certainly interpreted as I have just outlined by his contemporaries and co-workers such as Lashley.

If Behaviorism was to be significantly different from other approaches which preceded it, including the Darwin-Romanes approach, it must deny the reality of consciousness in humans and animals, or at least its knowability. In this regard, Watson is his own version of a consistent Darwinian. In fact, in a bizarre dialectical turn in the 1913 essay, he accuses those who argue for a phylogenetic continuum of consciousness of anthropocentrism, because "it makes consciousness as the human being knows it, the center of reference for all behavior" (Watson 1913, 459-460), just as Darwinian biology was anthropocentric in attempting first and foremost to describe the evolution of *Home sapiens*.

Behaviorism played well to the general public, especially the American public, because it promised a science that would birth a technology—the ability to control and shape behavior; with it we could rehabilitate criminals, educate children properly, produce a better society. With its contempt for genetic bases of behavior it fit perfectly into American optimism about social engineering and the ability to shape humans, just as we conquered the frontier and shaped nature. (This side of Behaviorism reached its culmination in the work of Watson's student, B. F. Skinner.)

Behaviorism also fit well with other early 20th century cultural tendencies, in particular with the reductive tendency manifest in that era to eliminate frills, excesses, and superfluities. This value may be found in diverse quarters: Schönberg's reaction against Wagner and Mahler, and others; the Bauhaus reaction against excessive ornamentation in art and design; the rise of formalism in criticism; all express the same spirit which also invaded science in the form of positivism. Thinkers like Mach, Einstein, and later the logical positivists all sought to excise metaphysical and speculative baggage from science; to clearly delineate the realm of science as the realm of the empirical and observable, a tendency which had been part of science since Newton. (The positivists also had political reasons and values which justified their hard empiricism—the elimination of meaningless but inflammatory rhetoric from political discourse.) Since animal consciousness could not become a direct empirical datum for us, it was automatically suspect on positivist grounds. Ironically, then, the phenomenalistic empiricism of Locke and Hume, which took animal consciousness as axiomatic, was stood on its head by their 20th century successors.

Indeed, while scholars debate the influence that Logical Positivism had directly on Behaviorism, there is no doubt it at least created an environment highly congenial to the elimination of consciousness. Indeed, as I have argued in my *Science and Ethics* (Cambridge University Press, 2006), positivism was a powerful force for removing both consciousness *and* ethics from legitimate scientific discourse, thereby accelerating what I have called "scientific ideology". In that book I trace the pernicious ethical consequences of this ideology for issues ranging from the treatment of research subjects to pain management in medicine, to science's image in the public mind.

To add insult to injury, Behaviorist historians throughout the 20th century wrote as if Watson was the logical and inevitable culmination of a variety of thinkers who succeeded Darwin. Boring, for example, cites Lloyd Morgan, Jacques Loeb, H.S. Jennings, E.B. Titchener, and Edward Thorndike as leading inevitably to Behaviorism (Boring 1957).

We all know that history is written by the victors. That notwithstanding, the tracing of psychology from Romanes to Watson is as egregious a distortion of the history of ideas I have ever encountered. In my book, *The Unheeded Cry* (Oxford 1989), I did something quite heretical and actually *read* the psychologist's cited as leading to Watson. Amazingly enough, *none of them ever even suggested the need for eliminating consciousness, indeed all presupposed it in their own writings.*

Consider, for example, the totally self-assured, unequivocal historical claim advanced by Marx and Hillix in their *Systems and Theories of Psychology* about the pivotal role of Conway Lloyd Morgan in paving the way for Behaviorism.

"Romanes was demonstrating continuity by finding mind everywhere; Morgan also wished to demonstrate continuity, but suggested that it might be done as well if we could find mind nowhere. Morgan's appeal to simplicity and rejection of anthropomorphism would seem, from a modern perspective, to have made the development of a scientific behaviourism inevitable." (Marx & Hillix 1967, 168)

They are here referring to the dogma (for Behaviorists) that Morgan's Canon eliminated consciousness. Sometimes erroneously seen as a special case of Occam's Razor, the Canon says with regard to an animal's behavior "In no case may we interpret an action as the outcome of the exercise of a higher psychical faculty, if it can be interpreted as the outcome of the exercise of one which stands lower in the psychological scale" (Morgan 1894, 53).

Anyone who reads Morgan as a proto-Behaviorist has not read Morgan. The Canon is not only not intended to eliminate consciousness, it again *presupposes* consciousness. For Morgan believes unequivocally that if consciousness exists *anywhere* on the phylogenetic scale, it must exist *everywhere*, at least in simple form, even in bare nature! He is in fact, a raving speculative metaphysician, a monist, a pan-psychist, a Spinozian, a believer that *everything* in nature has both a physical and psychological dimension. The Canon is simply meant to warn against confusing higher consciousness with lower, not to eliminate consciousness. Morgan's own words end any debate.

"We have [...] taken for granted the existence of consciousness, and the fact that there are subjective phenomena which we, as comparative psychologists, may study. We have also proceeded throughout on the assumption that subjective phenomena admit of a natural interpretation, as the result of a process or processes of development or evolution, in just the same sense as objective phenomena admit of such interpretation." (Morgan 1894, 323)

The truth notwithstanding, for much of the 20th century psychologist believed in the inexorable, logical, empirical victory of Behaviorism.

A number of questions obviously arise regarding the triumph of the Behavioristic/ Positivistic view of consciousness. First of all, surely the denial of animal mentation flew directly in the face of ordinary common sense? Secondly, but of primary moral importance, what were the moral consequences of wholesale denial of animal mentation as far as the moral status and treatment of animals was concerned?

It was certainly the case that the denial of consciousness in animals (or for that matter, in humans) was inimical to the basic tenets of ordinary common sense. Ordinary common sense never would have denied consciousness in animals, and most certainly not in humans! And ordinary common sense would certainly have been surprised by the stance of science. But, then, as today, ordinary people did not pay much attention to the claims of science (scientific illiteracy was rife then as now), and, unless the science went directly counter to their religious beliefs, as in evolution, did not care much about what scientists believed. People might, for example, have heard the Einsteinian implication that a ray of light shining from a fast train did not go any faster than a ray of light coming from a stationary source, or of the twin paradox, or of Schrödingers cat, and might even have experienced a moment of bafflement, but quickly shrugged and were not bothered—thinking "after all, scientists believe a lot of crazy things that strike us as odd."

As far as ethics and animals is concerned, the story is much more complex. In the first place, societal ethics (and the laws expressing it) *vis à vis* animal treatment were greatly limited—avoid deliberate, sadistic intentional unnecessary cruelty. But, by and large, animal treatment was not a moral issue—animals were to be provided with the necessities required for them to fulfil their human purposes. As we shall shortly see, this was presuppositional to the nature of agriculture. Anything much beyond that was ignored. A beautiful example of this can be found in a 1905 textbook of veterinary surgery, wherein the author laments that although anesthesia has been available since the 1860's, it is rarely employed in veterinary surgery, with the occasional exception of the canine practitioner, whose clients valued their animals beyond the dictates of economic necessity (Merillat 1906). Thus surgery on food animals was traditionally performed under restraint—"bruticaine" as veterinarians called it—and to a significant extent, is still done that way.

The moral implications of the denial of consciousness—even felt pain—to animals, did not become apparent until the second half of the 20th century, when social concern for animals began to surface, in the wake of major changes in the nature of animal use in agriculture and research, changes which significantly compromised animal well-being, and were abetted and perpetuated by the denial of animal consciousness among scientists, though not exclusively caused by that denial.

In the mid-twentieth century, animal use changed more precipitously and severely than had occurred since the advent of domestication. These changes ultimately had major impact on the belief in animal mind and on moral concern for animals, as we shall demonstrate. The most extreme change was in agriculture, by far the largest use of animals in society. Historically agriculture was based in good husbandry or care; placing animals into the optimal environment for which they had evolved, and augmenting their natural ability to survive and thrive by provision of food during famine, water during drought, help in birthing, medical attention, protection from predation. The relationship between humans and the animals they utilized for food, fiber, locomotion and power was a symbiotic one; both sides benefitted from the relationship—what has been referred to as "the ancient contract". This is dramatically illustrated in the 23rd Psalm where the Psalmist, seeking a metaphor for God's ideal relationship to humans, can find no better one then the shepherd:

"The lord is my shepherd, I shall not want. He leadeth me to green pastures; He maketh me to lie down beside still water; He restoreth my soul."

In other words, we ask no more of God than what the good shepherd provides to the sheep. A lamb in ancient Judea could not survive without a shepherd; the shepherd depended on his flock. Without a shepherd, the animals would be decimated by predators, famine and drought. With the shepherd, they lived decent lives while giving us milk, wool, and meat. But while they lived, they lived well. Indeed, Christian iconography vividly makes this point and celebrates the contract by portraying Jesus as both Shepherd and lamb.

To succeed in agriculture, one therefore had to know—and meet—animal physical and psychological needs, for the agriculturalist did well if and only if the animals did well. Husbandry became ingrained as an *ethical and prudential* imperative; proper care was essential to success. The only articulated ethic for animals required was the prohibition against deliberate, unnecessary, sadistic cruelty or outrageous neglect such as not feeding and watering. This prohibition was meant to capture the sadists and psychopaths unmoved by self-interest, and is present in the Bible, in medieval thought (where it is recognized that those who are cruel to animals are likely to be cruel to people), and in the criminal laws of all civilized societies since 1800.

It is very likely that what Hume had in mind when affirming that animal mind is obvious to all but the most benighted was animal users' understanding of their animals physical and mental states, an understanding presuppositional to working with them. Even contemporary veterinary scientists, asked to explain to agnostic researchers how to recognize pain in animals, responded by saying, in essence, "ask those who work with them on a daily basis, and whose business it is to know" (Morton & Griffiths 1985, 431-436).

But this ancient contract did not survive the emergence of modern science-based technology. By the mid-20th century, agriculture had became industrialized, with academic departments of Animal Husbandry rapidly transmuted into departments of Animal Science, defined in textbooks as the "application of industrial methods to the production of animals". Industry supplanted husbandry and agriculture became exploitative rather than symbiotic.

Whereas husbandry was about putting square pegs in square holes, round pegs in round holes, industrial agriculture forced square pegs into round holes, round pegs into oblong holes by use of "technological sanders"—antibiotics, vaccines, air-handling systems. The animals' natures (*telos* as I call it, following Aristotle) could be circumvented, yielding economic benefit, and severing animal welfare from productivity, impossible under husbandry. And with the industrial model came the irrelevance of animal thoughts and feeling, yielding what Ruth Harrison aptly called "animal machines"—parts of a factory. Understanding of animal thought and feeling became superfluous, rather than pre-suppositional to productivity; animal misery no longer impacted on agriculture success. Bitterly attesting to this was the 1981 Council for Agricultural Science and Technology (CAST) report on the welfare of food animals, which defined "animal welfare" as the animals being productive according to the human reasons for keeping the animals (CAST 1981, 1).

Thus the ideological agnosticism or atheism about animal mind inherent in Behaviorism and positivism meshed well with the revolution in animal agriculture. But this was not all. The mid-twentieth century also saw the rise of the massive amounts of animal research and testing. Though clearly productive of considerable benefit to humans and to animals in general, unlike the situation in husbandry agriculture, being an animal in research provided no benefit to the animals upon whom research was performed—they were inflicted with diseases, fractures, wounds, burns, lesions with no offsetting benefit. And thus another major animal use emerged violative of the ancient contract.

In biomedicine, i.e. in biological and medical research, in psychological research, and even in veterinary research and in veterinary practice, the Cartesian model of animals as non-conscious, biological machines was regnant. Perhaps the most extreme morally relevant example of this was both the ideological denial and complete disregard of felt pain in animals, pain being, after all, what a recent book on the history of human pain and its control calls in its title "the worst of evils". The denial of pain is of seminal importance for two reasons. First of all, it is the state of awareness most related to moral concern, so much so, that we saw that Bentham and Mill made it the *sine qua non* for moral status. If pain is denied, *a fortiori* more complex and abstract morally relevant mental states such as "suffering" would logically be ignored. More generally, felt pain is a very basic biological safeguard for an organism. If one denies simple pain consciousness in an animal, one is logically bound to deny more complex mental states which require greater sophistication of consciousness.

That felt pain was denied or ignored for much of the 20th century is easy to evidence objectively. As an architect and public advocate of federal legislation in the 1970's and 1980's that required control of pain in research animals, and which ultimately passed in 1985, I repeatedly came up against the denial of pain by the scientific community in both objectively documentable ways and in personal experiences, both sets of which are valuable to document.

On the objective front, the International Association for the Study of Pain (IASP) definition of pain until very recently required language as a necessary precondition for the ability to feel pain (shades of Descartes) thereby creating a belief that animals and neonatal humans (who until the 1990's were subjected to open heart surgery without anesthesia, restrained by paralytic drugs) could not be said to feel pain, i.e. did not. In essence, the same people who used animals as "pain models" for research turned around and denied that animals felt pain. Perfectly in harmony with this view was the complete failure of the first textbooks of veterinary anesthesia published in the U.S. to even acknowledge felt pain in animals or to raise any discussion of analgesia. (Anesthesia itself was tellingly referred to until very recently as synonymous with "chemical restraint".)

Finally, when I was asked by Congress to evidence the need for a law requiring pain control for research animals, I did a literature search on "laboratory animal analgesia" and then on "animal analgesia", and was amazed to find only two papers, one of which said, in essence, that there ought to be papers!

My personal experiences between 1976 (when we began to draft legislation) and 1985 (when it passed) better conveys the flavor of science's agnosticism about felt pain:

In 1979, I attended a conference on animal pain, where I debated a prominent scientist, with me defending the view that animals could feel pain, while he denied that claim. I thought we had enjoyed an amicable discussion until I returned to CSU, whereupon I found out that after the debate he called the Dean of Veterinary Medicine and told him that I was "a viper in the bosom of biomedicine" who should not be allowed to teach in a veterinary program!

In 1982, I was asked to respond to a noted pain researcher who gave a speech at a conference saying that since the electro-chemical activity in the cerebral cortex of dogs was different from that of humans, and the cerebral cortex was the area that processed pain, the dog "did not really feel pain as humans did". My refutation was singularly brief. I asked him, "As a prominent researcher in pain, you do your research on dogs". "Yes", he replied. "You extrapolate your results to people?" I queried. "Of course", he said, "that is why I do my work". "In that case", I said, "either your speech is false or your life's work is."

Around 1980, when I was developing and pressing the federal legislation for laboratory animals, I was invited by AALAS (American Association for Laboratory Science) to discuss my reasons for supporting legislative constraints on science on a panel with half a dozen eminent laboratory animal veterinarians. By way of making my point, I asked them all to tell me what analgesic would be of choice for a rat used in a limb-crush experiment, assuming analgesia did not disrupt results that were being studied. The consensus response was, in essence, "How should we know? We don't even know for sure if animals feel pain!" I will return to this anecdote shortly.

At the American Veterinary Medical Association pain panel convened in 1986 after the laws passed by Dean Hiram Kitchen at the request of Congress in response to researcher complaints that they knew nothing of animal pain and thus could not obey the new law, I was asked to write the prologue to the report. I did, and presented it to the group. I approvingly pointed out that according to the great *skeptical* philosopher, David Hume, few things are obvious as the fact that animals have thoughts and feelings, and that this point does not escape "even the most stupid", as we quoted earlier. A representative from NIMH (Natural Institute of Mental Health) stood up indignantly and declared, "If we are going to talk mysticism, I am leaving", and did, never to return.

I could proliferate such stories, but one serves as a capstone. After the laws passed, Dr. Robert Rissler, head of USDA/APHIS, was in charge of writing regulations interpreting them. As he related at a conference, he was particular concerned about the legal requirement stipulated in the law that accommodations for non-human primates, "enhance their psychological well-being." He told the audience that, as a veterinarian, he knew nothing of primates *or* "psychological well-being." So he went to the American Psychological Association Primatology Division, and asked for help. "Don't worry", he was told, "there is no such thing!" "Well there will be after January 1, 1987, whether you people help me or not", he astutely replied.

Science's ideological denial of consciousness, particularly pain, coupled with the ideological claim of science as "ethics-free", presented a formidable fortress, but one which burgeoning societal concern for animal treatment has successfully breached. As society has become conscious that new animal uses do not preserve the ancient fair contract with animals, and as interest in animals has been fueled by media coverage; philosophers like Singer, Regan, Sepontzis, and myself; celebrities; and by companion animals emerging as the paradigm for all animals in the social mind, society has demanded that laws ensure fair use—2400 state laws relevant to animal welfare were floated in 2004. The laboratory animal laws we have described were a significant juggernaut in forcing the scientific community to "re-appropriate common sense" about animal pain and about other aspects of animal consciousness. (The law also mandates control of distress, which the USDA wisely did not stress until recently, in order to allow agnosticism about animal pain to be overcome—there are now over 12,000 papers on pain in animals.)

With regard to animal agriculture, the situation is not as good. As we saw earlier, the industrial agriculture and agricultural science communities saw animal welfare as equated with productivity, were also agnostic about animal subjectivity, and further equated all forms of misery caused by production conditions with "stress", defined in terms of activation of the pituitary-adrenal axis—catecholamines were a measure of short-term stress, and cortico-steroids of long term. Agricultural science ignored the facts that "stress" is present during such pleasant experiences as sex and play, and the far more important fact proven by such scientists as John Mason (1971) and Jay Weiss (1972), that the stress response is modulated by animal *conscious* cognition, until well after this was known to other branches of science. In veterinary medicine, there is no knowledge or use to speak of regarding large animal analgesia, and in some cases, operative procedures are still done without anesthesia.

In Europe, ethical concerns about industrial agriculture, beginning in Britain in the 1960's, led gradually to the abolition of severe confinement practices, most dramatically represented by the Swedish law of 1988 that effectively banned animal agriculture of the sort still taken for granted in the U.S., and also to the study of animal consciousness and feelings with the realization that welfare is fundamentally about the animals conscious experiences of what matters to them. (This notion was pioneered in the early 1980's by Dawkins, Duncan, and myself.) The Swedish laws were followed by laws in other countries and EU regulations eliminating such practices as veal crates and sow confinement.

In the U.S., where much of the population is naive about animal agriculture, believing that farms are still "Old McDonald's" pastoral, bucolic entities, concern for farm animals did not grow along with concern for research animals. There are, however, signs that consciousness and concern for the suffering of farm animals is growing—the rapid growth in sales of "humane" meat products; the success of restaurant chains such as Chipotle and groceries such as Whole Foods; the development of audits for basic farm animal welfare by corporate restaurants; the publication of surveys indicating public demand for laws constraining the use of farm animals. Obviously, such burgeoning public moral concern about farm animals will ramify in ever-increasing attention to farm animal pain and consciousness and to a demand for research into animal experience of the sort pioneered by Marian Dawkins and Ian Duncan.

In my *Unheeded Cry*, I recounted other indications of and causes for scientists' disaffection with the denial of consciousness. It is clear that these forces, and neo-Darwinian interest in evolutionary continuity of consciousness, will continue to drive renewed scientific interest in these issues. Even if it does not, social concern with animal treatment will, as ordinary common sense clearly now perceives the connection between welfare and consciousness, and never doubts animal mentation, but rather is prone, if anything, to exaggerate its abilities.

In sum, the interplay between philosophy, science, and ethics manifested in the history of the waxing and waning of the legitimacy of talking about animal mind should serve as a salubrious counter to the standard story of how science changes. It is reasonable to predict that if societal concern for animal welfare continues to grow, and to demand practical ethical changes in animal use based in that concern, attention to the legitimacy of the study of animal mind will also continue to grow, particularly if there is research funding connected to such concern. As I once told Congress about science's disregard of animal pain: "If you appropriate a hundred million dollars for research into animal pain, few scientists will turn it down on ideological grounds."

REFERENCES

Bentham, J. (1948), An Introduction to the Principles of Morals and Legislation, New York: Hafner Press.

Boring, E.G. (1957), A History of Experimental Psychology, New York: Appleton-Century-Crafts.

CAST (1981), Scientific Aspects of the Aspects of the Welfare of Food Animals, Council for Agricultural Science and Technology (CAST) Report No. 91, November 1981.

Darwin, C. (1886), The Formation of Vegetable Mould Through the Action of Worms, with Observations on their Habits, New York: Dr. Appleton and Co.

Darwin, C. (1971), The Descent of Man and Selection in Relation to Sex, New York: Modern Library.

Feyerabend, P.K. (1975), Against Method, Atlantic Highlands, NJ: Humanities Press.

Hume, D. (1968), A Treatise of Human Nature, Oxford: Oxford University Press.

Locke, J. (1871), An Essay Concerning Human Understanding, Book II, New York: Dutton.

Marx, M., Hillix, W. (1967), Systems and Theories in Psychology, McGraw-Hill.

Mason, J.W. (1972) "A re-evaluation of the concept of 'non-specificity' in stress theory", Journal of Pscyhiatric Research 8, 323-333.

Merillat, L.A. (1906), Principles of Veterinary Surgery, Chicago, Illinois: Alexander Eger.

Mill, J.S. (1852), Principles of Political Economy, Volume 2, 3rd edition, London: John W. Parker and Son: 1852.

Morgan, C.L. (1894), An Introduction to Comparative Psychology, London: Walter Scott.

Morton, D.B., Griffiths, P.H.M. (1985), "Guidelines on the recognition of pain, distress, and discomfort in experimental animals and an hypothesis for assessment", Veterinary Record 20 April, 431-436.

Reiser, S. (1978), Medicine and the Reign of Technology, New York: Cambridge University Press.

Romanes, G.J. (1978), Animal Intelligence, London: Kegan Paul, Trench, Trubier and Co.

Ryder, R. (1999), "Darwinism, Altruism and Painience", www.ivu.org/ape/talks/ryder/ryder.htm (last access March, 2013).

Watson, J.B. (1913), "Psychology as the Behaviorist Views it", Psychological Review 20 Reprinted in W. Dennis (ed.) (1948), Readings in the History of Psychology, New York: Appleton-Century-Crofts.

Weiss, J. (1972), "Psychological factors in stress and disease", Scientific American 226/3, 101-113.

2. Animal Minds, Cognitive Ethology, and Ethics

Colin Allen & Marc Bekoff

In his 1975 book *Animal Liberation*, Peter Singer sought to revolutionize societal treatment of nonhuman animals by arguing that animal agriculture and animal experimentation cause conscious pain and suffering that is real and morally significant. With his 1976 book *The Question of Animal Awareness*, Donald Griffin sought to revolutionize the science of animal behavior by insisting that questions about animal consciousness should be placed firmly in the foreground of a new program of research he labeled 'cognitive ethology' (Griffin 1978). Both proposals immediately evoked a range of reactions, from enthusiasm to virulent attack. In the ensuing three decades little consensus has been reached about either.

Although Singer's arguments about ethical treatment of animals preceded Griffin's arguments about scientific understanding of animals, it is obvious why ethicists concerned with the former should be interested in the latter. Singer himself based the case for animal liberation on scientific evidence of behavioral and neurological homologies between humans and other animals (Singer 1990, 11-13). Cognitive ethology, by rejecting behaviorist strictures against attributing subjective states of awareness to nonhuman animals, offered the prospect of increased scientific support for the claim that animals are conscious in the ways that matter ethically.

In the past three and a half decades, animal ethics and cognitive ethology have both diversified significantly. Among ethicists, the Benthamite view that conscious experience of suffering is the fundamental moral issue remains prevalent, although many now also consider a range of cognitive capacities such as desires, prospective planning, and retrospective (or autobiographical) memory to be relevant to questions of what is morally permissible with respect to animals (e.g. DeGrazia 1996; Varner 1998).

In cognitive ethology, conscious awareness has remained a tough nut to crack, but there have been multiple studies on a broad range of cognitive abilities. Not all of these studies share Griffin's perspective on the aims or methods of animal cognition research.

These days, the entire field of animal cognition studies enjoys widespread exposure through television documentaries and the science sections of newspapers and magazines. Among the many studies that have made it into mainstream media are reports of dolphins (Reiss & Marino 2001), elephants (Plotnik et al. 2006), and magpies (Prior et al. 2008) apparently recognizing themselves in mirrors, starlings identifying recursive syntax violations (Gentner et al. 2006), chimpanzees who appear to know what others can see (Hare et al. 2001), crows fashioning tools (Kacelnik et al. 2006), monkeys rejecting unfair rewards (Brosnan & de Waal 2003), play and moral behavior in animals (Allen & Bekoff 2005; Bekoff 2007, 2010; Bekoff & Pierce 2009), fish rubbing inflamed lips (Sneddon et al. 2003), and rats laughing when tickled (Panksepp & Burgdorf 2003). Although the media coverage tends to be biased towards results that suggest human-like capacities in animals, there are exceptions, as with the coverage of a Norwegian government study denying that lobsters feel pain when immersed in boiling water that was widely reported in many major newspapers (e.g. Adam 2005). But on the whole, the public doesn't need much convincing that science supports the attribution of cognitive and emotional capacities to all vertebrate species, and perhaps some invertebrates too. Nevertheless, scientific skepticism about animal cognition and consciousness remains a significant factor in policy debates and it is important for philosophers who wish to engage such scientists to have a rich understanding of the origins of their skepticism. For example, that some scientists have presented evidence that mice (Langford et al. 2006), rats (Bartal et al. 2011), and chickens (Edgar et al. 2011) display empathy has not been factored into the Federal Animal Welfare Act in the United States. This is partly due to the fact that some influential scientists are unconvinced by the evidence, although political pressures from agriculture and industry are also a significant fact. Meanwhile, millions upon millions of these animals are used in highly invasive research with virtually no protection.

There are also important ethical frontiers where scientific information is inadequate and the conclusions are controversial; for example, fish. Braithwaite (2010) argues that "there is as much evidence that fish feel pain and suffer as there is for birds and mammals" but Cabanac et al.

(2009) maintain that there is no evidence for consciousness outside the *Amniota* (vertebrates adapted for terrestrial life, comprising the mammals, birds, and reptiles) and Rose (2002, 33) states: "The fundamental neural requirements for pain and suffering are now known. Fishes lack the most important of these required neural structures, and they have no alternative neural systems for producing the pain experience." Given the increasing use of fish as a cultivated food source, and for genetic and neurological studies in scientific research, the lack of a scientific consensus represents an obstacle to those who would argue the case for ethical concern about fish. Similarly, there is a small but burgeoning numbers of experiments on different species of fish indicating a surprising range of cognitive and learning capacities such as cooperative hunting in groupers and moray eels (Bshary et al. 2006), tool use in stingrays (Kuba et al. 2010), and so on,[1] yet the conclusions for welfare issues that might drawn from any of these studies are likely to be contested by a sizable portion of other scientists.

We see at least two areas where more sophistication about the scientific context would be beneficial to ethicists, and philosophers in general:

1. Philosophers' arguments would benefit from better understanding of the historical roots of ongoing controversies. It is not always accurate or helpful to dismiss skeptical questions from scientists about animal minds as a lingering relic of behaviorism or positivism. (It may be sometimes accurate, but rarely helpful to winning the argument.) Neither is it appropriate to treat some widely reported experiments in animal cognition as if their interpretations are a matter of scientific consensus. It is especially important to understand why loose references to 'cognitive ethology' by philosophers can signal ignorance of the field to scientists who are more deeply immersed in the relevant literature.
2. Philosophers need to distinguish more clearly among different features of animal cognition. Some scientists who are highly skeptical of animal consciousness are much less skeptical about notions such as memory, concepts, and attention. They may embrace the possibility of scientific investigation of these aspects of animal cognition while rejecting the association of cognitive ethology with the pursuit

---

1 | See Allen (2011) for a philosophically motivated review and discussion.

of consciousness. They may be more disposed to question behavioral evidence than neural evidence (Bekoff 2006a,b). Understanding the variety of approaches to phenomena such as learning is essential if such capacities are to form the foundation of scientifically-informed ethical reasoning about animals (Allen 2004a).

1. Sources of Controversy

"We submit that it is this very goal of investigating animal consciousness that, although grand and romantic, falls far outside the scope of a scientific psychology that has struggled for the better part of the past century to eschew such tantalizing, but ultimately unsubstantiable, analyses of subjective mental experience." (Blumberg & Wasserman 1995, 133)

"[I]t doesn't matter really how I know whether my dog is conscious, or even whether or not I do 'know' that he is conscious. The fact is, he is conscious and epistemology in this area has to start with this fact." (Searle 1998, 50)

"It really is something of a scandal that people's intuitions, in this domain, are given any weight at all." (Carruthers 2000, 199)

"It's important to blend 'science sense' with common sense. I maintain that we know that some non-human animals feel something some of the time, just as do human animals. It's nonsense to claim that we don't know if dogs, pigs, cows or chickens feel pain or have a point of view about whether they like or don't like being exposed to certain treatments. Who are we kidding? Frankly, I think we're kidding ourselves." (Bekoff 2006a, 33)

Unsubstantiable? A fact? A scandal? Nonsense to claim that we don't know? As the quotations above show, scientists and philosophers can be found on both sides of the question of animal consciousness. The only fact on which all these authors apparently agree is that the issue is unjustifiably controversial. They differ, of course, on where the blame for the controversy lies.

It is tempting (would be convenient) to dismiss the skeptics in general terms, and we can discern at least four strategies for doing so:

- *The sociopolitical strategy:* To dismiss the doubts as the product of scientists' vested interest in experimenting on live animals for their livelihoods.
- *The burden-shifting strategy:* To maintain that those who wish to deny mental states to animals bear the burden of proof against common sense.
- *The demon-dodging strategy:* To suggest that such skepticism sets a standard of proof that is too high for any empirical science to meet.
- *The progressivist strategy:* To claim that scientific scruples about animal minds are the result of an undue influence of (old-fashioned) positivistic philosophy of science on behaviorism.

In this essay, we shall have little to say about the sociopolitical strategy, which we think objectively unlikely to change the minds of skeptical scientists. Similarly, we think the burden-shifting strategy is, in its general form, unlikely to prove persuasive, for common sense has a poor track record when pitched against scientific progress. Appeals to common sense may reinforce popular support, but they won't gain the respect of the many scientists whose opinions remain influential when decisions materially affecting the lives of billions of animals get made. As long as scientific consensus on these matters remains elusive, skeptical attitudes are likely to harden if critics fail to appreciate the intellectual underpinnings of the skeptical position.

The demon-dodging and progressivist strategies are more promising insofar as they engage scientists with issues that are central to their enterprise. Questions about the limits of empirical investigation and about the meanings of theoretical terms are central to the history and philosophy of comparative psychology and ethology and prominent in the training given to students entering these fields. By and large, however, participants in the debate about animal minds (including ourselves in earlier writings) have failed to acknowledge the diversity of approaches within different scientific traditions. It has been easier to stereotype those coming from other perspectives as 'behaviorists' or 'mentalists' and reject the respective approaches in general outline than to engage with the specific details.

Our goal in this paper is to try to provide enough of an account of the origins of cognitive ethology to help ethicists to gauge for themselves how to balance skepticism and credulity about animal minds when communicating with scientists.

2. Cognitive Ethology

Griffin's term 'cognitive ethology' cleverly blended the anti-behaviorism of cognitive science with the evolutionary perspective of classical ethology. But, in fact, Griffin's original approach breaks significantly with both of these approaches. The origins of cognitive science are in the language-oriented tasks that defined Chomskyan linguistics and dominated early research in artificial intelligence and cognitive psychology. As such, at the time Griffin was writing, cognitive science was very much concerned with *human* intelligence (sometimes even *defined* as such) and, initially at least, cognitive scientists paid little attention to evolutionary questions. Neither was cognitive science particularly concerned with conscious processing. Computational theories of speech processing described cognitive processes that were assumed to be entirely unconscious, for instance.

Similarly, classical ethology was pursued in ways that were silent about questions of animal consciousness. Konrad Lorenz's popular writings about animal behavior often suggested rich mental lives for animals (Lorenz 1952), but Niko Tinbergen was openly opposed to the idea that addressing such issues had any scientific utility (Tinbergen 1963). Although ethologists used terms such as *intention movements*, they used them quite differently from how they are used in the philosophical literature. *Intention movements* refers to preparatory movements that might communicate what action individuals are likely to undertake next, and not necessarily to their beliefs and desires. Classical ethology was initially fixated on ideas of instinct and innateness and had little to say about learning or behavioral flexibility—the latter category being particularly important to Griffin's arguments for conscious awareness in nonhuman animals. Although Griffin's work was seminal, cognitive ethology soon took on broader significance than the study of consciousness alone. It can be defined as the comparative, evolutionary, and ecological study of nonhuman animal minds, including thought processes, beliefs, rationality, information processing, intentionality, and consciousness.

In response to criticism of the instinct concept (Lehrman 1953; Griffiths 2004) Tinbergen (1963) had identified four overlapping areas with which ethological investigations should be concerned: namely, evolution (phylogeny), adaptation (function), causation, and development (ontogeny). His framework is also useful for those interested in animal cognition (Jamieson & Bekoff 1993). The methods for answering questions in each of these areas vary, but all begin with careful observation and description of the behavior patterns that are exhibited by the animals under study. The information provided by these initial observations allows a researcher to exploit the animal's normal behavioral repertoire to answer questions about the evolution, function, causation, and development of the behavior patterns that are exhibited in various contexts. For example, the play bows used by all canid species to communicate about play are more stereotyped in coyotes than in wolves or domestic dogs because social play in coyotes is more likely to escalate into an aggressive encounter (Bekoff 1977). Further analysis of the placement of the bows during play bouts revealed that the bows functioned to communicate about the animals' intentions to engage in play (Bekoff 1995).

For a variety of reasons, however, not every scientist engaged in this kind of work willingly accepts the label 'cognitive ethologist' (Allen 2004b). Many of them reject it because they regard Griffin's approach as insufficiently experimental—a throwback to the excessive reliance on anecdotal reports of Darwin and Romanes—or because they regard the kinds of experiments that have been conducted under the banner of cognitive ethology as lacking the adequate experimental controls. It is not our goal here to analyze the merits or demerits of such views.[2] Rather our point is to explain why philosophers who appeal to 'cognitive ethology' to support their ethical views are likely to encounter resistance from various scientists who have alternative perspectives. It needs to be understood that not all scientists who investigate animal cognition are cognitive ethologists (Allen 2004b), not even all who are advocates for treating animals more humanely.

Self-identified proponents of cognitive ethology often fuel the skepticism of others. For instance, they explicitly trace the beginnings of cognitive ethology to Darwin's anecdotal cognitivism (Jamieson & Bekoff 1993) and they continue to argue that anecdotes and anthropomorphism have an important role to play in informing and motivating more rigorous study (Burghardt 1991; Bekoff 2006a, 2006b, 2007, 2010; Horowitz & Bekoff 2007). From our present-day perspective, however, it is hard to read Darwin (1871) or his protégé George Romanes (1882) without having the reaction that they erred too much on the side of credulity. Darwin appealed

---

2 | For critical discussion of Griffin's agenda see Jamieson & Bekoff (1993) and Crowley & Allen (2008).

to the reports of many 'excellent observers' to argue that there are only graded differences in mental capacity among the species. Accounts of insects feature prominently. Darwin's final work on earthworms attributes mental capacities to them that no scientist, to our knowledge, is currently investigating.[3] Romanes collected and published hundreds of anecdotes about animal intelligence, touting them as a first step towards a more systematic investigation. Romanes never got around to that investigation; thus he is remembered today only for his anecdotal approach, for example a story of ants "rescuing" another ant.

Reacting against Romanes, C. Lloyd Morgan had proposed, that "in no case may we interpret an action as the outcome of the exercise of a higher psychical faculty, if it can be interpreted as the outcome of the exercise of one which stands lower in the psychological scale" (Lloyd Morgan 1894, 53). Lloyd Morgan thought that consciousness (in different degrees) accompanied both 'higher' and 'lower' psychical faculties. But his principle, now known as 'Morgan's canon', soon became linked to the story of Clever Hans as one of the main rallying points for reformers seeking to eliminate mentalistic notions from psychology and put the study of animal behavior on an experimental footing. Students of animal behavior are brought up on the salutary tale of Clever Hans, a horse who fooled many observers into thinking that he could do arithmetic until it was demonstrated in a controlled experiment that Hans was 'simply' reacting to the body language of people who knew the answer. Of course, that Hans was so exquisitely sensitive to the postures of human beings is a fascinating observation in its own right, but one that was largely lost in the ensuing rush to champion the cause of controlled experimentation as an antidote to the 'natural' anthropomorphic tendencies of even the most sophisticated observers.

Glimmers of the idea that the scientific study of animal behavior and psychology should be conducted experimentally can be found in the 19th century, including in Darwin's own work on earthworms. But it is only in the 20th century that experimental approaches to animal behavior became the norm. Experimentation took two paths. In the laboratories of comparative psychologists, beginning with E.L Thorndike, there was an emphasis on control and measurement of the factors affecting learning, i.e. change of behavior as a function of external stimuli and rewards. In

---

3 | But see Crist (2002) for a discussion of Darwin's work in the present context.

the laboratories and fieldwork of the classical ethologists, the emphasis was on experiments which attempted to probe the innate or instinctual aspects of animal behavior, i.e. patterns of behavior which are relatively fixed within a given lineage. This difference of emphasis has many roots and many effects. Despite the differences, however, the comparative psychologists and the classical ethologists had, by the middle of the 20th century, effectively eliminated all explicit investigation of animal minds from the sciences.

Psychology had gone from the study of mind and behavior to being just the study of behavior. Among comparative psychologists, the radical behaviorism of J.B. Watson and B.F. Skinner exerted a strong influence in this respect. But not all comparative psychologists were or are radical behaviorists, and it is a mistake to label them all as such. Nor is it correct to assume that those schooled in behaviorist learning theory think there is no role for cognitive concepts in comparative psychology (Blumberg & Wasserman 1995; Zentall 2001). What comparative psychologists do share, regardless of their feelings about Skinnerian radical behaviorism, is an emphasis on the importance of controlled experiments, usually requiring laboratory conditions.

Meanwhile, many of the second generation of classical ethologists branched out into the fields of behavioral ecology and sociobiology. These branches of biology brought game theoretical approaches and other optimizing models to the biological study of animal behavior. By focusing on strategic outcomes without regard to the psychological mechanisms underlying behavior, these models supported the view that internal causes or subjective states were not essential components for a scientific explanation of animal behavior.

Comparative psychologists and ethologists alike claim to be the intellectual descendants of Darwin. But this means different things to different scientists. Although present-day learning theorists tend to cite Thorndike reverently, emphasizing the search for laws of general learning grounded in basic learning mechanisms that they claim are evolutionarily conserved, they also are well aware of evolved differences. Ethologists tend to emphasize the diversity arising from radiative adaptation of species to their environments, but cognitive ethologists have not managed to carry out a comprehensive program that relates cognitive variation to phylogenetic relationships.

Despite their different starting points, we see comparative psychologists and cognitive ethologists converging on several key points. All agree that the tractability of cognitive questions involves application of a diverse set of comparative methods in order to draw inferences about cognitive states and capacities. Comparative psychologists are becoming increasingly aware of ways in which their experimental apparatuses are not neutral pieces of equipment, but are highly tuned to the animal subjects in ways that implicitly reflect facts about niche-related specialization.[4] Captive settings are also proving to be important for cognitive investigation of evolved specializations such as seed caching in jays. Although these investigators are still cautious about drawing conclusions about subjective states, they nonetheless are more open to a broad range of cognitive questions than the standard behaviorist vs. mentalist dichotomy would suggest. Thus, for instance, Clayton and her colleagues have used seed caching to investigate episodic memory in scrub jays. These birds are able to remember what they cached, where they cached it, when they cached it, and who watched them cache it (see Emery & Clayton 2004 for a review).

While carefully conducted experiments in the laboratory and in the field are often able to control for the influence of variables that might affect the expression of behavioral responses, it is usually the case that there are variables whose influence cannot be accounted for. Field studies may be more prone to a lack of control, because the conditions under which they are conducted are inherently more complex and less controllable. An illustration of the concern for control is found in the explicitly cognitive ethological research of Cheney and Seyfarth (1990) on the meanings of vocal communication and mental processes of vervet monkeys. Cheney and Seyfarth played back pre-recorded vocalizations of familiar individuals to other group members to test what other group members knew about these individuals. Although they took pains to use the recordings only under conditions when the recorded animal was not visible or within hearing range of the focal animals of their experiments, these researchers remained concerned about their inability to eliminate "all visual or auditory evidence of the [familiar] animal's physical presence" (Cheney & Seyfarth 1990, 230). Under field conditions they could never be sure that

---

4 | For a discussion of the ways in which psychologists' mazes are tuned to rats, see Timberlake (2002).

the recorded animals could not be seen or heard by the other animals. Arguably, given their goal of understanding "how monkeys see the world", access to stimuli from different modalities may be important to consider. Legitimate worries about whether or not field experiments are adequately controlled, cannot be addressed in general terms, or rejected as manifestations of excessive skepticism. Specific concerns have to be addressed in the context of the specific experimental inference.

Ethicists who wish to make effective use of cognitive ethology in their arguments against skepticism about animal minds must consider the critics' points of view, and tailor their responses appropriately. Cognitive ethology is by no means a mature discipline whose results can be cited without controversy. There is also a long way to go before having an adequate data-base from which claims about the taxonomic distribution of various cognitive skills that might be relevant to ethics can be put forth.

3. Who Says Animals Don't Suffer?

We have been pushing the idea that to convince anyone of anything, you have to know what position they are starting from. When preaching to the choir, some things can be taken for granted. But quoting scripture will rarely convince an atheist.

This is not to say that the truth or soundness of arguments is relative to an audience—just that their effectiveness is. Neither are we advocating saying whatever it takes to win an argument. Believing P, but recognizing that it may be ineffective to use or try to convince the audience of P in an argument, does not license one to say not-P instead—one must instead find a way to give a convincing argument without using either.

Against a background of common-sense ideas about whether nonhuman animals experience pain and suffering, more detailed neurological, physiological, and behavioral studies can help resolve difficult cases. But against a more general skepticism about animal consciousness (e.g. Carruthers 1989, 2000), the scientifically agreed upon facts about neural, behavior, and physiological similarities between humans and other animals may not be convincing at all.

It is tempting to dismiss the most trenchant of skeptics in the way suggested by Searle (quoted above). One might think it's just obvious that dogs experience pleasure and pain—just look at them wagging their tails, or listen to them whimpering. Suggesting otherwise is *in some contexts* going to be treated as nonsense—liable to get you laughed out of the room. But in other contexts it's not obvious at all. Tail wagging is hardly likely to convince the skeptical scientist or philosopher who might insist on a higher standard of proof than is set by common sense (and profess to be scandalized by the intuitions of ordinary folk).

The reference to a 'higher' standard of proof immediately introduces a value judgment since 'higher' suggests 'better'. And this, indeed, is the way both scientists and philosophers, think about their standards. Scientists have a long and successful history of undermining common sense, of showing that things that seem obvious—that the earth doesn't move for example—are mistakes. Philosophers, with even higher (perhaps impossible?) standards of proof have rather less to show for their much longer history of professional skepticism. But still, by challenging the dogmas of the day, philosophers may help to create an environment in which new ideas can flourish. Nevertheless, it remains an open question: whose standards are the right ones for evaluating answers to questions about animal pain and suffering?

Even this question implicitly begs another question by presupposing something that it should not. Why assume that any single standard of evaluation is *the* right one? Typically, we apply different standards for different purposes. What counts as knowledge in my kitchen may not count as knowledge in the chemistry lab, and whether I am willing to say that I know whether the soufflé will rise depends on who is asking.

Many people from various walks of life have an intense interest in issues of animal pain and suffering. For many of them, the professional skeptic's extreme view that only humans have conscious experiences can be quickly dismissed. "Doesn't he have a dog?" they ask, with a dismissive wave of the hand. From this perspective, there's no need to inspect the arguments because the conclusions are so obviously false. Yet if the skeptic is Peter Carruthers, he has a theory of consciousness (Carruthers 2000)—perhaps a wrong one, but a theory nevertheless—which is more than those who wave their hands. Against the background of this theory, which links consciousness to higher-order thoughts about thoughts, only certain things would count as evidence of consciousness. Wagging tails isn't among them.

How might comparisons between humans and animals prove useful for assessing the experiential states of an animal? Our response should be no surprise by now: it depends who you are talking to. Some people want to be assured that their common sense judgments about animal experiences can be mapped onto physiological and anatomical similarities between humans and nonhuman animals. For such people, such comparisons are likely to be highly useful. Others will want more than this. They might point out, for example, that for any similarity one can present, there are also dissimilarities. Humans have significantly more neural tissue than rats, dogs, or monkeys, presumably allowing more sophisticated forms of cognitive processing. Without a theoretical reason for connecting physiology and behavior to conscious experience, it's hard to say exactly how useful these comparisons are. No matter what one says about the analogies between human and nonhuman physiology, a more detailed description will reveal differences that *might* be relevant to questions about conscious experience. Without anything more to say, arguments based on similarities can always be undermined by pointing out differences.[5]

This is, of course, a double-edged sword. Anyone wishing to argue that certain disanalogies between humans and animals provide grounds for denying conscious experiences to animals, must also give an argument for attributing conscious experience in the one case and not the other. Such an argument is most likely going to have to provide a theoretical reason for linking certain physiological processes to conscious experience, or for thinking that certain forms of sophisticated cognitive mechanisms are required for conscious experience.

Ethicists, like almost everyone else, have typically adopted rather simplistic ideas linking physiology and behavior to function—in this respect they are hardly worse off than almost anyone else writing on this topic. Although critical, this remark is supposed to be constructive, intended to encourage all to be more explicit about the standards of evidence that are in play. Our own view is that greater sophistication about the functions of pain and other conscious states will provide a better framework for assessing the evidence in contexts where the interpretation is in doubt. Common ideas about the function of pain are too unspecific. It is not unusual, for instance, to see it claimed that the capacity to experience adverse states is to protect the animal from harm. This is so generic as to be true also of the immune system, and of various completely unconscious withdrawal reflexes. As such, then, it says nothing about why conscious experiences should be especially implicated in responses to harmful situations, and

---

5 | See Allen (2004a) for a more detailed discussion of analogy arguments.

therefore nothing about why certain responses should be considered as indicating conscious pain or suffering.

Common sense tends to focus on the cries or vocalizations of animals, but there needs to be caution about what is casually inferred from vocalizations. For instance, if a rat receives a mildly painful electric shock to its tail, this produces antinociception (reduced responsiveness to subsequent noxious stimuli) in the rat's tail for up to 10 minutes. But during this same period rats will vocalize more rapidly to the same stimulus (King et al. 1996; Grau 2002). These results caution against simple reliance on reflexive measures when trying to determine the pain experienced by an animal subjected to an aversive stimulus (Allen et al. 2005) and they specifically raise questions about the functional interpretation of rat vocalizations. But this is not to say that vocalizations can never be informative about animal pain. For instance, Puppe et al. (2005) analyzed piglet vocalizations before, during, and after unanesthetized castration, and found that high frequency calls associated with stress occurred most during the surgical portion of the procedure. Recognizing that it is a legitimate scientific question whether any particular animal vocalization provides a measure of conscious pain is not the same as conceding the blanket skeptical view that vocalizations never show anything about pain.

Both the present authors participated in an exercise concerning the ethics of research involving animals that was conducted by the United Kingdom's Nuffield Council on Bioethics (Nuffield 2006). We were asked to comment on the possibility of defining concepts such as 'experience', 'distress', 'harm', 'suffering', and 'well-being' in relation to humans and animals. We were also asked how these concepts can be distinguished. But these terms aren't all on the same level. Anyone looking for a definition of 'experience' has rather different worries in mind than someone seeking a definition of 'harm' or 'well-being'—the last two concepts can both be defined with respect to non-sentient organisms such as trees (or even, in the case of 'harm', for things that aren't living at all, such as buildings). Depending on who is asking, different definitions of these terms will be more or less convincing. How important for defining 'harm' are notions like consciousness, self-consciousness, or self-awareness? While we can define harm without any of these, the resulting notion of harm may not be relevant to those who are interested in ethical questions about the treatment of animals. So even our definitions must be calibrated to the intended audience. (It is not possible to turn to science for resolution because such terms, if they are defined at all, are done so only controversially.)

Consultants were also asked to say how these theoretical terms would be applied to three different species used in research: rats, dogs, and primates. But the question is too abstract. Does anyone seriously think that dogs suffer but rats don't? If so, let us see why they think it before deciding how to respond. Or is the question intended more narrowly, e.g., do rats suffer less than dogs when given similar electric shocks? This question has a better chance of being answered without getting sidetracked into dealing with general skeptical worries, since the question itself presupposes the possibility of suffering. If we agree that there is suffering associated with shock, and we can find its physiological, behavioral, and neurological correlates in one species, then we can assess the correlates in other species, or in genetically modified animals, in order to make a comparative judgment. Brain imaging can be used to figure out the extent and ramifications of reactions to painful stimuli. Anyone who insists that none of this adds up to an attribution of suffering to any animal has much more general worries that will have to be addressed on their own terms.

Concepts such as 'pain', 'suffering', 'distress' and 'happiness' are regularly applied to animals with a high degree of intersubjective agreement. Is this justifiable? Why not? As often happens in public debates about animal welfare, the Nuffield consultants were not provided with any specific arguments against applying these concepts to animals. Could recordings of activity in an animal's brain help decide their applicability? A justification in terms of neuroanatomical convergence is available, but without knowing the specific source of the uncertainty it is impossible to say whether more brain measurements will convince the skeptic. We don't tell physicians that they must withhold attributions of suffering to each other in the absence of brain measurements, so why should we demand such measures before attributing pain to animals? Is a capacity for verbal self-report the deciding factor? These questions are not intended to short circuit arguments, but to highlight the extent to which the adequacy of any response is hard to assess in the absence of a specific challenge.

4. BACK TO ETHICS

Studies which emphasize cognitive sophistication of nonhuman animals are highly congenial to the work of many ethicists. Philosophers working on applied questions about the ethical treatment of animals have increasingly turned to science (and not just the media reports) to bolster their arguments (e.g., Rachels 1990; DeGrazia 1996; Varner 1998). The kinds of results offered by cognitive ethology and comparative psychology are attractive to ethicists not just for the fuel they seem to provide for normative claims about the proper treatment of nonhuman animals qua moral patients, but also because some of these results put pressure on some widely held views in ethical theory about the nature of moral agency. Some ethical theories (especially Kantian accounts) build requirements for sophisticated cognitive or linguistic abilities into their accounts of the nature of ethical judgments and actions. Straightforwardly applying such theories would appear to exclude nonhuman animals from the domain of moral agents. But evidence that monkeys reject unfair rewards (Brosnan & de Waal 2003) or that the give and take of play behavior may foster cooperation and fairness (Allen & Bekoff 2005; Bekoff & Pierce 2009) requires reconsideration of the view that moral judgment or action are exclusively human capacities (see also Gruen 2002). Thus, the potential significance of recent scientific work on animal minds for both theoretical and applied ethics is huge. Nevertheless, this work has scientific critics who cannot be dismissed in a generic fashion. It cannot be straightforwardly imported. Rather, the critics' arguments, objections, and suggestions for alternative experiments and explanation must be considered case-by-case.

Among applied ethicists who write about the morality of our treatment of animals credence seems more frequent than skepticism about animal mind. This may be a self-selection effect since those who write on this topic usually do so because they care deeply about how animals are treated. Overly credulous reliance on the kinds of studies mentioned above can make ethical arguments appear weak, especially to some of the more skeptical scientists (Allen 2006). A similar point can be made about appeals to common sense, although those who argue that scientific data ('science sense', Bekoff 2006a) and common sense should be considered side-by-side in arguments about how we treat other animals are making a valid point about how such arguments operate in many practical contexts, where there is interest in what the theories imply, but where people must also make decisions based on more immediate and intuitive judgments about what the animals in their care are experiencing.

The demands of practical ethics in the castration barn can make the more skeptical challenges to common sense seem completely ungrounded in any real experience with animals. But, for scientists at least, that skepticism is born of specific failures of common sense. Although some scientists do express a kind of blanket skepticism about animal minds, it is usually the case that this skepticism is rooted in specific criticisms of particular studies. Ethicists would do well to go beyond the progressivist strategy of dismissing scientific reluctance about animal minds wholesale, as the product of bad philosophical arguments about the nature of science (Rollin 1989), or the demon-dodging strategy of dismissing scientific reluctance as the product of excessive skepticism that should not be "permitted to infect science" (Jamieson 2002, 68). In this paper we have attempted to describe the field of cognitive ethology and related scientific approaches to animal cognition in a way that brings some of the complexity of the field to the fore. Our hope is that doing so will enable ethicists to avoid certain pitfalls that might arise from having too simplistic a classification scheme that identifies all comparative psychologists as strict behaviorists and defenders of animal mind as cognitive ethologists. The bottom line is that when arguing with scientists about animal minds there's no substitute for detailed empirical knowledge of the cases in question.[6]

REFERENCES

Adam, D. (2005), "Scientists Say Lobsters Feel no Pain", Guardian Unlimited, February 8, 2005, http://www.guardian.co.uk/animalrights/story/0,11917,1408050,00.html.
Allen, C. (2004a), "Animal Pain", Noûs 38/4, 617-643.
Allen, C. (2004b), "Is Anyone a Cognitive Ethologist?", Biology & Philosophy 19, 589-607.

---

[6] | We would like to thank Robert Francescotti and Gary Steiner for comments on earlier drafts of this essay. This essay originally appeared in The Journal of Ethics in 2007 and is reprinted here with permission. It was slightly updated in March 2012.

Allen, C. (2006), "Ethics and the Science of Animal Minds", Theoretical Medicine and Bioethics 27/4, 375-394.

Allen, C. (2011), "Fish Cognition and Consciousness", Journal of Agricultural and Environmental Ethics, online first: preprint doi:10.1007/s10806-011-9364-9.

Allen, C., Bekoff, M. (1995), "Cognitive Ethology and the Intentionality of Animal Behaviour", Mind and Language 10/4, 313-28.

Allen, C., Bekoff, M. (1997), Species of Mind: The Philosophy and Biology of Cognitive Ethology, Cambridge, MA.: MIT Press.

Allen, C., Bekoff, M. (2005), "Animal Play and the Evolution of Morality: An Ethological Approach", Topoi 24/2, 125-135.

Allen, C., Fuchs, P.N., Shriver, A., Wilson, H. (2005) "Deciphering Animal Pain", in: M. Aydede, M. (ed.), Pain: New Essays on the Nature of Pain and the Methodology of Its Study, Cambridge, MA.: MIT Press, 352-366.

Bartal, I.B.A., Decety, J., Mason, P. (2011), "Empathy and Pro-Social Behavior in Rats", Science 334, 1427-1430.

Bekoff, M. (1977), "Social Communication in Canids: Evidence for the Evolution of a Stereotyped Mammalian Display", Science 197, 1097-1099.

Bekoff, M. (1995), "Play Signals as Punctuation: The Structure of Social Play in Canids", Behaviour 132, 419-429.

Bekoff, M. (2006a), "Animal Emotions and Animal Sentience and Why They Matter: Blending 'Science Sense' With Common Sense, Compassion, and Heart", in: J. Turner, J. D'Silva (ed.), Animals, Ethics and Trade, London: Earthscan Publishing, 27-40.

Bekoff, M. (2006b), Animal Passions and Beastly Virtues: Reflections on Redecorating Nature, Philadelphia: Temple University Press.

Bekoff, M. (2006c), "Animal Passions and Beastly Virtues: Cognitive Ethology as the Unifying Science for Understanding the Subjective, Emotional, Empathic, and Moral Lives of Animals", Zygon (Journal of Religion and Science) 41/1, 71-104.

Bekoff, M. (2007), The Emotional Lives of Animals, New World Library: Novato, California.

Bekoff, M. (2010), The Animal Manifesto: Six Reasons for Expanding Our Compassion, New World Library: Novato, California.

Bekoff, M., Allen. C. (1997), "Cognitive Ethology: Slayers, Skeptics, and Proponents", in: R.W. Mitchell, N. Thompson, L. Miles (ed.) (1997),

Anthropomorphism, Anecdote, and Animals: The Emperor's New Clothes?, Albany, NY: SUNY Press, 313-34.
Bekoff, M., Jamieson, D. (ed.) (1996), Readings in Animal cognition, Cambridge, MA.: MIT Press.
Bekoff, M., Pierce, J. (2009), Wild Justice: The Moral Lives of Animals, Chicago: University of Chicago Press.
Blumberg, M., Wasserman, E.A. (1995), "Animal Mind and the Argument From Design", American Psychologist 50, 133-144.
Braithwaite, V. (2010), Do Fish Feel Pain?, Oxford: Oxford University Press.
Brosnan, S.F., de Waal, F.B.M. (2003), "Monkeys Reject Unequal Pay", Nature 425, 297-299.
Bshary, R., Hohner, A., Ait-el-Djoudi, K., Fricke, H. (2006), "Interspecific Communicative and Coordinated Hunting Between Groupers and Giant Moray Eels in the Red Sea", PLoS Biology 4/12, e431. doi:10.1371/journal.pbio.0040431.
Burghardt, G.M. (1991), "Cognitive Ethology and Critical Anthropomorphism: A Snake With Two Heads and Hognose Snakes That Play Dead", in: C.A. Ristau (ed.), Cognitive Ethology: the Minds of Other Animals, San Francisco: Erlbaum, 53-90
Cabanac, M., Cabanac, A.J., Parent, A. (2009), "The Emergence of Consciousness in Phylogeny", Behavioral Brain Research 198/2, 267-272.
Carruthers, P.M. (1989), "Brute Experience", Journal of Philosophy 86, 258-269.
Carruthers, P.M. (2000), Phenomenal Consciousness: A Naturalistic Theory, Cambridge: Cambridge University Press.
Cheney, D.L., Seyfarth, R.M. (1990), How Monkeys See the World: Inside the Mind of Another Species, Chicago: University of Chicago Press.
Crist, E. (2002), "The Inner Life of Earthworms: Darwin's Argument and Its Implications", in: M. Bekoff, C. Allen, G. M. Burghardt (ed.), The Cognitive Animal: Empirical and Theoretical Perspectives on Animal Cognition, Cambridge, MA: MIT Press, 3-8.
Crowley, S.J., Allen, C. (2008), "Animal Behavior: E Pluribus Unum?", in: M. Ruse (ed.), Oxford Handbook of Philosophy of Biology, New York: Oxford University Press, 327-348.
Darwin, C. (1871), The Descent of Man and Selection in Relation to Sex, New York: D. Appleton & Company.

DeGrazia, D. (1996), Taking Animals Seriously: Mental Life and Moral Status, Cambridge: Cambridge University Press.

Edgar, J.L., Lowe, J.C., Paul, E.S., Nicol, C.J. (2011), "Avian Maternal Response to Chick Distress", Proceedings of the Royal Society B, doi: 10.1098/rspb.2010.2701

Emery, N.J., Clayton, N.S. (2004), "The Mentality of Crows: Convergent Evolution of Intelligence in Corvids and Apes", Science 306, 1903-1907.

Grau, J. (2002), "Learning and Memory Without a Brain", in: M. Bekoff, C. Allen, G.M. Burghardt (ed.), The Cognitive Animal: Emprical and Theoretical Perspectives on Animal Cognition, Cambridge, MA: MIT Press, 77-88.

Griffin, D.R. (1976), The Question of Animal Awareness: Evolutionary Continuity of Mental Experience, New York: Rockefeller University Press.

Griffin, D.R. (1978), "Prospects for a Cognitive Ethology", Behavioral and Brain Sciences 4, 527-538.

Griffiths, P.E. (2004), "Instinct in the '50s: The British Reception of Konrad Lorenz's Theory of Instinctive Behavior", Biology and Philosophy 19/4, 609-631.

Gruen, L. (2002), "The Morals of Animal Minds", in: M. Bekoff, C. Allen, G. M. Burghardt (ed.), The Cognitive Animal: Emprical and Theoretical Perspectives on Animal Cognition, Cambridge, MA: MIT Press, 437-442.

Horowitz, A., Bekoff, M. (2007), "Naturalizing Anthropomorphism: Behavioral Prompts to Our Humanizing of Animals", Anthrozoös 20/1, 25-35.

Jamieson, D. (2002), Morality's Progress, New York: Oxford University Press.

Jamieson. D., Bekoff, M. (1993), "On Aims and Methods of Cognitive Ethology", Philosophy of Science Association 2/1, 110-24.

Kacelnik, A., Chappell, J., Weir, A.A.S., Kenward, B. (2006), "Cognitive Adaptations for Tool-Related Behaviour in New Caledonian Crows", in: E.A. Wasserman, T.R. Zentall (ed.), Comparative Cognition: Experimental Explorations of Animal Intelligence, Oxford: Oxford University Press, 515-528.

King, T.E., Joynes, R.L., Meagher, M.W., Grau, J.W. (1996), "The Impact of Shock on Pain Reactivity II: Evidence for Enhanced Pain", Journal of Experimental Psychology: Animal Behavior Processes 22, 265-278.

Kuba, M.J., Byrne, R.A., Burghardt, G.M. (2010), "A New Method for Studying Problem Solving and Tool Use in Stingrays (Potamotrygon castexi)", Animal Cognition 13/3, 507-513.

Langford, D.J. et al. (2006), "Social Modulation of Pain as Evidence for Empathy in Mice" Science 213, 1967-1970.

Lehrman, D.S. (1953), "A Critique of Konrad Lorenz's Theory of Instinctive Behavior", The Quarterly Review of Biology 28/, 337-363.

Lloyd Morgan, C. (1894), An Introduction to Comparative Psychology, London: Walter Scott.

Lorenz, K. (1952), King Solomon's Ring: New Light on Animal Ways, New York: Crowell.

Nuffield Council (ed.) (2005), The Ethics of Research Involving Animals, London: Nuffield Council on Bioethics. http://bit.ly/rc6fL1.

Panksepp, J., Burgdorf, J. (2003), "'Laughing' Rats and the Evolutionary Antecedents of Human Joy?", Physiology and Behavior 79/3, 533-547.

Puppe, B., Schön, P.C., Tuchscherer, A., Manteuffel, G. (2005), "Castration-Induced Vocalisation in Domestic Piglets, Sus scrofa: Complex and Specific Alterations of the Vocal Quality", Applied Animal Behavior Science 95/1, 67-78.

Rachels, J. (1990), Created from Animals: The Moral Implications of Darwinism, New York: Oxford University Press.

Rollin, B. (1989), The Unheeded Cry: Animal Consciousness, Animal Pain, and Science, Oxford: Oxford University Press.

Romanes, G. (1882), Animal Intelligence, London: Routledge & Kegan Paul.

Rose, J. (2002), "The Neurobehavioral Nature of Fishes and the Question of Awareness and Pain", Reviews in Fisheries Science 10/1, 1-38.

Searle, J. (1998), "Animal Minds", Etica & Animali 9, 37-50.

Singer, P. (1975), Animal Liberation, New York: Ecco Press Books.

Singer, P. (1990), Animal Liberation, 2nd edition. New York: New York Review of Books.

Sneddon, L.U., Braithwaite, V.A., Gentle, M.J. (2003), "Do Fishes Have Nociceptors? Evidence for the Evolution of a Vertebrate Sensory System", Proceedings of the Royal Society of London B 270, 1115-1121.

Timberlake, W. (2002), "Niche-Related Learning in Laboratory Paradigms: The Case of Maze Behavior in Norway rats", Behavioural Brain Research 134: 355-374.

Tinbergen, N. (1963), "On the Aims and Methods of Ethology", Zeitschrift für Tierpsychologie 20, 410-433.

Varner, G. (1998), In Nature's Interests? Animal Rights, and Environmental Ethics, New York: Oxford University Press.

Zentall, T.R. (2001), "The Case for a Cognitive Approach to Animal Learning and Behavior", Behavioural Processes 54, 65-78.

3. A Form of War
Animals, Humans, and the Shifting Boundaries of Community

Justin E.H. Smith

1. Introduction

The modern conception of moral status, in which humans are supposed to have absolute moral commitment to all other humans, while having no properly moral commitments, but only indirect ones, to the vast majority of other animals, is the result of a long and complex genealogy, and one that has yet to be written. If I speak of genealogy here it is because, with Nietzsche (1887), Foucault (1975), and Bernard Williams (1994), I wish to suggest that an investigation into the deep historical sources of a common assumption of the modern world might reveal, at the same time, the extent to which this assumption is merely or largely verbal, serving as the *ad hoc* account we give of a system of practices which only begins to make sense when we consider the way these practices emerge out of a world that did not share our assumptions.

But how could the human-animal dichotomy have a genealogy at all? What could be more deep-seated, more natural, than to divide the world into 'us' and 'them' in just this way? It is certainly true that the idea that humans are a variety of animal is a very new one, a Victorian invention, and one that has not managed to significantly change the way we speak and think about the human-animal relationship. No matter what we retain from biology classes, our own folk-taxonomy continues to take 'animal' as the intermediate category between 'human' and 'plant', and the emphatic phrase 'non-human animal' continues to strike even those of us who insist that humans are in fact animals as a bit forced. But if we have had trouble recently accepting that humans are animals, nonetheless the default assumption throughout most of human history has been that animals are themselves people, if not exactly in the same way we are. Animals and humans were for most of the history of *homo sapiens* members of a single, all-encompassing community, in which each member was thought capable of a certain kind of rational activity grounded in intention and in anticipation of the future; in which members of each kind had reciprocal obligations towards members of all other kinds (even if these obligations did not involve refraining from killing, whether one was to refrain or not was not centrally determined by whether the creature in question was an animal person or a human person); and in which there was no meaningful division between nature and culture, or between the boundaries of the human world and the vast expanses of inhuman and indifferent wilderness that surround it.

Nietzsche and Williams were interested, each in his own way, in determining how we came to account for the range of ways we treat other human beings, and in each case the answer had to do with the invention of something we call 'morality' over the course of Western history. I want to suggest in turn that if morality is new, and the loss of a view of the world on which animals are persons is also new, it may be that these two developments are part of a package. That is, coming to think of people as having something we might call 'moral status', rather than just being governed by shame and necessity, or by prohibitions that impose themselves as if from outside as quasi-physical forces rather than flowing from within as a result of one's autonomous agency, involved a corresponding need to sharply determine the boundaries of the realm of beings endowed with such status. The extension of moral status to *all* human beings, to put this another way, might have as its corollary the limitation of moral status to *only* human beings.

From an earlier model on which beings derived their importance from, let us say, their ecological role in a socio-natural theater that included human beings, a new picture emerged on which moral status had to be articulated in terms of criteria based upon the internal capacities of the different kinds of creature. The question was no longer: Do these creatures play a vital role in the ecology that includes us?, but rather: Are these creatures inwardly like us? Wherein this likeness is to consist would be a question that would receive different answers over the course of history, but most would be variations on the idea that, whereas we have rational souls, or reason, or agency, or language, or recursive language, or a developed neocortex, they do not. The exact way in which these distinctions were to make all the difference, or in which practical consequences were to follow from them, was never entirely clear. As Richard Sorabji (1995) has noted, "they lack syntax, therefore we may eat them", is hardly a compelling inference.

On the account I wish to articulate, the discovery that there is something universally shared by human beings, regardless of country or clime, regardless of whether the humans in question are friends or enemies, meant at the same time that species became the sole criterion for the determination of the bounds of community. Human beings came to have moral status because they had this new thing, morality, and for the first time the range of what you can or cannot do to them came to be determined by this new internal capacity. At the same time, the range of what you can do to beings that are not characterized by that internal capacity grew without limit. The genealogy of morality, as the key defining feature of all human beings, goes together with what we might call the genealogy of animality: the creation of that class of beings that, as non-human, lies outside of the sphere of moral consideration altogether.

Yet the account we give of where our moral commitments lie is often grossly out of synch with our practices, and in this connection I want to suggest that species boundaries are far less important than the account we give of our moral commitments would lead one to believe. In fact, while we are committed to a basic division between the beings that have moral status and the beings that lack it, and this division for the most part extends only up to the boundaries of the human species (notwithstanding the minimal animal welfare laws in a handful of developed countries), there is another division dictating practice, one that cuts across species boundaries and that divides beings, both human and non-human, into two basic categories, which we might call 'the protected' and 'the unprotected'. There are animals, and people, that can be exterminated without consequences; and there are animals, and people, whose injury disrupts the ordinary course of things, or at least appears to disrupt it. On this division, moral status does not flow from the kind of being an individual living thing is, still less from its neurophysiology or the evidence it gives of having a rich internal life or of being intelligent.

'Animal' as a category that informs the way we speak and reason about the reach of our moral commitments coexists with a set of rules governing what we may or may not do to different kinds of creature that seems not to take the human-animal dichotomy as fundamental. Sometimes, philosophers notice the gap between the way we reason and the way we act, and when they do the usual reaction is to suppose that our actions are out of step with right reason. Thus Cass Sunstein observes that "people who love... pets, and greatly care about their welfare, help ensure short and painful lives for millions, even billions of animals that cannot easily be distinguished from dogs and cats" (Sunstein 2005, 3). But these pet-lovers are not necessarily guilty of a contradiction, for they never claimed to consider anatomical or neurophysiological similarity between, say, cows and dogs, to be the criterion for equal treatment. This may be the preferred criterion of Peter Singer, Tom Regan, and others who wish to argue for the rights of animals on the basis of their capacity, evidently equal to ours, to suffer. But the pet-loving carnivore has her own, coherent means of easily distinguishing between the two kinds of being: the dog belongs to the class of pets, the steer to the class of food.

Evidently social kinds such as food-animal, pet, vermin, and so on, are often more relevant indicators of what can and cannot be done to them than the matter of their species membership. Philosophers are in general less able to see this than anthropologists, since the former tend to suppose, with Kant, that the categories of our understanding, which make possible an understanding of the world in general, are themselves the *a priori* structures of understanding; anthropologists on the other hand tend to believe, with Emile Durkheim and Marcel Mauss, that the categories we have at our disposal for our understanding of the natural world took shape in the first instance from our experience of some unique form or other of social reality. Thus Durkheim and Mauss wrote in 1902 that, originally, "[s]ociety was not simply a model which classificatory thought followed; it was its own divisions which served as divisions for the system of classification. The first logical categories were social categories; the first classes of things were classes of men, into which these things were integrated." (Durkheim & Mauss 1902, 66-67) If we can agree that, at a certain subscientific level of taxonomy that we share with the 'primitive' societies of interest to Durkheim and Mauss, natural kinds have their parallels in social kinds, it is no longer so surprising to note that there are street people in just the same way as there are street dogs, and there are people who can be exterminated by fighter jet or by machete massacre in just the same way as vermin are dealt with by pest-control professionals. When I say 'in just the same way' what I mean is that these animals and these humans belong to the same class not just in an analogical sense; rather, the range of possible actions towards a certain animal or human is determined by the fact that it is conceptualized as belonging to a distinctly social category that may contain either animals or humans. The usual reaction to atrocities against humans is to recoil in horror and declare that humans should not be treating one another like animals. But what this reaction fails to capture is that not every animal is treated atrociously, and when they are treated atrociously this is not necessarily in recognition of their animality.

The extension of morality to all and only human beings, I want to say, is one that causes a bit of confusion in the way we talk, but that leaves us to act more or less as we always have. In fact, in practice, we are familiar both with the figure of the *homo sacer* in Agamben's (1998) sense, as well as with all sorts of highly protected animals: cherished pets, endangered wildlife, sacred cows. There are people who may be treated with arbitrary cruelty, and animals that must be treated with the utmost solicitude. Again, the usual reaction to this fact is to suppose that people are confused, in the sense that they are acting in violation of their own commitments. Sunstein is not alone in his condescension to the pet-loving steak-eater. But what if the different ways we treat dogs and cattle, respectively, has nothing to do with the fact that they are animals and we are not?

One obstacle, perhaps, to accepting this is the corollary suggestion that the range of ways we treat people, in different circumstances (say, a raid on an enemy village, or, by contrast, volunteering at the soup kitchen), has little to do with the fact that they are human, and so are we. The danger associated with dislodging moral commitment from the kind of creature a creature is, a kindhood that is supposed to flow from its internal constitution, and instead associating moral commitment with the way that creature shows up in our ecology, is that this would be to overturn the now millennia-long tradition of moral universalism vis-à-vis other humans. It would also, however, help us to come to terms with the fact that we do, in fact, have a variety of commitments to a range of different kinds of creature, and these commitments do not necessarily flow from their internal constitution, whether this is conceptualized in terms of an immaterial soul, or in terms of a complex nervous system.

2. Humans and Animals in Deep History

I aim to reveal some of the pretheoretical commitments that underlie human relationships with animals, and I have described this task as a sort of genealogy. There is a danger, of course, of lapsing into the sort of uninformed and romantic speculation about the distant past of which Nietzsche is plainly guilty in the *Genealogy*. But fortunately some things may now be said with confidence about what the first several hundred decades of human existence were in fact like; and cautious conjectures may be made about how this long chapter makes itself felt in our own lives. At best, attention to the anthropology and the archaeology of hunter-gatherer societies might turn out to be usefully 'untimely' in much the same way that Williams and Nietzsche considered their use of Greek antiquity to be. It is not that one might derive from an imagined past a model for how we ought to be, but rather that an honest exploration of the foreign country of the past can help to reveal the contingency of our own commitments.

Now a consideration of pre-modern attitudes towards animals that is not only untimely but also unromantic will acknowledge the evidence for massive, wasteful slaughter of animals by members of hunter-gatherer societies. The Plains Indians, for example, are known to have driven vastly more bison to their deaths, through the so called *pis'kin* or corralling method, than could possibly be used for human consumption. Hunter-gatherers were not 'green', and to say that they lived in a single socio-natural community with other living beings is not at all to suggest that they had values of the sort towards which conservationists today hope to steer our society. Indeed, what made human community with nature and other living beings possible was that nature was not something to which humans felt they had to return, or from which they felt they had been cut off to begin with. To suppose that traditional ideas about nature and the other living beings in nature flowed from a 'respect' for the 'intrinsic value' of these things, a respect conceptualized on the model of today's conservationism, is as anachronistic as supposing that a prehistoric hunter considered his principle activity and source of livelihood to be a 'good line of work'.

Of course, to say that hunting was not 'work' in any meaningful sense is not to say that hunter-gatherer societies fell short of the mark of distinctly human activity. There is a widespread view, going back most importantly to Marx and Engels, that history itself begins when humans begin transforming the environment in pursuit of their own goals, when humans stop merely collecting, and begin producing. As Maurice Godelier puts it, "humans have a history because they transform nature" (Godelier 1986, 12). Yet recently the very idea of 'prehistory' has been criticized as setting up a buffer zone between the humanities discipline of history on the one hand and the natural-scientific domain of paleoanthropology on the other, which makes historians feel comfortable about their neatly contained discipline, but also arbitrarily cuts them off from the source of a good deal of what it was that was, so to speak, driving humans when they entered what the humanists are willing to recognize as the historical era (Lord Smail 2008). From another direction, some anthropologists have disputed the traditional view according to which the shift from hunting and gathering to pastoralism and agriculture amounted, at least from the inside, to the discovery of production and consequently to the emergence of a distinctly human way of relating to the natural world. Tim Ingold cites the case of the crop-growing people of the Mount Hagen region of Papua New Guinea. "Completely absent from the Hagen conception", he writes, "is the notion of a domestic environment 'carved out' from wild nature. *Mbo* [the word for the activity of planting] does not refer to an enclosed space of settlement, as opposed to the surrounding of the bush or forest. Hageners do not seek to subjugate or colonize the wilderness... *Rømi* [the antonym of '*mbo*'] is simply that which lies outside the limits of human care and sociability." (Ingold 1996, 18) On the basis of examples such as this, Ingold argues that the shift away from hunting and gathering was not necessarily conceptualized by those involved in the shift as one towards production, or as one that sets the human world over against the natural one.

This is significant since pastoralism, as a mode of production generally thought to have radically displaced hunting and gathering, is really not so far from our own world as we might think. Some of the earliest and most important texts to which historians (in the narrow sense) have access are the records of pastoralist societies. These include the *Rig Veda* of northern India and the Hebrew Bible of the eastern Mediterranean. We may locate the textual traditions of Greek and Roman antiquity at only a partial remove from the values and world-view of pastoralism: sometimes the concerns of the countryside are occluded from sight (as in the dialogues of Plato, which take place in a center of commerce), but sometimes they come back to the center of attention (as in Virgil's *Georgics*). We have *access*, in other words, to a world in which human beings in some sense dominated animals, had the power of life and death over them, yet did not have anything like a sense of the 'moral status' of animals and of the responsibility towards them that flows from this, and also certainly did not believe that one may conduct oneself in any way one chooses towards the animals encountered over the course of a life.

Consider the rules governing horse sacrifice in the *Rig Veda*, or Evans-Pritchard's well-known account of the attention and benevolence that a Nuer cattle herd lavishes upon the cow under his care. In each case, we are looking at highly rule-governed domains of human activity, but it would be a mistake to suppose that these rules have anything at all in common with, say, the animal protection laws that have sprung up in the Western world since the 19th century, or, in the case of the horse sacrifice, with the abattoir regulations that are intended to ensure a 'humane' slaughter. The Nuer treats his cow well, but not because it has 'moral status'. He treats it well because the cosmos rotates around it. Nor does the Nuer conceive his relations with the cow as flowing from human dominion over nature, or the transformation of nature in accordance with human will. Rather, the cow functions as a sort of fixed reference point that gives context and meaning to human action. As Evans-Pritchard summed up the motivations underlying a Nuer's actions, *"cherchez la vache* is the best advice that can be given to those who desire to understand Nuer behaviour" (Evans-Pritchard 1940, 19). All this suggests that if we are going to pinpoint the moment of the shift in the way we conceptualize animals, we will not be able to do this principally by charting shifts in the dominant mode of production.

Of course, at just the same time as the Nuer cattle herd is lavishing his care on his prize bull, he is also likely ready to exterminate any would-be predators without a second thought. These predators might be very much like the bull with respect to neurophysiology or behavioral capabilities. Was the Nuer, then, contradicting himself? Of course not. The contradictions only begin to grow when we commit ourselves, against our actual practices, to the idea that the rules of conduct towards a being flow from its moral status, which in turn flows from its interior nature and capabilities.

3. Out of Sight, Out of Mind

Whether living in societies based on collection or on production, most pre-industrial people had to confront animals much more regularly than we, and in a way that was much more likely to have an influence, depending on the outcome of the human-animal encounter, on the quality of their human lives. Animals were phenomenally salient in a way that they are not now: a regular and significant part of the landscape of daily opportunities and obstacles. In classical antiquity, Aristotle still recognized that hunting is a form of war. He explains in Book I of the *Politics*, in fact, that the hunting of animals and the subjugation of peoples by force are in fact just two aspects of the same general activity, an activity approved by nature herself:

"Now if nature makes nothing incomplete, and nothing in vain, the inference must be that she has made all animals for the sake of man. And so, in one point of view, the art of war is a natural art of acquisition, for the art of acquisition includes hunting, an art which we ought to practice against wild beasts, and against men who, though intended by nature to be governed, will not submit; for war of such a kind is naturally just." (*Politics* 1256b 20-25)

Though there were still of course skirmishes being fought, in an important sense the war against animals, if not against human beings intended by nature to be ruled, had already been decisively won by the time Aristotle wrote. We might speculate that the human victory over animals (or at least over our megafauna competitors) in the hunting war was directly related to the detheriomorphization of the gods in Greek antiquity, and the corollary elevation of human beings to an exceptional status among living things in the singular way in which their actions, intentions, schemings, and even their bare physiology, mirrors those of the gods.

Consider by contrast the Cree of central Canada, who traditionally had to give thanks and reverence to the bear, in order that it should 'give itself' to them in the hunt. What is most central to the lives of a human group, what is most wrapped up with its continuing vitality, easily becomes elevated to something like a divine status (this is also the case for a number of agrarian societies such as the Mesoamerican societies based on cults surrounding the grains they cultivate, as well as for pastoralist societies such as the Nuer). But in a marketplace in the center of a complex democracy, it could easily appear that dealings with other people are singularly relevant to one's continued vitality. Now I do not wish to lapse into crude reductivism here as to the origins of philosophy and of the core values of the West, such as humanism and moral universalism. But I only wish to point out what should in fact be quite obvious, that the status accorded to animals in different human societies has a good deal to do with the way animals show up in what I have been calling the 'ecology' of a human life, and they do not show up in the lives of the people in the societies that gave rise to and sustained philosophy in at all the same way that they do in the lives of hunters and pastoralists.

For Aristotle, animals are interesting but not intimate, worthy objects of study but not members of a shared community. In an elegant passage of *On the Parts of Animals*, Aristotle takes the time to justify having an interest in animals at all. "Every realm of nature is marvellous", Aristotle writes,

"and as Heraclitus, when the strangers who came to visit him found him warming himself at the furnace in the kitchen and hesitated to go in, is reported to have bidden them not to be afraid to enter, as even in that kitchen divinities were present, so we should venture on the study of every kind of animal without distaste; for each and all will reveal something natural and something beautiful." (PA I 5, 17-23)

Aristotle is reminding his contemporaries of something they might have forgotten: that animals are divine. Of course, we should not see him as appealing here for a revival of the theriomorphic gods of Greece's neighbors and predecessors to the east, for Aristotle's conception of divinity here is of nothing more than that which reveals natural order and purpose. And so the philosopher sets out to study the generation, parts, motion, and progress of animals, and if there is any religious sense in this undertaking, it is fully subordinated to the aim of understanding. Other than in the ten books of the *History of Animals*, Aristotle's animals have nothing to do with the animals of fables and allegories: what is natural and beautiful in the parts of animals is interesting in its own right, not in view of what it enables one to say about human beings. Aristotle is thinking about animals, not with animals.

In large part for this reason, although Aristotle is without question the greatest zoologist in antiquity, others who are not nearly so great are in many ways better able to communicate common ideas about the intellectual and behavioral capacities of animals, and about the nature of the human-animal relationship. The 3rd-century historian Claudius Aelianus, also known as Aelian, devotes much of his multi-book treatise *On Animals* to reciting anecdotes about animals that are capable of planning for the future, feeling emotional attachment, outsmarting humans, and so on. But the capabilities he attributes to them already show that these are exceptional, and thus worthy of being communicated. Consider this rich, and very typical, passage:

"Here again I may as well speak of the peculiarities of animals [...] Baboons and goats are lecherous, and it is even said that the latter have intercourse with women—a fact which Pindar also appears to marvel at. And even hounds are said to have assaulted women, and indeed it is reported that a woman in Rome was accused by her husband of adultery, and the adulterer in the case was stated to be a hound. And I have heard that baboons have fallen madly in love with girls and have even raped them, being more wanton than the little boys in the all-night revels of Menander. The partridge is extremely lecherous and given to adultery... The hog is implacable and devoid of justice; at any rate these creatures eat one another's dead bodies. And the majority of fishes do the same. But the most impious of all is the hippopotamus, for it even eats its own father." (*On Animals* VII, 19)

One noteworthy feature of Aelian's observations here is that the animals are described in normative, and thus human terms, but at the same time their praiseworthy or blameworthy actions are supposed to flow from their very natures, and thus to pertain to a given kind universally. Thus *the* hippopotamus eats its father, which is to say hippopotamuses just are patriphagous. But if this is just what animals of this kind do, then how can it possibly be impious? We will return below to the curious way animals are often spoken of, in which a species as a whole becomes the moral and ontological equivalent of a single human individual. For now it is sufficient to comment that Aelian's mixture of registers—human-like psychology with animal necessity, the moral with the natural, the exceptional with the universal—was, Aristotle's major contribution aside, the standard way of speaking about animals until the early modern period, and one of the available ways of speaking about animals long after the early modern period.

Dennis Des Chene notes that in the modern period "[t]he concept animal is charged not only with designating a class of creatures, real and imagined, but also with supplying a contrast to the human" (Des Chene 2006, 216). Animals came to be conceptualized as humanity's contrast class, as the inversion of what a human being was thought to be. But what did this inversion look like?

We are of course familiar with the model of the animal-machine associated with Descartes and the rise of mechanical philosophy in the early 17th century. To some extent, certainly, the mechanization of nature in the early modern period, and of animal generation, development, structure, and motion along with it, served to intensify human exceptionalism. Yet we might have reason to doubt that this part of the story, though so often emphasized, is the one that really tells us about transformations in human conceptualization of animals in the modern period. After all, Descartes believed that human bodies are machines as well; the difference between humans and animals was for him that the human being is itself not a body at all, but a soul, while animals are entirely body. But the machine model had to do with explaining the motion of natural bodies, not 'objectifying' animals. There is simply no evidence from the early modern period that philosophers who believed that animals are machines were any more eager to objectify animals through scientific experiment than were the philosophers who continued to adhere to the old model, according to which animals have their own animal souls. G. W. Leibniz, for example, was a staunch opponent of the Cartesian doctrine of the animal-machine, yet in at least one early text, the *Directiones ad rem medicam pertinentes* of 1671, we find the philosopher arguing that dogs are more useful for studying the inner workings of the body than are humans, since, he explains "we can cut them open how and when we please" (Smith 2011, Appendix 1).

In this text Leibniz is also very enthused about some of the experimental work being done in the London meeting hall of the Royal Philosophical Society. Most intriguing was the work of a certain Richard Lower, a Cornish physician who in 1669 had published a *Tractatus de corde* [*Treatise on the Heart*]. Lower was not working alone, and indeed he appears to have been encouraged in his experiments by other members (many of higher rank than he) of the Royal Society. Thus we learn from the society's journal, the *Philosophical Transactions of the Royal Society* about "[t]ryals Proposed by Mr. [Robert] Boyle to Dr. Lower, to Be Made by Him for the Improvement of Transfusing Blood Out of One Live Animal into Another." Boyle goes on to enunciate a list 'Queries' for Lower to answer:

- Whether a fierce dog, by being quite new stocked with the blood of a cowardly dog, may not become more tame or vice versa?
- Whether a transfused dog will recognize his master?
- Whether characteristics peculiar to a breed (e.g., the scent of bloodhounds) will be abolished or impaired if a spaniel's blood is transfused into a bloodhound?
- Whether rejuvenation will occur if an old, feeble dog is given the blood of a young, vigorous one?

We know from the text of the *Tractatus de corde* that Lower took Boyle up on many of these suggestions. The most active period of animal experimentation in the Royal Society seems to have peaked in the 1660s, when researchers were concerned mostly with questions about respiration and the circulation of the blood, areas in which, it could easily be presumed, not much differed from species to species. William Harvey, with his discovery of the blood's circulation, did not settle the question once for all as to why it circulates and of what vital functions it sees to. Next to those performed with the air pump, experiments involving transfusion were among the most common of those performed by the Royal Society (and it is worth noting as well that many of the air-pump experiments on animals were also concerned with blood—namely, with the oxygenation of the blood through respiration).

Before a transfixed public at Greshame College, in 1666 Lower performed dog-to-dog transfusions, in which two dogs were connected together by means of tubes, and blood was made to flow out of one, into the other, and back again. The record shows that of all the members of the audience at the experiment on transfusion, only the legendary diarist John Evelyn registered any squeamishness. A few years later, in 1670, Evelyn writes in his diary of being "forc'd to accompanie some friends to the Beare-garden" in London, to watch a dog-fight. "[T]he Irish Wolfe dog exceeded", he relates, "which was a tall Gray-hound, a stately creature in deede, who beat a cruell Mastife". Evelyn goes on: "One of the Bulls tossd a dog full into a Ladys lap as she sate in one of the boxes at a Considerable height from the Arena: there were two poore dogs killed; & so all ended with the Ape on horse-back, & I most heartily weary, of the rude & dirty passetime, which I had not seene I think in twenty years before." (5 June, 1670; Evelyn 1995, 175)

Was the Royal Society just another scene of rude and dirty pastimes? One thing that the historian of animal experimentation cannot help but notice is that the dog was often taken as the ideal test subject not just because of the relative similarity of its internal anatomy to ours, but also because its expressions of pain or displeasure are for us so easy to read and understand. Who after all really knows whether the parakeet in the vacuum chamber is suffering from lack of oxygen, or just flapping its wings as some mechanical response? Far from it being the case that the famous new animal-machine doctrine of the 17th century made vivisection permissible, it is rather precisely because the vivisectionists knew that dogs *do* have feelings that they were such useful *Ersätze* in experiments known to involve suffering. Dogs were moreover useful because they were so forgiving: they can be put through the same torture over and over again without growing resentful. Thus Lower tells of one test subject who, "once its jugular vein was sewn up and its binding shackles cast off, promptly jumped down from the table and, apparently oblivious of its hurts, soon began to fondle its master, and to roll on the grass to clean itself of blood" (Lower 1669).

What is thus more revealing than studying the way philosophers changed their metaphysical models of animals, perhaps, is a consideration of the way in society as a whole changed the way it related towards animals, not just the animals that served in scientific experiment, but also farm animals, food animals, vermin. Noëlie Vialles highlights some important changes in the late 18th and early 19th centuries in her *Animal to Edible*, an ethnographic study of the slaughterhouses of southern France:

"While [the relocation of slaughtering to the town limits] certainly had to do with a town-planning policy concerned about public hygiene, exiling the abattoir was also, through that very policy, an expression of the profound shift in sensibilities with regard to such realities as death (human or animal), suffering, violence, waste and disease, miasmas, and finally animals themselves." (Vialles 1994, 19)

Vialles notes that private slaughtering by butchers in their central shops was prohibited in France under Napoleon, and that this brought about an effective "dissociation of slaughtering and butchering". The butcher does not have blood on his hands; he simply deals with a commodity that, by the time it reaches his shop, has been thoroughly de-animalized. The blood-stained hands now belong to the abattoir laborer, an unseen, abstract figure beyond the city limits, who certainly will never make it into any illustrated children's book about our town, its buildings and people.

With this in mind, we might suppose that the greatest shift in the perception of animals over the course of the modern period had to do with the fact that a great many animals that have a direct impact on human lives, as nutriment, ceased to be perceived at all. They did not have to be re-conceptualized as animal-machines in order for this to happen; they had to stop being conceptualized as animals of any sort, but instead as commodities. As for the animal-machines objectified in scientific experiments from the mid-17th century on, the machine model was certainly conducive to the advancement of scientific discovery, but it does not appear to have been necessary to presuppose this model in order to justify the experimentation morally. Compared to the secret slaughter in the abattoirs, the experiments of the Royal Society have more in common with religious sacrifice than with pure objectification. The animals were offered up to science *because* they were animals, whether conceived on the machine model or otherwise, and qua animals they were worthy of interest as 'something natural and something wonderful', even if this involved killing where Aristotle was content to remain at the level of non-interventionist observation.

Here, indeed, in contrast with what has been said above about the shift from hunting to pastoralism, it is much more to a change in the mode of production, and to a consequent change in the ecology of modern human life, than to any shift in the scientific elite's conceptual model of animal bodies, that we should look in trying to understand one of the most remarkable features of our current, seemingly inconsistent relationship to different kinds of animal: some are protected, while billions of others are brought into being, made to suffer, and then slaughtered every year so that they may be consumed like any other commodity. There is no thanks given to them, no reverence. They are not part of our social world at all (a social world that is no longer socio-natural), let alone the center of the cosmos. One common exclamation at the sight of the horrible treatment of human beings by other human beings (say, deportation in cattle cars) has it that 'they are being treated like animals'. In fact the animals implicated in the system of factory farming are not even being treated like animals, if we understand animals to be a certain kind of other, different from us yet phenomenally salient, occupying a place in our ecologies and in our minds.

4. THE STACKED DECK OF INTELLIGENCE

At the same time as certain animals were deanimalized over the course of the modern period, to the extent that they were reconceptualized simply as a food commodity in an earlier stage of production, candidacy for protection came to be understood, increasingly, in terms of the ability of a given creature to perform feats generally associated with the human sphere of interests. The ability to perform these feats came to be associated with 'intelligence'. Such a conception of intelligence, and by implication of moral worth, has been articulately criticized by Elizabeth Costello, J.M. Coetzee's fictional defender of animals in his novel, *The Lives of Animals* (1999). Costello takes Kafka's fable of an ape's report to a scientific academy as an illustration of her views about the vain search for a test of animal intelligence. The ape in the story, now a cultivated, language-endowed gentleman, reminisces about his earlier, merely animal stage, shortly after his capture in Africa. He tells how he was subjected to various experiments in which, for example, scientists hung a banana from the ceiling in order to see whether he had the requisite 'intelligence' to stack blocks together and climb up them to reach his reward. This sort of experiment takes a number of things for granted. Among other things, although it purports to be testing for something human-like, it does not allow for the possibility of individual whim; it does not allow for the possibility of a response such as Zira's, the fictional chimpanzee in the film *Escape from the Planet of the Apes* (1971), who cannot help but exclaim, when the human scientists try a similar experiment on her, "but I simply loathe bananas!". The fact that experiments such as these *require* a certain course of action in order for the creature to be deemed intelligent suggests that what is being tested for is not really intelligence in any meaningful, human sense—since humans are permitted to have arbitrary whims and individual tastes—but rather a certain automatism that reproduces the kind of action of which a human being is capable, e.g., stacking blocks, but in the pursuit of a species-specific goal, a goal that a creature must have simply in view of the kind of creature it is, and that for that reason is not the result of a human-like willing, e.g., the will to obtain a banana.

If 'being intelligent' is defined as 'being like us', we may anticipate in advance that non-human animals are doomed to fail any possible intelligence test. We may also predict that the more distant a creature is from *homo sapiens* in its evolution, the greater will be its challenge in demonstrating to human researchers that it, too, is intelligent. A parallel problem has been confronted by researchers attempting to conceptualize what extra-terrestrial intelligence might look like. What if, for example, an alien race has evolved that communicates by means of electrical signals? What if, now, we are already surrounded by such species? What if a species of electrical eels has its own Beethovens and Kurt Gödels, communicating their beautiful compositions or penetrating discoveries through media we have not yet even thought to investigate as potential reflections of intelligence? Even if this is a foolish example, it reveals a real problem: as long as it is human beings who are designing the intelligence tests, non-humans are predetermined to come up short.

Recent scientific research is, thankfully, starting to overturn the old criteria for the measurement of the richness of internal life, and instead of asking of animals that they show us their ability to solve puzzles we design for them, researchers are instead focusing on the way different species relate to members of their own group in the pursuit of species-specific ends. One thing that has become apparent is that, in our own species, much intelligence is in fact social intelligence: the ability to interact with other humans in subtle and complex ways. But we also know, now, that the mechanisms underlying human social relations are just the same endocrinologically, and much the same neurologically, as those that cause walruses, say, to prefer to live in groups rather than to live alone. Thus one study on social relationships in rodents concludes that while extrapolation to humans and other primates must be made with caution, "the neural systems and chemicals responsible for social behavior [in rodents] depend on conserved neuroendocrine systems and thus may be highly relevant to behavior in other species." (Carter et al. 2009, 136)

Still, the old habit of standardized testing dies hard, and an important question remains as to what constituency, exactly, an individual animal represent when it takes an intelligence test. When a child takes an IQ test, it is clear that she stands alone, that the results will be considered only as a measure of her intelligence, but not as a measure of humanity. An individual animal, in contrast, when it takes a test involving blocks and bananas, is held up as a representative of its entire kind. Sometimes, individual animals are even held up as representatives of the animal kingdom as a whole. Consider the BBC News item of 9 March, 2009, concerning a chimpanzee in a zoo in Sweden that had stockpiled rocks as part of a plan to throw them later on at the zoo's visitors. "There has been scant evidence" until now, the article observes, "that animals can plan for future events". One chimp in a zoo in Sweden is made to tell us something about 'animals' in general, while a child prodigy, or for that matter a child dullard, tells us in her exceptional or mediocre test results only about herself.

Of course, the Swedish chimp tells us nothing at all about 'animals': its ability to plan for the future says nothing about whether fruit flies or tapeworms are able to do the same. What is meant by 'animals' here, we may suppose, is actually 'some non-humans'. If capacities that are jealously guarded as the exclusive property of human beings are found to occur anywhere beyond the human species, the thought seems to be, then they may as well occur everywhere. In the end, however, no amount of experimental evidence will suffice to convince those with an *a priori* conviction that animals cannot plan for the future, or entertain a concept of the self, or absence, or the like, that they were in fact mistaken. Anything a non-human animal does can always be explained, if one chooses, in terms of 'instinct'. Take planning. Of course we all already knew that squirrels, bees, and countless other species go about their business in a way that appears to anticipate future states. Why does this not count as "planning for future events"? The answer is that in squirrels and bees this activity is only instinctive, which is to say programmed into them simply in virtue of what they are, and not requiring any conscious agency in order to execute it. The chimp's stone storage is of interest because it is thought to be rare; if all chimps did it it would reveal nothing at all. This, again, means that in an important sense it is *a priori* impossible to detect the existence of other intelligent species, since intelligence is taken as something that can only show up exceptionally. And yet, again, while whatever is universal is taken to be merely instinctive and so not indicative of intelligence, what is not universal but exceptional, such as the storage of stones, is taken to say something about 'animals' as a whole.

What is going on here? It seems that in general humans hope to be able to explain everything animals do in terms of automatism or instinct, and that journalists regularly hope to create a sensation by providing evidence to the contrary. But what this scenario leaves out is the possibility that different creatures will manifest different capacities, in part in view of the kind of creatures they are, in part in view of the opportunities and challenges their environments present to them. This scenario leaves out, moreover, the possibility that there is simply no such thing as 'animals', conceived as a discrete class of entities that lies between the vegetable and the human in the same way that the human was long thought to lie between the animal and the angelic. 'Animal', on the reading I am suggesting, is an uninformative umbrella term, one that fails to pick out a set of kinds of creature with similar internal natures and capabilities.

5. ANIMAL AND HUMAN, GENERAL AND PARTICULAR

One striking difference between the way we tend to conceptualize human beings and the way we tend to conceptualize animals is that, in the latter case, a species as a whole may be represented by one individual. Thus Aelian tells of the impious hippopotamus, just as folk legends often tell of 'the bear' or 'the crow', as if there were only one, or rather, as if any one representative will do just as well as any other. This is a habit that continues in story-telling about animals today. Thus in Roald Dahl's children's story *Fantastic Mr. Fox* (1970), 'fox' seems to function as a surname for the vulpine protagonist, while his human enemies are not, for their part, 'Mr. Man'. There can be no Mr. Man, even in a children's story, because men are always individuals, each with his or her own irreducible uniqueness, while individual animals are instantiations of a kind that itself seems to be on an ontological and moral par with the individual human being. Thus in traditional sayings an animal kind will have a psychological profile that might match that of a single individual human (Mr. Jones might be sly as a fox, but Mr. Brown would never be only as swift as a given individual hare, and a given individual dog would certainly never be, say, as lazy as Mr. Smith). Correlatively, when conservationists speak about the loss of biodiversity, it is generally implicit that it is the animal species as a whole that is the morally relevant entity: individual zebras can be culled from a population, just as long as the population itself continues to thrive; every human being, in contrast, has protected status, and culling is out of the question, at least as an explicit policy.

The one circumstance in which culling of human populations becomes possible (even if we still would not call it that), arises when a foreign ethnic group has been conceptualized in the way that animals are conceptualized in fables, not as irreducible individuals, but as, e.g., the Jap or the Hun. In a controversial article, Francisco Gil-White (2001) has argued that human beings are innately disposed to cognize other racial groups by means of the same module responsible for folk-biological taxonomizing of animal species. On this line of thinking, the default mode of cognition of Japanese people (for anyone who is not Japanese, that is), is as 'the Jap', just as the default mode of cognition of foxes is through their imagined representative, 'Mr. Fox'. Now what moral universalism is supposed to do is to ensure that we not think in this way about the members of other human groups, while in contrast *Fantastic Mr. Fox* is still a harmless entertainment. But it is no secret that moral universalism can easily be suspended under circumstances of demographic and ecological competition (a competition often conceptualized as 'political'). When this happens, does it not seem to be a *reversion* to a more basic way of cognizing, rather than a perversion of our natural or regular way?

More than one prominent theory of the origins of the religious life sees it as rooted in an attempt to absolve the guilt that arises from aggression and violence. We are religious because we are violent, and we are violent simply because it is in our natures. According to Walter Burkert in his influential work, *Homo necans*, for most of human history social solidarity was achieved through "through a sacred crime [hunting and war] with due reparation [the rituals associated with these]" (Burkert 1983, xiv; see also Girard 1979). He argues that "[s]acrificial killing is the basic experience of the 'sacred'. *Homo religiosus* acts and attains self-awareness as *homo necans*. Indeed, this is what it means 'to act', *rezein, operari* (whence 'sacrifice' is *Opfer* in German)—the name merely covers up the heart of the action with a euphemism" (Burkert 1983, 3). In this respect, for Burkert those progressive social scientists are mistaken who "attempt to locate the roots of the evil" of violence while setting out from "short-sighted assumptions, as though the failure of our upbringing or the faulty development of a particular national tradition or economic system were to blame" (Burkert 1983, 1).

I do not wish either to defend or to refute Burkert's specific thesis here. It is enough to draw inspiration from his suggestion that both war and hunting are part of the same complex of human behaviors, a complex that required the creation of a counter-complex, that of ritual, religion, and, eventually, morality, in order to repair for the transgression of the originating complex. If this is the case, then one thing that becomes clear is that there is a knowable mechanism at work in the periodic dehumanization of human groups, a dehumanization that functions almost as a precondition of being able to go to war against them. It is a dehumanization in the sense just considered, that from being a group of sundry irreducible individuals they are now conceived, in the way in which we regularly conceive animals, as interchangeable instances of the same kind. We might in this sense modify Aristotle's claim above by saying that war is a form of hunting, and that it is made possible by the rescinding of the irreducible moral status of individual human beings, and its replacement with the default perspective humans take on animals: as Mr. Fox, or as Brer Rabbit, or 'that filthy varmint'. The rescinding of moral status is possible, indeed easy, along Burkert's lines, because the war/hunting complex comes first in the order of things, and the morality/religion complex was only erected subsequently in order to modulate or regulate an existence that is fundamentally defined by the first of these.

6. Conclusion

I have been suggesting that, whatever our moral theory tells us about the way moral status flows from the internal nature of a being, in fact our attribution of this status to some creatures, and our withholding of it from others, has much more to do with the way these creatures show up in our ecology, or fail to show up there. The theory of animals that enables the system of factory farming is not the Cartesian animal-machine model, or anything of the sort. The theory, such as it is, is much sooner the one that has always been available to anyone capable of understanding an allegorical fable: individual creatures are reduced ontologically to interchangeable instances of a kind, and this kind in turn is conceptualized as having a unique property or end (what Leibniz would have called the *officium* of a species).

At its most anodyne, this conception of animals permits us to see entire species as manifesting a single psychological trait of the sort we would ordinarily ascribe to individual human beings (e.g., slyness, laziness), but it is fundamentally no different than the conception that enables us to see cattle as 'beef on the hoof'. In this latter case, the very *raison d'être* of the creature is to provide meat to humans; if the meat is temporarily stored as part of the body of an 'individual' living creature, this does not change the creature's ultimate *telos* or end-towards-which. The Stoic philosopher Chrysippus already dared to say in the 3rd century BCE that a pig's soul functions in the pig's body no differently than salt in cured ham. The reason pigs exist at all is to be eaten by human beings, he thought. For a while their meat is held together by a soul, later it is held together by salt. Thus Cicero ponders in his 1st-century BCE work *On the Nature of the Gods*: "And the pig? What else is it but food? It has a soul, Chrysippus says, in order to keep it from rotting; the soul takes the place of salt, for it is destined to serve as nourishment for man." (*De natura deorum* II, 64) It makes no difference that, in English as in Latin, 'meat' is a mass noun (that is, we speak of 'some meat', but not, ordinarily, 'the meats'), while 'pig' is a count noun. In fact, one of the most usual ways of performing the conceptual transformation that deanimalizes animals—that is, that takes them out of the ecology of reciprocal obligations and places them in the economy of commodity production—is by shifting to a mass noun in speaking of an ensemble of otherwise individual animals. Think of 'cattle'.

That the system of factory farming requires deanimalization—the rescinding of the status of individual creature from the animals involved, a status that in traditional hunting and pastoralist societies was not rescinded, but indeed all that much more present in the moment of killing—shows that if hunting was a form of war, and if the current system of meat production bears some ancestral link to hunting, then what we have today is a form of war that could not have been imagined in earlier societies. It is a war that costs the victors nothing, and in which the losers are already vanquished simply in virtue of being born.

The purpose here, anyway, is not to decry the current state of things, but only to seek to understand how it came to be. I have been trying to show that the range of things one may or may not do to another creature does not really flow from that creature's species affiliation, or even from a consideration of where it lies in the supposedly fundamental division between humans and animals. After all, humans *are* in fact capable of doing horrible things to other humans. The presumption I have been questioning, that the range of what we may or may not do to animals flows from a theory of their internal natures, seems related to a corollary presumption, that the range of things we *must not* do to other humans flows from an awareness of their internal natures, or of their possession of something we call 'moral status'. But if we accept Burkert's advice that we should not interpret breakdowns in the force field that moral status is supposed to uphold as mere "faulty developments in particular economic or national traditions", then we quickly see that there is a different, and deeper, system of rules that governs what may or may not be done to other creatures, a system that does not take the question whether those other creatures are humans or animals to be the most salient one. In this system, it is the way the other creature shows up in the ecology of our lives, and the way different courses of action towards it are thought to influence the balance and well-being of the socio-natural theater in which we act, that determines what may or may not be done to it. With Nietzsche and Williams, I suspect that the difficulty we have in discerning this deeper system has something to do with the invention of morality, a thing supposed to be shared by all and only human beings, and with the idea that it is from this that our actions towards other human beings, but not towards other animals, flows.

References

Agamben G. (1998), Homo sacer: Sovereign Power and Bare Life, Stanford: Stanford University Press.
Burkert, W. (1983), Homo necans: The Anthropology of Ancient Greek Sacrificial Ritual and Myth (tr. P. Bing), Berkeley, CA: University of California Press.
Carter, C.S., Boone, E., Grippo, E.J., Ruscio, M., Bales, K.L. (2009), "The Endocrinology of Social Relationships in Rodents", in: P.T. Ellison & P.B. Gray (ed.), The Endocrinology of Social Relationships, Harvard: Harvard University Press, 121-137.
Coetzee, J. M. (1999), The Lives of Animals, Princeton: Princeton University Press.
Des Chene, D. (2006), "'Animal' as Category: Bayle's Rorarius", in: J.E.H. Smith (ed.), The Problem of Animal Generation in Early Modern Philosophy, Cambridge: Cambridge University Press, 215-231.
Durkheim, E., Mauss, M. (1902), "De quelques formes primitives de classification. Contribution à l'étude des répresentations collectives", Année sociologique 6, 1-72.
Evans-Pritchard, E.E. (1940), The Nuer: A Description of the Modes of Livelihood and Political Institutions of a Nilotic People, Oxford: Oxford University Press.
Evelyn, J. (1995), The Diary of John Evelyn (ed. G. de la Bédoyère), London: The Boydell Press.
Foucault, M, (1975), Surveillir et punir. Naissance de la prison, Paris: Gallimard.

Gil-White, F. (2001), "Are Ethnic Groups Biological 'Species' to the Human Brain?", Essentialism in our Cognition of Some Social Categories", Current Anthropology 42/4, 515-554.

Girard, R. (1979), Violence and the Sacred, Baltimoe, London: Johns Hopkins University Press.

Godelier, M. (1986), The Mental and the Material: Thought, Economy and Society, London: Verso.

Ingold, T. (1995), "Growing Plants and Raising Animals: An Anthropological Perspective on Domestication", in: D. R. Harris (ed.), The Origins and Spread of Agriculture and Pastoralism in Eurasia, Washington: Smithsonian Institution Press, 12-24.

Lord Smail, D. (2007), On Deep History and the Brain, Berkeley, CA: University of California Press.

Nietzsche, F. (1985), Zur Genealogie der Moral [1887], in: Werke: Kritische Gesamtausgabe, ed. G. Colli & M. Montinari, Berlin, New York: De Gruyter.

Smith, J.E.H. (2011), Divine Machines: Leibniz and the Sciences of Life, Princeton: Princeton University Press.

Sorabji, R. (1995), Animal Minds and Human Morals: The Origins of the Western Debate, Ithaka, NY: Cornell University Press.

Sunstein, C.R. (2004), "Introduction: What Are Animal Rights?", in: M.C. Nussbaum, C.R. Sunstein (ed.), Animal Rights: Current Debates and New Directions, Oxford: Oxford University Press, 3-18.

Vialles, N. (1994), Animal to Edible, Cambridge: Cambridge University Press.

Williams, B. (1994), Shame and Necessity, Berkeley CA: University of California Press.

4. Cognition and Community

Gary Steiner

1. A Traditional Prejudice

It has long been a commonplace in Western philosophy that a being's moral status is in some important sense a function of its cognitive abilities. This assumption has been employed since antiquity as the basis for conferring full moral status on human beings and something less—either inferior moral status or, on the view of some philosophers, no moral status at all—on non-human animals. The putative reasoning behind the claim of human moral superiority is that human beings, in virtue of their rationality, are capable of kinds of experience and sophisticated forms of action that are impossible for non-rational beings; to the extent that all and only human beings are rational, whereas no animals are rational, it follows (so the tradition tells us) that human beings are categorically superior cognitively and hence morally to animals.[1]

The crux of this way of viewing the comparative moral status of human beings and animals is the idea that the capacities for reason and language are the key to full moral status. The tradition envisions a *scala naturae* with rational beings at the top and non-rational beings located somewhere beneath rational beings. Cosmopolitan thinkers from the Stoics to Kant take such a hierarchy for granted, and they employ it as the basis for arguing that human beings are entitled to use animals, along with other natural beings, as resources for the satisfaction of human desires. Some thinkers, notably Aristotle, go so far as to make distinctions among

---

[1] | In the following I take it for granted that human beings are animals. For the sake of simplicity, when I refer to animals I mean non-human animals; the reader may take references to humans as a shorthand for human animals.

human beings based on rational capacity. Aristotle excludes slaves and women from citizenship on the grounds that neither possess sufficient rational capacity to discharge the functions of citizenship; he argues that only a subset of humanity, namely males possessing a free nature, possess rational capacity in sufficient degree to merit active participation in the administration of the polis, an entity that by its nature aims at the pursuit of virtue and hence is by its very nature a moral entity (Aristotle, *Politics* 1.5 at 1254b10-25, 1255a1-3; 1.13 at 1260a14-18).

This assumption about the relationship between rational capacity and moral status finds expression in Aristotle's views about animals as well. Animals, Aristotle asserts in Book I of the *Politics*, exist entirely for the sake of human beings, which is to say that the natural telos of an animal is to satisfy human desires (Aristotle, *Politics* 1.8 at 1256b14-21). Some interpreters have argued that Aristotle is simply conveying a popular, philosophically ungrounded sentiment when he makes this statement early in the *Politics*.[2] Indeed, it is the only place in Aristotle's writings in which he states categorically that animals exist for the sake of human beings (Dierauer 1977, 155, 240). But even if Aristotle is not clearly committed to the servitude status of animals as a cosmic principle, he develops the prejudice of human superiority in ways that anticipate the entire subsequent history of Western thinking about the relative moral status of humans and animals.

Central to Aristotle comparative analysis of human and animal experiential capacities is his distinction between deliberative choice and volition, a distinction that anticipates the contemporary contrast between action and behavior. On Aristotle's view, to be a fully functioning rational agent is to be capable of rational deliberation (*bouleusis*) and deliberative choice (*proairesis*). Beings that act rationally make their choices on the basis of knowledge; choice in this sense "involves reason and thought" concerning the proper means to be employed in pursuing desired ends (Aristotle, *Nicomachean Ethics* 3.2 at 1112a16, 3.3 at 1112b12). We deliberate about matters within our power "in which the event is obscure", such as how a doctor can best to bring about or preserve good health in a patient, and how one can best acquire or preserve material wealth (Aristotle, *Nicomachean*

---

2 | Nussbaum suggests that in presenting this view, Aristotle is simply "stating the appearances", not making "a serious theoretical statement" (Nussbaum 1978, 96).

Ethics 3.3 at 1112b1-13). In order to be capable of deliberative choice, an agent must be able to seize upon ends as such and consider the relative merits and drawbacks of the various courses of action that might be pursued in the service of particular ends. If a being is not rational (such as an animal) or is not fully rational (such as a child, a slave, or, presumably, a woman), then that being must depend on others to deliberate on its behalf. Only those beings fully capable of deliberation are agents in the authentic sense of the term: *ago, agere* signifies acting or doing, and acting in the fullest sense is purposive conduct that is guided by one's own reason.

If women, children, and slaves cannot act in this sense, then *a fortiori* neither can animals. But whereas women, children, and even slaves have some share in reason—Aristotle writes that even though the slave "has no deliberative capacity at all", it nonetheless "participates in reason enough to apprehend" a rational principle—animals "cannot even apprehend reason" but instead simply "obey their passions" (Aristotle, *Politics* 1.12 at 1260a12-14, 1.5 at 1254b21-23). The behavior of animals is not action in the strict sense but instead is something less: It is "voluntary" (*ekousion*) behavior driven by appetite (*epithumia*); as such, it "relates to the pleasant and the painful" rather than being guided by any kind of rational consideration (Aristotle, *Nicomachean Ethics* 3.2 at 1111b11-17). Animals, on this view, do not reflect on ends in a way that discloses the relative merits and drawbacks of different possible courses of action; instead, they are moved by their passions or appetites in such a way that Aristotle considers it a misnomer to call the conduct of animals "choice". As John of Damascus and Saint Thomas Aquinas would later argue, *non agunt sed magis aguntur*: animals do not act but rather are acted upon (Aquinas, *Quaestiones disputate de veritate*, q. 22, art 4, resp). Hence animals are not agents in a sense that would recommend including them in any kind of community with human beings, least of all in a moral community. Human beings, too, often act on the basis of their appetites (as well as on the basis of *thumos* or spirited desire), but animals can act only on the basis of appetites and spirited desire, whereas human beings can employ reason to regulate their desires. This is what, for Aristotle, constitutes the crucial difference between what we today would call action in human beings and behavior in animals.

Aristotle sets the tone for the subsequent history of Western thinking about the moral status of animals when he categorically excludes animals from community with human beings. It is one thing to say that the lack of reason and language in animals makes it impossible for us to have certain sorts of relationships with them, such as bonds of friendship. But it is quite another to say that because animals do not share in reason with us, we may treat them in any way we wish, and that in particular we may use them as resources for the satisfaction of our desires, without the least moral scruple. If animals lack the capacities that would make them moral agents and hence beings with whom we share bonds of mutual respect, then they must be the utter opposite of moral agents. They are so removed from moral considerability that they must be objects of utter moral disregard—not objects of moral enmity, not immoral beings (which are at least capable of moral correction), but categorically *amoral* ones. Animals are *aloga* and hence amoral. And in fact Aristotle, even though in his zoological writings he attributes a variety of sophisticated cognitive capacities to animals (even speculating that some birds may possess articulate voice, which presupposes rational capacity), excludes animals from the moral sphere altogether on the grounds that they are incapable of moral agency.[3] Aristotle states that "there is nothing common [*koinon*]" to humans and animals, just as there is nothing common to a free person and a slave *qua* slave; but there can be relationships such as friendship with a slave *qua* person, inasmuch as a slave "can share in a system of law [and] be party to an agreement", whereas there can be no such relationships between human beings and animals. In particular, the lack of anything common to humans and animals that would enable animals to participate in a system of law and enter into reciprocal agreements means that animals are categorically excluded from the sphere of justice (Aristotle, *Nicomachean Ethics* 8.11 at 1161b1-8). This means that nothing we do to animals can be considered an injustice; we owe them nothing, and may use them as we please.

Indeed, Aristotle excludes animals from ethics generally, and for the same reason: Lacking rational and linguistic capacity (*logos*), animals are incapable of engaging in the practices that would merit inclusion in the moral community. Aristotle excludes animals from any share in *eudaimonia* and hence from the moral sphere on the grounds that they lack the capacity for rational contemplation (Aristotle, *Nicomachean Ethics* 10.8 at 1178b24-32). Animals can neither contemplate ends nor deliberate about

---

3 | For a discussion of Aristotle's attribution of varieties of intelligence to animals in his zoological writings, see Steiner (2005) 72-76.

the means toward chosen ends; completely incapable of choice, animals are imprisoned in a kind of eternal present in which they are moved by their drives toward objects of desire and specifically toward objects that promise pleasure and away from objects that threaten pain. To be a member of the moral community, in contrast, is to be capable of rising above the promise of pleasure and the spectre of pain, and to direct one's actions on the basis of rational insight into the good and the true, as well as on the basis of having formed a stable and enduring state of character (*ethos*) whose possessor habitually pursues virtue and habitually avoids vice.

Aristotle's commitments about the differences between human moral agents and animals set the stage for the tradition of political thinking known as contractualism. Thinkers from Epicurus to John Rawls have seized upon Aristotle's notion that a being must be able to "share in a system of law and be party to an agreement" in order to have a share in justice; and they have categorically excluded animals from the sphere of justice on the grounds that animals are *aloga*, fundamentally lacking in the capacities for reason and language. Not terribly long ago, John Rawls proposed that "justice [holds] only in our relations to human persons" because "the capacity for a sense of justice is necessary in order to be owed the duties of justice" (Rawls 2000, 441, 448). In articulating this perspective, Rawls was restating the inner logic of a prejudice that extends back to antiquity: that all and only those beings that are capable of being moral agents, which is to say that all and only those beings that possess full rationality and the ability to reflect on ends and deliberate about means, have any direct moral status. All other beings have at best what Kant would call "indirect" moral status, which means that we have duties to treat such "other" beings in certain ways (e.g., to avoid being cruel to them) not because they possess any inherent dignity or worth, but simply because by treating them well we render ourselves more likely to treat moral agents properly. One of Kant's ideas in this connection was that, if we express cruelty toward animals, we will be more likely to be cruel to human beings; in this respect he was following a line of reasoning offered long before him by Saint Thomas Aquinas (Kant 1996, 192f; 1997, 212; Aquinas 1920-25, 197; 1997, 904). In themselves, animals have no direct moral worth and do not merit our moral concern; at best they are simply "a practicing ground for virtue", an elaborate kind of object—not mere Cartesian machines, Kant assures us, but living beings capable of having representations—that we may use in any ways we wish as long as these uses do not hinder us in our pursuit of cosmopolitan community with our fellow human beings (DeGrazia 1996, 43). Kant assures us that animals are not mere Cartesian machines, but instead are living beings capable of having representations. But that does not stop Kant from classifying animals in the category of mere "things", beings utterly lacking in direct moral worth, and from setting up a stark contrast between such things and moral agents or "persons" possessing inherent dignity and meriting membership in the same sort of moral community that Aristotle had reserved for human beings (Kant 1987, sec. 90, pp. 356-357nn64, 66).

Kant implicitly follows the formula first presented by Aristotle and more recently embraced, if only implicitly, by Rawls: All and only those beings that possess rationality possess full moral status. Only such beings are capable of progressive self-improvement and of taking on reciprocal duties of justice that bind us in community with other rational agents. For his own part, Rawls equivocates somewhat on the question whether this means that animals are excluded from moral consideration altogether. He states that his theory of justice has limits, and that in particular "no account has been given of right conduct in regard to animals and the rest of nature. [...] A correct conception of our relations to animals and to nature would seem to depend upon a theory of the natural order and our place in it" (Rawls 2000, 448). What is striking about this assertion is that in making it, Rawls betrays no awareness of the history of thinking out of which his own theory of justice emerges, a history that long ago articulated a theory of the natural order and our place in it—indeed, a highly anthropocentric theory that leaves little if any room for a robust sense of moral obligation toward animals.

More than anyone else, it was the Stoics who articulated the theory of the natural order that has served as the essential background for Western thinking about the moral status of animals. The Stoics, like Aristotle before them, view animals as instrumentalities for the satisfaction of human needs and desires. More than that, the Stoics formalize Aristotle's instrumental view of animals into a cosmic principle according to which animals were created expressly for the sake of human beings. Human beings, as rational, are destined for the attainment of a cosmopolitan standpoint from which they, along with the gods, will contemplate the eternal *logos* that can be appreciated only by rational beings. Animals, as fundamentally non-rational or *aloga*, exist to satisfy the material needs of humans who, disburdened of these needs, are thereby freed for the task of contemplating the eternal *logos* of nature (Cicero, *De natura deorum* 2.133; Diogenes Laertius 7.138; Epictetus, *Discourses* 1.16.1-5, 2.10.3).[4]

Saint Augustine would incorporate this anthropocentric prejudice into his thinking when he maintained that we need have no moral scruples about causing animals pain and killing them for our own purposes. Like Aristotle and the Stoics before him, Augustine stresses that no sort of community prevails between humans and animals, and that "for this reason, by the most just ordinance of their Creator, both their life and their death [viz., the life and death of animals] are subject to our needs" (Saint Augustine 1998, bk. 1, ch. 20, 32). Indeed, "to refrain from the killing of animals and the destroying of plants is the height of superstition [...] there are no common rights between us and the beasts and the trees" (Saint Augustine 1966, bk. 2, ch. 17, sec. 54, 102). Animals are so far removed from community with humans—so lacking in anything *koinon* to humans, as Aristotle put it—that we need not even concern ourselves with the suffering we cause animals, let alone with the fact that we customarily deprive animals of their lives: "We can perceive by their cries that animals die in pain, although we make little of this since the beast, lacking a rational soul, is not related to us by a common nature." (Saint Augustine 1966, ch. 2, ch. 17, sec. 59, 105) For Augustine as for Aristotle before him and Kant after him, that which would be relevantly *koinon* to humans and animals would be not just any sort of experiential capacity but specifically the capacity for rational thought (Saint Augustine 1998, bk. 1, ch. 20, 32). To lack this capacity is to stand insuperably outside the moral community.

Even though they exclude animals from any sort of community with humans (and *a fortiori* from the moral community), thinkers such as Saint Thomas Aquinas and Kant recognize that we might well assert duties of compassion toward animals. As noted earlier, Kant calls such duties indirect, which means that they are not owed directly to animals but are duties "with regard to" them. Thus duties of compassion toward animals are really, like all genuine duties, ultimately duties to humanity. Inasmuch as duties and rights are reciprocal concepts—to have a duty to another is to be obliged not to interfere with that other's enjoyment of a specific right—to say that animals are not direct beneficiaries of duties is to say that they are not direct possessors of rights. And indeed this is the position taken

---

4 | For a more detailed discussion of the Stoics' views regarding animals, see Steiner (2005), 77-92.

by contractualist thinkers from Epicurus to Rawls. Rawls asserts that "certainly it is wrong to be cruel to animals and the destruction of a whole species can be a great evil. The capacity for feelings of pleasure and pain and for the forms of life of which animals are capable clearly imposes duties of compassion and humanity in their case." But these sorts of considerations "are outside the scope of justice, and it does not seem possible to extend the contract doctrine so as to include them in a natural way" (Rawls 2000, 448). Because animals cannot have a sense of justice, there is no "natural way" to consider them to be beneficiaries of justice.

What, then, is the precise nature of duties of compassion toward animals, provided that it makes sense to suppose that we have such duties? It cannot be that we owe compassion to animals as a matter of justice; duties of compassion must be of a different nature than duties of justice. On the contractualist view, justice is a relation that prevails between beings that are able to enter into reciprocal agreements of non-harm or non-interference. Justice in this sense is a matter of fairness among equally-empowered rational beings who can recognize and respect the reciprocal relationship between rights and duties or responsibilities. If I have a right, say, to own property, then others have a comparable right to own property; the notion of fairness precludes a situation in which some are entitled to own property while others are not. Of course, certain rights may be sacrificed, as when felons lose the right to own firearms; but in such situations, the deprivation of the right is a consequence of someone having violated the terms of the contract calling for mutual respect of rights. In each case in which someone has a right, others have a corresponding duty not to interfere with the bearer's enjoyment of that right. The underlying idea of the contractualist conception of rights and duties is that all members of the community of contractors agree to abide by certain rules governing the enjoyment of rights, in particular rules prohibiting interference with the rights of others.

Thus the contractualist notion of rights is based on the notion of a *quid pro quo*: I have duties to respect the prerogatives of others only to the extent that, *and because*, those others have corresponding duties to respect rights that I possess. In essence, I owe others only what they owe me. And it is possible to enter into a reciprocally-binding (which is to say, contractual) relationship of rights and duties only if both parties to the agreement are rational agents, beings who can contemplate what rights and duties are in general, consider the nature and implications of particular rights and duties, and can endeavor to respect the prerogatives of others and protect their own interests. To the extent that animals are *aloga*, the thinking goes, animals are incapable of all these things and hence cannot coherently be considered to be participants in the sphere of justice—in particular, animals cannot have any right to justice because they cannot be bound by duties of justice.

But again, then, what is the precise status of putative duties of compassion toward animals? Can a contractualist thinker consistently speak of such duties toward animals? It would seem that this can make sense only if it is possible to detach the notion of such a duty from the corresponding notion of a right. John Finnis makes a very telling statement when he maintains that "those who propose that animals have rights have a deficient appreciation of the basic forms of human good". Finnis sees the entire notion of rights not simply in terms of reciprocal justice relations but as irretrievably bound up with the kinds of good of which only human beings are capable. Human good, Finnis believes, is fundamentally different than whatever sorts of good animals are capable of participating in, inasmuch as human but not animal experience is "expressive of decision, choice, reflectiveness, commitment, as fruition of purpose, or of self-discipline or self-abandonment, and as the action of a responsible personality". Justice, on this view, is oriented exclusively on "respect for human good" and has no reference whatsoever to any other sort of good, regardless of anything we might believe about the supposed richness of animal experience or the supposed dignity of animal life (Finnis 1980, 194f).

Finnis conceives of rights not simply as pertinent to justice relations, but more importantly as entitlements that only rational agents can possess. Accordingly, animals cannot be said to have a right to our compassion. Can human beings, then, be said to have duties of compassion toward animals? What, exactly, does Rawls have in mind when he says that we can be said to have such duties? It seems to me that the acknowledgment of duties of compassion toward animals can be understood in only one of two ways in the context of contractualist thought: either our duties of compassion are indirect, which is to say that we really owe nothing to animals, or the assertion of duties of compassion is an implicit acknowledgment of something that thinkers such as Finnis are unwilling to recognize: that there is a sphere of rights and duties that transcends the sphere of justice understood as a set of reciprocal fairness relations among rational agents, such that we can be said to have certain sorts of duties toward animals and perhaps even that animals can be said to have certain sorts of rights. The idea that there is a sphere of right or good that transcends merely human goods brings with it idea that there is a way of owing something to a being even if that being owes nothing to me, i.e., the sense of duty in this larger sphere of good or right is not based on a *quid pro quo* but instead follows from something crucial about animal experience that even Rawls had to acknowledge, namely, that animals are capable of "feelings of pleasure and pain and for [certain] forms of life", and that these capacities rather than any sort of rational capacity are sufficient as the basis for recognizing that animals have rights.

2. ARE ANIMALS REALLY *ALOGA*?

Given the extent to which the Western philosophical tradition has emphasized the idea that animals lack rights (on the grounds that animals lack language and rationality), many people find it surprising that the tradition has included a number of heterodox voices proclaiming that animals possess sophisticated forms of subjective experience and that animals therefore should be accorded what modern thinkers have conceptualized as rights. In the Fifth Set of Objections to Descartes's *Meditations*, Pierre Gassendi poses a challenge to the traditional classification of animals as *aloga*. In the *Meditations* Descartes makes a strict metaphysical distinction between mind and body that reinforces his contention in the *Discourse on Method* that animals are purely corporeal beings and hence utterly incapable of reason or language (Descartes, *Discourse on Method*, Part 5). Gassendi places the burden on Descartes "to prove that the power of thought is something so far beyond the nature of a body that neither a vapour nor any other mobile, pure and rarefied body can be organized in such a way as would make it capable of thought" (Gassendi 1984, 183). Unlike Descartes, Gassendi acknowledges that "although man is the foremost of the animals, he still belongs to the class of animals"—something that, as we have seen, Aristotle acknowledges only to forget it as soon as he directs his attention to the political and moral sphere (Gassendi 1984, 188). This commonality between human beings and animals—in particular the fact that both are embodied beings that have a sensory encounter with the world—makes the complete denial of understanding or thought in animals highly implausible:

"You say that brutes lack reason. Well, of course they lack human reason, but they do not lack their own kind of reason. So it does not seem appropriate to call them *aloga* except by comparison with us or with our kind of reason; and in any case *logos* or reason seems to be a general term, which can be attributed to them no less than the cognitive faculty or internal sense. [...] The difference [between humans and animals in this regard] seems to be merely one of degree." (Gassendi 1984, 189)

Gassendi urges Descartes to recognize that even though animals may not be capable of human speech, they are evidently capable of their own forms of speech. As I noted in passing earlier, even Aristotle, in his zoological writings, observes on several occasions that birds seem to be possessed of articulate speech, which Aristotle believes is generally a sign of rationality. And even if we are not willing to grant that 'speech' is a term that may appropriately be applied to animals, recent work in cognitive ethology has made it increasingly difficult to deny that many animals exhibit sophisticated capacities for communication with their conspecifics.

Descartes's adherence to strict metaphysical dualism and his conception of embodiment as pure mechanism prevents him from taking seriously the proposition that *logos* can take non-human forms such as the forms of intelligence and communication found in a wide variety of animals. As Bernard Williams once noted, Descartes is committed to an "all or nothing" view of consciousness according to which a being either possesses the full range of mental capacities (including self-awareness, language, and abstract rationality) or lacks them altogether, and according to which animals are mere biological mechanisms "with no experience of any kind" (Williams 1978, 284).[5] Gassendi's challenge is precisely to this strict either-or between full rationality and inert passivity. Gassendi takes it for granted that the varieties of animal ingenuity reflect some sort of inner awareness; he questions Descartes's assumption that sensation is fundamentally different in humans and in animals, and specifically Descartes's contention that sensation is a mode of thought in the former and a simple mechanistic process akin to mercury rising in a thermometer in the latter (Descartes' letter to Plempius for Fromondus, October 3, 1637; Author's Replies to the Fourth Set of Objections; *The Passions of the Soul*,

---

5 | On the controversy surrounding this interpretation of Descartes's views about animal experience, see Steiner (2005), 287n62.

art. 16, 38). The crux of Gassendi's challenge to Descartes is that there is something essentially *koinon* to humans and animals, namely, something about the nature of our embodied sensory encounter with the world: humans and animals alike have inner states of awareness that differ not in kind but merely in degree. Gassendi's point is that subjective experience can take many forms, and that the seeming lack of capacities for language, logic, mathematics, and the like in animals is no bar in principle to their having their own forms of communication and ways of reckoning with the contingencies of life. Descartes had attempted to dismiss all apparent signs of intelligence in animals as cases of instinct (Descartes, *Discourse on Method*, Part 5; letter to the Marquess of Newcastle, November 23, 1646). But why assume that any behavior that falls short of full discursive rationality must be nothing more than mere instinct? Does such an assumption not beg the question of forms of subjective experience different than our own? And what does such persistent question-begging in the history of Western philosophy reveal about those who have proclaimed such a decisive gulf between human beings and animals? Why this almost desperate insistence on human uniqueness?

Gassendi is by no means the first philosopher in the West to challenge the strict Aristotelian distinction between the discursive rationality of humans and the comparatively diminished experience (which Descartes refused even to acknowledge) of animals. Presocratic thinkers such as Pythagoras and Empedocles had argued for a commonality of soul between human beings and animals. And in the first century C.E., Plutarch issued a strong challenge to the Stoic denial of reason in animals. His *Moralia* includes three texts on animals, in the course of which Plutarch argues for duties of justice toward animals on the grounds that animals are rational, urges the reader to consider reasons why animals are superior to human beings, and challenges the propriety of eating animal flesh (Plutarch 1995). The crux of Plutarch's reasoning, like Gassendi's nearly sixteen centuries after him, is that "nothing is endowed with sensation [*aisthesis*] which does not also partake of intelligence [*synesis*]" (Plutarch 1995, 960D, 327f; 961A, 329). Aristotle had made a strict distinction between beings characterized by sensitive or locomotive soul and those moved in addition by rational soul; neither he (in his psychological and political writings, at any rate), nor Descartes after him, allowed for the possibility of a being possessing any kind of reason or *logos* other than the full-blown discursive and linguistic rationality exhibited by human beings. In attributing intelligence to all sentient beings, Plutarch expresses a recognition of the need to see sentient life as a continuum and to make fine distinctions between types and degrees of intelligence. Every day the annals of contemporary cognitive ethology expand with our increasing knowledge of the diverse forms of animal intelligence, from the seed-caching abilities of scrub jays to the communicative abilities of vervet monkeys and dolphins to the sophisticated classificatory capacities of pigeons and parrots. But the world hardly needed to wait for the turn from behavioral to cognitive ethology in the past generation to gain an appreciation of the sophisticated cognitive abilities of animals. As noted earlier, Aristotle himself chronicles a remarkable array of examples of animal ingenuity in his zoological writings, in some instances even attributing *synesis* to certain animals.[6] More recently, in arguing for a continuity rather than a radical discontinuity between the cognitive and emotional capacities of human beings and animals, Darwin was simply doing justice to insights about animal experience that Aristotle had sought to forget just as quickly as he had assembled them.

One of the great mysteries of the Western philosophical tradition is why so many thinkers have proclaimed the categorical superiority of human beings over animals when others, such as Plutarch, have expressed a clear awareness of two facts: that differences in experiential capacities between humans and animals are at most matters of degree rather than of kind, and that these differences ultimately have no moral significance whatsoever. Plutarch expresses a sensitivity to both of these considerations, but the cumulative force of many of the exaggeratedly anthropomorphic examples he gives is such that his writings on animals have had little impact on our culture's values and thinking about the moral status of animals. Neither the suggestion that fish swimming in cube formation reflects that they possess knowledge of geometry, for example, nor Plutarch's account of one army of ants ransoming a grub in exchange for the return of the corpse of one of its soldiers from an opposing army, seems to have had the intended effect of convincing many readers that animals relate to the world in ways that depend on modes of intelligence traditionally thought to be the exclusive possession of humans (Plutarch 1995, 967E-F and 979E-F).

---

6 | For this and other attributions of sophisticated mental capacities to animals in Aristotle's zoological writings, see Steiner (2005), 72ff.

In the fourth century C.E., Porphyry presented a more systematic and somewhat less fanciful refutation of traditional prejudices about the experiential capacities and the moral status of animals. In *De abstinentia* (*On Abstinence from Killing Animals*), Porphyry seeks to convince his friend Castricius, a lapsed vegetarian, of the injustice of killing animals and eating their flesh. Porphyry notes that animals have been revered in a number of world traditions, notably by the Egyptians, who recognized that animals have "almost the same soul" as human beings, namely a rational soul (Porphyry 2000, 4.9.1; 4.10.1, 106f). Porphyry takes this to mean that "*logos* [can] be seen in absolutely all animals", even though we may be incapable of understanding the *logoi* expressed by other animals (Porphyry 2000, 3.2.4; 3.3.3-4, 80f). "The complexity and diversity of their [viz. animals'] speech demonstrates that it has meaning: animals are heard to speak differently when they are afraid, when they are calling, when they are asking to be fed, when they are friendly and when they are challenging to a fight." (Porphyry 2000, 3.4.2, 82) Of course, Porphyry is not immune to the same sorts of (what this author takes to be) fanciful moments of anthropomorphizing found in Plutarch, as when Porphyry interprets the story of Chrysippus's dog to demonstrate that "dogs understand dialectic" (Porphyry 2000, 3.6.3). Chrysippus's dog is pursuing prey and comes to a three-fold fork in the road. The dog sniffs at two of the paths and, not smelling the prey there, immediately heads down the third path without smelling it first. Like Porphyry, Sextus Empiricus takes this story to be a refutation of the Stoics, Sextus going so far as to assert that the story confirms that the dog can draw logical inferences involving "repeated applications of the fifth-undemonstrated argument-schema" (Sextus Empiricus 1996, 98). But the reader, Porphyry seems to want to say, need not take this sort of conclusion entirely seriously in order to recognize the inadequacy of the Aristotelian-Stoic treatment of the dog's behavior as something like blind instinct: for even Aristotle acknowledges that animals teach their young and learn from us as well as from each other (Porphyry 2000, 3.6.5). And it is clear that many animals "seem to surpass us in perception", that they "know everything that relates to their advantage", that they "devise their home with regard to their means of living and their security", and the like (Porphyry 2000, 3.8.3; 3.9.4-5, 85f). Even if it is plausible to suppose that some of these capacities are matters of instinct (as some of them presumably are even in human beings), research into animal behavior has made it increasingly implausible to suppose that the many instances of adaptation, problem-solving, and ingenuity exhibited by animals can be explained through the traditional appeal to instinct. If we are inclined to resist the suggestion that animals and not just humans possess *logos*, this is because our consciousness and our inclinations have been shaped by several millennia of thinking that have sought to emphasize the differences rather than the continuities between ourselves and animals. What thinkers such as Porphyry urge us to consider is whether *logos* is best understood in the narrowly anthropocentric terms in which it has been construed by the dominant voices in the tradition, namely, in terms of symbolic language and discursive rationality. Perhaps the most incisive modern challenge to this anthropocentric conception of *logos* was articulated by Schopenhauer, who, arguing specifically against Kant, suggested that any creature that has eyes has knowledge and "the identity of a consciousness" (Schopenhauer 1958, 30). Kant had conceded that animals are living beings that experience representations; but he had attributed the capacity for understanding or knowledge, and the capacity for self-awareness (the transcendental unity of apperception) exclusively to rational beings. Kant, as noted earlier, classifies animals as "things" rather than as "persons", thereby categorically denying animals rational capacity: for Kant, a being either possesses both reason and understanding (the faculty of knowledge), or it possesses neither of them. Schopenhauer maintains against Kant, and in a way that (in this author's judgment) is truer to the facts of animal experience, that many beings can and do possess understanding and knowledge even though they are not capable of reason in the sense of symbolic language and discursive rationality. Schopenhauer thus provides an account of understanding (logos) that makes it possible to see the flexible and adaptive behavior of animals as signs of intelligence and of a grasp of causal relations in the world, rather than seeking to force animal behavior into the narrow and question-begging confines of instinct.

But Schopenhauer, like Plutarch and Porphyry, goes further. His willingness to acknowledge the continuity between human and animal modes of intelligence is accompanied by a willingness to rethink the basic terms of justice and the question whether we ought to recognize duties of justice toward animals. Where the tradition had proclaimed that a being must be rational, linguistic, and self-conscious in a specifically human sense in order to be a beneficiary of justice, Schopenhauer urges the contrary conclusion that "virtue and holiness result not from [the capacity for reflection], but from the inner depth of the will, and from its relation to knowledge" (Schopenhauer 1958, 58). Not only does any being with eyes possess the capacity for understanding and knowledge, its possession of that capacity qualifies it as a member of the moral community and specifically as a beneficiary of justice. In challenging the traditional prejudice that only human beings participate in the *logos*, thinkers such as Plutarch, Porphyry, and Schopenhauer are not simply taking up an abstract question of fact about the cognitive abilities of animals. Instead they are issuing a revolutionary challenge to the traditional assumption that human beings are morally superior to animals, and all three go so far as to insist that human beings have duties of justice toward animals.

3. IMPLICATIONS FOR COMMUNITY AND THE NOTION OF JUSTICE

It is one thing to suggest, as Rawls does, that we might have duties of compassion toward animals. But it is quite another, and something much more demanding, to assert that we have duties of justice toward animals. For duties of compassion require not that we *refrain* from engaging in certain sorts of practices involving animals, but simply that we *feel sorry* for the sacrifices that we exact from animals in the course of using them to satisfy our desires. Thus some authors urge us to follow the example of native American groups such as the Cree, in apologizing to animals in the course of slashing their throats and consuming them, as if such an apology could erase the act of violence that we commit against animals in killing them for our purposes, and as if our own situation were in the most remote sense at all like that of groups of people whose very lives depend on the killing and consumption of animals. But one need only consider how often and how customarily we subjugate and kill animals nowadays in our culture, and do so "with compassion", in order to recognize the disingenuousness of such a suggestion. The entire contemporary animal welfare movement, replete with its cheerful invocations of "happy meat", that current shibboleth of multinational corporations such as MacDonald's and KFC, serves as an index of the hypocrisy of all suggestions that an acknowledgment of animal sentience can be rendered consistent with animal husbandry and the killing of animals for human consumption-- particularly given the fact that the vast majority of people, and certainly most if not all people reading this essay, have no need whatsoever to consume animal products in order to lead a healthy and prosperous life.[7]

As noted in the first part of this essay, contractualist thinkers, whose thought has long dominated Western reflections on the notion of justice, insist that a being must be capable of entering into explicit reciprocal agreements in order to be considered a beneficiary of justice. Contractualists define justice in terms of mutually-binding agreements of non-harm or non-interference, and they see the historical turn to justice in our culture as a turn away from an animalistic, violent form of life. Some of the earliest texts in Western culture attest to such an understanding of the notion of justice. In his *Works and Days*, Hesiod speaks of a time when Zeus bestowed justice not on animals but rather on human beings. "Here is the law [*nomos*] as Zeus established it for human beings; / as for fish, and wild animals, and the flying birds, / they feed on each other, since there is no idea of justice among them; / but to men he gave justice [*dike*], and she in the end is proved the best thing / they have" (Hesiod 1959, 51). Justice is the "best thing" we have, inasmuch as it elevates us above the status of animals, which visit violence upon one another in their quest for survival. As beneficiaries of *dike*, human beings are able to use reciprocal agreements to establish and preserve peaceful interrelationships with one another. Should anyone violate the terms of these agreements, there will be clear sanctions imposed on the transgressor; and prior knowledge of these sanctions functions as a deterrent against transgression.

Hesiod, like Ovid after him, frames the turn to justice in terms of a pagan *Verfallsgeschichte*: once upon a time, humans lived in a golden age characterized by peaceful interrelationships among humans and between humans and animals, but humanity devolved into a state of violence that made Zeus's bestowal of justice necessary to prevent human beings from destroying themselves (Hesiod 1959, 105-201, 31-43). In the golden age humanity enjoyed ease and abundance, and "the fruitful grainland yielded its harvest to them / of its own accord". Implied here is the vegetarian repose in terms of which Milton would later characterize the Garden of Eden in *Paradise Lost* (book five, ll. 303-7). In the course of subsequent ages, human beings begin to age, perpetrate "reckless crime against one another", and engage in "evil war and [...] terrible carnage". Whereas ani-

---

7 | For the classic text on the limitations of the "animal welfare" movement, see Francione (1996); (2009), 67-128.

mals, such as the hawk who kills the nightingale, naturally and appropriately obey the law that might makes right, human beings are meant to follow a different and higher law, namely, Zeus's law of justice; human beings are meant to "listen to justice" and not "to practice violence" (Hesiod 1959, 207-211, 43, 213, 275).

To "listen to justice" is to emulate the peaceful conditions that prevailed in our prelapsarian "golden" state. By characterizing the turn to justice as an ascent above animality and a movement toward the divine, Hesiod sets the terms of the dominant discourses about human-animal relations in the history of Western thought: he proclaims a hierarchy in which human beings are superior to animals in virtue of being able to eschew violence and follow the peaceful way. Any Thrasymachus who proposes that justice is that which is to the advantage of the stronger is simply following the law that governs Hesiod's hawk: that might makes right. For Hesiod as for Plato, and indeed for the entire subsequent history of Western thought about society, the capacity to refrain from violence and to practice mutual respect is precisely what distinguishes us from animals.

But does this capacity truly make us superior to animals in the sense that we need recognize no duties of respect or non-harm toward animals? Does the fact that we cannot enter into formal, recpirocal agreements with animals entail that we may treat animals in any way we wish, at least as long as we do so "compassionately"? Implicit in Hesiod's story is the idea that we enter into a state of peace with other human beings by means of a *quid pro quo*: we abandon violence provided that other human beings do so as well. But is the *essence* of our desire for peace ultimately to be understood in terms of such a *quid pro quo*? Is there not something more at work in our desire to follow the peaceful way, something that makes us recoil at the prospect of inflicting avoidable harm on sentient beings quite apart from any concern for what we have to gain by refraining from violence, and quite apart from any concern for whether the others to whom we extend our respect are capable of appreciating and returning the gesture?

The views articulated by Plutarch, Porphyry, and Schopenhauer on the question of justice toward animals all express at least an incipient appreciation of the inherent value of animals and of the need to ground the idea of justice in a non-anthropocentric sense of kinship and common cause with all conscious, purposive beings. That this appreciation is merely incipient is evident from the fact that each of these thinkers places qualifications on our duties of justice toward animals. For his own part, Plutarch recants his view that the sphere of justice unites human beings and animals. In volume 12 of the *Moralia*, Plutarch criticizes the Stoics for having excluded animals from the sphere of justice; he goes to great lengths to describe the many cognitive capacities of animals and to show that many animals themselves have a sense of justice (as when a dog went to great lengths to avenge the death of his master), and he bases his call for justice toward animals on their evident intelligence and sociability (Plutarch 1995, 969E-F, 979B-C).[8] At the end of *De esu carnium*, Plutarch explicitly links his criticism of the Stoic conception of justice to the imperative to avoid killing and eating animals (Plutarch 1995, 999A-B). Even if animals lack *logos* in the specifically human sense and cannot enter into reciprocal agreements of non-harm with us, we nonetheless owe them justice in virtue of their participation of their own kinds of *logos* and in virtue of the many evident ways in which their lives and aspirations are bound up with and are comparable to our own. Animals "are entitled by birth and being" to the enjoyment and "duration of life" (Plutarch 1995, 994E, 549).[9] Plutarch recognizes, and suggests that even animals recognize, that there will be situations in which necessity forces us to kill animals; but he insists that we kill and eat animals not out of necessity but simply for the sake of pleasure, hence he deplores the practice of meat eating. "Nature disavows our eating of flesh" (Plutarch 1995, 994E-F, 551).

Late in his life, however, Plutarch retreats from this strong insistence on justice for animals and calls for comparatively less demanding duties of compassion toward animals. In his *Life of Marcus Cato*, he writes that "we know that kindness has a wider scope than justice. Law and justice we naturally apply to men alone; but when it comes to beneficence and charity, these often flow in streams from the gentle heart, like water from a copious spring, even down to dumb animals" (Plutarch 1985, 317). Whether

---

8 | The reader should not be misled by the suggestion in the latter passage that land but not sea animals are owed duties of justice. This text takes the form of a debate about the relative capacities and merits of land and sea animals, and the passage in question is part of a case on behalf of land animals; the part of the text that argues on behalf of sea animals includes equally strong arguments, including the suggestion that „the dolphin is the only creature who loves man for his own sake" rather than „for utilitarian reasons only" (Plutrach 1995, 984C, 471).

9 | See also Plutrach (1995), 994B, 547: "Nature appears to have produced [animals, at least tame ones] for the sake of their beauty and grace."

the translator of *De esu carnium* is right to interpret this softening of Plutarch's views as an indication that his early defense of animals was nothing more than "a foible of Plutarch's early manhood" must forever remain a matter of idle speculation (Plutrach 1995, 537 [introductory note by William C. Helmbold]). More important than the question why Plutarch lost his resolve on the question of justice toward animals is the power of his argumentation in the *Moralia*, in particular the challenge he poses to the traditional assumption that the moral worth of a being is dependent on the extent to which its experiential capacities resemble those of humans.

A similar if less pointedly anthropocentric qualification regarding the moral status of animals is found in Porphyry's argumentation in *De abstinentia*. Porphyry builds a case for justice toward animals by drawing out the implications of the Stoic doctrine of *oikeiosis*, a kinship doctrine that the Stoics interpret anthropocentrically so as to proclaim a fundamental distinction between humans and animals. The doctrine of *oikeiosis* focuses on the idea that every being has a fundamental regard first of all for itself and its own bodily integrity, and by extension for its family and in particular for its offspring.[10] The Stoics acknowledge that animals as well as humans participate in these first two stages or levels of *oikeiosis*, that of self-regard and that of regard for one's immediate kin or offspring. But the Stoics, because they deny *logos* to animals, deny that animals participate in the third and broadest circle of kinship, that of regard for all members of one's own kind or species. Or perhaps they deny *logos* to animals precisely *in order to* deny animals participation in the third level of *oikeiosis*: for beings who participate in that third level are able to recognize their kinship with all members of their own kind, regardless of whether they have any actual, immediate acquaintance with those other members. The Stoics attribute to human beings the capacity to recognize obligations of justice toward all other human beings, strangers and friends alike. Because animals are *aloga*, the Stoics maintain, animals are governed entirely by impulse (Orme), cannot scrutinize their perceptions rationally, and hence cannot establish principles according to which they could recognize their inner kinship with strangers of their own kind. Even the most sociable animals, such as bees and ants, the Stoics note, do not establish bonds of mutual respect with other, stranger communities of bees or ants. Only hu-

---

[10] | For a more detailed account of the doctrine of oikeiosis, see Steiner (2005), 88ff.

man beings can do this; this is enough for the Stoics to conclude that we have no bonds of kinship with animals, and hence that we have no obligations of justice toward animals.

Porphyry criticizes the arch anthropocentrism of the Stoics, and seeks to revise the doctrine of *oikeiosis* so as to argue for a highest, most encompassing bond of kinship not merely among humans but among all sentient beings. Porphyry's arguments about animal ingenuity, adaptation, and the like are designed to "show that animals are rational; in most of them *logos* is imperfect, but it is not wholly lacking. So if, as our opponents [viz. the Stoics] say, justice applies to rational beings, why should not justice, for us, also apply to animals?" (Porphyry 2000, 3.18.1, 90) Porphyry conceives of justice not in terms of mutually advantageous contractual arrangements, but rather in terms of "restraint and harmlessness towards everything that does not do harm. [...] the essence of justice is that the rational rules over the irrational, and the irrational follows" (Porphyry 2000, 3.26.9-10, 98). To be rational in this sense is to acknowledge that all sentient beings, all those who participate in the *logos* to some extent or other, can be harmed in ways in which non-sentient beings such as plants cannot be harmed; thus justice does not extend to plants (Porphyry 2000, 3.18.2, 90: Plants "appear to be quite incompatible with *logos*"). In arguing that we have duties of justice toward animals, Porphyry recognizes that animals (most, at any rate, if not all) are incapable of the degree of reason that would enable them to take on reciprocal obligations of non-harm toward us. He also recognizes that there will be times when we must inflict harm on animals. "Nature concedes and provides for harm inflicted, up to a point, on necessities [...] but to destroy other creatures gratuitously and for pleasure is total savagery and injustice." Just because we must sometimes inflict harm upon some animals, it does not follow that we are entitled to place ourselves in a state of war with all animals at all times (Porphyry 2000, 3.18.3-5, 90). A fundamental bond of justice is the starting point from which we should regard our relations with animals: rather than seeing peaceful relations with animals as a modification of or departure from a basic relation of enmity and violence with animals, we ought to regard violence toward animals as a regrettable but sometimes unavoidable departure from an underlying bond of peaceful kinship with animals.

A reader could hardly be reproached for inferring from Porphyry's arguments and from the title of his text that he is an advocate of universal vegetarianism. After all, when he lists the things without which human beings cannot survive, he names "air and water, plants and crops" but makes no mention of animal flesh (Porphyry 2000, 3.18.4, 90). And yet Porphyry does not argue that all human beings ought to practice vegetarianism. He writes that "my discourse will not offer advice to every human way of life: not to those who engage in banausic crafts, nor to athletes of the body, nor to soldiers, nor to sailors, nor orators, nor to those who have chosen the life of public affairs, but to the person who has thought about who he is and whence he has come and where he should try to go" (Porphyry 2000, 1.27.1, 40). Porphyry's arguments are directed in Neoplatonist fashion to those among us who aspire to take part in "the Olympics of the soul", those who would seek to transcend the conditions of embodiment toward an ideal of spiritual purification (Porphyry 2000, 1.31.3, 43). Indeed, the Neoplatonist strain in *De abstinentia* stands in an uneasy tension with the many passages in which Porphyry presents what modern thinkers would call a direct duties approach to animals: on the one hand we are told that practices such as eating meat arouse our passions and therefore are incompatible with the aspiration to achieve spiritual enlightenment, while on the other hand we are told that animals are beloved of the gods and that we should respect the inherent dignity of animals. It remains for the contemporary reader to resolve this tension, and in particular to confront the question whether Porphyry's reasons for excluding so many people from the duty to eschew animal flesh have any force within the context of contemporary society and consciousness. In doing so, one would do well to ponder whether, if he had been writing today rather than nearly two thousand years ago, Porphyry might have argued not simply for vegetarianism but for universal veganism.

Perhaps he would not have. For it is not enough to suppose that thinkers such as Plutarch and Porphyry stopped short of advocating universal vegetarianism, not to mention veganism, simply because they were unenlightened by modern liberal political theory and its concepts of individuality and rational agency. One immediately thinks of Kant, with his classification of animals as mere "things" and his denial of direct duties toward animals. Schopenhauer, too, ultimately succumbs to anthropocentric prejudice in the course of arguing for duties of justice toward animals. Schopenhauer recognizes that the first principle of justice, whether it be the kind that prevails contractually among humans or that among sentient beings generally, is to refrain from harming others. The former sense of justice, that which prevails among humans, calls on us primarily to respect one another's property rights (Schopenhauer 1995, 149). Justice in this sense is "temporal", and the function of the state is to enforce it. But Schopenhauer recognizes another, transcendent form of justice that he calls "heavenly" or "eternal" (Schopenhauer 1995, 152: True justice is *"ourania"*; Schopenhauer 1958, 350). Even in a state of nature, quite apart from human conventions, we have an obligation to avoid doing harm (Schopenhauer 1958, 359). This obligation to avoid doing harm wherever possible is not mitigated by the fact that there will always be a great deal of unavoidable suffering in nature. Our capacity for compassion discloses for us the imperatives of justice and the rightness of engaging in acts of self-sacrifice on behalf of others (Schopenhauer 1958, 376, 378; 1995, 152).

To accept the duty to sacrifice one's individual interests for the sake of others is to embrace justice in its purest form—purest in the sense that I gain nothing from acts of self-sacrifice but instead perform certain actions out of pure compassion for another. Justice in this sense is not a *quid pro quo* but rather takes the form of a unilateral expression of concern for the other. Thus the ideal of cosmic justice requires something that the contractualist ideal of justice does not: namely, that I recognize and act on certain duties even though I have nothing to gain from doing so. The ideal of cosmic justice also dispenses with a requirement that is essential to contractualism: the requirement that beneficiaries of justice be capable of conceptualizing justice. This is the crux of the dispute between those who believe that we can have no duties of justice toward animals and those who believe that we can. Those who think that animals are categorically excluded from justice relations believe so because animals are unable to assert anything like an interest or a right. Those who believe that we have eternal or cosmic duties of justice toward animals believe that animals need not be able to think about or conceptualize what is owed to them in order for something to *be* owed to them. Animals merit consideration and respect quite apart from whether they can demand consideration and respect. Schopenhauer even believes that there is such a thing as "an *inborn* principle of giving others their due", and that what is "due" to conscious beings such as animals is consideration and respect very much like the consideration we customarily extend to other human beings (Schopenhauer 1995, 138f).

For all that, however, Schopenhauer falls into the anthropocentric trap of arguing that our duties toward animals are less demanding than our duties toward human beings. Schopenhauer purports to derive a recognition of duties of justice toward animals from feelings of compassion: Our sense of fellow-feeling or kinship with animals makes us recognize that "in all essential respects, *the animal* is absolutely identical with us" and that we have cosmic duties not merely of mercy but of justice with regard to animals, just as we have with regard to our fellow human beings (Schopenhauer 2000, 372, 375). But Schopenhauer ultimately conflates duties of justice with duties of compassion, rather than recognizing that feelings of compassion ought to lead us to recognize rights in animals that we must treat as inviolable once we have recognized them. Far from advocating vegetarianism, let alone veganism, Schopenhauer proceeds from an assertion of duties of justice toward animals to the contradictory conclusion that practices such as meat eating can be justified. "Sympathy for animals should not carry us to the length of having to abstain from animal food, like the Brahmins; for in nature the capacity for suffering keeps pace with intelligence, and thus man would suffer more by going without animal food, especially in North America, than the animal does through a quick and always unforseen death" (Schopenhauer 1995, 182).[11]

The reasoning that Schopenhauer offers in justification of meat eating is of a piece with that offered by Bentham, who is more commonly thought of as a champion of animals. In the passage in *An Introduction to the Principles of Morals and Legislation*, so often cited, in which Bentham asserts that "the question is not, Can they [viz. animals] *reason?* nor, Can they *talk?* but, Can they *suffer?*" he goes on make a statement that is much less often cited: that when we kill animals for food, "we are the better for it, and they are never the worse. They have none of those long-protracted anticipations of future misery which we have. The death they suffer in our hands commonly is, and always may be, a speedier, and by that means a less painful one, than that which would await them in the inevitable course of nature. [...] We should be the worse for their living, and they are never the worse for being dead" (Bentham 1948, 310-311n). Schopenhauer puts the point in the following way: Animals lack the capacity for reflective awareness (*Besonnenheit*); they cannot contemplate the remote past or the distant future, hence their ability to suffer pain and loss is inherently less than that of human beings (Schopenhauer 1974, 151). "The absence of reason restricts the animals to representations of perception immediately

---

11 | See also Schopenhauer (2000), 373-375, where he hints that vivisection may be justified by great utility to human beings.

present to them in time, in other words to real objects. We, on the other hand, by virtue of knowledge in the abstract, comprehend not only the narrow and actual present, but also the whole past and future together with the wide realm of possibility." (Schopenhauer 1959, 84) "In consequence, the animals have infinitely less to *suffer* than we have, because they know no other sufferings than those directly brought about by the *present.*" (Schopenhauer 1959, 60, 36)

It is this putatively inferior capacity for suffering in animals that makes it permissible to kill and eat them, and perhaps even to experiment on them as well. But does it really make sense to suppose that because animals cannot contemplate past and future as such, their sufferings are in principle less than the sufferings that human beings can experience? Or is this simply the extreme manifestation of an anthropocentrism that would argue practically anything in order to justify the subjection of animals? Consider the analogy of a young child who learns that she must visit the dentist, and who is inconsolably terrified at the prospect: can her suffering in such a situation truly be said to be less than that of an adult who must visit the dentist but who has considerably more experience with the dentist and knows exactly what is in store? Or what about the case of an animal that is engaged in a fight for its life: are we really to suppose that this animal's life matters any less to it than my life would matter to me in such a situation? Are there any rational grounds for supposing that an animal ought to be gratified to be deprived of its life by human beings who want to eat it, rather than being killed by some deadly non-human adversary?

However we may ultimately answer these sorts of questions, we must proceed with an intimate awareness that human beings do not typically answer them in a detached, objective fashion but instead often concoct putative reasons designed to conceal underlying selfish motivations. In the case of our relations with animals, these motivations are clear: we like the taste of animal flesh and other animal products; our lives are made considerably easier by the use of animals as beasts of burden; and, perhaps most importantly, we have an almost desperate desire to distinguish ourselves from animals and proclaim that we are in some essential sense above nature. All these motivations are at work when Mill asserts that "human beings have faculties more elevated than the animal appetites" and that therefore it is "better to be a fool dissatisfied than a pig satisfied" (Mill 1998, 138, 140). They are equally at work when Brillat-Savarin attributes transcendent status to the human capacity to enjoy cuisine: "Animals feed themselves; man eats; only man, possessed of spirit, knows how to eat" (Brillat-Savarin 1842, 9; Brillat-Savarin goes on to argue that only the French truly know how to eat). In the end, we have to ask ourselves in all sobriety whether wine is the sort of transfiguration of the grape that elevates us above nature and the "merely" animal, whether bread signifies our connection with the holy or whether, as Francis Ponge urged, it is ultimately "less an object of respect than of consumption" (Ponge 1942). For the way in which we ultimately answer the question of the inner meaning of an activity as arguably quotidian as eating will tell us everything about the way in which we ultimately answer the question whether we have duties of justice toward animals.

References

Aquinas, T. (1920-25), The 'Summa Theologica' of St. Thomas Aquinas, 22 vols., trans. the Fathers of the English Dominican Province, vol. 10, London: Burns Oats and Washbourne.
Aquinas, T. (1997), Basic Writings of St. Thomas Aquinas, 2 vols., ed. Anton C. Pegis, vol. 2, Indianapolis: Hackett.
Bentham, J. (1948), An Introduction to the Principles of Morals and Legislation, New York: Hafner/Macmillan.
Brillat-Savarin, J.A. (1842), Physiologie du goût: Méditations de gastronomie transcendentale, Paris: Charpentier.
DeGrazia, D. (1996), Taking Animals Seriously: Mental Life and Moral Status, Cambridge: Cambridge University Press.
Dierauer, U. (1977), Tier und Mensch im Denken der Antike: Studien zur Tierpsychologie, Anthropologie und Ethik, Amsterdam: Grüner.
Finnis, J. (1980), Natural Law and Natural Rights, Oxford: Clarendon.
Francione, G.L. (1996), Rain Without Thunder: The Ideology of the Animal Rights Movement, Philadelphia: Temple University Press.
Francione, G.L. (2009), "Reflections on Animals, Property, and the Law and Rain Without Thunder", in: G.L. Francione, Animals as Persons: Essays on the Abolition of Animal Exploitation, New York: Columbia University Press.

Gassendi, P. (1984), Fifth Set of Objections, in: R. Descartes, The Philosophical Writings of Descartes, vol. 2, trans. J. Cottingham, R. Stoothoff, D. Murdoch, Cambridge: Cambridge University Press.
Hesiod (1959), Works and Days, in: Hesiod, trans. R. Lattimore, Ann Arbor: University of Michigan Press, 276-9.
Kant, I. (1987), Critique of Judgment, trans. W.S. Pluhar, Indianapolis: Hackett.
Kant, I. (1996), "The Doctrine of Virtue", in: M. Gregor (ed.), The Metaphysics of Morals, Cambridge: Cambridge University Press.
Kant, I. (1997), Lectures on Ethics, ed. P. Heath, J.B. Schneewind, trans. P. Heath, Cambridge: Cambridge University Press.
Mill, J.S. (1998), Utilitarianism, in: J.S. Mill, On Liberty and Other Essays, ed. J. Gray, Oxford: Oxford University Press.
Nussbaum, M.C. (1978), Aristotle's De Motu Animalium, Princeton: Princeton University Press.
Plutarch (1985), Life of Marcus Cato 5.2, in: Plutarch's Lives, vol. 2, Greek with English trans. by B. Perrin, Cambridge: Harvard University Press; London: William Heinemann.
Plutarch (1995), Whether Land or Sea Animals are Cleverer, Beasts are Rational/The Eating of Flesh, in Moralia, vol. 12, Greek with English trans. H. Cherniss, W.C. Helmbold, Cambridge: Harvard University Press.
Ponge, F. (1942), "Le pain", Le Parti pris des choses: Collection poésie, Paris: Éditions Gallimard.
Porphyry (2000), On Abstinence from Killing Animals, trans. G. Clark, Ithaca: Cornell University Press.
Rawls, J. (2000), A Theory of Justice, revised ed., Cambridge: Bellknap/Harvard University Press.
Saint Augustine (1966), The Catholic and Manichaean Ways of Life, trans. D.A. Gallagher, I.J. Gallagher, Fathers of the Church, vol. 56, Washington, D.C.: Catholic University of America Press.
Saint Augustine (1998), The City of God against the Pagans, ed. and trans. R.W. Dyson, Cambridge: Cambridge University Press.
Schopenhauer, A. (1958), The World as Will and Representation, vol. 1, trans. E.F.J. Payne, Indiana Hills, CO: Falcon's Wing Press.
Schopenhauer, A. (1974), The Fourfold Root of the Principle of Sufficient Reason, trans. E.F.J. Payne, La Salle, IL: Open Court.

Schopenhauer, A. (1995), On the Basis of Morality, trans. E.F.J. Payne, Providence/Oxford: Berghahn Books.

Schopenhauer, A. (2000), "On Religion", in: A. Schopenhauer, Parerga and Paralipomena, vol. 2, trans. E.F.J. Payne, Oxford: Clarendon Press.

Sextus Empiricus (1996), Outlines of Pyrrhonism, in: Sextus Empiricus, The Skeptic Way: Sextus Empiricus's "Outlines of Pyrrhonism", trans. B. Mates, Oxford: Oxford University Press

Steiner, G. (2005), Anthropocentrism and Its Discontents: The Moral Status of Animals in the History of Western Philosophy, Pittsburgh: University of Pittsburgh Press.

Williams, B. (1978), Descartes: The Project of Pure Enquiry, Harmondsworth: Penguin.

Part Two
Animal Autonomy and Its Moral Significance

5. Mental Capacities and Animal Ethics

Hans-Johann Glock

1. WHY MORAL STATUS DEPENDS ON MENTAL CAPACITIES

Do at least some non-human animals (henceforth simply 'animals') have minds comparable to those of humans? The question is both complex and vexed. It has exercised philosophers, scientists, theologians, lawyers, artists and laypeople at least since antiquity. At present it is treated intensively from a variety of methodological perspectives in subjects ranging from evolutionary biology and neurophysiology through ethology, archaeology, psychology and linguistics to the philosophy of mind and language (see Allen 2010; Andrews 2010; Wild 2008; Perler & Wild 2005; Lurz 2009). It is also prominent in the wider public sphere, on account of its moral and legal implications. Again, this interest in the question of how we should treat animals goes back to antiquity. Indeed the two topics—animal minds and animal ethics or animal welfare—have been intertwined from the outset—as indicated by the title of Sorabji's seminal Animal Minds and Human Morals.

In some respects, however, the increasing intrusion of moral concerns has had a baneful influence on recent debates about animal minds. In contributions to animal ethics one rarely encounters a dispassionate attitude and a weighing of pros and cons. Many protagonists do not approach the problems *sine ira et studio*, as the ancients would have put it. For instance, the voluminous The Animal Ethics Reader (Armstrong & Botzler 2003) features an annotated bibliography concerning theories of animal ethics. As luck would have it, however, all the contributions in favour of raising the moral status of animals turn out to be utterly brilliant, while the sceptics are guilty of various mistakes, such as 'ignoring scientific data'. Indeed, for some animal rights theorists, a neutral approach to the problems and the toleration of competing positions amounts to nothing less than 'betraying one's own values'. Indeed, R. Garner would consider it the 'worse (sic!) indictment' of his book if it failed to condemn our current treatment of animals (Garner 2005: 13). Instead one might have thought that the worst indictment for a self-avowed survey of the debate would be if it distorted the claims and arguments on whatever side, or if it reached conclusions that are incorrect or unwarranted.

There is reason to suspect more than the usual degree of ideological interference. On occasion, factual and conceptual claims about animal minds as well as moral principles seem to be adopted because of pre-established views on the moral status of animals. Of course it is perfectly legitimate to be interested in the topic of animal minds because of its moral, political and legal repercussions. And it is not just legitimate but imperative to discuss what implications the possession or lack of mentality should have for our treatment of animals, their treatment by ethologists included (see Bekoff & Jamieson 1991). What is illegitimate is to tailor one's view of animal minds to suit one's ethical (or unethical) prejudices. Alas, in many cases verdicts on animal minds appear to be motivated neither by empirical observations nor by conceptual clarifications, but by a desire to affirm or deny that animals are worthy of various degrees of moral and legal consideration, a desire that has not been subjected to critical scrutiny. By contrast, the rational procedure is to decide on the moral status of animals on the basis of their possession or lack of morally relevant properties.

Some virtue ethicists are in danger of succumbing to a similar vice. According to them our treatment of animals should not be guided by rational argumentation concerning the moral significance of features possessed by animals. Rather, it is a matter of our moral experience, in particular of the concern we have with leading a virtuous life, which will create an indescribable pull against cruelty towards animals (see Diamond 1991, chs. 13-14; Hursthouse 2000, 165-166). Such versions of virtue theory portray our moral thinking and our moral lives as more self-regarding and egocentric (as opposed to egoistic) than it ought to be and, I hope, is. They appear ultimately concerned only with achieving a biography they can feel proud of, rather than with making the world a better place. At the same time, virtue theory provides an important corrective to ethical perspectives that focus exclusively on other-regarding aims and obligations. And virtue theory has important contributions to make to animal ethics in particular, in that it invokes and explores notions of well-being and flourishing that can be applied to all living creatures, while at the same time taking on a different content with respect to different species.

My own stance on these issues stands in the tradition of the enlightenment and, more specifically, of analytic philosophy. Nevertheless, it should be acceptable even to a recent movement that purports to be sceptical or even hostile to such a rationalist perspective. According to the so-called 'vulnerability approach', human beings should not exploit animals which are vulnerable in some respects, for example susceptible to harm or dependent on humans for their well-being or survival (e.g. Clement 2003; Linzey 2009). This contrasts with the so-called 'psychological approach' of earlier animal rights activists, according to which animals should be protected on account of their mental capacities. Even according to the vulnerability approach, however, our treatment of animals should be guided by their morally relevant properties. It is just that those properties are not the mental capacities, but rather their vulnerabilities.

The moot question is how mental capacities and vulnerabilities might come apart. I can detect two areas in which the contrast between vulnerability and psychological approach can make for a real difference as regards the moral consequences. Aristotelians and Neo-Aristotelians distinguish between three basic kinds of living things according to their capacities: plants, animals and humans (see Hacker 2007). All of them have needs, animals and humans have perception and agency, only humans have intellect or reason. This hierarchy must be taken with more than a pinch of salt. As regards its extension, the Aristotelian classification is not a hard and fast one, and it may not be fruitful or even applicable to certain types of organisms. Connected to this last point is the fact that the Aristotelian distinction is no longer state of the art as regards the life sciences. The latter distinguish fungi from plants, and separate both from animals according to the source of energy—the former being autotrophic, the latter being heterotrophic. Nevertheless it remains legitimate and fruitful to distinguish organisms according to the Aristotelian criteria. For the latter have a close connection not just to our everyday concerns in dealing with non-human organisms, but also to the topic of the mental.

Now, the first potential contrast between mental capacities and vulnerabilities arises if one follows the Aristotelian tradition one step further, namely by insisting that only the higher faculty of reason (nous) qualifies as genuinely mental. For in that case sentience, the archetypal form of vulnerability, does not yet amount to anything mental. However, this

Aristotelian demarcation of the mental is neither wide-spread at present nor in line with our established use of the term 'mental' and its cognates in everyday parlance or the behavioural sciences. By contrast, it is in line with our established notion of the mental to draw the line at creatures that possess sensory capacities. Prince Charles notwithstanding, therefore, plants do not possess mental capacities. Yet this is where a second potential contrast arises. Because of having needs, plants are vulnerable in a non-metaphorical sense. For their needs can be either satisfied or frustrated. And there is at least a case for holding that the needs of plants possess some moral weight, however slight it may be and however low its place in a hierarchy of moral demands. Wanton frustration of the requirements of plants—in particular their wanton destruction—may well be regarded as bad for moral reasons, reasons that cannot be reduced to prudential or aesthetic ones, for instance.

Nevertheless I shall set aside the vulnerability approach in the remainder of this essay. Our topic is animal minds and their moral implications. And the possession of certain psychological capacities such as sentience or intentions or thoughts about the future is both necessary and sufficient for the kind of susceptibility to harm that the vulnerability approach itself focuses on (see Blasimme, Sandis, Bortolotti, this volume). The net result of these considerations is: what kind and degree of moral consideration various types of animals are worthy of depends principally on their mental capacities, widely conceived, rather than the other way around. As I hope to show, it hinges in particular on whether animals are capable of experiencing pain, of acting intentionally or for reasons, of having beliefs and desires, of having emotions, and of entertaining plans about the future.

In the Western philosophical tradition, to which I shall confine myself, animal minds and animal ethics loomed large until early modern philosophy, but were sidelined thereafter. Their revival occurred only in the twentieth century.

As regards animal ethics, Leonard Nelson (1932) provided an exemplary early discussion. Unfortunately, his contribution has largely been ignored. The gradual expansion of animal welfare debates was fuelled by various economic and social developments, notably the rise of factory farming and its entry into public conscience. But the veritable explosion since the 1970s is largely due to the work of Anglophone analytic philosophers like Peter Singer (1975) and Tom Regan (1983).

5. Mental Capacities and Animal Ethics

As regards animal minds, Charles Darwin and his early followers showed a keen interest.[1] But this interest was expunged by the rise of behaviourism in the nascent subject of psychology. The behaviourists sought to overcome the reliance on introspection as regards human psychology and the reliance on anecdotes of the kind invoked by the early Darwinists as regards animals. What is needed instead, they argued, are intersubjectively accessible and strictly controlled data. From a behaviourist perspective, mental notions tended to be suspect even when applied to humans. They were definitely on the index when it came to animals. Instead, the behaviourists explained even complex and apparently intelligent animal activities solely by reference to stimulus-response mechanisms, whether innate or acquired ('conditioned'). Behaviourism was in turn superseded by the so-called cognitive revolution, as regards human psychology since the 1950s, as regards comparative psychology since the 1970s. Like most revolutions, that one was a mixed blessing. As regards comparative psychology, however, it had one indisputably positive result. The rise of so-called cognitive ethology led to definite advances in the methods for observing and experimenting on animal behaviour, both in the laboratory and in the wild. These in turn led to astonishing discoveries concerning the intelligence and behavioural capacities not just of primates, cetaceans and other mammals (notably dogs and pigs), but also of species from other taxa, such as parrots, Caledonian crows and octopuses.

Nevertheless, such empirical discoveries do not simply settle by themselves the question of animal minds, let alone the moral questions

---

1 | Thus Darwin wrote: "There is no fundamental difference between man and the higher mammals in their mental faculties". Yet he also acknowledged: "Of the high importance of the intellectual faculties there can be no doubt, for man mainly owes to them his predominant position in the world" (Darwin 1874, ch. II/798 and ch. V/868). Note the potential tension between the two statements. If the predominance of humans over all other higher animals is more than a matter of degree—as all the evidence suggests—this militates against insisting that the difference in the underlying mental faculties is one of degree rather than kind. Darwin himself only elaborated on the mental proximity between humans and animals as regards the emotions (Darwin 1872). But his follower Romanes (1881) developed a ranking of species according to intelligence, according pride of place to dogs. Another early Darwinist, Asa Gray (1880), may have been the first to draw explicit moral conclusions from the common evolutionary origins of humans and animals.

concerning our treatment of animals. I shall indicate why in the next, loosely speaking methodological section. In the sequel I shall discuss the applicability to animals of several mental notions that are plausibly connected to various kinds of moral status—sensation, interests, beliefs and desires, intentional agency and reasoning (scts. 5.3-7). As this list shows, it is not my ambition to discuss all mental properties that have been fingered for conferring a special moral status. Thus autonomy, free will, self-consciousness and personhood will at most be mentioned in the context of other mental capacities. I shall also leave aside a question that has attracted a lot of attention recently, namely whether animals are not just objects but also subjects of moral consideration, i.e. whether they are capable of moral beliefs and sentiments (see de Waal 2006; Bekoff & Pierce 2009).[2] Even without a complete survey, it will transpire that there are no theoretical reasons for denying that animals have intrinsic moral value. At the same time such value comes in varying degrees, depending on the mental capacities concerned. In the final section I shall tentatively suggest that there are nevertheless reasons for drawing a qualitative distinction between the moral status of animals and that of humans.

2. METHODOLOGICAL PROLEGOMENA

Some of the questions raised by animal welfare are not within the remit of philosophy. This holds in particular for the question of whether some of the morally contentious ways in which animals are currently treated—notably in the field of animal experimentation—actually produce the benefits for human beings that they are claimed to yield, and whether they are the only or even most efficient ways of achieving these benefits (see Garner 2005, 17; Rowlands 2002, 28-31; Francione & Watson 2000). Whether

---

2 | In so far as they are, and in so far as these sentiments include not just conspecifics but also human companions, this might qualify them for a higher moral status even if moral status is a function of the degree to which a creature can interact with us morally and emotionally (see sct. 5.8). This would still fail to satisfy contractualists, who insist that only creatures able to enter into some kind of agreement with us can be fully-fledged beneficiaries of moral consideration. Furthermore, I remain sceptical about the claims made on behalf of the moral lives of animals.

some controversial treatment of animals is unnecessary or even harmful for its intended beneficiaries depends exclusively on empirical issues, notably in human and veterinary medicine.

In other respects, the territory needs to be divided between practical philosophy, theoretical philosophy and the empirical sciences investigating animals. The latter two are involved in assessing what mental capacities animals have, the former in reflecting on the moral relevance of these capacities. Some authors interested mainly in the moral and political aspects of animal welfare tend to downplay the question of animal minds at the expense of moral considerations. For instance, Garner suggests that 'by and large advocates of inequality [between humans and animals] do concur with cross-species egalitarians that humans do cause animals to suffer. The difference then is not primarily about the degree of suffering but on the degree to which this suffering is justified' (Garner 2005, 16). But first, the question of whether animals suffer pain at all is contested (see sct. 5.3). Secondly, the contested issues proliferate in number and complexity when it comes to more complex mental features that are of potential moral import. Even the seemingly innocuous idea that higher animals have beliefs is subject to intense debate. Thirdly, the separation of animal attributes from moral principles concerning these attributes is not always clear-cut or straightforward. For instance, the question of whether suffering matters may depend not just on moral principles but also on what other mental capacities animals possess. Suffering which can be anticipated or remembered is arguably more important than suffering, which is confined to the present.

That the empirical sciences are central to establishing the extent and nature of animal mentality is obvious. Theoretical philosophy also has a vital contribution to make, however. One reason why the topic of animal minds is so complex is that it poses problems of a distinctively conceptual kind. What mentality, if any, one can attribute to animals depends not just on the empirical findings (whether observations in the field or experiments in the laboratory) and theories of disciplines like comparative psychology and cognitive ethology. It also depends on what one makes of heavily contested concepts like that of a mind, of thought, of consciousness, of behaviour, etc. The philosophical task in this area consists not in collecting new empirical data about animal behaviour, its neurological causes or its evolutionary origins, but in clarifying what it is to possess various mental properties, and hence under what conditions such properties can be ascribed to organisms. This is not to say that one needs a cast-iron precise definition of these properties in advance of empirical theory-building. But it is to say that such theory-building must be accompanied by conceptual reflection on the provisional understanding of mental concepts that inform specific lines of research, methods and conclusions (see Allen & Bekoff 1996, 236-7).

As regards animal minds, there are two opposing stances. Differentialists maintain that there are crucial qualitative differences separating us from animals; assimilationists insist that the differences are merely quantitative and gradual. The most important variant of differentialism is lingualism. It denies on a priori grounds that animals without a language can have mental capacities at all, or at least the 'higher' mental capacities required for moral status. This raises the question of whether there are conceptual connections between the possession of language on the one hand, and the capacity to act, to act for reasons, and to reason on the other.

I shall approach these issues from a third-person perspective. Such a perspective is not committed to the behaviourist idea that mental phenomena are reducible to behavioural dispositions. It merely holds that the connection between the mental and the behavioural is conceptual rather than merely factual. Our mental terms would not mean what they do unless there were characteristic manifestations of mental phenomena, at least in some situations. A third-person perspective on animal minds, in particular, is adopted both by laypeople and by empirical scientists. Unsurprisingly so.

Our mental vocabulary does not capture genetic or neurophysiological differences, let alone putative 'private' experiences that can never be revealed. Instead, it captures differences in the kinds of behavioural and perceptual capacities human beings are interested in. We are social primates by nature. Our languages include mental terms mainly because of our fundamental need to describe, explain, predict and otherwise understand the behaviour and behavioural dispositions of other human and non-human animals, and because of the equally fundamental need to express these mental phenomena, thereby also providing such information to other humans. No room here for the inner glow sought by Cartesians, or the neural mechanisms that captivate many contemporary philosophers.

What we require is a perspective which is both more naturalistic and more realistic. Mental and biological phenomena reveal themselves only when we go beyond the brain and consider not just the whole organism, but the organism in the context of its environment, in the context of its form of life, as both Wittgensteinians and cognitive ethologists might put it.

Mental phenomena as defined by our existing mental concepts must be capable of being manifested in behaviour. The moot question is whether certain mental features can only be manifested in linguistic behaviour, and for what morally relevant features, if any, this holds.[3] In addressing that question, one needs to consider not just extant species and their actual behavioural repertoire, but also what kind of behaviour non-linguistic creatures are capable of in principle. For lingualism to be correct, even animals very much like us in their facial expressions, gestures, and non-linguistic behavioural patterns must lack the mental capacities under consideration, simply because they lack linguistic competence. As regards animal ethics, however, we may safely concentrate on the behavioural capacities of extant species.

3. Sensation

The question of whether animals can experience sensations, in particular pleasure and pain, is of obvious moral relevance. There are countless studies of the behavioural and physiological reactions of animals to harmful stimuli (see, e.g., Allen 2004; Braithwaite 2010). And that vertebrates, at any rate, have sensations and are capable of perceiving their environment should be obvious. Nonetheless it has been contested (e.g. Harrison 1991). That animals can feel pain tends to be doubted especially by those who, in the wake of Nagel, conceive of all sentience in terms of qualia, mysterious inner goings-on accessible only to their respective owners. It has also been denied outright.

Thus Bermond (2003, 80) confidently declares pain to be an emotion, ignoring the difference between a sensation like pain, with a bodily location, and bodily feelings like hunger on the one hand, and emotions on the other. He rightly links the issue of pain to that of consciousness. But

---

3 | Constraints of space rule out a more thorough defence of a third-person perspective. This would require a lengthy discussion of the conceptual connections between mind and behaviour and a rebuttal of objections like those advanced by Searle. See Glock (2009); Dupré (1996).

he then dismisses out of hand arguments for the presence of pain in animals, even in species that possess higher cognitive capacities. Such capacities, he avers, are no indicator of consciousness, since cognitive processes in humans such as speaking or calculating need not be conscious. Yet it is surely imperative here to consider what kind of consciousness is at issue.

At the most basic level, there are states of mere consciousness. Such consciousness has no object. It stands in contrast to various states of sleep and unconsciousness. It is something one may lose and later regain, and it comes in degrees: one can be more or less conscious in this sense. Subject to this qualification, mere consciousness is a precondition of all other forms of consciousness. Organisms can be in occurrent mental states or undergo occurrent mental processes only to the extent to which they are conscious in this sense. Some of these states or processes are intentional, i.e. they have an object or content, a thing, state of affairs, etc. at which they are directed. Here one can speak of transitive consciousness, consciousness of something. But others lack such an object. This holds not just of sensations like pain, but also of moods (see Glock 2001). Here one might speak of states of intransitive consciousness.[4]

Finally, there is self-consciousness or self-awareness. This is a particular variant of transitive consciousness. In it one is conscious of oneself

---

4 | My terminology is inspired by Rosenthal (1986) on the one hand, Malcolm (1984), Bennett and Hacker (2003, ch. 9) on the other. The latter's contrast between intransitive (i.e. mere) and transitive consciousness does not accommodate the difference between being awake on the one hand, and being in either intentional or *non-intentional* states on the other. The former's 'creature consciousness' corresponds to my mere consciousness, except that it signifies the capacity of a subject rather than a kind of state, which Rosenthal calls 'state consciousness'. Rosenthal further distinguishes between 'transitive consciousness'— which roughly corresponds to my notion—and intransitive consciousness, which is my mere consciousness. Using Rosenthal's terminology without subscribing to his theory of consciousness, Bermond's mistake lies in thinking that being in pain requires transitive rather than merely intransitive consciousness, and hence that creature consciousness does not suffice for susceptibility to pain. The mistake can also be diagnosed in terms suggested by Dretske (1995, 101). It consists in thinking that any state one is 'conscious with', any state being in which makes a subject conscious, notably an experience, must also be a state the subject is 'conscious of'.

and of one's properties. A special case of self-consciousness—though the one philosophers tend to be obsessed with—is consciousness of one's own mental phenomena (states, processes, abilities, etc.). All forms of consciousness discussed so far are potential objects of self-consciousness, for those subjects who possess that advanced capacity. I can be aware of being awake, of being depressed, or of fretting about an exam. But these other forms of consciousness need not be confined to subjects capable of self-consciousness.

Bermond's denial of pain even in creatures with cognitive capacities trades on a confusion between a state one is conscious of, which requires a form of self-consciousness, and a state of consciousness, i.e. a state of mere sentience, or of being intransitively conscious, or of being transitively conscious of something. Genuinely cognitive processes must involve at least some intentional states. Hence they presuppose transitive consciousness, and by implication sentience. However, they do not require any self-awareness or self-reflection. One needs to be conscious of something, yet this need not be one's own mental states. What is more, the capacity to suffer pain does not even require cognitive processes and hence transitive consciousness. It only requires sentience and intransitive consciousness.

To be sure, genuine sentience is more than a disposition to react to stimuli. A real sensation must be felt by its subject—there is no difference between having a sensation and feeling a sensation. Most sensations also have a hedonic or affective dimension. Pain, for instance, must have an aversive dimension and be felt as bad. And in that case, one might argue in Bermond's defence, it must involve some kind of self-consciousness. The subject feels or experiences a mental state of the subject. All of these steps are sound, except for the last. Feeling or experiencing a pain is to be contrasted with nociception, a mere reaction to noxious stimuli. But it does not constitute even a minimal case of self-consciousness. For, as Wittgenstein argued persuasively, in my view, the subject of a pain does not stand in a genuine relation to a bona fide object which is part of its own mental furniture (see Glock 1996). Feeling a pain is simply being in pain. It is a modification of subjects that are capable of affective responses displayed in behaviour, facial expressions and bodily demeanour.

At this juncture, Bermond's second cavil comes into play. Against the idea that the behavioural repertoire shows animals to be susceptible to pain he invokes various scenarios in which pain is divorced from behaviour in particular: there can be pain without pain behaviour and pain behaviour without pain. This is correct. But if it were sufficient reason to disregard behaviour altogether, it would open the flood-gates to a general skepticism about other minds rather than casting particular doubt about animal sensation. For in humans we encounter pain without linguistic pain behaviour and linguistic pain behaviour without pain. Bermond further compounds his error when he defends the unrestrained separability of pain and pain behaviour by reference to the alleged fact that both have different neurophysiological loci, namely, respectively, cortical and subcortically (Bermond 2003, 81-2). This is to confuse the de facto physiological separation of the vehicles of different mental capacities with a conceptual separation of the capacities themselves (on the difference between an ability, its exercise and its vehicle see Kenny 1989, ch. 5).

A differentialist line similar to that of Bermond is taken by Carruthers (1989). He subscribes to a higher-order theory of consciousness. According to such a theory, 'a conscious state is a mental state whose subject is aware of being in it' (Lycan 2001, 3). From this he, along with other higher-order theorists, concludes that only creatures with second-order mental states have conscious mental states. And that covers only human beings and perhaps primates with a 'theory of mind', beliefs about the beliefs of other subjects. But the definition is at odds with the established distinction between being in a state of consciousness—e.g. a state of thinking about Mary—and being conscious of such a state— e.g. becoming aware that one is constantly thinking about Mary. And if it is meant as a stipulative definition, one which bestows a novel meaning on 'conscious' and its cognates, then sensations simply need not be conscious in this sense.

For those who doubt or deny animal consciousness, sensitivity to the environment is supposed to be insufficient to prove sentiency. But consider complex animals with sense-organs, bodily demeanour and facial expressions resembling ours. When such animals are awake, alert and 'negotiate the world' on the basis of the information provided by their senses, it makes no sense to insist that they do so unconsciously. Unless this were to mean—perversely—that they may not be aware of their own states of consciousness. Yet the latter is by no means a prerequisite for being aware of one's environment. Au contraire, self-consciousness is often a distraction. Conversely, 'being available to thought'—i.e. being a potential object of self-awareness—is not a precondition for a mental state to be conscious in the sense of intransitive or transitive consciousness, let alone of mere consciousness. To suppose otherwise is once more to confuse intransitive and transitive consciousness with self-consciousness and reflection.[5]

Finally, from the third-person perspective advocated in the previous section, there cannot be a universal and radical separation of pain from pain behaviour. There are pains to which we do not pay attention. But there cannot be pains that are principally and deeply unconscious. Otherwise the difference between the concept of pain and the concept of bodily damage is lost. Furthermore, if nothing counted as a typical behavioural manifestation of pain in pertinent circumstances, our current concept of pain would lose its grip. Finally, the claim that the behavioural manifestations of the mental must be linguistic is particularly implausible with respect to sensations. For here both the occasion and the reaction (not to mention the physiological and neurophysiological mechanisms) are very similar in humans and the higher animals (see Glock 1996, 95-7, 176-7; 2009, 234-6.).

4. Interests

On this topic I start out from the pioneering work of Leonard Nelson (1932). He devised what remains the most auspicious argument for animals having moral rights.

P1 All and only creatures that have interests have moral rights
P2 Animals have interests
C1 Animals have moral rights.

In his influential discussion of Nelson's argument, Fry accepts P1, while contesting P2. His reasoning runs as follows.

---

5 | For other criticisms see de Grazia (1996), 114; Garner (2005), 29-33. In fact, Carruthers (1992) grants that some animals may possess sentience and Carruthers (2004) that animals are capable of suffering, yet without subjectivity. Unfortunately, I have been unable to fathom what precisely that caveat amounts to and how it is supposed to be compatible with the fact that animals can feel pain.

P3 Only creatures that have beliefs can have interests in a sense that can sustain P1
P4 Only creatures with language can have beliefs
C2 Animals do not have interests (≡ ¬ P2)
C3 Animals do not have moral rights (≡ ¬ C1)

In arguing for P3, Fry distinguishes between 'two logically distinct senses of interest' (Fry 1980, 51). The first, weaker, sense is that in which something can be in the interest of something else.

(I) X is in the interest of A iff x has a good or well-being to which x is conducive.

The second, stronger, sense is that in which a subject can have an interest in something.

(II) A has an interest in X iff A wants X.

Fry's distinction is well-taken. His weaker sense of interest corresponds roughly to the aforementioned notion of needs. Fry is right to concede that animals can have interests in the weak sense. They have 'a good or well-being that can be harmed or benefited'. He insists, however, that this must be insufficient for sustaining P1, since even 'manmade/manufactured objects' can have interests in this weak sense. '[...] just as it is not good for a dog to be deprived of a certain amount of exercise, it is not good for prehistoric cave paintings to be exposed to excessive amounts of carbon dioxide'. This claim is based on confusing the good or well-being of the humans that employ the artifacts with a good of the artifacts themselves. Exposure to excessive amounts of carbon dioxide will destroy the cave paintings, no doubt. Yet the cave paintings have no good or well-being of their own, they can only be more or less useful or attractive to humans. Only animate objects have an intrinsic flourishing, however the latter is to be identified. Even leaving aside this unwarranted assimilation of animals to artefacts, Fry's argument fails to convince. For his defence of P4 is inadequate. He maintains that when we say

(1)   A believes that p

what we mean is that

(2)   A holds the declarative sentence 'p' to be true.

But (1) and (2) do not have the same truth-conditions, let alone meaning. If A is a human who does not know any English (yes, such people do exist!), (2) is false, while (1) may nonetheless be true. Furthermore, we do not strictly speaking hold sentences true in the first place. What is true or false are what sentences express—something of the form 'that p'—rather than sentences of the form 'p'. The notion of holding true applies in the first instance to things of the form 'the proposition that p'. But one need not be capable of holding true the proposition that p in order to simply believe that p (see Glock 2003, 118-26, 266; 2010, 18-9).

In addition to his lingualist, and indeed Anglo-centric analysis of belief, Fry offers three considerations in support of P4. First, in order to have the concept of belief a creature must be able to distinguish between true and false beliefs. Secondly, in order to be able to distinguish between true and false beliefs a creature must have 'some awareness of, ..., how language connects with, links up with reality'. Thirdly, in order to have some awareness of how language connects with the world, a creature must possess a language. The first claim is correct, the second and by implication the third are unclear. In any event, none of them is pertinent in the context of his argument. For the question raised by P3 is not whether animals can distinguish between true and false beliefs—which would require them to have the concept of belief—but whether they can have beliefs that are true or false. Fry would need to show that having beliefs requires having the concept of belief. A line of reasoning later advanced by Davidson (2001, ch. 7) would fill this lacuna, and further demonstrate that the concept of belief in turn requires language. But it is unsound (see Glock 2003, 286-293).

Fry maintains that the sense of 'want' which is at issue in (II) amounts to 'desire'. Moreover, he offers his opponent a final life-line, namely that there may be a class of desires—'simple desires'—which are independent of beliefs—contrary to P3. He regards that option as insufficient to sustain the Nelsonian argument, since the dog could not display his awareness of such desires. Once more, however, the relevance of this failure remains unclear. Why should simple desires have to be such that the subject is aware of them?

Ultimately, the crux of Fry's differentialist reasoning is simply this: Are animals barred from having interests in the stronger sense that would sustain moral rights (as in P1 and P3)? Fry's explanation of the stronger sense of interest in (II) makes this dependent on animals being able to want or desire things. Quite properly so. Let us grant for the sake of argument at least that a creature can desire something only if it is also capable of believing something—as maintained by P3. Even then Fry would have to demonstrate that belief and desire require language.

5. BELIEFS AND DESIRES

That last claim is not just unsupported by argument, it is also implausible. Both in everyday life and in science we explain the behaviour of higher animals by reference to their beliefs, desires, intentions, goals, purposes, wants, etc. In the animal case no less than the human case we employ intentional verbs, and we render the behaviour of a subject A intelligible by reference to the fact that A believes that p, desires X, wants to Φ etc.

The trouble is, of course, that this practice has been challenged by linguists. Some of them reject it outright. Others grant the legitimacy of the practice, provided that it is understood as a potentially misleading yet useful or even indispensable *façon de parler*. But why should we not take intentional explanations of animal behaviour at face value?

The standard linguist reproach is that of anthropomorphism. Taking intentional explanations of animal behaviour literally, the story goes, amounts to reading human traits and abilities into phenomena where they have no place. Indeed, according to Davidson, employing intentional explanations in the case of animals is just as anthropomorphic as employing them in the case of a heat-seeking missile (Davidson 2001, 102).

Davidson's analogy misses the mark, however. We regard attributing thoughts to animals not just as convenient, as he would have it, but as entirely justified. For, unlike attributing desires and beliefs to complex missiles, such attributions are not based on technological ignorance but on a biological insight, namely that the life and behaviour of animals shows them to have both wants and perceptual capacities. Davidson might reply that the alleged insight is merely an illusion of Aristotelian folk-biology.

Animal behaviour, the reply continues, could be fully explained by reference to physiological processes, if our knowledge of physiology were sufficiently advanced. However, this invites the question of why human behaviour should resist such explanation. Davidson has a well-known response: human action defies psychophysical laws because it is based on propositional attitudes forming a holistic web. But of course he could not invoke that response in the present context without presupposing that animals, unlike humans, lack propositional attitudes, which would obviously beg the question at issue.

Admittedly, Davidson has produced a raft of independent arguments to the effect that animals can't "think", that is, have "thoughts" like beliefs (believing that p) or desires (desiring that p be the case).[6] These have been debated intensively for some time now, and they have been found wanting (see, e.g. Glock 2003, ch. 9). Instead of rehearsing once more the well-known rebuttals of Davidson's lingualism, let me instead produce what I regard as a compelling argument to the effect that animals can have thoughts in Davidson's sense, that is, intentional states like belief and desire.

My starting-point is the fact that at least higher animals with sense organs are capable of perception. This claim is not accepted by everyone, alas.[7] But it should be accepted as an incontrovertible datum by anyone

---

6 | Like Davidson, I am wary of the idea that these intentional states are relations to propositions (see Glock 2003, 264-267). For this reason I avoid the popular terminology of 'propositional attitudes' and instead employ 'thinking' or 'having thoughts' in the technical sense of being in an intentional state.

7 | There are, I am informed, die-hards who insist that animals are capable only of reacting to proximal stimuli and not of perceiving distal objects. This behaviourist fairy-tale (or should that be 'horror story'?) ignores the difference between primitive organisms and higher animals. The latter possess differentiated sense-organs and a central nervous system with perceptual centres. They are also capable of adjusting their behaviour in complex and flexible ways in accordance to the deliverances of their senses. And all primates, at least, perform well on object permanence and identity tasks (Seed & Tomasello 2010, 409). The behaviourist is also at a loss to explain why humans displaying the same kind of capacities are doing more than reacting to proximal stimuli. If the behaviourist assumption were true, it would no longer be clear why the noises emitted by humans should be of a qualitatively distinct kind, one which evinces beliefs and desires.

who is genuinely interested in animal mentality, and in the differences between plants, animals and humans, rather than in merely spelling out the implications of a pet philosophical ideology. Once this starting-point is granted, however, it is well-nigh impossible to deny that animals can 'think' in the sense of believing (knowing, etc.) that something is the case. For seeing is believing! That is to say, a creature that is capable of perception is ipso facto capable of belief. To be more precise, perceiving that p implies either knowing that p, if 'perceiving' is used as a factive or success-verb; or it implies merely believing that p, if it is not.[8] In either event, it amounts to a case of thinking that p as defined above.

However, one can distinguish two kinds of perception, fact-perception and object-perception. The lingualist might insist that animal perception does not include perceiving that p, but is confined to perceiving X, i.e. to perceiving objects, persons, situations, events, etc.[9] But this response is implausible.[10] The perceptually guided reaction of complex animals to their environment can only be explained by a capacity to perceive that p. For instance, the dog refrains from grabbing the bone while it lies on the table, something it has been trained not to do; yet the dog grabs the bone as soon as it is placed in its bowl. This action is neither explained by the

---

8 | I have phrased the matter in this fashion because I do not want to commit myself to the idea—enshrined in the traditional definition of knowledge as true, justified belief—that knowing that p implies believing that p.
9 | Thus Dretske (2004) distinguishes between 'seeing things' and 'seeing facts', maintaining that only the latter is conceptual.
10 | Intentional verbs occur mainly in three sentential forms:

A)   A   Vs (thinks/believes/expects, etc.)   that p
B)   A   Vs (intends/plans/means, etc.)   to Φ
C)   A   Vs (loves/desires/thinks about, etc.)   X

Following this scheme, fact-perception is a case of type A intentionality, object-perception a case of type C intentionality. Some analytic philosophers have contended that both type B and type C intentionality can be reduced to type A intentionality. This would further strengthen my case against lingualism, since it implies that any creature capable of perception is ipso facto capable of fact perception. But there are reasons for being sceptical about the prospects of such a reduction. See Glock (2001).

dog seeing a bone, nor by its seeing a bowl, nor even by its seeing a bone and a bowl. It is only explained by the dog seeing that the bone is in the bowl. The linguist cannot avoid this conclusion by insisting that the dog simply perceives (sees, smells, etc.) the bone in the bowl. For either the apposition 'in the bowl' is restrictive, and simply serves to identify what bone the dog sees; in that case the dog seeing the bone in the bowl goes no further towards explaining its behaviour than the dog simply seeing a bone. Or 'in the bowl' is shorthand for 'being in the bowl'; in that case perceiving the bone in the bowl would explain the dog's behaviour. However, perceiving the bone being in the bowl is simply perceiving that the bone is in the bowl by another name. The explanatory power of the ascription can be purchased only by imputing fact-perception, whether explicitly or implicitly. Consequently there is no way around the admission that some animals can perceive that something is the case, just as we can. We can summarize this result through the following argument:

P5   The reaction of complex animals to their environment can only be explained by a capacity to perceive that p.
P6   If A perceives that p, then either A knows that p or A (merely) believes that p.
C4   Complex animals can know or believe that p.

6. Agency

There is a sense of agency connected to the active voice of grammar, in which even inanimate objects can act. But action takes on moral significance if it is intentional in the sense that it is goal-directed, voluntary or performed for a reason. Now, acting for reasons may simply mean acting in a way that is subject to intentional explanation. In that case, animals can act for reasons. As mentioned above, we have no better explanations for the complex behaviour of some animals than by reference to beliefs, desires and intentions. And we have no license for disparaging these explanations as a mere façon de parler. This result by itself is morally significant. Everything else being equal, one ought not to frustrate the intentions of a creature. However, the idea of acting for a reason can also be construed in potentially more demanding ways, which at the same time might also impose higher moral barriers.

In fact, the very idea of acting for a reason can be spelled out in two fundamentally different ways. First, there is an understanding of acting for a reason which can be labelled as psychologistic, internal or subjectivist. It goes back at least to Hume, and at present it is epitomized by Davidson (1980). According to this subjectivist conception,

(III) A is capable of acting for a reason iff A's actions are to be explained by reference to mental states of A (beliefs and 'pro-attitudes' like desires and intentions).

Subjectivism insists that the beliefs and desires invoked in intentional explanations are mental states of the agent—states of desiring or wanting something and states of believing something.

By contrast, according to recent revisionists, the reasons for which agents act are not mental states of the agent herself. Instead, they are objective facts or states of affairs which, save for special cases, concern the agent's environment rather than her own mind. In so far as the reasons for which an agent acts can be said to be beliefs and desires at all, they are not subjective states of believing or desiring, but what is believed or what is desired (e.g. Hornsby 1997; Dancy 2000; Stout 2005; Alvarez 2010). An agent A acts for a reason if A acts on account not of her own beliefs, but on account of facts or states of affairs, on account of how things are (from A's perspective). Accordingly,

(IV) A is capable of acting for a reason iff A can act in the light of reasons, that is, in the light of facts (as A sees them).

Unlike certain biological or economic conceptions of rationality, this objectivist conception of reasons does not disregard the subject's perspective (see Glock 2009). Although A's reasons for Φ-ing are states of affairs, they are states of affairs which make Φ-ing good or attractive in A's eyes (either instrumentally or intrinsically), that is, from the agent's own perspective.

In spite of important differences, objectivists tend to agree on two points. First, A's reasons for Φ-ing is something that makes Φ-ing good or valuable in A's eyes; secondly, what makes Φ-ing good or valuable in A's eye is (by and large) not A's believing something to be the case, but what is believed to be the case. There is a powerful rationale for both claims. My reason for Φ-ing is what I specify in response to the question "Why are you Φ-ing?"; and this answer typically takes the form "Because p" rather than "Because I believe that p". My reason for taking an umbrella is that it is raining, not that I believe that it is raining; for it is the weather rather than my own mental state that makes taking an umbrella good or bad in my eyes.

This is not the place to develop and defend a watertight version of objectivism. What matters for present purposes are two points: firstly, there are noteworthy reasons for adopting such an account; secondly, such an account removes an important obstacle to crediting animals with the capacity to act for reasons.

The obstacle arises from the idea that rational agency requires that the agent be able to act in the light of reasons. The action makes sense to the agent (as the rational or a rational thing to do), given those reasons. And this implies that the agent is aware of those reasons. At this point the contrast between subjectivism and objectivism makes a crucial difference. For subjectivism the reasons in the light of which A acts are subjective states antecedent to A's action. In Davidson, for instance, A's reason for Φ-ing is A's mental state of believing that p will lead to q, in combination with her mental state of desiring that q.

Now, if reasons for action are subjective states of agents, acting in their light seems to require A to entertain thoughts about A's own thoughts. More specifically, it appears to require A to think about or represent its own states of believing and desiring. To put it more grandly, animals would have to possess not just consciousness of their environment, but self-consciousness, awareness of their own beliefs and desires. The same would hold if the reasons in the light of which A acts were psychological facts about A, e.g. the fact that A believes that p, desires X or wants to Φ.

Such self-consciousness may be beyond the ken of animals. But the apparent obstacle does not even arise on the objectivist account of reasons for action. According to objectivism, reasons for action are facts or states of affairs, or at any rate things which are believed rather than subjective states of believing. This immediately removes the threat posed to the idea of animals acting in the light of reasons. For animals are capable of acting in the light of facts or states of affairs, i.e. in the light of how things are in their environment or of how they perceive them to be. This is just a corollary of their having cognitive capacities. In particular, animals are able to perceive and hence to believe and know things.

According to some objectivists, reasons for action include not just facts the agent is aware of, but also goods or goals—things desired as well as things believed. Yet this does not pose a threat to the claim that animals can act in the light of reasons. That animals possess conative powers is at least as clear as that they possess cognitive powers. They have not just needs of the kind invoked in some externalist conceptions of rationality, but also wants, and they can pursue goods or goals and avoid things. In addition, higher animals have and adopt purposes or goals of their own, namely the goals they pursue, the ends for the sake of which they act (Hacker 2007, 130-140, 160-164). They can also evaluate states of affairs—or, in a more realistic ethological idiom, features of their environment—in the sense of responding to them as good or bad (e.g. attractive or threatening), and they can act accordingly.

A linguist might insist nonetheless that animals cannot act for reasons, while conceding that there are reasons why they act. For instance, the elephant drinks from the well because it is thirsty. But on the lingualist's gloss of that statement, the 'because' refers not to something objective that makes drinking good from the elephant's perspective, but simply to an inner state leading to outward behaviour. In that case, the alleged 'reasons why' animals act would simply be internal causes, rather than reasons as objectivists understand them. So this apparent compromise is at best open to subjectivists (see Glock 2012).

The upshot is that animals are capable of acting in the light of reasons, provided that these are construed as they should be: as objective features of the environment assessable from the perspective of agents.

7. REASONS, REASONING AND CHOICE

Even without appealing to subjectivism, some lingualists deny that animals can act in the light of reasons, on the grounds that they cannot reflect on their reasons (e.g. Hacker 2007, 204, 236, 240; McDowell 1996, 70; Frankfurt 2004, 18-19; Brandom 2010).

Admittedly there is one mental power that does presuppose the power to reflect on reasons, namely the power to deliberate. But as we shall see, it need not presuppose the ability to justify one's action verbally. Even more problematic is the idea that one can only act for a reason, in response to reasons, if one is able to reflect on reasons, at least if the latter requires the agent to entertain self-conscious thoughts about certain things (facts, goals) being her reasons (i.e. thoughts of the form 'My reason for Φ-ing is that p'). Indeed, there is a positive argument for keeping the having of reasons separate from reflecting on reasons: A couldn't develop a capacity to reflect on A's reasons if A didn't have reasons to begin with (MacIntyre 1999, 56).

Linguists could respond, however, that there is no genuine gap between a creature that can act for reasons and one that can reflect on these reasons. Without the capacity for reflection and hence, the story continues, without the gift of language, an agent cannot act for a reason. Having reasons and being able to reflect on them come as a package.

But how can this holistic response account for the intermediate stages that lie between the human infant, who can neither act for reasons nor reflect on them, and the adult, who can do both? Furthermore, how can lingualism do justice to the intentional explanation of animal behaviour? Unlike machines or plants, animals can act for purposes, adopt purposes of their own, and adapt their behaviour to circumstances in pursuit of these purposes. Yet it is unclear what this could amount to, if such animals could not act in the light of facts pertinent to achieving those purposes. For instance, we explain a well-known behaviour among some chimpanzees by saying that they batter nuts with hard stones in order to, or for the purpose of cracking them. This implies that they act on account of the fact that nuts crack when treated in this way. Furthermore, great apes, among other taxa, are capable of organizing their behaviour in the light of what they perceive, remember, etc., in such a way that they distinguish means from ends, notably by showing awareness of the fact that one and the same end can be achieved by different means and that one and the same means—for instance a tool—can serve different ends, etc. (Tomasello & Call 1997, 318; Hurley 2006, 148-149).

Nevertheless there may be a case for insisting that in order to act for reasons in the fullest sense, it does not suffice to be responsive to reasons (something feasible for animals on an objectivist construal); the agent must also be capable of operating with reasons. After all, the reasons of fully linguistic creatures are closely tied to how they reasoned or could have reasoned. And such deliberation or practical reasoning seems to be the prerogative of language users.

According to a plausible account, practical reasoning takes the following form (Kenny 1989, 43-45):

P7   X is to be brought about
P8   If I Φ then X
C5   So I'll Φ!

By contrast to theoretical reasoning, the conclusions of practical inferences are not assertions but resolves or expressions of intentions. This does not count in favour of lingualism, however. As regards context (problem), demeanour (e.g. head scratching) and result (problem solution), the behaviour of chimpanzees, for instance, resembles that of human beings. They interrupt an activity, examine an obstacle, pursue a certain solution, discard one type of tool in favour of another, resume their activity in a purposeful and determined fashion. All of this is accompanied, moreover, by gestures and grimaces displaying displeasure, hesitation, resolve and satisfaction. In short, it is perfectly possible for non-linguistic creatures to manifest not just intentions but also choices, resolves or decisions.

A more serious difficulty for the idea of animal reasoning is that P8 and C5 are 'I-thoughts', which seem to require self-consciousness and thereby language. However, there are forms of self-awareness which do not presuppose consciousness of one's own mental phenomena (states, processes, etc.), let alone consciousness of a 'self', and which do not require language. Great apes and dolphins, for instance, can recognize themselves, i.e. their own bodies, in mirrors and are also aware of their own status and role within complex social groups (Plotnik et al. 2006; Tomasello & Call 1997, Part II). The crucial point is that P8 and C5 require only such simple self-awareness, namely awareness of one's own actions and their consequences. What is more, this kind of self-awareness is already implied by the very idea of intentional action. For behaviour can only be explained by reference to reasons if it is under the control of the agent, and such control clearly presupposes awareness of what one is doing. Similarly, one can ascribe wants and goals to an agent A only if A is capable of recognizing having attained what A wants. Yet this again implies self-awareness of a minimal kind. Nor should we be all that surprised to learn that some animals are aware of what they are doing. This is a straightforward outgrowth of kinaesthetic knowledge and essential to the survival of higher animals that need to adapt their behaviour to changing circumstances in an intelligent manner.

The issue of reasoning is also central a lingualist line of thought inspired by Aristotle. Our talk of animals wanting things notwithstanding, these Aristotelians contend, animals do not possess a will—a claim congenial to Fry. For the will is the capacity for rational choice, and this requires the ability to reason, the ability to weigh up or assess the alternatives. Just now we have discussed whether animals might in principle be capable of practical reasoning. The question of whether animals—including extant specimen—can engage in rudimentary forms of practical or theoretical reasoning is contested and would require a lengthy discussion in its own right (see Allen 2006; Glock 2009). Even if the answer should turn out to be negative, however, this does not rule out animal choice. Rational choice in the sense of choice being based on explicit reasoning is one thing. Choice in the sense of choosing in an intelligent and deliberate manner between different options in pursuit of one's goal is another. Some animals can and do assess alternatives, and they can and do choose in a deliberate way, i.e. one which is controlled and responsive to the situation.[11] For instance, chimpanzees choose tools for cracking nuts or hunting insects in a foresightful way, often out of sight of the location in which the tool is to be used. Furthermore, as indicated above, this process closely resembles human instrumental reasoning in concrete situations. Complex non-linguistic creatures can weigh the conflicting claims of objective features of the situation, including their own behaviour, and act accordingly. As mentioned before, they can also have and adopt purposes or goals, that is the ends for the sake of which they act.

For those animals that can choose both means and ends, certain moral principles kick in. It is morally wrong to frustrate the preferences and choices of others, unless these preferences compete with other, more important preferences, or with overriding norms and values. At a more advanced moral level, agency, acting for a reason and choice are essential to our self-understanding as persons. And either mediated through that last notion or for their own sake, they are also held to be essential to various kinds of moral status (see, e.g., Stoecker 2009, 270). In this vein, Griffin (2008) contends that agency provides the sole ground for human rights. There are two ways of blocking adverse consequences of this claim for animal welfare. For one thing, one can reject the idea that personhood is a prerequisite for certain levels of moral status—in line with the vulner-

---

11 | See Glock (2010). Note that 'acting deliberately' as understood here—and, I venture to say, in ordinary parlance—does not require deliberation in the sense of explicit reflection on one's reasons.

ability approach mentioned at the start. For another, one can repudiate the 'agential conception of persons' (Reader 2010). These strategies are not mutually exclusive, of course. In fact, both of them presuppose that animals possess some mental capacities. For vulnerabilities presuppose capacities, indeed some mental capacities are susceptibilities—to stimuli, objects or facts in the case of sensation, object-perception and fact-perception, respectively. To suppose otherwise is to put a gloss on the notion of a capacity that is too literalistic. A capacity, and in particular a mental capacity, need not always be a potential for acting on other things, it may also be a susceptibility to be influenced or informed. Perception, for instance, is a kind of cognitive receptivity, a capacity to receive information from the environment. In any event, moreover, opponents of the agential conception merely claim that patiency is just as essential to personhood as agency, being the flipside of the latter. As a result, they cannot and do not deny that patiency presupposes agency and its various mental prerequisites.

8. Moral Epilogue
(or: What Humans Owe to Each Other)

So far I have argued that the moral status of animals depends to a large extent on their mental capacities. I have also resisted various differentialist claims concerning mental capacities with potential moral implications. Concerning sensations, interests, beliefs, agency and choice, at any rate, a priori arguments for qualitative differences between humans and animals have been found wanting. Nevertheless I incline to the view that the moral status of humans is qualitatively distinct from that even of higher animals. Our moral obligations towards each other are of a different order from our moral obligations towards animas.

This may appear incoherent, but in fact it is not. Indeed, some of the considerations that I invoked against differentialism may also show that there are morally relevant differences between animals and us. It is just that these differences may not be well captured by venerable strict dichotomies such as: we experience pain, they only react to bodily damage; we have interests, they merely have wants; we believe propositions, they at best perceive objects; we act for reasons, they only behave mechanically; we communicate by way of language, the best they can do is signal; and so on, and so forth.

Take the case of thinking. From the third-person perspective adopted in section 5.2 ascribing thoughts makes sense only in cases where we have criteria for identifying thoughts. In Quine's memorable phrase, 'No entity without identity' (Quine 1969, 23). Something must count as thinking that p rather than that q, otherwise ascriptions of thoughts are vacuous. This means that thoughts, although they need not actually be expressed, must be capable of being expressed. And only a very restricted range of thoughts can be expressed in non-linguistic behaviour. To use Wittgenstein's famous example, a dog can think that its master is at the door, but not that its master will return the day after tomorrow (Witttgenstein 1967, 174, §650, see also §§342, 376-378). The reason is that its behavioural repertoire is much to restricted to display such a thought. Arguably, this verdict applies not just to thoughts about the distant past and future. It also applies to, e.g., a capacity for knowing necessary truths, the possession of a moral sense and a sense of beauty, a sense of history, a sense of dignity, and forms of self-consciousness that concern one's own death and ultimate aims.

The potential moral repercussions are wide-ranging. Here is a real-life recent controversy. I have chosen it not in order to pronounce on the moral and legal rights and wrongs, but only in order to illustrate what kind of consideration is relevant, given the considerations advanced so far. In 2008, the animal experimentation committee of the Canton of Zurich prohibited experiments on macaque monkeys, which would have involved delaying their access to drink by a few hours in order to increase the appreciation of the apple juice reward they would be offered on mastering a new task. This would violate the 'dignity of [non-human] organisms' (*Würde der Kreatur*) guaranteed by the Swiss constitution, the committee opined (see Abbott 2008).

Now, it is quite normal for macaques in the wild to experience such delays. One might insist, however, that this does not legitimize our inflicting such a treatment on them. But the idea of dignity as standardly understood, both in everyday parlance and in moral discourse, gets only a tenuous grip here. It is dubious to credit macaques with a sense of dignity, e.g. thoughts of the kind 'I am being manipulated here solely for the benefits of others'. To be sure, the idea of 'dignity' which the Swiss constitution extends to animals does not include the kind of absolute ban on instrumentalization—on treating a subject exclusively as a means to an end, that the constitution applies to humans. Instead, it is a matter of recognizing the 'intrinsic value' of animals, something that must be taken into account and weighed against the interests served by using them for human purposes.

In that case, however, the term 'dignity' may well turn into an idle wheel. Approval of the experiments should simply turn on weighing the suffering of the macaques—who can feel thirsty—against the theoretical and practical interests served by the experiments. For legal reasons, the committee's original verdict on the experiments did not concern a far more contentious issue which featured in the later verdict of the Swiss federal court, namely that the subjects were subsequently to be killed to study their brains under a microscope. As regards that procedure, the crucial consideration to emerge from my considerations is this: in so far as an animal lacks a concern about or plans for its own future, killing it cannot be faulted on the grounds of thwarting these plans.

Next consider the case of communication. Paid-up Chomskians notwithstanding, some enculturated great apes, cataceans and parrots have acquired linguistic skills which display at least some of the features traditionally claimed to set language apart from animal systems of communication (see, e.g., Savage-Rumbaugh, Shanker & Taylor 1998; Hurley & Nudds 2006, Part VI). Admittedly, no animal seems capable of acquiring linguistic skills that include semantic productivity and syntactic recursion. As Jane Goodall remarked in a recent interview, however: 'Why should that matter?' when it comes to our treatment of these specimen.

The potential for morally relevant differences lies elsewhere, in my view. First, these symbolic skills are not part of the typical developmental pathways of even the most intelligent animal species in their natural environments. They are inevitably lacking in most individual specimen. Secondly, even symbol-trained animals seem incapable of the kind of disinterested sharing of information and cooperation that characterizes human communication and interaction (Tomasello 2008; Tomasello & Rakoczy 2003). These unique features of our form of life have yet unexplored implications for ethics. Our ability to interact with even the most advanced animals, to share ideas, responsibilities and aspirations with them, are severely restricted. And this provides succour to the idea that our obligations towards living human beings are of a different order from those towards animals.

At this point many readers approaching this essay from the perspective of applied ethics will have grown impatient. Don't these considerations apply equally to so-called 'marginal cases', especially to severely handicapped humans that do not even have the potential to acquire the capacities I have emphasized? The answer is: Up to a point. Weighing the interests of such individuals against other interests cannot be faulted on some of the grounds mentioned above, such as plans for the future, linguistic communication and the kind of cooperation that they render possible. For related reasons, contractualist considerations do not apply to marginal cases.

Contractualism is right to link morality to human interaction. But it errs in thinking that this interaction must take the form of entering into some kind of agreement that is either explicit or at least explicable. That is a highly evolved and specialised phenomenon. Once we take into account simpler forms of interaction, differences between our relations with marginal cases and our relations with animals come back into view. We should not underestimate the importance of facial expressions, gestures and bodily demeanours that are distinctly human in spite of being simple. And even less should we underestimate that we begat and gave birth to these individuals. We are human beings, and we value human life. If taking this lesson to heart makes one a speciecist, then so be it. The popular accusation that taking this stance also opens the floodgates to racism relies on an assumption which is both unwarranted and sinister, namely that there are barriers to communication and interaction between members of different races that resemble even remotely and in kind the barriers to communicating and interacting with animals.

Irrespective of what our obligations towards marginal cases are, they do not detract from the unique importance that cognitive capacities of a social and linguistic kind have for our moral lives. While these may be absent in individual specimen, no human society could function without the special powers of foresight, communication and cooperation (see Glock 2012). And this very much includes special powers of moral behaviour and judgement.

In order to set our moral obligations towards each other apart, we do not need the problematic blanket contention that only we think and communicate. Insisting that we think and communicate about a lot more and in a lot more complex fashion may just be enough. For in this case, a difference in quality may arise out of a difference in quantity. That at any rate is one Hegelian and Marxist idea which may be due for a revival.

Be that as it may, the topic of animal minds remains paramount in tackling questions of animal welfare, anyway you cut up the pie. With this conclusion we are back at the start of this essay. Nevertheless, the journey has not been futile. Along the way I hope to have shown that many prominent lingualist arguments against attributing morally relevant mental features to animals fail. I also hope to have indicated why this need not diminish our special sense of responsibility and care for each other.[12]

REFERENCES

Abbott, A. (2008), "Swiss Court bans Work on Macaque Brains", Nature 453, 833.
Allen, C. (2004), "Animal Pain", Noûs 38, 317-43.
Allen, C. (2006), "Transitive Inference in Animals; Reasoning or conditioned associations?", in: S. Hurley, M. Nudds (ed.), Rational Animals?, Oxford: Oxford University Press, 175-186.
Allen, C. (2010), "Animal Consciousness", in: E. Zalta (ed.), The Stanford Encyclopedia of Philosophy, http://www.science.uva.nl/~seop/entries/consciousness-animal/.
Allen, C., Bekoff, M. (1999), Species of Mind: The Philosophy and Biology of Cognitive Ethology, Cambridge/Mass.: MIT Press.
Alvarez, M. (2010), Kinds of Reason, Oxford: Oxford University Press.
Andrews, K. 2010, "Animal Cognition", in: E.N. Zalta (ed.), The Stanford Encyclopedia of Philosophy, http://www.science.uva.nl/~seop/entries/cognition-animal/.
Armstrong, S.J., Botzler, R.G. (eds.) (2003), The Animal Ethics Reader, London: Routledge.
Aydede, M. (ed.) (2006), Pain: new essays on its nature and the methodology of its study, Cambridge, MA: MIT Press.
Bekoff, M., Jamieson, D. (1991), "Reflective Ethology, Applied Philosophy, and the Moral Status of Animals", Perspectives in Ethology 9, 1-47.
Bekoff, M., Jamieson, D. (eds.) (1996), Readings in Animal Psychology, Cambridge, MA: MIT Press.

---

12 | This paper has benefited enormously from comments by Frank Esken, Peter Hacker, and Markus Wild, and from discussion at a workshop in Essen organised by Neil Rougley. I also wish to record my sincere gratitude to the Hanse-Wissenschaftskolleg, Delmenhorst for awarding me a fellowship enabling me to write this article.

Bekoff, M., Pierce, J. (2009), Wild Justice, Chicago: University of Chicago Press.
Bennett, R.M., Hacker P.M.S. (2003), The Philosophical Foundations of Neuroscience, Oxford: Blackwell.
Bermond, B. (2003), "The Myth of Animal Suffering", reprinted in: S. J. Armstrong, R.G. Botzler (eds.), The Animal Ethics Reader, London: Routledge, 79-85.
Brandom, R. (2010), "Conceptual Content and Discursive Practice", Grazer Philosophische Studien, (81) 13-35.
Braithwaite, V. (2010), Do Fish feel Pain, Oxford: Oxford University Press.
Carruthers, P. (1989), "Brute Experience", Journal of Philosophy 86, 258-269.
Carruthers, P. (1992), The Animals Issue, Cambridge: Cambridge University Press.
Carruthers, P. (2004), "On Being Simple-Minded", American Philosophical Quarterly 41, 205-220.
Clement, G. (2003), "The Ethics of Care and the Problem of Wild Animals. Between the Species III", http://cla.calpoly.edu/bts/issue_03/03clement.htm (accessed April 2010).
Dancy, J. (2000), Practical Reality, Oxford: Oxford University Press.
Darwin, C. (1871), "The Descent of Man", in: E.O. Wilson (ed.) (2006), From so Simple a Beginning: the four great works of Charles Darwin, London: Norton.
Darwin, C. (1872), "The Expressions of the Emotions in Man and Animals", in: E.O. Wilson (ed.) (2006), From so Simple a Beginning: the four great works of Charles Darwin, London: Norton.
Davidson, D. (1980), Actions, Reasons and Causes, Oxford: Oxford University Press.
Davidson, D. (2001), Subjective, Intersubjective, Objective, Oxford: Oxford University Press.
Diamond, C. (1991), The Realistic Spirit, Cambridge, MA: MIT Press.
De Grazia, D. (1996), Taking Animals Seriously, Cambridge: Cambridge University Press.
Dretske, F. (1995), Naturalizing the Mind, Cambridge, MA: MIT Press.
Dretske, F. (2004), "Seeing, Believing and Knowing", in: R. Schwartz (ed.) Perception, Malden: Blackwell) 268-86.
Dupré, J. (2002), Humans and Other Animals, Oxford: Oxford University Press.

Francione, G.L. (2000), Introduction to Animal Rights, Philadelphia: Temple University Press.

Frankfurt, H. (2004), The Reasons of Love, Princeton: Princeton University Press.

Fry, R.G. (1980), Interests and Rights: the case against animals, Oxford: Clarendon.

Garner, R. (2005), Animal Ethics, Cambridge: Polity.

Glock, H.J. (1996), A Wittgenstein Dictionary, Oxford: Blackwell.

Glock, H.J. (1997), "Philosophy, Thought and Language", in: J. Preston (ed.), Thought and Language, Cambridge: Cambridge University Press, 151-169.

Glock, H.J. (2001), "Intentionality and Language", Language and Communication 21, 105-18.

Glock, H.J. (2003), Quine and Davidson on Language, Thought and Reality, Cambridge: Cambridge University Press.

Glock, H.J. (2009), "Can Animals Act for Reasons?", Inquiry 52, 232-255.

Glock, H.J. (2010), "Can animals judge?", Dialectica 64, 11-34.

Glock, H.J. (2011), "The Anthropological Difference", in: C. Sandis et al. (eds.), Human Nature, Cambridge: Cambridge University Press.

Goodin, R. (1985), Protecting the Vulnerable, Chicago: University of Chicago Press.

Gray, A. (1880), Natural Science and Religion, New York: Charles Scribner's Sons.

Griffin, J. (2008), On Human Rights, Oxford: Oxford University Press.

Hacker, P.M.S. (2007), Human Nature: the Categorial Framework, Oxford: Blackwell.

Harrison, P. (1991), "Do Animals Feel Pain?", Philosophy 66, 25-40.

Hornsby, J. (1997), Simple Mindedness, Cambridge, MA: Harvard University Press.

Hurley, S. (2006), "Making sense of animals", in: S. Hurley, M. Nudds. (eds.), Rational Animals, Oxford: Oxford University Press, 139-171.

Hurley, S., Nudds, M. (eds.) (2006), Rational Animals, Oxford: Oxford University Press.

Hursthouse, R. (2000), Ethics, Humans and Other Animals, London: Routledge.

Kenny, A.J.P. (1989), The Metaphysics of Mind, Oxford: Oxford University Press.

Linzey, A. (2009), Why Animal Suffering Matters, New York: Oxford University Press.
Lurz, R. (ed.) (2009), The Philosophy of Animal Minds, Cambridge: Cambridge University Press.
Lycan, W. (2001), "A Simple Argument for a Higher-Order Representation Theory of Consciousness", Analysis 61, 3-4.
MacIntyre, A. (1999), Dependent Rational Animals, London: Duckworth.
Malcolm, N. (1984), "Consciousness and Causality", in: D. M. Armstrong, N. Malcolm (eds.), Consciousness and Causality, Oxford: Blackwell.
McDowell, J. (1996), Mind and World, Cambridge, MA: Harvard University Press.
Nelson, L. (1932), Vorlesungen über die Grundlagen der Ethik, Göttingen: Verlag Öffentliches Leben.
Perler, D., Wild, M. (eds.) (2005), Der Geist der Tiere, Frankfurt: Suhrkamp.
Plotnik, J.M., de Waal, F., Reiss D. (2006), "Self-recognition in an Asian Elephant", Proceedings of the National Academy of Sciences 103/45, 17053-17057.
Quine, W.V. (1969), Ontological Relativity and Other Essays, New York: Columbia University Press.
Reader, S. (2010), "Agency, Patiency and Personhood", in: T. O'Connor, C. Sandis (ed.), A Companion to the Philosophy of Action, Oxford: Wiley-Blackwell.
Regan, T. (1983), The Case for Animal Rights, London: Routledge and Kegan.
Romanes, G. (1881/1977), Animal Intelligence, Washington D.C.: University Publications of America.
Rosenthal, D. (1986), "Two Concepts of Consciousness", Philosophical Studies 49, 329-59.
Rowlands, M. (2002), Animals Like Us, London: Verso.
Savage-Rumbaugh, S., Shanker, S., Taylor, T. (1998), Apes, Language and the Human Mind, Oxford: Oxford University Press.
Seed, A., Tomasello M. (2010), "Primate Cognition", Topics on Cognitive Science 2, 407-19.
Singer, P. (1975), Animal Liberation, New York: New York Review Books.
Sorabji, R. (1994), Animal Minds and Human Morals, London: Routledge.
Stoecker, R. (2009), "Why Animals Can't Act", Inquiry 52, 255-71.
Stout, R. (2005), Action, London: Acumen Press.

Tomasello, M. (2008), Origins of Human Communication, Cambridge, MA: MIT Press.

Tomasello, M., Call, J. (1997), Primate Cognition, Oxford: Oxford University Press.

Tomasello, M., Rakoczy, H. (2003), "What makes Human Cognition Unique?", Mind and Language 18, 121-47.

de Waal, F. (2006), Primates and Philosophers, Princeton: Princeton University Press.

Wild, M. (2006), Die Anthropologische Differenz, Berlin: de Gruyter.

Wild, M. (2008), Tierphilosophie zur Einführung, Hamburg: Junius.

Wilson, E.O. (ed.) (2006), From so Simple a Beginning: the four great works of Charles Darwin, London: Norton.

Wittgenstein, L. (1967), Philosophical Investigations, Oxford: Blackwell.

6. The Question of Belief Attribution in Great Apes
Its Moral Significance and Epistemic Problems

Robert W. Lurz

1. INTRODUCTION

A number of philosophers, legal scholars, and primatologists have argued that, on the grounds of their biological and mental similarities to human beings, great apes should be granted certain basic legal rights (Cavalieri & Singer 1993; de Waal 2006).[1] Often cited on this list of mental similarities is the purported ability of great apes (specifically chimpanzees and bonobos) to empathize or more generally to attribute mental states to others. But the results of a number of recent mindreading (or theory-of-mind) studies suggest that various non-anthropoid ape species may well be capable of attributing simple perceptual states and goal-directed actions to others, making it rather unlikely that great apes are the only non-human species capable of attributing mental states (e.g., Tschudin 2001; Kuroshima et al. 2002; Bugnyar & Heinrich 2005; Flombaum & Santos 2005; Santos et al. 2006; Topál et al. 2006; Kaminski et al. 2006; Wood & Hauser 2008; Emery & Clayton 2008).[2] Thus, if the ability to attribute mental states is to play a role in justifying a moral distinction between

---

1 | It is important to note that on the basis of such arguments, Spain's parliament recently approved a resolution for the legal recognition and protection of the rights of life, liberty, and freedom from torture for the great apes.
2 | There is a vocal dissenting minority, however, who maintain that these animals are at best merely gifted behavior-readers (Heyes 1998; Povinelli & Vonk 2006; Penn & Povinelli 2007).

great apes and other animals, then it will need to be the ability to attribute a distinctive type of mental state.

To date no animal other than the great ape has shown any evidence of being able to attribute beliefs. What is more, it is plausible that belief attribution, unlike any other kinds of mental-state attribution, may mark an important moral difference among mindreading animals. For belief-attribution—at least of the kind that apes and other animals are likely capable—would appear to require the possession of a concept similar to our own psychologically and morally relevant concept of a self. If animals evolved the ability to attribute belief, then arguably they did so because it provided them with a more effective means of predicting others agents' (e.g., conspecifics, predators, prey) behaviors. Thus, it quite plausible that belief-attributing animals, if they exist, view the animals to which they attributed beliefs as individuals capable of acting on their beliefs. Furthermore, it is plausible that the kinds of beliefs that animals are most likely to be capable of attributing will be perceptually-based beliefs—beliefs that the animal understands as resulting from a target's present or past perceptual states. As we shall see in the next section, most researchers studying mindreading abilities in apes (as well as other animals) assume that apes rely upon something like the principle that seeing leads to believing as their method of attributing beliefs to targets. The principle, of course, presupposes that the individual animal that comes to have the belief is the very same individual that has or had the earlier perceptual state. The principle presupposes the existence of an enduring, unified psychological subject.[3] Perceptual-state attribution and goal attribution, on the other hand, carry no such a presupposition. The reason for this, to put it somewhat metaphorically, is that perceptual-states and goal-directed actions lie much closer to the edge where the mind meets the world. As a result, the principles that would govern an animal's attribution of such states to another need not require it presupposing the existence of an enduring, unified psychological subject. Rather, in attributing such states, the animal need only presuppose the existence of an enduring animal body that at different times has different perceptual states and goal-directed actions. These different perceptual states and goal-directed acts, however, need not be viewed by the animal as standing in any sort of dependency relation as perceptually-based beliefs stand to the perceptual states that lead to them.

---

3 | See Welker (1988) for a similar line argument on this point.

The animal, in other words, need not understand that within the same enduring animal body, one mental states leads to another. But beliefs are connected to the external world in a more indirect manner, by way of their relation to other mental states such as perceptions and intentions. Hence, in attributing a belief to another, an animal will need to understand that within the same enduring individual, one state of mind (perception) leads to another (belief). And that is the notion of an enduring, unified psychological entity.

Thus, as a result of these two features of belief attribution, animals that are capable of attributing beliefs would need to view targets as genuine psychological subjects—as individuals that act on reasons (beliefs) and endure long enough so that their earlier perceptual states lead to their later beliefs. Such an understanding of other animals is a rudimentary version of our own psychological and moral notion of selves. And so if apes are capable of attributing beliefs, then they, unlike other mindreading animals, will likely possess a nascent conception of other animals as selves. Is this morally significant? Arguably so. The more similar an animal's mind is to our own (especially with respect to the more noble or valued features of mind), the more morally significant it becomes for us. This, after all, is the moral principle that underlies the above authors' reasons for crediting great apes, but not other animals, with legal rights. The ability to understand other animals (human and nonhuman) as selves in the above sense, as opposed to mere organic, animated (even perceiving and sensing) bodies in motion, is undoubtedly an important element in our own moral and psychological development (see McGinn 1995). Thus it is not implausible to speculate on the basis of these points that if there is any moral distinction to be made between the great apes and other animals on the basis of their possessing the ability to attribute mental states, it will be on the basis of their ability to attribute beliefs.

This point regarding the moral significance of belief attribution in great apes seems to me (at any rate) to be relatively unproblematic compared to the epistemic and methodological question of how we might ever come to know whether great apes are capable of attributing beliefs. At the moment, there is considerable disagreement among empirical researchers over this question. On the one hand, there are philosophical arguments (Davidson 2001; Bermúdez 2003, 2009) that purport to show the a priori impossibility of belief attribution in animals, and a couple of empirical studies with chimpanzees that appear to confirm this conclusion (Call & Tomasello

1999; Kaminski et al. 2008). And on the other hand, there are a couple of empirical studies with chimpanzees that have produced what appear to be opposite findings (O'Connell & Dunbar 2003; Krachun et al. 2009).

I do not believe that the philosophical arguments or the empirical studies on either side of this debate are particularly persuasive. Since I have argued elsewhere (Lurz 2007; 2008; see also Lurz forthcoming) that the philosophical arguments against belief attribution in animals are invalid, I focus here on the empirical side of the debate. I shall argue that those studies that have been taken to indicate that chimpanzees are incapable of belief attribution provide, at best, rather weak support for this hypothesis, and that those studies that have been taken to indicated that chimpanzees may be capable of belief attribution fail to provide any evidence of genuine belief attribution over and above perceptual-state attribution or behavior-reading. What is needed to move the debate and the field forward, I argue, is a fundamentally new experimental approach for testing belief attribution in chimpanzees (as well as other great apes), one that is capable of distinguishing genuine belief-attributing subjects from their perceptual-state and behavior-reading counterparts. In the last section of the paper, I present just such an experimental protocol.

Although the focus of this essay is on the epistemic and methodological problems associated with answering the question of belief-attribution in chimpanzees (as well as other great apes), it should not be forgotten that the question itself, as argued above, has a potentially important moral significance, as well.

2. Belief Attribution Studies With Chimpanzees

Two types of experiments protocols have been used to test for belief attribution in chimpanzees and other animals. The first type, commonly called the cooperative knowledge-ignorance paradigm, is designed to test an animal's ability to choose between containers indicated by either a knowledgeable experimenter or an ignorant one. In Call and Tomasello (1999), for example, a chimpanzee observes an experimenter hide bait in one of two containers behind a screen. Another experimenter, acting as the communicator, sees the container that is baited and then turns his back. The screen is removed and the hider switches the locations of containers in front of the ape. The communicator returns, indicates a container by placing a marker on it, and the ape is allowed to choose between the containers. Call and Tomasello discovered that in such tests, their apes consistently choose the marked (empty) container over the unmarked (baited) one, despite the fact that in the control tests, the apes were able to ignore the marked container for the unmarked (baited) one, but only if they saw the food transferred from one container to the next. The researchers interpreted the results as indicating an inability in the apes to attribute beliefs.

It was thought by some that the chimpanzees failed the cooperative knowledge-ignorance test because it involved cooperative communication regarding the location of hidden food, a type of communicative act that is not part of the natural behavioral repertoire of chimpanzees (see Hare & Tomasello 2004). This, in turn, prompted Kaminski et al. (2008) to run a competitive version of the knowledge-ignorance experiment. In their experiment, two chimpanzees (a subject and a competitor) participated in a competitive game over a highly desirous piece of food (e.g., a grape) hidden beneath one of three cups on a sliding table in a middle area (see figure 1).

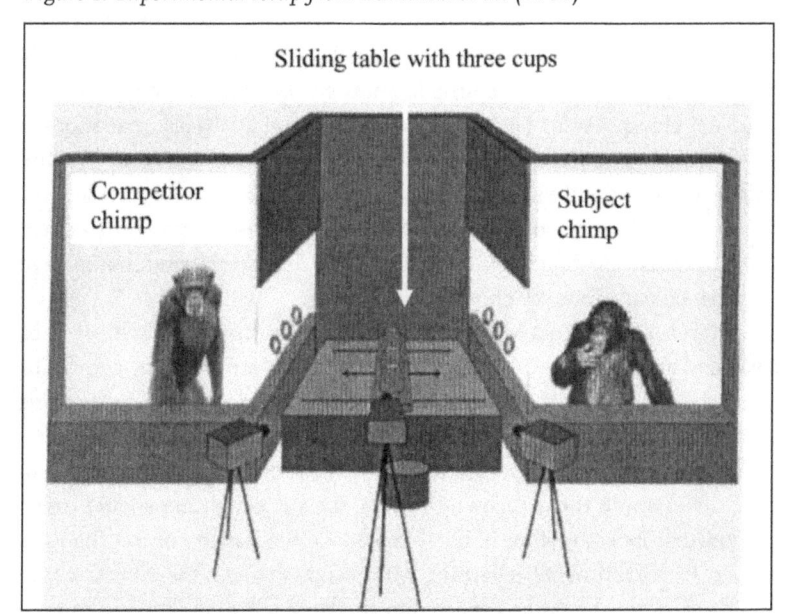

Figure 1: Experimental setup from Kaminski et al. (2008)

At the start of the game, the chimps watch while an experimenter baits one of three cups on the table. After the baiting, a screen is raised in front of the competitor, blocking its view of the middle area. The screen also signals to the subject chimp that its competitor is blind to the events that will shortly transpire in the middle area. Once the screen is raised, the experimenter performs one of two types of manipulations on the cups and bait in front of the subject chimp. In the unknown-lift trials, the experimenter removes the bait from underneath the cup and then places it back underneath the cup. In the unknown-shift trials, the experimenter removes the bait from underneath the cup and places it under a different cup. After this, a screen is raised before the subject chimp, blocking its view of the middle area. The screen before competitor is then removed, and the table with the cups is slid to the competitor's side. The competitor is allowed to choose a cup by pointing at it. If the baited cup is chosen, then the food underneath it is removed and given to the animal; the cup is then returned to the table. If an unbaited cup is chosen, then the animal is shown that the cup is empty and receives no reward; the empty cup is then returned to the table. The subject chimp, of course, cannot see which cup the competitor has chosen; although from its prior training in the experiment, it knows that the competitor has selected a cup at this point and has received the hidden bait if it chose correctly. After the competitor has made its choice and the cups returned to their original locations, the screen before the subject chimp is removed. The table is then slid to the subject chimp's side. The subject chimp is now allowed to make one of two choices: it is allowed to choose a cup on the table which (depending upon the competitor's choice) may or may not have the highly desirous piece of food underneath, or it is allowed to choose a cup that has been placed insides its booth which it knows has a less preferred, but guaranteed, food (e.g., monkey chow) reward inside.

Kaminski and colleagues hypothesize that if the subject chimp is capable of attributing beliefs, then it should understand that the competitor in the unknown-shift trials is likely to choose the empty cup on the table, given its false belief regarding which cup is baited; the subject chimp in such trials would be expected to choose the higher-quality baited cup on the table. But in the unknown-lift tests, the subject chimp should understand that its competitor is likely to choose the baited cup on the table, given its correct belief regarding which cup is baited; the subject chimp in these trials should be expected to choose the low-quality (but guaranteed) baited cup inside its booth. Kaminski and colleagues found no such preferential choosing on part of the subject chimp. In fact, the subject chimps were just as likely to choose the high-quality baited cup on the table in the unknown-shift tests as they were in the unknown-lift tests. The authors took these results, plus the findings from Call and Tomsello (1999), as positive support for the hypothesis that chimpanzees are unable to attribute beliefs.

Negative results are always tricky to interpret. And although Kaminski et al.'s interpretation of the above findings is plausible, it is not the only plausible interpretation. Here is another. It is quite possible that the subject animal in the test condition is confused by the novel introduction of the screen before the competitor while the experimenter manipulates the bait. When this screen is lowered and then another is raised in front of the subject animal, the subject animal may not understand that at this point the competitor is choosing a cup on the table. For all the subject knows, nothing is happening behind the screen in the critical test, or perhaps the subject (not unreasonably) assumes that the experimenter is extending to the competitor the same courtesy of lifting or shifting the bait around as he did for the subject. Either way, the subject animal may well think that when the screen before it is removed, it is actually choosing first, not after, the competitor. This would explain why subjects in the unknown-lift and unknown-shift tests choose the higher-quality baited container on the table at the same rate—they assume that in both cases, they are choosing first. It is not unreasonable, then, to suppose that chimpanzees' failures on the knowledge-ignorance experiments are not indicative of their inability to attribute beliefs but of their difficultly with understanding when the competitor has chosen and when he has not. This problem, however, could be addressed by some type of sound cue, such as a buzzer, which sounded whenever the competitor makes a choice. The subject animal could then use the sound cue as evidence that the competitor is choosing a container behind the screen during the test trials.

As mentioned above, there have been some positive results from different versions of the cooperative knowledge-ignorance experiment with chimpanzees. In O'Connell and Dunbar (2003), for example, one of four chimpanzees tested performed significantly better than chance in the critical test condition. In their study, one chimp, Josie, showed an ability to discriminate between when an experimenter had a correct belief about the position of a peg (used to indicate the baited drawer) and when the experimenter had a false belief about the peg's position (see figure 2). Josie consistently chose the baited pegged drawer on the true-belief tests and the non-pegged (but previously pegged) baited drawer on the false-belief tests.

Figure 2: Experimental setup from O'Connell & Dunbar (2003)

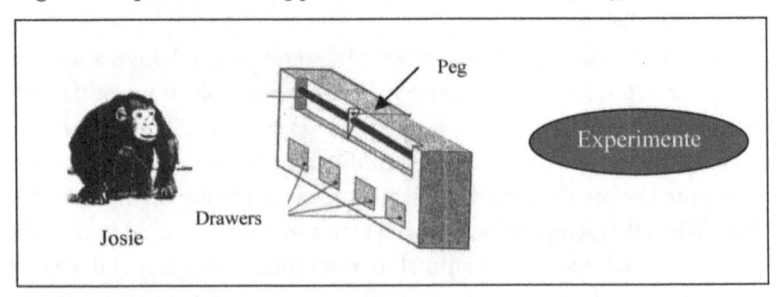

And so, one might ask, isn't this enough to say that chimpanzees are capable of attributing beliefs? I am afraid not. The knowledge-ignorance protocol, unfortunately, is not sensitive enough to distinguish between subjects that genuinely attribute beliefs from those that merely attribute the physically observable grounds or the perceptual-states that are associated with such beliefs.[4] The results of O'Connell and Dunbar's study, for example, can be just as well explained either in terms of a behavior-reading hypothesis or in terms of a perceptual-state attribution hypothesis. On the former, Josie's performance can be explained in terms of her learning to choose the drawer that was originally marked by the experimenter regardless of whether it was still currently marked at the time of her choosing; and on the latter hypothesis, Josie's performance can be explained in terms of her following the perceptual-state attribution rule to choose the drawer over which the experimenter last saw the peg. Neither of these alternative hypotheses credits Josie with attributing beliefs to the experimenter, merely those physically observable grounds or perceptual states that are associated with such beliefs in the experimenter.

---

4 | See Lurz (2009, forthcoming), as well as Povinelli & Vonk (2006), Penn & Povinelli (2008), and Heyes (1998), for a fuller discussion of the problem of experimentally distinguishing genuine mindreading animals from their complementary behavior-reading counterparts.

More recently, Krachun et al. (2008) ran a competitive knowledge-ignorance experiment that used looking-time as a measure. In the experiment, a chimpanzee competed with a human competitor for food hidden in one of two containers. In the false-belief test, the chimpanzee observed one of the two containers being baited behind a screen while the competitor watched. The screen was removed, and while the competitor left the room or turned around, the chimpanzee witnessed the experimenter switch the locations of containers. The competitor returned to the table and "unsuccessfully" reached for the empty container. The chimpanzee was then allowed to choose. Krachun et al. discovered that although chimpanzees failed to choose the baited container on false belief trails, they looked more at the baited container on these trials than in the true belief control trials. Krachun et al. guardedly suggest that these results may indicate a possible implicit understanding of false belief in chimpanzees.

A chief problem with Krachun et al.'s study, however, is that the chimpanzees' differential looking-times on the test trials were not indicative of the animals' anticipation of where the competitor would reach, but rather, as Krachun et al. acknowledge, their level of uncertainty over which container to choose. The fact that the chimpanzees looked more often at the unbaited container in the false-belief trials than in the true-belief trials indicated that the animals were less certain of their choices in the former than the latter trials. But their being less certain of their choice in the false-belief test may have little to do with their understanding the competitor's false belief. As Krachun et al. point out, there were reasons for the animals to be uncertain in the false-belief test that had nothing to do with the competitor's false belief. In the false-belief trials, but not in the true-belief trials, the experimenter performed the switching of the containers in a deceptive manner—smiling mischievously and glancing occasionally at the door or the competitor's back. This may have suggested to the animals that something was underhanded, perhaps making them wonder whether the competitor's indicated choice of containers (by his "unsuccessful" reaching) was a reliable indicator of the hidden food as it had been in the past. Also, in the warm-up and pre-test trials of the experiment, the competitor always had direct line to gaze with the containers while the experimenter manipulated them. It was only on the false-belief test that the competitor's line of gaze of to the containers was first blocked or absent while the experimenter switched them. This difference between these preceding trials and the false-belief test may have made the animal feel uncertain, or confused, about whether the container indicated by the competitor was the baited container. From its previous experience, the chimpanzee may have thought that the competitor's indicative gestures were reliable because the competitor had direct line of gaze with the manipulation of the containers. When this condition was absent in the false-belief test, the chimpanzee may have become less certain of the reliability of the competitor's indicative gesture.

Two guiding principles can be taken from this brief survey. First, a belief-attribution test in chimpanzees should be one in which the animal is required to predict a competitor's action on the basis of attributing a belief. And second, the test must be capable of distinguishing between genuine belief attributing chimpanzees and their perceptual-state attributing or behavior-reading counterparts. Section 6.4 below describes a false-belief test that satisfies these two conditions.

3. THEORETICAL BACKGROUND: THE ARM THEORY

The experimental protocol outlined below is based upon an appearance-reality mindreading (ARM) theory, various versions of which have been defended over the years by Humphreys (1980), Gallup (1982), and Carruthers (1996). According to ARM, mental-state attribution in animals evolved for the express purpose of anticipating agents' behaviors in those situations in which the animals' behavior-reading counterparts could not. In many cases, the way things perceptually appear to a target animal is a better predictor of its behavior than the way things objectively are. Behavior-reading animals—animals that are unable to attribute mental states—can appeal only to the latter sorts of objective, observable, mind-independent facts (e.g., facts about the target animal's past behaviors, or its line of eye gaze to an object in the environment). Mindreading animals are able to appeal to the subjective way things perceptually appear to the target animal to predict its behavior. It is hypothesized that mental-state attribution in animals evolved as a result of their coming to introspect their own ability to distinguish appearance from reality, using this introspective distinction for the purpose of anticipating other agents' behaviors.

Of course, other agents can sometimes see through deceptive appearances and act on what they believe to be really occurring in the environment. And so, on the ARM theory, mental-state attribution in animals should reflect two levels of development. The first level involves perceptual-state attribution, wherein the animal is able to anticipate a target's behavior in terms of how it represents the world perceptually appearing to the target. The second level of development is belief attribution, wherein the animal is able to anticipate a target's behavior in terms of how it thinks the target believes things are.

To test ARM empirically we need an experimental method capable of distinguishing (a) those animals capable of attributing perceptual states (e.g., seeing or visually appearing) from (b) those capable of attributing perceptual states and beliefs. All of the belief-attribution studies surveyed above, unfortunately, rest upon a particular view of the difference between belief attribution and perceptual-state attribution that prevent them from experimentally distinguishing (a) and (b). The view itself, quite correctly, is based upon an undeniable fact about beliefs and perceptions—namely, that past veridical perceptions (e.g., having seen the baiting of cup x) can sometimes lead a subject to later act on a false belief at a time when the veridical perception no longer exists (e.g., after the deceptive switching of the bait's location, the competitor now incorrectly believes that the bait is under cup x). The studies, therefore, assume that if chimpanzees are capable of attributing beliefs, and not just occurrent perceptual-states, then they should be able to predict a target's behavior on the basis of his/her currently held false belief in the absence of the veridical perception which caused to it. The chief problem with this approach is that a target's currently held false belief will always be confounded with his/her having had a past veridical perception (as well as his/her having had a direct-line-of-gaze to the perceived object), and, as a result, the animal's successful prediction of the target's action can just as well be explained in terms of it attributing a past veridical perception (or a past direct-line-of-gaze to an object) to the target as it can in terms of it attributing a currently held false belief.

Luckily there are two other ways of understanding the difference between belief attribution and perceptual-state attribution that escape this problem. Both of these approaches reflect a distinctive feature of belief vis-à-vis perception—namely, revisability and abstractness. A distinctive feature of beliefs (at least, as a kind of mental state) is that they are revisable in light of countervailing evidence in the way perceptual states (as a kind) largely are not.[5]

---

5 | The notion of 'revisability' here is similar to Jonathan Bennett (1976) notion of 'educatability', which he also took to be the distinguishing mark of beliefs vis-à-vis perception.

As a result of measuring the lines in a Muller-Lyer diagram (see figure 3), for example, one's belief about the lines' unequal length changes despite their continuing to look unequal, and this change in one's belief naturally leads to a change in one's behavior.

Figure 3: Muller-Lyer diagram

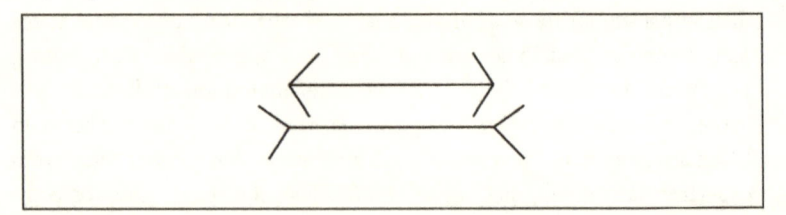

Thus an animal capable of attributing beliefs, and not just perceptual-states, is expected to be sensitive to the behavioral difference between (1) a target that perceives an object as F but has been presented with evidence that the object is really *not* F, and (2) a target that perceives an object as F but has not been presented with such countervailing evidence. In Lurz (2009, forthcoming), I have described a number of innovative experimental protocols for testing chimpanzees' and other animal's sensitivity to this epistemic difference; so I shall not discuss those here.

The other distinctive feature of belief (and thought in general) is its ability to allow subjects to represent facts or properties in the world that cannot be represented by means of perception alone. Such facts and properties are routinely called 'abstract.' Of course, abstractness comes in degree, and so it is unlikely that there will be any sharp distinction between perception and cognition on this dimension. Be this as it may, the point here is merely that the more abstract a fact or property which a mental state represents the more the state belongs to cognition. And this is surely correct. Although I do not have a metric of abstractness to offer, it is surely the case that representing an object as having a second-order (or determinable) property (i.e., a property that is defined in terms of other properties) is more abstract than representing an object's first-order (determinate) properties (i.e., properties that are not defined in terms of other properties). Consider, for example, the second-order (determinable) property of having shape in general. Intuitively, representing an object has having shape in general is more abstract than representing it as square or circular, for example. And for similar reasons, representing a pair of objects as being same/different in shape in general is more abstract than representing them as having the same/different determinate shape (e.g, as both being square).

Following Premack (1983), cognitive scientists have come to call relations of same/difference in second-order (determinable) properties of color or shape second-order relations and relations of same/difference in determinate colors or shape first-order relations, taking mental representations of the former (abstract) relations as a mark of genuine cognition. It would be ideal, then, in developing a test for belief-attribution in chimpanzees to run an experiment that tested the apes' capacity to attribute representations of second-order relations to targets. Just such a protocol can be developed, I believe. Chimpanzees and other great apes, after all, are known for their distinctive talent in solving and responding to relation matching problems that arguably require representing abstract, second-order relations or properties (see Smith et al. 1975; Premack 1983; Thompson et al. 1997; Vonk & MacDonald 2002; Vonk 2003; Vonk & MacDonald 2004).[6] The idea behind the experimental protocol that I am proposing here is to exploit this unique cognitive talent in chimpanzees and see whether they can attribute such abstract representations (i.e., beliefs) to others.

---

6 | Thompson & Oden (2000) go further and interpret the success of chimpanzees on such tasks as evidence that the animals judge the sameness/difference of the relations exemplified by the different pairs. All that is being assumed above, rather, is that the chimpanzees represent the abstract, second-order relations exemplified by each of the different pairs. On this point, it relevant to note that Penn et al. (2008) have argued that chimpanzees could pass relation matching tasks by simply representing the level of variability existing between the items in a pair and by learning the conditional rule 'if the between-item variability of the sample pair is low/high, then select the pair in the choice display that has a between-item variability that is low/high.' The chimps, on such a view, are certainly not credited with understanding relations about relations. Nevertheless, they are credited with representing the between-item level of variability of a pair, which Penn et al. acknowledge, is a representation of an abstract, second-order relation. Thus Penn et al.'s interpretation of the relation matching data is quite consistent with the argument made here.

4. Testing the Attribution of Abstract Representations by Chimpanzees

The following experimental protocol is modeled on Kaminski et al.'s (2008) competitive knowledge-ignorance paradigm, correcting for the problem noted above. The protocol has three initial training phases before the critical competitive tests are administered.

Generalized relation matching test phase. In this phase of the experiment, the chimpanzees are trained on a generalized relation matching problem similar to that used by Burdyn and Thomas (1984) with monkeys. A sample pair of shapes is placed on top of the display apparatus (figure 4). On a shelf below the sample pair, there is a striped and a checked container, one of which contains a hidden food reward inside. Both containers have bells attached to them that make a sound when the containers are manipulated by the experimenter. After the sample objects are placed, the apparatus is slid over to the side of the chimpanzee's cage, indicating that it is to point to one of the two containers. The chimpanzee is trained to point to the striped container if the sample objects on top of the apparatus are similar in shape, and to point to the checked container if they are different (irrespective of the sample object's color or size). Correct choices are rewarded by the experimenter lifting the container that was indicated and giving the hidden food (e.g., a grape) to the chimp and then lifting the other container and showing the chimp that it is empty. Incorrect choices are not reward; rather, the experimenter simply lifts the container indicated, showing that it is empty, and then lifts the second container, showing that it is baited.

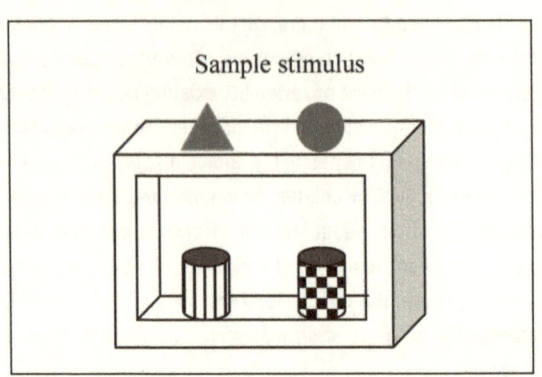

Figure 4: Apparatus for relation matching test

Occluded sample object test. Before testing, two occluder boxes (e.g., shoeboxes with slits in their sides for inserting shapes) are fastened at opposite ends of the top of the apparatus (see figure 5).

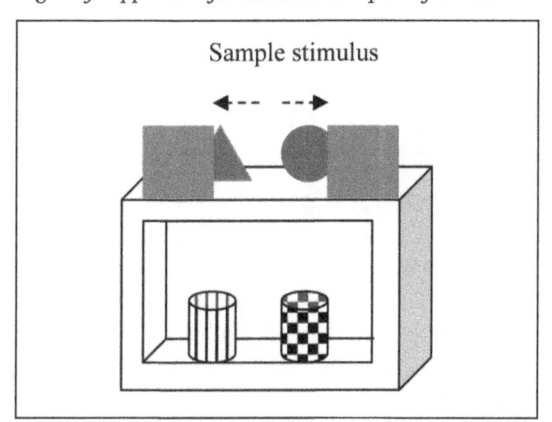

Figure 5: Apparatus for occluded sample object test

The animal is first shown the sample objects in front of the occluders, and then each object is inserted ¼ of the way into its respective occluder. The chimps are trained (if training is needed) to select the appropriate container for the actual second-order relation of the sample pair. If training is required, the chimps' comprehension of the task can be tested by giving them a test with novel sample objects.

There is, incidentally, abundant empirical evidence showing that chimpanzees (as well as many other species of animal) interpret the shapes of occluded objects much in the way that humans do (see Fujita 2006 for review). Thus it is quite plausible to suppose that chimpanzees would see the occluded objects in figure 5, for example, as being a triangle and a circle. This, of course, would need to be tested.

Deceptive sample object test. This test is just like the occluded sample object test except "deceptive" sample objects are used. These objects are such that after being inserted into their respective occluders, they give the appearance of having a second-order relation (sameness/difference in shape) that they do not in fact possess. For example, in figure 6, the inserted sample objects appear as if they have the same shape; whereas in figure 7, the inserted sample objects appears as if they have different shapes.

Figure 6 and 7: Deceptive occluded objects

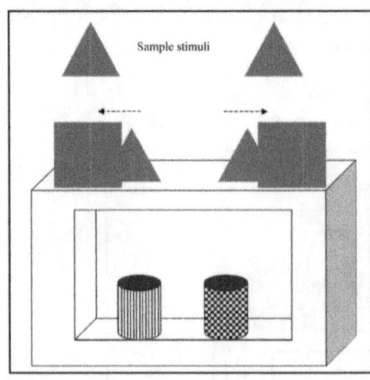

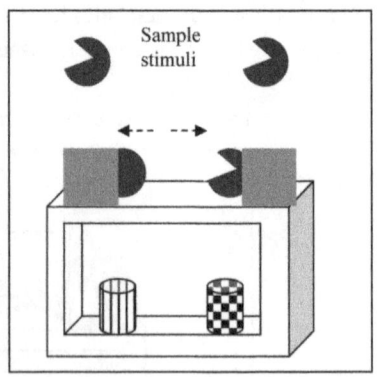

The chimp is trained (if training is needed) to select the correct container for the sample objects presented. Again, if training is required, the chimps' comprehension of the task can be tested by testing them on a novel pair of deceptive objects.

It is important to note that the deceptive-sample-object test here is designed to test the chimpanzees' ability to distinguish an occluded object's apparent shape from its real shape. It is, therefore, an appearance-reality discrimination test. To date researchers have not investigated whether chimpanzees (or any other animals) can distinguish appearance from reality in cases of occluded objects.[7] However, it does not seem a priori implausible to think that some chimpanzees might pass the deceptive-sample-object test with novel stimuli.

Introduction to the competitive game. In this phase of the experiment, the chimps are introduced to a competitive game with a human competitor, similar to the one used in Kaminski et al. (2008). The subject chimp and the human competitor compete for the reward (a grape) in a relation matching task. To introduce them to the rules of the game the chimps are trained on a simplified version of the game. On this version of the game, the experimenter places two sample objects on top of the apparatus (but not inserting them into the occluder boxes) while the chimp and the competitor watch (see figure 8 below minus the screen and occluder boxes).

---

7 | Krachun et al. (2009) received positive results with an appearance-reality task using magnifying and minimizing lenses.

Figure 8: Possible set-up for competitive game

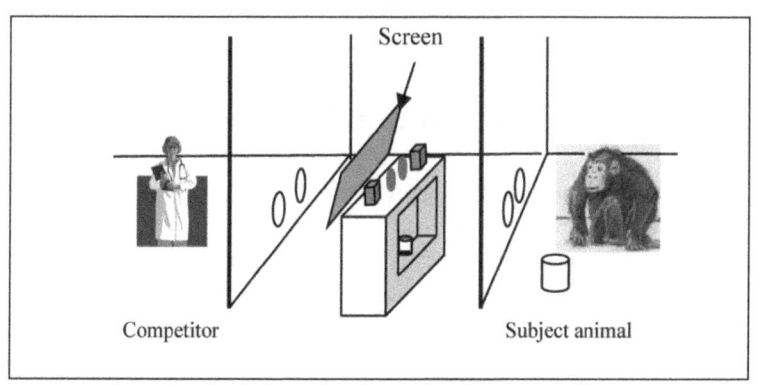

The window in the middle of the apparatus allows the chimpanzee to observe the competitor's direction of gaze and behavior on the other side of the arena. The apparatus is then moved over to the competitor's side of the arena. The chimpanzee then observes the competitor pointing to the correct container and the experimenter lifting the container and giving the grape to the competitor. When the competitor chooses first, he/she always chooses the correct container on the apparatus. In lifting the container, the experimenter always causes the bells to jingle, which act as an auditory cue that the competitor has made a choice. After the competitor chooses, the container is replaced and the apparatus is moved to the chimp's side of the arena, indicating that it is allowed to choose a container. In all trials of the game, the chimp (as in Kaminski et al.'s second experiment) is given the option to choose a container on the apparatus, with the potential of yielding a high-quality food reward, or the "safe" option of choosing a container in its cage with a low-quality food reward (e.g., monkey chow). If the chimp's initial choice after the competitor has chosen is a container on the apparatus, then the experimenter shows the chimp that the indicated container, as well as the non-indicated containers, is empty. The chimp is only allowed the low-quality food reward in the game when the container in its cage is its initial choice.

The game is played again, this time allowing the chimp to choose first. After the chimp chooses, the apparatus is moved toward the competitor, allowing him/her to choose. If the chimp chooses the correct container on the apparatus, then it receives the high-quality food reward. If it chooses the incorrect container, then it is shown that the container is empty and the chimp gets no reward. And if it elects to choose the low-quality food container, it is rewarded with the low-quality reward. The game is played a number of times using the same set of sample objects until the chimp consistently chooses the correct container on the apparatus when it is allowed to choose first and the low-quality food container when it is allowed to choose second.

A modified version of the game is played next with the experimenter inserting the sample objects ¼ of the way into their respective occluder boxes while both contestants watch. The game is then played as described above. This occluded-sample-object version of the game is played until the chimp consistently chooses the correct container on the apparatus when it is allowed to choose first, choosing the low-quality food container when it is allowed to choose second.

Once the chimps reach criterion on this version of the game, they are allowed to play a variant of the game in which the experimenter uses a screen to block the competitor's view of the sample objects while they are being placed on the apparatus, as well as another screen used to block the chimp's view of the competitor's choice. Four test conditions and one control are run.

Non-deceptive condition. A screen is used to block the competitor's but not the chimp's view of the top of the apparatus while the experimenter places two sample objects on top of the apparatus (see figure 8 above). The experimenter slides each of the sample objects ¼ of the way into their respective occluders and then removes the screen, enabling the competitor to see the occluded sample objects. The apparatus is then moved to the chimp's side or the competitor's side. Before the chimp or the competitor chooses, a screen is drawn in front of the see-through window, preventing any potential observation on the part of the non-choosing subject regarding the choosing subject's choice of containers. However, even though the screen prevents the chimp from seeing the competitor making his/her choice, the sound of the bells on the container will indicate to the chimp that the competitor has made a choice. (This addresses the problem noted above with Kaminski et al. (2008) study.) As with the simplified version of the game, if the human competitor chooses first, then he/she will always choose the correct container. In such a case, the chimp should choose the low-quality food container. On the other hand, if the chimp chooses first, then it should choose the correct contained on the apparatus.

Deceptive condition. This test condition is just like the above except that a deceptive pair of sample objects is slid ¼ way into their respective occluders, giving the appearance of the objects having a second-order relation that they do not really have. See figures 6 and 7 above for examples. It is critical, however, that in this test condition whatever pair of determinate shapes (same or different) that the sample objects *look* to have, that pair of determinate shapes is not possessed by any of the sample objects used in the other test conditions. So, for example, if the pair of determinate shapes that the sample objects *look* to be are (as in figure 6) both triangles, then a triangle-triangle pair is not to be used in any of the other test conditions; likewise, if the pair of determinate shapes that the sample objects *look* to be are (as in figure 7) a circle and a packman, then the circle-packman pair is not used in any of the other test conditions. Since there is an open-ended number of shape pairs that one can use as sample objects, eliminating those that are the same as the apparent shape pairs used in the deceptive tests should not create any significant difficultly. The point of doing this, which will be made clearer below, is to distinguish second-order belief-attributing subjects from mere first-order perceptual-state-attributing subjects.

After the deceptive sample pair is in place, the screen is removed, allowing the competitor to see the occluded objects. The apparatus is then moved to one side of the arena. Again, a screen is drawn in front of the see-through window, blocking the view of the contestant's choice. On this test trial, if the competitor chooses first, then he/she will choose the wrong (empty) container on the apparatus.[8] Thus, if the chimp is capable of attributing beliefs involving second-order relations, then it ought to understand that the competitor in this case mistakenly believes that the sample objects have a second-order relation (sameness/difference in shape) that they do not really have. Thus, on the basis of this attribution, the chimp should anticipate the competitor choosing the wrong container on the apparatus and should select the correct container when its turn comes.

Completely occluded condition. This condition is just like the others except that the experimenter places the sample objects behind their respective occluders so that only the chimp can see them (see figure 9).

---

8 | It is preferable that the competitor not make any distinctive sound of disappointment in choosing the wrong container. Doing so would only introduce a potentially confounding variable.

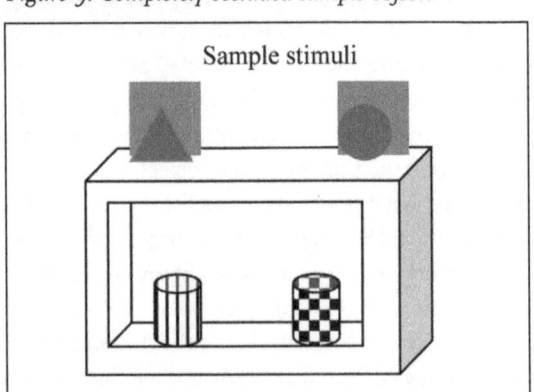

Figure 9: Completely occluded sample objects

The screen is then removed, allowing the competitor to see the occluder boxes but not the sample objects behind them. Again, if the competitor chooses first, then he/she will choose the wrong container on the apparatus. Thus, if the chimp chooses second in this test condition, it ought to understand that competitor could not see the sample objects and is unlikely to select the correct container on the apparatus. The chimp should, then, select the correct container on the apparatus when it is allowed to choose.

Control condition. This is just like the other test conditions except that the experimenter does not slide the sample objects into their occluders or behind them but places them in the open between the two occluders, as was done on the simplified version of the game. Again, after the placement of the sample objects, the screen is removed, allowing the competitor a view. If the competitor chooses first, then he/she will choose the correct container. And so, if the chimp chooses second, then it ought to understand that the competitor is likely to have chosen correctly, and it should therefore choose the "safe" option when it is allowed to choose.

As stated in the description of the various test and control conditions, the subject chimp, if capable of attributing beliefs involving second-order relations, is expected to choose a container on the apparatus more often in the deceptive and completely occluded tests when choosing second than in the non-deceptive or control tests, and to choose the "safe" option more often in the non-deceptive and control tests when choosing second than in the other two tests.

However, the chimpanzees would not be expected to perform in this way if they were capable of attributing only first-order perceptions. Although such perceptual-state attributing chimps could very well understand that the competitor in the deceptive test mistakenly perceives the pair of sample objects as having certain determinate shapes (e.g., triangle-triangle or circle-packman) that they really do not have, the chimps would be unable to predict what the competitor is likely to do as a result of his having such illusory first-order perceptions. For in none of the previous test trials has the chimpanzee had the opportunity to attribute such first-order perceptions to the competitor. Recall that the pair of shapes that the sample objects *look* to have in the deceptive test trials have never been possessed by any of the sample objects in the other test conditions. The competitor, for example, has never been shown looking at a triangle-triangle pair or a circle-packman pair (occluded or otherwise) before. Thus, a first-order perceptual-state attributing chimp—though capable of understanding that the competitor sees the sample pair as being (say) an occluded triangle-triangle pair or as an occluded circle-packman pair—is incapable of predicting what the competitor is likely to do as result of having this deceptive first-order perception. Hence, such chimps are not expected to choose in the same way that their second-order belief attributing counterparts are.

And if the chimps were behavior-readers, incapable of attributing mental states of any type, then they would be expected to perform quite differently on the deceptive test condition from their second-order belief attributing counterparts. Failing to understand that the competitor has a false belief regarding the second-order relation of the sample objects, the behavior-reading chimps would not be expected to treat such a trial any differently from the way they treated the non-deceptive test trials—in both cases, they would be expected to predict that the competitor will choose the correct container on the apparatus if he/she chooses first.

Thus, unlike any test used in the past, or currently being used, this belief-attribution test has the power to distinguish genuine belief attributing chimpanzees from their perceptual-state attributing and behavior-reading counterparts. It has been the challenge of designing an experimental protocol capable of making this distinction that has severely retarded progress in animal mindreading research (see Heyes 1998; Povinelli & Vonk 2006; Penn & Povinelli 2007; Lurz 2009; Fitzpatrick 2009). The proposed experimental protocol has the potential to move the field forward.

5. Conclusion

If chimpanzees and other great apes prove capable of attributing beliefs, then, I have argued, this may justify a moral distinction between them and other animals. However, the question of whether chimpanzees and other great apes are capable of attributing beliefs is still very much an open question. More sensitive tests are needed. I have outlined just such a test that I think will work.[9] The rest is in the hands of empirical researchers.

Acknowledgments: I wish to thank Marietta Dindo for her very helpful comments on an earlier draft of this essay.

References

Bennett, J. (1976), Linguistic Behaviour, Indianapolis: Hackett.
Bermúdez, J. L. (2003), Thinking without Words, Oxford: Oxford University Press.
Bermúdez, J. L. (2009), Mindreading in the Animal Kingdom, in: R. Lurz (ed.) (2009), The Philosophy of Animal Minds, Cambridge: Cambridge University Press.
Boysen, S., Kuhlmeier V. (2002), "Representational Capacities for Pretense With Scale Models and Photographs in Chimpanzees (Pan troglodytes)", in: R. Mitchell (ed.), Pretending and Imagination in Animals and Children, Cambridge: Cambridge University Press.
Bugnyar, T., Heinrich, B. (2005), "Ravens, Corvus Corax, Differentiate Between Knowledgeable and Ignorant Competitors", Proceedings of the Royal Society B 272, 1641-1646.
Burdyn, L., Thomas, R. (1984), "Conditional Discrimination With Conceptual Simultaneous and Successive Cues in the Squirrel Monkey (Saimiri sciureus)", Journal of Comparative Psychology 4, 405-13.
Call, J., Tomasello, M. (1999), "A Nonverbal False Belief Task: The Performance of Children and Great Apes", Child Development 70, 381-395.
Carruthers, P. (1996), Language, Thought and Consciousness, Cambridge: Cambridge University Press.

---

9 | See Lurz (forthcoming-a, and forthcoming-b) for other belief-attribution tests for a variety of animal species.

Cavalieri, P., Singer, P. (eds.) (1993), The Great Ape Project: Equality Beyond Humanity, New York: St. Martin's Press.

Davidson, D. (2001), Subjective, Intersubjective, and Objective, Oxford: Oxford University Press.

de Waal, F. (2006), Primates and Philosophers: How Morality Evolved, Princeton: Princeton University Press.

Emery, N.J., Clayton, N.S. (2008), "How to Build a Scrub-Jay That Reads Minds", in: S. Itakura, Fujita, K. (ed.) (2008), Origins of the Social Minds, Tokyo: Springer.

Fagot, J., Wasserman, E., Young, M. (2001), "Discriminating the Relation Between Relations: The Role of Entropy in Abstract Conceptualization by Baboons (Papio papio) and Humans (Homo sapien)", Journal of Experimental Psychology 27, 316-28.

Fitzpatrick, S. (2009), "The Primate Mindreading Controversy: A Case Study in Simplicity and Methodology in Animal Psychology", in: R. Lurz (ed.), The Philosophy of Animal Minds, Cambridge: Cambridge University Press.

Fujita, K. (2006), "Seeing What is Not There: Illusion, Completion, and Spatiotemporal Boundary Formation in Comparative Perspective", in: E. A. Wasserman, T. R. Zentall (eds.), Comparative Cognition, Oxford: Oxford University Press.

Flombaum, J., Santos, L. (2004), "Rhesus Monkeys Attribute Perceptions to Others", Current Biology 15, 447-452.

Gallup, G. (1982), "Self-Awareness and the Emergence of Mind in Primates", American Journal of Primatology 2, 237-248.

Gergely, G., Nadasdy, Z., Csibra, G., Biro, S. (1995), "Taking the Intentional Stance at 12 Months of Age", Cognition 56, 165-193.

Hare, B., Tomasello, M. (2004), "Chimpanzees Are More Skillful in Competitive Than in Cooperative Cognitive Tasks", Animal Behaviour 68, 571-581.

Heyes, C. (1998), "Theory of Mind in Nonhuman Primates", Behavioral and Brain Sciences 21, 101-148.

Humphrey, N. (1980), "Nature's Psychologists", in: B. Josephson, V. Ramachandran (ed.), Consciousness and the Physical world, Oxford: Pergamon Press.

Kaminski, J., Call, J., Tomasello, M. (2006), "Goats' Behaviour in a Competitive Food Paradigm: Evidence for Perspective Taking?", Behaviour 143, 1341-1356.

Kaminski, J., Call, J., Tomasello, M. (2008), "Chimpanzees Know What Others Know, But Not What They Believe", Cognition 109, 224-234.

Krachun, C., Carpenter, M., Call, J., Tomasello, M. (2009), "A Competitive Nonverbal False Belief Task for Children and Apes", Developmental Science 12, 521-535.

Krachun, C., Call, J., Tomasello, M. (2009), "Can Chimpanzees Discriminate Appearances From Reality?", Cognition 112, 435-450.

Kuroshima, H., Fujita, K., Fuyuki, A. (2002), "Understanding of the Relation Between Seeing and Knowing by Tufted Capuchin Monkeys (Cebus paella)", Animal Cognition 5, 41-48.

Lurz, R. (2007), "In Defense of Wordless Thoughts About Thoughts", Mind and Language, 22, 270-296.

Lurz, R. (2008), "Animal Minds", in: Internet Encyclopedia of Philosophy, http://www.iep.utm.edu/ani-mind/.

Lurz, R. (2009), "If Chimpanzees Are Mindreaders, Could Behavioral Science Tell? Toward a Solution to the Logical Problem", Philosophical Psychology 22, 305-328.

Lurz, R. (forthcoming-a), Mindreading Animals, Cambridge, MA: MIT Press.

Lurz, R. (forthcoming-b), "Can Chimps Attribute Beliefs? A New Approach to Answering an Old Nettled Question", in: R. Mitchell, J. Smith (eds.), Minds of Animals, New York: Columbia University Press.

Menzel, E., Savage-Rumbaugh, E. S., Lawson, J. (1985), "Chimpanzees (Pan troglodytes) Spatial Problem Solving With the Use of Mirrors and Televised Equivalents of Mirrors", Journal of Comparative Psychology 99, 211-217.

McGinn, C. (1995), "Animal Minds, Animal Morality", Social Research 62, 731-747.

O'Connell, S., Dunbar, R. I. M. (2003), "A Test Comprehension for False Belief in Chimpanzees", Evolution and Cognition 9, 131-140.

Penn, D. C., Povinelli, D. (2007), "On the Lack of Evidence That Non-Human Animals Possess Anything Remotely Resembling a 'Theory of Mind'", Philosophical Transactions of the Royal Society B 362, 731-744.

Penn, D., Hoyloak, K., Povinelli, D. (2008), "Darwin's Mistake: Explaining the Discontinuity Between Human and Nonhuman Minds", Behavioral and Brain Sciences 31, 109-178.

Poss, S., Rochat, P. (2003), "Referential Understanding of Videos in Chimpanzees (Pan troglodytes), Orangutans (Pongo pygmaeus), and Chil-

dren (Homo sapiens)", Journal of Comparative Psychology 117, 420-428.
Povinelli, D., Vonk, J. (2006), "We Don't Need a Microscope to Explore the Chimpanzee's Mind", in: S. Hurley, M. Nudds (eds.), Rational Animals, Oxford: Oxford University Press.
Premack, D. (1983), "The Codes of Man and Beast", Behavioral and Brain Sciences 6, 125-167.
Santos, L, Nissen, A., Ferrugia, J. (2006), "Rhesus Moneys, Macaca Mulatta, Know What Others Can and Cannot Hear", Animal Behavior 71, 1175-1181.
Smith, H., King, J., Witt, E., Rickel, J. (1975), "Sameness-Difference Matching From Sample by Chimpanzees", Bulletin of the Psychonomic Society 6, 469-471.
Thompson, R., Oden, D., Boysen, S. (1997), "Language-Naïve Chimpanzees (Pan troglodytes) Judge Relations Between Relations in a Conceptual Matching-to-Sample Task", Journal of Experimental Psychology 23, 31-43.
Thompson, R., Oden, D. (2000), "Categorical Perception and Conceptual Judgments by Primates: The Paleological Monkey and the Analogical Ape", Behavioural Processes 35, 149-161.
Topál, J., Erdőhegyi, Á., Mányik, R., Miklósi, Á. (2006), "Mindreading in a Dog: An Adaptation of a Primate 'Mental Attribution' Study", International Journal of Psychology and Psychological Therapy 6, 365-379.
Tschudin, A. (2001), "'Mindreading' Mammals? Attribution of Belief Tasks With Dolphins", Animal Welfare 10, S119-127.
Vonk, J. (2003), "Gorilla (Gorilla gorilla) and Orangutan (Pongo abelii) Understanding of First- and Second-Order Relations", Animal Cognition, 6, 77-86.
Vonk, J., MacDonald, S. (2002), "Natural Concept Formation by a Juvenile Gorilla (Gorilla gorilla gorilla) at Three Levels of Abstraction", Journal of the Experimental Analysis of Behaviour 78, 315-332.
Vonk, J., MacDonald, S. (2004), "Levels of Abstraction in Orangutan (Pongo abelii), Categorization", Journal of Comparative Psychology 118, 3-13.
Welker, D. (1988), "On the Necessity ofBbodies", Erkenntnis 28, 363-385.
Wood, J., Hauser, M. (2008), "Action Comprehension in Non-Human Primates: Motor Simulation or Inferential Reasoning?", Trends in Cognitive Sciences 12, 461-465.

7. Ape Autonomy?
Social Norms and Moral Agency in Other Species

Kristin Andrews

1. INTRODUCTION

Once upon a time, not too long ago, the question about apes and ethics had to do with moral standing—do apes have interests or rights that humans ought to respect? Given the fifty years of research on great ape cognition, life history, social organization, and behavior, the answer to that question seems obvious. Apes have emotions and projects, they can be harmed, and they have important social relationships.

Today the question is more likely to be about whether apes have morality in some sense—whether they are autonomous agents, have social norms, moral emotions, or even abstract concepts of right and wrong. Some argue that given what we now know, the great apes do fall into the sphere of what we might call moral agents (de Waal 2006; Bekoff & Pierce 2009). From field research, we know that within species, great ape communities differ from one another in their methods of food processing and social interaction to an extent that is recognized as cultural (McGrew 1992; Whiten et al. 1999; van Schaik 2003). And from captive research we know that great apes can recognize intentions and goals (Uller 2004; Call et al. 2004; Warneken & Tomasello 2006) as well as others' emotional states (Parr & Hopkins 2000; Parr 2001). There is evidence of prosocial behavior in chimpanzees including consolation behavior (comforting individuals who are subject to aggressive attacks) (Fraser et al 2008; Fraser & Aureli 2008) and helping behavior (Hirata 2003; Melis et al. 2006). Indeed, de Waal argues that great apes are capable of empathy, act to help others in flexible and creative ways, and engage in reciprocal exchanges of goods and services (de Waal 2006; 2009).

There have been two approaches to endorsing moral agency in nonhuman animals. One approach, taken by de Waal, is to see moral agency as on a continuum, so that he sees a smooth continuity between moral and amoral agents, just as he sees a smooth continuity between human and nonhuman minds. This allows him to conclude that many species have morality to some degree, since he takes empathy and reciprocity to be jointly sufficient for entry into the domain of moral agent, and he thinks many species demonstrate primitive versions of these requirements. De Waal concludes that many animals have a moral sense, though one that is not as developed as the human moral sense.

The other approach is to be a pluralist about kinds of moral agency, and argue that an animal who lacks many of the cognitive capacities of adult humans can still be a moral agent because there are different kinds of moral agents, and animal species can have their own form of morality. This view is defended by Bekoff and Pierce (2009) who argue that some species have a distinct form of morality that is not a precursor to human morality. Because they take *morality* to mean "a suite of other-regarding behaviors that cultivate and regulate complex interactions within social groups" (Bekoff & Pierce 2009, 82), they take the complexity of animal behavior, social organization, and cognitive flexibility to demonstrate that other species have morality in this sense. Central to the view is that different species have different norms, and that this makes animal morality species-relative. Despite their differences, important similarities between species include the capacities for empathy, altruism, cooperation and perhaps a sense of fairness. Unlike de Waal's focus on the mechanisms of morality, Bekoff and Pierce are more interested in the existence of those beneficial behavioral regularities, which they identify functionally in terms of the benefits offered to the group.

However, there are certain theoretical barriers toward considering either de Waal's empathy and reciprocity or Bekoff and Pierce's other-regarding behaviors as sufficient criteria for moral agency. A moral agent is someone who can be held responsible for her behavior, whose behavior can appropriately be judged morally acceptable or not. This suggests that there is something cognitive about morality that isn't reflected in Bekoff and Pierce's approach. But the mechanisms that de Waal suggest may not be sufficient. Consider the following passage from the entry on moral agents in *The Routledge Encyclopedia of Philosophy*:

"Moral agents are those agents expected to meet the demands of morality. Not all agents are moral agents. Young children and animals, being capable of performing actions, may be agents in the way that stones, plants and cars are not. But though they are agents they are not automatically considered moral agents. For a moral agent must also be capable of conforming to at least some of the demands of morality." (Haksar 1998)

Here the question shifts from the nature of moral agency to the question of what counts as a demand for morality. Of course answers to that question will vary, because a demand of morality can only be answered from within the framework of a moral theory, and different moral theories will provide different answers. Subsequently, different moral theories will draw different conclusions about which individuals are included as moral agents. For example, it is plausible that a psychopath that is impaired in empathic understanding may not be considered a moral agent in the Humean sense, but could still be a moral agent in a Kantian framework, so long as his rational abilities are not impaired. Principlist views might require knowledge of moral rules, characterological views might require knowledge of moral valiances associated with personality traits, and particularist theories will stress the importance of procedural knowledge and skill in recognizing moral saliencies of situations. Depending on one's moral theory, a demand of morality might include the ability to follow the Categorical Imperative, the ability to compute utility, the ability to emotionally relate to others, or the ability to understand and develop the virtues. And while it's true that all these theories share the view that a moral agent must be able to evaluate the actions of others, they differ when it comes to what counts as a moral evaluation, and thus the cognitive capacities required for meeting the demands of morality would vary.

This disagreement accentuates the burden for those who want to argue that animals do have morality. Since the null hypothesis is that animals are not moral agents, it will require more work to defend the view that nonhumans have morality in some sense. The additional burden is due to the fact that there is no consensus on the properties required to be a moral agent. As a result, any argument for moral agency can be deflected by claiming that the properties identified in a species are irrelevant or not sufficient for moral agency. The lack of consensus on moral theory also makes it easier to find direct arguments against the claim that animals have morality. That's because one can find one property associated with some account of moral agency and argue that animals lack that property, and hence cannot be moral agents.

For example, the recent discussions of animal morality that have focused on the ability to understand the moral sentiments have been criticized not on empirical grounds, but on philosophical ones (e.g. Wright 2006; Korsgaard 2006; Kitcher 2006; Singer 2006). Frans de Waal argues that great apes, as well as dolphins and elephants, demonstrate empathy in behaviors such as targeted helping, consolation, cooperation, and sensitivity to fairness (de Waal 2006). However, the critics argue that these behaviors do not count as moral behaviors, because humans have some capacity that the animals lack. That is, while animals might do the right sort of thing, they may not do it for the right reasons (if they are even acting for reasons at all). It isn't the behavior that matters, but the mechanisms that drive the behavior. The issue then becomes the sort of capacity required to make the moral-looking behavior into truly moral behavior.

I will look at one capacity that is sometimes thought to be a necessary condition for moral agency—a theory of mind. A theory of mind is the ability to understand that self and others act for reasons, and that propositional attitudes drive behavior. As we will see, there are several reasons for thinking that this capacity is required for moral agency. However, I will argue that this concern should not lead one to conclude that great apes cannot be moral agents, even for those who think it unlikely that any non-human species has a theory of mind. While there is no current evidence that great apes have anything like the philosopher's representational concept of belief (Call & Tomasello 2008), this is no reason to reject the possibility that they are moral agents. My aim is to undermine in-principle arguments against animal moral agency by showing that moral agency is possible without a theory of mind. I will argue that great apes have other cognitive capacities that can fulfill the same functions that are sometimes seen as requirements for moral agency, such as knowing the likely consequences of an action by predicting the participants' behaviors and emotional responses. This argument is based on my work on the evolution of mindreading (understood narrowly as the ability to attribute representational mental states such as belief), according to which the drive to explain behavior is fundamental to the development of theory of mind (Andrews 2009, 2012). The need to explain behavior is, in turn, driven by a recognition of the behavior as norm-violating. If recognizing social norms drives the development of metacognitive social abilities such as theory of mind, and the existence of social norms implies the existence of moral agency, then theory of mind is not a necessary condition for moral agency.

2. Moral Behavior and Theory of Mind

With a theory of mind come the concepts of belief and desire, and with those concepts comes the understanding that people act for reasons that consist of their beliefs and desires. An impoverished mother chooses to forgo eating nutritious food herself because she believes she cannot afford nutritious food for both her and her children, she wants her children to be healthy, and she believes they need nutritious food for healthy development. These days, some people are quick to make judgments about people who subsist on fast food, and might call into question the woman's fast-food-eating behavior. But those same people, once they realize the woman's reason for her food choice, would likely change their mind about her behavior as morally suspect, and perhaps even see her as a tragic hero. Knowing another's reason for action allows us to make a better-informed judgment about the behavior in question.

A full-fledged moral agent will be someone whose behavior can be seen as moral or immoral, and someone who can judge her own action and others' actions through a normative lens. At minimum, she must be an intentional agent who purposefully affects change in her environment. On this minimal conception, two things must hold: (1) the individual must be autonomous; (2) the individual must understand the consequences of her actions. For each condition, having a theory of mind seems to be implicated: insofar as autonomy requires knowing someone's reasons for action, it would require a theory of mind; since knowing the consequences of an action requires being able to predict behavior, and having a theory of mind has been touted as extremely beneficial in predicting behavior, theory of mind seems to be involved here as well.

One response to such worries is to argue that great apes do have a theory of mind, and hence these requirements do not interfere with their possible moral agency. I will not take this path, because I think that we don't currently have conclusive evidence on this point. This is due both to problems with the methodologies used to study theory of mind in other species, and with our understanding of theory of mind in humans (Andrews 2005, 2012). I will argue that theory of mind is not needed for either condition. Let us now examine each of the conditions in turn.

3. Autonomy

Having reasons for actions, or having autonomy, or being an intentional agent are different ways of stating one demand of morality that cuts across moral theories. An autonomous agent will understand that her actions have consequences, and she can evaluate those consequences. I will assume the generic account of autonomy given by Christman: "to be autonomous is to be one's own person, to be directed by considerations, desires, conditions, and characteristics that are not simply imposed externally upon one, but are part of what can somehow be considered one's authentic self" (Christman 2009). Here an autonomous agent is contrasted with an individual whose every act is controlled by external forces such as fixed action patterns. An animal could be an autonomous agent if his behavior is flexible and the result of internal cognitive processes rather than a reflex or some species-typical behavior. For animals with flexible behavior, the question is then whether the internal processes are of the right sort.

I will defend an umbrella view of autonomy, which includes both diagnostic features and constitutive cognitive capacities. The diagnostic element takes seriously our acceptance of children as moral agents. The cognitive capacities involved will be related both to this developmental approach and the evolutionary one I sketched above. My view is at odds with one view that has been widely discussed in the animal morality context, namely Korsgaard's Kantian approach. Let me introduce her view in order to use it as a foil for the umbrella account.

Following Kant, Korsgaard argues that all nonhuman animals lack the rational processes necessary for autonomy (Kant 1798; Korsgaard 2006). On Korsgaard's view animals lack autonomy because they lack what she calls *normative self-government* which is the ability to decide whether an act is justified and then act from that judgment rather than from one's desire. She writes:

"What it [normative self-government] requires is a certain form of self-consciousness: namely, consciousness of the grounds on which you propose to act *as grounds*. What I mean is this: a nonhuman agent may be conscious of it as *fearful* or *desirable*, and so as something to be avoided or to be sought. This is the ground of his action. But a rational animal is, in addition, conscious *that* she fears or desires the object, and *that* she is inclined to act in a certain way as a result. That's what I mean by being conscious of the ground *as a ground*. She does not just think about the object that she fears or even about its fearfulness but about her fears and desires themselves." (Korsgaard 2006, 113)

Korsgaard understands self-consciousness as consciousness about one's beliefs and desires—one's reasons—which is another way of describing having a theory of mind. A straightforward argument that moral agency requires having a theory of mind begins with the idea that moral agency requires autonomy, and autonomy requires acting for reasons, which in turn requires realizing that you have reasons for performing an action. Since reasons for action are sets of beliefs and desires that motivate behavior, and having a theory of mind is the ability to think about beliefs and desires, it follows that acting for reasons requires having a theory of mind. Or so the argument goes.

But we shouldn't let it go too far, at least in terms of the question of ape moral agency. Besides being an argument from within a Kantian framework, and hence rather irrelevant for other moral theories, the consequences of this view lead to counterintuitive conclusions about human children, who we should want to retain in the sphere of moral agents. While doing so, however, it is important to see what we can retain as well as what we should jettison from Korsgaard's account. I will question the notion that the ability to consider one's own beliefs and desires is the only internal process that can generate something like normative self-government. I also want to make clear that this discussion isn't intended to criticize Korsgaard's project, only its applicability to the question at issue, which is whether we can make sense of children as moral agents without a theory of mind, and hence potentially apply that status to other apes as well.

So, on to the diagnostic aspect. If a moral agent needs explicit knowledge of her reasons for action and the ability to analyze them, it would follow that children, who do not even begin to understand belief until around 4 years old (Wellman et al. 2001), and who don't recognize some of the implications of belief attributions until mid-childhood (Apperly & Robinson 2001; 2002; 2003) are not autonomous agents. Even worse, it would follow that teenagers, who appear to be impaired at considering their own reasons for action (Pillow 1999; Morris 2000; Moshman 2004), are also outside the sphere of moral agency. At nine years-old, a child who burns a cat would not have acted immorally, on this view, because he isn't yet endowed with the cognitive capacities for evaluating his reasons for action. However, such a child will likely grow up to engage in anti-social behavior toward humans; we know what sort of a moral agent he will turn into. Rather than considering the nine year-old anti-social child as amoral, our common response is to retain moral language and judgments in describing the child and his actions. Psychologists who study moral cognition also base their work on the intuition that young children are within the sphere of the moral, as when Kohlberg asked what sort of moral reasoning ten year-old boys engaged in (Kohlberg 1971), and when Turiel and colleagues examined whether toddlers have a distinction between moral and conventional rules (Turiel & Nucci 1978).

While we take children to be responsible and in the sphere of the moral, we don't hold them fully responsible for their actions, as is reflected in the leniency given to children who commit crimes. Because children and adolescents are still developing their cognitive capacities and their ability to control their impulses and emotions, they are limited in what they *can* do, and hence are limited in what they *should* do. But this doesn't mean that children are not moral agents, and that their behavior cannot be categorized as good or bad. It just means that they have some degree of moral agency. And while children are limited to varying degrees during development, we start to treat them as moral agents when they become mobile and not entirely dependent on a caregiver.

Human children are seen as moral agents because they have degrees of the cognitive capacities required for normative self-government, and they live in a world of social norms that they can grow into and that their behavior is evaluated and shaped in terms of. Insofar as there are degrees of these cognitive capacities, there are also degrees of normative self-government. But as soon as an individual begins to attempt to shape her own behavior, we take her to have entered into the domain of moral agency, whatever mechanisms drive the attempt for self-betterment.

The case of children raises questions about whether a consideration of reasons for action, and hence a theory of mind, is the mechanism necessary for being an autonomous agent. To determine what those mechanisms might be, we can turn back to Christman's definition of autonomy: "to be autonomous is to be one's own person, to be directed by considerations, desires, conditions, and characteristics that are not simply imposed externally upon one, but are part of what can somehow be considered one's authentic self" (Christman 2009). We can appeal to this definition in order to ask about the cognitive capacities required in the case of children, and then turn to the question of whether apes have them.

Christman points to two requirements for autonomy: being directed by internal considerations, and being one's own person. I suggest that we can identify an individual who is directed by internal considerations by examining whether she can distinguish intentional from nonintentional action. An intentional action is done purposefully, and is often described as being done for reasons. If someone can sort intentional actions from other kinds of actions, then there is at least an implicit recognition that these two kinds of actions are different, and that some actions are the responsibility of the agent, and others are not. While it would be experimentally difficult to determine whether nonhuman apes understand some of their own actions as intentional and others as unintentional, there is ample evidence that they understand this distinction in others. And, though it does not directly follow, we can infer that the individual who understands this about others likely also understand this about herself, given the dearth of human subjects who can understand others' mental states but not their own. (This view is even consistent with Carruthers's (2009) argument that mindreading others evolved before the ability to know one's own mind, because he is not committed to there being any developmental lag between using one's mindreading capacity on a third party and one's self; what is unique about his view is that mindreading supersedes any introspective access to one's own mind).

There is ample evidence that apes and human children understand intentional action in terms of individuals having goals and intentions. In one study, Uller found that chimpanzees, like human children (Gergeley et al. 1995), seem to perceive the behavior of geometric shapes moving in the right way as intentional (Uller 2004). For both humans and chimpanzees, a violation of expectation paradigm was used to measure the subjects' responses. In the child study, Gergerly concluded that the infants' surprise response to 'irrational' behavior suggests that they attribute goals and rationality to the geometric shapes. In another study, Call and colleagues found that chimpanzees are more impatient with humans who are unwilling to give them food compared with humans who are unable to give them food; they beg more from the capable person who is unwilling than they beg from the person who is unable to access the visible food (Call et al. 2004). In addition, Jensen found that in an experimental setting chimpanzees will punish a conspecific who steals their food, by pulling a rope that causes the food to fall out of reach of both individuals. However, when the food is taken away by a human and given to the conspecific, the chimpanzee will not punish by pulling the rope (Jensen et al. 2007).

There is one study that suggests chimpanzees do not understand capability, and since understanding capability is necessary for distinguishing between intentional and unintentional actions, this study challenges the dominant view (Vonk & Subiaul 2009). In the study, chimpanzees are given the opportunity to beg for food from one of two humans, one of whom is unable to supply the food. Across a number of experimental conditions, the researchers found that the chimpanzees did not beg from the capable human significantly more often than from the incapable human, thus suggesting that the chimpanzees are unable to make this distinction. However, I have argued that this experiment fails to pick out the distinction (Andrews 2012). In the experimental set-up, the humans were not actually rendered incapable; instead, different apparatuses were used to suggest that movement was restricted, though in fact the human could have maneuvered around the barriers. Given the concerns with this study and the findings of other studies, I think that the received view, that chimpanzees are sensitive to intentional agency, and can distinguish between intentional action and nonintentional action, is justified.

The second aspect of Christman's definition is being one's own person, and acting from one's authentic self. I interpret this as the ability to self-create rather than having one's self as given, since self-creation requires deliberately changing oneself.

The ability to self-create by purposefully changing oneself has not been given direct attention by great ape researchers or developmental psychologists. However, the observation that children spontaneously begin practicing adult actions as part of play at an early age influenced Maria Montessori's development of her early childhood education methods, many of which have been positively evaluated by developmental psychologists (Lillard 2005). Like human children, great apes engage in observational learning (Whiten 2000, Tomasello et al. 1987; Call & Tomasello 1994). Orangutans will position themselves so that they are only a few inches away from the behavior that they are observing, and will subsequently attempt the behavior themselves (Call & Tomasello 1994). Some scientists think that great apes practice behaviors in order to develop competences (Anne Russon, pers. communication). More research on the issue of practice within the social learning project can help to determine whether and to what extent the great apes act to purposefully change themselves.

There are other areas of research that are ripe for exploring the question of self-improvement. Both human infants (Gartstein & Rothbart 2003) and many nonhuman animal species, like adult humans, have identifiable personality factors. Six personality factors have been identified in chimpanzees[1] (King & Figueredo 1997) and five in orangutans (Weiss, King, & Perkins 2006)[2]. The personality research program could take on the question of whether individuals understand their own personality traits, and whether they act to modify them. Such self-help activity would be compelling evidence for self-improvement.

While there may be prima facie reason for thinking that a moral actor needs to have a theory of mind because of considerations of autonomy, I think we should reject this connection. Autonomy, in the present context, is better understood as an umbrella concept, and while it can be defined in such a way as to require theory of mind, defining it that way excludes not only nonhuman animals, but many humans as well. Rather, following de Waal if we understand autonomy as a concept on a gradation that includes a number of different cognitive capacities, we can make sense of our inclusion of children into the sphere of the moral, and we can better understand the variety of cognitive capacities that may be involved in moral activity. One of these capacities is surely a theory of mind, but other capacities include the ability to recognize intentional agency and the ability to learn from others and from experience. There is evidence that great apes have these capacities to some extent, and that insofar as one wants to cast a wide moral net, great apes may be included alongside young humans and unreflective adults.

---

1 | The chimpanzee personality factors include correlates for all the human ones (Neuroticism, Extraversion, Openness to Experience, Agreeableness, and Conscientiousness) plus a factor for Dominance.

2 | Orangutans showed only the correlates to Neuroticism, Extraversion, Agreeableness, and Dominance, but also showed a factor that is a combination of Conscientiousness and Openness that was called Intellect.

4. CONSEQUENCES OF ONE'S ACTIONS

While the first requirement I gave for being a moral agent has historically been associated with Kant's moral theory, the second requirement is more aligned with consequentialist thinking, and is based on the role moral knowledge plays in moral agency. Plausibly, a moral agent needs to have some degree of knowledge about how her actions will affect another. But this requirement entails that we must predict how our actions impact others; we must be generally accurate predictors of behavior. And, one might argue, a theory of mind is necessary for accurately predicting intentional behavior.

The ability to see oneself and others as acting from beliefs and desires is often thought to be a necessary condition for the human ability to copiously and successfully predict behavior, and an ability that evolved to allow our ancestors to succeed in a complex Machiavellian social environment. One familiar account of the evolution of belief/desire attribution comes from the Social Intelligence Hypothesis, according to which human cognitive ability evolved as a result of our ancestors' complex social environment, rather than pressures of the physical environment. The pressures that come from living among others created a need to become better psychologists who are able to make better predictions of behavior, and these pressures led to the development of mental state concepts and a corresponding logic (Humphrey 1978; Jolly 1966). Behavioral and neurological evidence supports the claim that there is a correlation between sociality and cognitive abilities in a number of different taxa, and one explanation for the extraordinary social and cognitive abilities in humans stems from our success in confronting the task of better predicting and manipulating others' behavior (Byrne & Whiten 1988, Dunbar 1998). The story goes like this: In large social groups it is necessary to accurately predict the behavior of conspecifics. Having a theory of mind allows people to make more accurate predictions of behavior, because it lets a predictor understand someone's reasons for action (or the causes of action). Since theory of mind requires the postulation of theoretical entities such as belief and desire, and it requires the development of some mechanism for using these theoretical entities to make predictions of behavior, only a sophisticated cognitive agent should be able to develop it.

I have challenged the premise that a theory of mind is necessary for making accurate predictions of behavior in such environments (Andrews

2009, 2012). I argue that a theory of mind is not necessary to predict the behavior of individuals who lack a theory of mind, and is not even the predominant method used to predict adult human behavior. Rather, I argue that adult humans predict from their understanding of the person *qua* person, not from their understanding of the person as a container for beliefs and desires. We develop our models of people by using a host of heuristics, and develop our predictions from our understanding of an individual's personality traits, stereotypic qualities, past behavior, emotional state, similarity to self, and so forth. Such models might include some propositional attitudes, but they need not. Thus, in a world without a theory of mind one could predict behavior using the same general process, by appeal to the model of the target; it's just that the model would lack any reference to belief. In our world, which is rich with belief attribution, we only use predictions based on propositional attitudes when the model at hand fails. And the model only fails in unusual or unfamiliar situations.

If all this is right, then reason attribution is not an automatic process for humans, but rather a deliberate and controlled process that is appealed to only when the agent deems it necessary. Given my account of predicting behavior, I challenge the claim that an appeal to propositional attitudes is necessary for moral cognition, and I claim that the version of the Social Intelligence Hypothesis that uses theory of mind to explain the correlation between sophisticated cognitive abilities and complex social groups cannot be correct. This is because in a world without mindreading, the kind of predictions one couldn't make would be predictions in anomalous or bizarre situations. Quotidian predictions would follow directly from the model, since the model was developed on the basis of quotidian situations. It would only be behaviors that are outside the norm that one would have difficulty in predicting. It might be tempting to claim that a theory of mind is needed to predict behavior in such situations, and I think that temptation leads to truth, with one caveat. In order to predict behavior in an anomalous situation, we must first seek to understand the situation. The odd situation and the odd behavior are things that need to be construed, and the act of construal consists of formulating an explanation for the behavior. A successful explanation will resolve the affective tension that drove the need to explain the behavior in the first place, and it will include additional information that can be added to the model. In some cases, the only information that will resolve that tension will be a belief attribution, and in those cases, having a theory of mind will be needed to make a prediction of behavior. However, note that the prediction is derivative of the explanation. That is, one must first be able to explain behavior in terms of belief before being able to predict in terms of belief. Thus, predicting behavior based on the attribution of beliefs and desires relies on a prior ability to construe behavior as being caused by beliefs and desires.

These considerations drive the argument that an understanding of a society's standards or normative rules is necessary for developing a theory of mind. This is because the ability to explain behavior develops before or alongside the development of a theory of mind, and in order to explain behavior in terms of beliefs, the explainer must have recognized the situation as anomalous. That is the explainer must have recognized that the actor was behaving outside the range of normal behavior, and the construal of the situation as anomalous implies at least an implicit understanding of society's norms.

An immediate objection is to deny that the norms that are identified are moral norms, and to claim that they are instead merely conventional norms. While moral norms may be taken to be universal, authority independent, and involve concepts such as help, harm, justice, rights, and cooperation, conventional norms are not universal, authority depending, and don't involve the moral concepts. Rather, conventional norms are seen as "behavioral uniformities which coordinate interactions of individuals within social systems" (Nucci & Turiel 1978). Turiel's research on children's early recognition of conventional vs. moral violations was based on assumptions about the nature of the distinction between moral and conventional, something that moral philosophers have, despite their best efforts, not managed to come to consensus on (Kelly et al. 2007). Recent work on the moral/conventional distinction suggests that children and adults may not see a clear distinction between the two in some cases; for example, Nichols found that children, and to a lesser extent college students, responded to etiquette violations that involved disgusting behaviors in the same way they respond to moral transgressions (Nichols 2002, 2004). Given their analysis, Kelly et al. write that there is "a growing body of evidence justifying substantial skepticism about *all* the major conclusions that have been drawn from studies using the moral/conventional task" (Kelly et al. 2007).

I agree that there is reason to reject the distinction. Norms of convention may be based on the harm concept, and what appears to be a distinction may simply be two ends of a continuum. For example, the conventional norm against chewing gum might be a norm about avoiding harm, though low level or distant harm. One can tell a story about why children ought not chew gum in class: it gets all over the place, dried up balls under desks and gooey pieces stuck on the bottom of shoes. This causes harm in the sense of annoyance or disgust to the person who encounters the used pieces of gum, and might cause harm in the long run if resources that could be used to teach students are funneled into an expensive janitorial service. What causes these sorts of harms may depend on the other conventions of the society. Littering and leaving dog droppings are two behaviors that became seen as harmful in the west within recent memory, and social norms changed due to shifts in how people feel about such behaviors.

Nonetheless, there may still be some important theoretical distinction between moral and conventional rules, and there may be borderline cases that are less clear. What such a distinction may consist of takes us back to the concern I raised at the beginning of the paper; different moral theories will identify different necessary features of morality. Cleanly dividing norms into moral and conventional cannot be done outside any particular moral framework. But if the lay folk don't see a distinction, and the ethicists cannot agree on what a distinction would amount to, perhaps there is reason to think that it is nothing more than a theoretical construct.

A second concern is that my argument only requires having implicit knowledge of the social norms, and implicit knowledge is not open to the self-reflective analysis that is required on some accounts of autonomy. On my account, it is sufficient to have procedural knowledge how to act in the face of norm violations; I want to count individuals as having a degree of autonomy even if they fail to have explicit knowledge of the moral norms. As in my response to the last objection, here too I want to appeal to what people actually do. There is reason to suspect that most humans don't have explicit moral knowledge of at least some moral norms. One reason to suspect this is so comes from a series of studies on adult human moral reasoning. In these studies, Hauser and colleagues found that adult humans confabulate when providing moral justification for their response on how to respond to a trolley problem (Hauser et al. 2007). And in other studies, Jonathan Haidt found that insofar as adults make reference to moral principles, it is only *post hoc* and *ad hoc* attempts to rationalize their emotional reactions to moral situations (Haidt 2001). This result suggests that either adult humans don't have privileged access to all the norms they use when making moral judgments, or they don't use principles when making moral judgments.

To illustrate, consider a literary example. Huck Finn is a character who implicitly tracked the moral norms, even though he also knew that the legal principles of his society were in conflict with his intuitions. After lying to a man about having seen Jim, the runaway slave that Huck was floating down the Mississippi with, we hear Huck's inner soliloquy:

"They went off and I got aboard the raft, feeling bad and low, because I knowed very well I had done wrong, and I see it warn't no use for me to try to learn to do right; a body that don't get STARTED right when he's little ain't got no show—when the pinch comes there ain't nothing to back him up and keep him to his work, and so he gets beat. Then I thought a minute, and says to myself, hold on; s'pose you'd a done right and give Jim up, would you felt better than what you do now? No, says I, I'd feel bad—I'd feel just the same way I do now. Well, then, says I, what's the use you learning to do right when it's troublesome to do right and ain't no trouble to do wrong, and the wages is just the same? I was stuck. I couldn't answer that. So I reckoned I wouldn't bother no more about it, but after this always do whichever come handiest at the time." (Twain 1885, 118)

This example illustrates that a person can live according to norms without being able to offer reasons for action in terms of those norms or even without the ability to recognize them as norms.

Just as Huck Finn was able to track norms that he wasn't explicitly aware of, the great apes may also be able to follow norms (and norm violations) without requiring any metacognitive awareness of such norms. I have discussed some of the evidence about norms in ape societies elsewhere (Andrews 2009). But here let me point to some of the findings from the ape culture literature. Culture research involves collaborations between researchers who study wild apes across different sites. The typical ape behaviors are listed, and researchers indicate whether or not that behavior is seen among their community. Using this method, we know that there is great behavioral variation within species of great apes, and that this variation does not reflect only behavior on the environment, but social behavior as well.

A good example of a sophisticated social behavior that involves something that looks like group norms is the group hunting behavior of the Tai forest chimpanzees in the Ivory Coast (Boesch 2005). There are cultural differences in hunting; some chimpanzee communities do not hunt at all, even though there are monkeys in the surroundings. In other communities chimpanzees hunt alone. But in the Tai forest, chimpanzees only hunt in groups, and each group member fulfills a particular role. In a four-member hunting party, the roles are Driver (who initiates a hunt by forcing the prey to move through the trees in a single direction), Blocker (who climbs trees to herd the prey toward the Driver), Chaser (who climbs under the prey to capture it), and Ambusher (who quietly climbs in front of the prey to block escape). Roles are determined functionally and flexibly, and may change during the course of the hunt depending on the positioning of the individuals and the monkey. The chimpanzees take on the role that they ought to take on, given the situation. After the hunt, the meat is shared between the hunters depending on their role in the hunt. Drivers and Ambushers rarely capture the monkey, and they receive about three times less meat than do the captors (Boesch 2002; Boesch & Boesch-Achermann 2000). However, if an Ambusher accurately predicts the prey's behavior, and the behavior of the other hunters, then he is given just as much meat as the captors. The hunting and meat-sharing behavior looks like a group norm because the group expects that meat be shared in this way, and each individual acts to enforce the expectation.

Other ape behaviors, such as the special treatment of infants in chimpanzee societies, have been argued by primatologists to serve as what they call proto social norms (von Rohr et al. 2011). Chimpanzee infants are given deferential treatment by other community members. Newborn chimpanzees are extremely interesting to other community members, and adults will watch intently but not try to approach the new member of their group. Juveniles and older infants, however, act on their interest by trying to approach or touch the new infant, which leads the mother to act hostilely or defensively; these young chimpanzees quickly learn not to approach newborn infants. Once infants are old enough to venture away from their mother, adults are extremely tolerant of infants climbing over them and even stealing their food or tools. Adults are also reported to self-handicap when playing with infants. A violation the norms regarding infants, such as infanticide or other aggressive acts towards infants, often results in an uproar of vocal protest from adult females, and can also cause third party intervention. The authors take such behaviors to be a potential proto social norm because they involve behavioral regularities that, when violated, elicit bystander reactions, including punishment (in the sense of indignation toward the transgressor) and the expression of moral emotions.

I hope to have made the prima facie case that there can be sensitivity to the normative without the advanced cognitive capacities required to consider reasons for action. Without a theory of mind, one can have moral knowledge of the society's norms and standards in the sense of tracking such norms, and that coupled with a motivation to follow the society's norms results in a moral status that is not unlike that of many humans.

5. Ape Moral Agency

I've challenged the two central arguments connecting theory of mind to moral agency. If theory of mind develops from an understanding of moral norms, then some moral knowledge is antecedent to having a theory of mind. In addition, I have raised some worries about the consistency of holding both that most humans are moral agents and that most humans are limited in their ability to engage in the kind of normative self-government required by Korsgaard. I suggest that there are other cognitive mechanisms that could be used to engage in self-governing and self-creation.

But let me clearly state the limitations of my argument. I have not shown that great apes should be considered moral agents, but only that the prima facie case against ape moral agency, based on the idea that they lack a particular cognition capacity, is not warranted. However, this discussion has suggested a kind of upper limit to the sort of moral agency that apes might have. I have argued that one can have knowledge of the norms of society without a theory of mind, and one can have the cognitive capacities needed to change oneself without a theory of mind. Taken together, it follows that without a theory of mind one could still purposefully act to become a better group citizen, one could know that there are such moral norms, want to conform to them, and control one's behavior so as to better conform to them.

While this describes the upper level of the kind of moral agency available to a creature without a theory of mind, it still describes something that is identified as a level of morality. Without a theory of mind, one can still participate in Kohlberg's conventional stage of moral development, in which one recognizes and acts so as to follow the group's rules. While such an individual may remain there, it is only from within the perspective of a particular moral theory that we can conclude that he does not count as a moral agent.

At any rate, once at the conventional level of morality, one has some concept of acceptable and unacceptable, good and bad, right and wrong. And at this point the individual has entered the domain of the normative.

REFERENCES

Andrews, K. (2005), "Chimpanzee Theory of Mind: Looking in All the Wrong Places?", Mind and Language 20/5, 521-536.
Andrews, K. (2009), "Understanding Norms Without a Theory of Mind", Inquiry 52/5, 433-448.
Andrews, K. (in preparation). Persons as We Know Them: A Pluralistic Folk Psychology, Cambridge, MA: MIT Press.
Apperly, I.A., Robinson, E.J. (2001), "Children's Difficulties Handling Dual Identity", Journal of Experimental Child Psychology 78/4, 374-397.
Apperly, I.A., Robinson, E.J. (2002), "Five-Year-Olds' Handling of Reference and Description in the Domains of Language and Mental Representation", Journal of Experimental Child Psychology 83/1, 53-75.
Apperly, I.A., Robinson, E.J. (2003), "When Can Children Handle Referential Opacity? Evidence for Systematic Variation in 5- and 6-Year-Old Children's Reasoning About Beliefs and Belief Reports", Journal of Experimental Child Psychology 85/4, 297-311.
Bekoff, M., Pierce, J. (2009), Wild Justice: The Moral Lives of Animals, Chicago: University of Chicago Press.
Boesch, C. (2005), "Joint Cooperative Hunting Among Wild Chimpanzees: Taking Natural observations seriously", Behavioral and Brain Sciences 28/5, 692.
Boesch, C. (2002), "Cooperative Hunting Roles Among Tai Chimpanzees", Human Nature 13/1, 27-46.
Boesch, C., Boesch-Achermann, H. (2000), The Chimpanzees of the Tai Forest: Behavioural Ecology and Evolution, Oxford: Oxford University Press.
Byrne, R., Whiten, A. (eds.) (1988), Machiavellian Intelligence: Social Expertise and the Evolution of Intellect in Monkeys, Apes, and Humans, New York: Oxford University Press.

Call, J., Tomasello, M. (2008), "Does the Chimpanzee Have a Theory of Mind? 30 Years Later", Trends in Cognitive Science 12/5, 187-192.
Call, J., Tomasello, M. (1994), "The Social Learning of Tool Use by Orangutans (Pongo pygmaeus)", Human Evolution 9/4, 297-313.
Call, J., Hare, B., Carpenter, M., Tomasello, M. (2004), "'Unwilling' Versus 'Unable': Chimpanzees' Understanding of Human Intentional Action", Developmental Science 7/4, 488-498.
Carruthers, P. (2009), "How We Know Our Own Minds: The Relationship Between Mindreading and Metacognition", Behavioral and Brain Sciences 32/2, 121-182.
Christman, J. (2009), "Autonomy in Moral and Political Philosophy", in: E.N. Zalta (ed.), Stanford Encyclopedia of Philosophy, http://plato.stanford.edu/archives/spr2011/entries/autonomy-moral/.
Dunbar, R.I.M. (1998), "The Social Brain Hypothesis", Evolutionary Anthropology 6/5, 178-190.
Fraser, O.N., D. Stahl, Aureli, F. (2008), "Stress Reduction Through Consolation in Chimpanzees", Proceeding of the National Academy of the Sciences 105/25, 8557-8562.
Fraser, O.N., Aureli, F. (2008), "Reconciliation, Consolation and Postconflict Behavior Specificity in Chimpanzees", American Journal of Primatology 70, 1114-1123.
Gartstein, M.A., Rothbard, M.K. (2003), "Studying Infant Temperment Via the Revised Infant Behavior Questionnaire", Infant Behavior and Development 26/1, 64-86.
Gergely, G., Nadasdy, Z., Csibra, G., Bíró, S. (1995), "Taking the Intentional Stance at 12 Months of Age", Cognition 56/2, 165-193.
Goodall, J. (1986), The Chimpanzees of Gombe: Patterns of Behavior, Cambridge, MA: Harvard University Press.
Haidt, J. (2001), "The Emotional Dog and Its Rational Tail: A Social Intuitionist Approach to Moral Judgment", Psychological Review 108/4, 814-834.
Haksar, V. (1998), "Moral Agents", in: E. Craig (ed.), *Routledge Encyclopedia of Philosophy*, London: Routledge, 1998. Retrieved January 14, 2004, from http://www.rep.routledge.com/article/L049.
Hare, B., Call, J., Agnetta, B., Tomasello, M. (2000), "Chimpanzees Know What Conspecifics Do and Do Not See", Animal Behaviour 59/4, 771-785.

Hare, B., Call, J., Tomasello, M. (2001), "Do Chimpanzees Know What Conspecifics Know?", Animal Behaviour 61/1, 139-151.

Hauser, M., Cushman, F., Young, L., Jin, R.K.X., Mikhail, J. (2007), "A Dissociation Between Moral Judgments and Justifications", Mind and Language 22/1, 1-21.

Hirata, S. (2003), "Cooperation in Chimpanzees", Hattatsu 95, 103-111.

Humphrey, N. (1978), "Nature's Psychologists", New Scientist 29, 900-904.

Jensen, K., Call, J., Tomasello, M. (2007), "Chimpanzees Are Vengeful But Not Spiteful", Proceeding of the National Academy of the Sciences 104/32, 13046-13050.

Jolly, A. (1966), "Lemur Social Behavior and Primate Intelligence", Science 153, 501-506.

Kant, I. (1798/1977), Anthropologie in pragmatischer Hinsicht (translated as Anthropology from a Pragmatic Point of View), Carbondale: Southern Illinois Press.

Kelly, D., Stich, S., Haley, K.J., Eng, S.J., Fessler, D.M.T. (2007), "Harm, Affect, and the Moral/Conventional Distinction", Mind and Language 22/2, 117-131.

King, J.E., Figueredo, A.J. (1997), "The Five-Factor Model Plus Dominance in Chimpanzee Personality", Journal of Research in Personality 31/2, 257-271.

Kitcher, P. (2006), "Ethics and Evolution: How to Get Here from There", in: S. Macedo, J. Ober (eds.), Primates and Philosophers: How Morality Evolved, Princeton: Princeton University Press, 120-139.

Kohlberg, L. (1971), From Is to Ought: How to Commit the Naturalistic Fallacy and Get Away with It in the Study of Moral Development, New York: Academic Press.

Korsgaard, C. (2006), "Morality and the Distinctiveness of Human Action", in: S. Macedo, J. Ober (eds.), Primates and Philosophers: How Morality Evolved, Princeton: Princeton University Press, 98-119.

Lillard, A.S. (2005), Montessori: The Science Behind the Genius, New York: Oxford University Press.

McGrew, W.C. (1992), Chimpanzee Material Culture: Implications for Human Evolution, Cambridge: Cambridge University Press.

Melis, A.P., Hare, B., Tomasello, M. (2006), "Chimpanzees Recruit The Best Collaborators", Science 311, 1297-1300.

Nichols, S. (2002), "Norms With Feeling: Towards a Psychological Account of Moral Judgment", Cognition 84/2, 221-236.

Nucci, L.P., Turiel, E. (1978), "Social Interactions and the Development of Social Concepts in Preschool Children", Child Development 49/2, 400-407.

Nichols, S. (2004), Sentimental Rules: On the Natural Foundation of Moral Judgment, Oxford: Oxford University Press.

Parr, L.A. (2001), "Cognitive and Physiological Markers of Emotional Awareness in Chimpanzees (Pan troglodytes)", Animal Cognition 4/3-4, 223-229.

Parr, L.A., Hopkins, W. . (2000), "Brain Temperature Asymmetries and Emotional Perception in Chimpanzees, Pan troglodytes", Physiology and Behavior 71, 363-371.

Plooij, F.X. (1978), "Some Basic Traits of Language in Wild Chimpanzees", in: A. Lock (ed.), Action, Gesture, and Symbol: The Emergence of Language, New York: Academic Press, 11-131.

Singer, P. (2006), "Morality, Reason, and the Rights of Animals", in: S. Macedo, J. Ober (eds.), Primates and Philosophers: How Morality Evolved, Princeton: Princeton University Press, 140-160.

Smetana, J. (1981), "Preschool Children's Conceptions of Moral and Social Rules", Child Development 52, 1333-1336.

Tomasello, M., Carpenter, M. (2005), "The Emergence of Social Cognition in Three Young Chimpanzees", Monographs of the Society for Research in Child Development, 70/1, 1-131.

Tomasello, M., Davis-Dasilva, M., Camak, L., Bard, K. (1987), "Observational Learning of Tool-Use by Young Chimpanzees", Human Evolution 2/2, 175-183.

Turiel, E., Nucci, L. (1978), "Social Interactions and the Development of Social Concepts in Preschool Children", Child Development 49, 400-407.

Twain, M. (1884/1885), The Adventures of Huckleberry Finn, New York: Charles L. Webster and Company.

Uller, C. (2004), "Disposition to Recognize Goals in Infant Chimpanzees", Animal Cognition 7/3, 154-161.

van Schaik, C.P., Ancrenaz, M., Borgen, G., Galdikas, B., Knott, C.D., Singleton, I. (2003), "Orangutan Cultures and the Evolution of Material Culture", Science, 299/5603, 102-105.

von Rohr, C.R., Burkart, J.M., van Schaik, C.P. (2011), "Evolutionary Precursors of Social Norms in Chimpanzees: A New Approach", Biology and Philosophy 26/1, 1-30.
Vonk, J., Subiaul, F. (2009), "Do Chimpanzees Know what Others Can and Cannot Do? Reasoning About 'Capability'", Animal Cognition 12/2, 267-286.
de Waal, F. (1996), Good Natured: The Origins of Right and Wrong in Humans and Other Animals, Cambridge, MA: Harvard University Press.
de Waal, F. (2006), Primates and Philosophers: How Morality Evolved, Princeton: Princeton University Press.
de Waal, F. (2009), The Age of Empathy: Nature's Lessons for a Kinder society, New York: Harmony Books.
Warneken, F., Tomasello, M. (2006), "Altruistic Helping in Infants and Young Chimpanzees", Science 311/5765, 1301-1303.
Weiss, A., King, J.E., Perkins, L. (2006), "Personality and Subjective Well-Being in Orangutans (Pongo pygmaeus and Pongo abelii)", Journal of Personality and Social Psychology 90/3, 501-511.
Wellman, H.M., Cross, D., Watson, J. (2001), "Meta-Analysis of Theory-of-Mind Development: The Truth About False Belief", Child Development 72/3, 655-684.
Whiten, A., Goodall, J., McGrew, W.C., Nishida, T., Reynolds, V., Sugiyama, Y., et al. (1999), "Cultures in Chimpanzees", Nature 399/6737, 682-685.
Whiten, A. (2000), "Primate Culture and Social Learning", Cognitive Science: A Multidisciplinary Journal 24/3, 477-508.
Wright, R. (2006), "The Uses of Anthropomorphism", in: S. Macedo, J. Ober (eds.), Primates and Philosophers: How Morality Evolved, Princeton: Princeton University Press, 83-97.

8. The Nonhuman Roots of Human Morality

Evelyn B. Pluhar

1. INTRODUCTION

When we perceive others as beings with the same inherent value we claim for ourselves, not regarding them as mere ladder rungs or obstacles to our own advancement, we are taking the moral point of view. Immanuel Kant's best known version of the Categorical Imperative bids us to treat others as "ends in themselves", not solely as means for the realization of our goals (Kant 1989). Is morality the exclusive province of humans? The ability to conceive of, comprehend and act upon moral principles—moral agency—is discernible in typical mature human beings. We perceive (although we may not always follow) the imperative to consider the interests of others and how those others will be affected by our decisions. When we heed these imperatives, even when the others are not loved ones, no personal benefit is expected, and our lives might even be lost, we are not merely taking the moral point of view; we are being virtuous. Does our species stand apart from nature by exemplifying moral agency? A positive answer is often taken for granted; moreover, it is thought to place us *above*, not merely apart, from all other beings. According to this anthropocentric perspective, humans are the most, perhaps the only, morally significant beings on the planet. Nonhumans may be included to some degree in our moral deliberations, but their interests would in general be trumped by ours. However, neither science nor scientifically informed philosophy supports anthropocentrism. Biology, neurology, ethology, and psychology make it increasingly evident that the roots of moral agency, including empathy and altruism, are to be found in nonhuman animals.

Anthropocentrism is hard to overcome, however, since it is so closely connected to our kind's view of us and our place in the order of things.

Some who believe that humankind has been divinely designed for preeminence object to what they see as the devaluation of our species. Remarkably, as we shall now see, those who believe that nature alone, through a combination of chance and selection, shaped all living beings, often join their spiritually opposed brethren in asserting human preeminence.

2. Theistic[1] and Atheistic Views on Human/ Nonhuman Linkage

Resistance to any linkage of human sensibilities and behavior to nonhuman traits has often come from anthropocentric theists, who see any such suggestion as an assault on morality itself. Since Charles Darwin published *The Origin of Species* in 1859, many have fought the theory of evolution on moralistic grounds. Dr. Braswell Deen, Chief Justice of the Georgia Court of Appeals in the United States, has colorfully expressed this opinion: "This monkey mythology of Darwin is the cause of permissiveness, promiscuity, pills, prophylactics, perversions, pregnancies, abortions, pornography, pollution, poisoning, and the proliferation of crimes of all types." (Lynch 2007) Parents sharing Deen's view genuinely fear that teaching evolution in classrooms will degrade and corrupt their offspring.

Many of us find such fears misguided and misinformed: one would be hard-pressed to find condom-equipped, pornography-addicted, polluting, poisoning gangs of (non)human primates swelling the crime statistics. To be fair, however, one must note that one of Darwin's most ardent supporters, Thomas Huxley, helped to fuel such ideas by comparing humans striving to be moral with gardeners ever vigilantly pulling noxious weeds from their flowerbeds. Morality is a constant battle with nature, in his view: "Let us understand, once for all, that the ethical progress of society depends, not on imitating the cosmic process, still less in running away from it, but in combating it." (Huxley 2004) Primatologist Frans de Waal (2006) attributes what he terms "the Veneer Theory" to evolutionists like Huxley: only a razor-thin layer of civilization separates humans from their brutal animal natures. Ironically, some theists share the view that moral-

---

1 | For the purposes of this paper, "theism" refers to affirmation of the existence of an omnipotent, omniscient, omnibenevolent creator of the universe.

ity is all too easily subverted by amoral and immoral urges, fearing that evolutionary ideas serve as excuses for unbridled selfishness. Worse, they see the scientific account of human origins as an attack on theism itself. What is to keep one's basest impulses in check if divine retribution is seen as a fairy tale?

Scientifically informed theists, by contrast, see no conflict between evolutionary theory and the divine creation of the universe. They are not disturbed by the notion of literal kinship with all other life forms, seeing in such kinship confirmation of divine purpose. Philosopher and theologian Andrew Linzey (2009) articulates this position eloquently. Other philosophers and scientists take the weight of scientific evidence as powerful support for a contemporary argument from design, holding that what is known about the origin of the universe and the evolution of life forms is best explained by the hypothesis of a vastly intelligent, powerful creator. Philosopher Richard Swinburne (2004) appeals to inductive logic and physics, noting that the conditions present at the "Big Bang" had to have fallen in a very narrow range for universal expansion, and eventually human-style life, to have been possible. "The Anthropic Principle" holds that initial conditions were precisely what life, including human life, required to develop (Barrow & Tipler 1986). Astrophysicist Stephen Hawking states that, "If the rate of expansion one second after the Big Bang had been smaller by even one part in a hundred thousand million million, the universe would have recollapsed before it ever reached it's present size (Hawking 1988, 121-122)." Unlike many scientists, Hawking was earlier willing to go out on a theological limb in the face of such numbers: "It would be very difficult to explain why the universe should have begun in just this way, except as the act of a God who intended to create beings just like us" (Hawking 1988, 127).[2] (The reaction of physicists like Leonard Susskind, who rejects appeals to supernatural agency, is more typical: "Is it any wonder that the Anthropic Principle makes many physicists very uncomfortable?" (Susskind 2006, 8)

Theistic Author Dinesh D'Souza (2009), like Swinburne, also sees design at work rather than chance: "The universe is tailor-made for life on earth." Geneticist Francis Collins, leader of the research team that decoded the human genome, agrees in finding this compelling evidence for divine creation. Like Swinburne, Collins appeals to inductive logic. In a de-

---

2 | As we shall shortly see, he has recently retracted this view.

bate with atheist and evolutionary biologist Richard Dawkins (Van Biema 2006), Collins cites the literally astronomical numbers at the time of the Big Bang, adding, "If you are willing to consider the possibility of a designer, this becomes a rather plausible explanation for what is otherwise an exceedingly implausible event—namely our existence." (Collins 2006, 52)

Dawkins counters that one gets nowhere by trying to explain the "vastly improbable" by invoking an allegedly even more improbable God (Van Biema 2006). Moreover, a purely scientific theory accounting for our existence might turn out to be true. He and some astrophysicists (e.g. Dyson & Goldsmith 2004) suggest the possibility of a "multiverse" consisting of a great many universes, filled with "bangs", most of which would fizzle because of the wrong gravitational constant. Perhaps we simply got lucky. Hawking now agrees with this view, writing with his co-author Mlodinow that if the multiverse possibility is true, "our universe seems to be one of many" (Hawking & Mlodinow 2010, 164). Collins' reply to the multiverse argument is that there is no evidence for this admittedly speculative proposal. Absent any evidence for multiple universes, Occam's Razor bids us to offer the simplest explanation required to account for this universe: the God hypothesis. Dawkins believes that Occam's razor cuts his way instead, eliminating any recourse to a *deus ex machina* (Van Biema 2006). Hawking now joins Dawkins in holding that the God hypothesis is superfluous: "It is not necessary to invoke God to light the blue touch paper and set the universe going" (Hawking & Mlodinow 2010, 180). As for the Anthropic Principle, all the humans made possible by such a perfectly fine-tuned Big Bang can be accounted for in purely scientific terms: "Only a very few [universes] would allow creatures like us to exist. [...] Although we are puny and insignificant on the scale of the cosmos, this makes us in a sense the lords of creation-" (Hawking & Mlodinow 2010, 9)

Are we indeed? It is fascinating that both scientifically informed theists such as Collins and D'Souza and atheists such as Dawkins, while they part company theologically, agree on a very key matter: we humans stand out as the only moral beings on our planet. Collins (2006) argues that "a moral sense" appears to be unique to humans, rejecting the view that a purely evolutionary explanation can be given of altruism. D'Souza agrees:

"We humans—atheists no less than religious believers—inhabit two worlds. The first is the evolutionary world; let's call it Realm A. Then there is the next world; let's call this Realm B. The remarkable fact is that we, who live in Realm A, nevertheless have the standards of Realm B built into our natures. This is the voice of morality, which makes us dissatisfied with our selfish natures and continually hopeful that we can rise above them." (D'Souza 2009, 182)

Dawkins comes to the same conclusion as his theistic opponents. At the end of *The Selfish Gene*, after arguing his thesis that every living being is driven to preserve its genes, he finds that human animals have it in them to be exceptions: "We, alone on earth, can rebel against the tyranny of our selfish replicators." (Dawkins 2006, 201) When Dawkins first wrote this in 1976, he was accused of being inconsistent with what readers took to be his biological determinism. He has kept the sentence while adding an explanatory endnote in his 30th Anniversary Edition, arguing that our complex brains allow us to override our genetic drive, for example by using contraception (ibid., 332). Why not a morality override as well? Thomas Huxley expressed the same view nearly a century earlier, when he said we had to rip the rank weeds out of the garden as fast as they poked through the soil if we are to progress morally (Huxley 2004).

As biology, psychology, and ethology reveal, the human "exceptionalism" expressed by these theists and nontheists alike is more mistaken than correct. Let us take a closer look at the "garden" anthropocentrists believe themselves to inhabit. In what follows, we will consider examples of nonhuman animal behavior drawn from various sources. One such source is "narrative ethology". As Bekoff and Pierce (2009) note, these accounts by animal behavior experts rise above anecdotal evidence because they are shaped by years of informed interpretation. Examples from field settings, confined areas (e.g., zoos), and laboratory settings will be considered. Some anecdotal evidence will also be included, however, drawn from personal experience and from publicly documented occurrences. Given the weight of the evidence from all of these different sources, it is plausible to attribute altruism and empathy to nonhumans.

3. The Evolutionary Basis of Altruism

As many critics of Social Darwinism have pointed out (e.g., de Waal 2006; Hauser 2007[3]), those who took evolution to mean that "survival of the fittest" requires ruthless struggle against competing life forms were simply mistaken. They imagined a jungle "red of tooth and claw" where the strongest eliminated the weakest. Leaping from that which allegedly "is" to that which "ought" to be, Social Darwinists embraced the "might makes right" maxim. Friedrich Nietzsche is the most eloquent spokesperson of this view: "The weak and the failures shall perish: first principle of *our* love of man. And they shall even be given every possible assistance. What is more harmful than any vice? Active pity for all the failures and all the weak: Christianity." (Nietzsche 1961, 570)

Such views can take no comfort from Darwinian theory. "Fitness" for individuals is measured in reproductive success. For beings living in groups, as humans and many nonhumans do, such success requires the stability that nurturing, bonding, cooperation, adaptability, and reciprocity make possible. Altruistic behavior, behavior directed towards the care of others, has crucial survival value.

There was confusion on this score for many decades, however; biologists wondered how a trait that would benefit the group could also directly benefit an altruistic member, particularly if the individual sacrificed him or herself for another. How can this be reproductive fitness? Richard Dawkins' (2006) answer to this puzzle is his "selfish genes" hypothesis. Well below the level of conscious motivation, genes push to replicate themselves in other living beings. Helping, saving, even sacrificing one's own life for one's biological kin, perpetuates those genes.

The selfish gene hypothesis has explanatory value. De Waal (2009) writes that parental care, the ultimate in perpetuating one's genes, is probably the foundation of empathy and altruism. Without concern, car-

---

3 | On August 21, 2010 Hauser was found guilty of academic misconduct by Harvard University (Wade 2010). Three of the articles he published in recent years were accused of containing some fabricated data. Dr. Hauser redid the experiments for two of the questioned publications and was able to replicate the results. He retracted one 2002 article in the journal Cognition when he could not replicate the results. In this paper, I have not relied on that or the other initially disputed research in any way.

ing, helping, the children, the social unit, and ultimately the species die. Parental instincts push progenitors exactly in the direction their genes would "want" them to go, even at great sacrifice to their own wellbeing.[4] Dawkins' hypothesis would also account for the fact that bonds formed with others tend to correlate with our genetic closeness to them. The outstanding example would be children. The bonds usually become more attenuated as relatedness decreases. We retain a bond, however weakened compared to that with immediate family, to our species. Animals usually have stronger bonds with conspecifics than they do with individuals of other species. Preference for one's own family and group has deep, albeit alterable, roots.

Nonetheless, social animals will often display caring behavior towards those not related to them. How can this be accounted for in evolutionary terms? Another part of the explanation (but not the whole part, as I shall argue below) is provided by the notion of reciprocity. This is compatible with the selfish gene hypothesis. Caring, generous group members tend to receive rewards from those they help, which in turn enhances their own survival chances. De Waal reports, for example, that a chimpanzee who spontaneously grooms another chimpanzee is very likely to be gifted with tasty leafy branches from the beneficiary later that day (de Waal, 2009). There is no reason to assume Machiavellian intent on the part of the groomer; fortune—really, nature—favors the generous. Chimpanzees who are helped by another to secure food are much more likely to share the food with the helper than they are to share if they procured the food on their own (de Waal 1989).[5] Social non-primates reciprocate as well, includ-

---

4 | Documentary film director Luc Jacquet spent a year in Antarctica with his crew recording the life cycle of the Emperor Penguins (Jacquet 2005). The lengths to which parents of an egg (which must be protected from temperatures as low as 128 degrees below zero Fahrenheit if it is to hatch) will go to help their offspring survive are astounding. Mothers and fathers take turns protecting their young, forgoing food for as long as six months while the other makes the dangerous trek to obtain food for regurgitation upon return. Emperor Penguins are beyond model parents.

5 | While chimpanzee society is replete with reciprocally beneficial acts, it would be a mistake to conclude that chimpanzees live in primarily peaceful, harmonious groups. See *Chimpanzee Politics* (de Waal 2007). The male drive for dominance has brutal consequences, including what we humans call murder when

ing dolphins (Conner et al. 1999) and blood-sharing vampire bats (Hauser 2007). Bekoff and Pierce document numerous instances of reciprocity in different species (2009). Humans familiar with cats or dogs can easily supply their own examples. Cats or dogs will groom one another if they are friends and do each other different favors as well. My husband and I had set out large plates of salad festooned on top with vegetarian "steak" strips. One of our feline companions, Lindi, jumped on the dining room table while we were bringing other food from the kitchen. When we returned, she was not only tearing into the strips; she was throwing down some pieces to her gobbling brothers under the table—quite a testimonial to the company producing the fake steak!

Reciprocity and genetic kinship do help to explain the evolutionary advantage of altruism, but they are not the whole explanation. Many human and nonhuman animals will help others, even give their lives for others, when no reciprocity is possible and no kinship is present. De Waal relates that instances of altruism among chimpanzees are very numerous. One example concerns a disabled elderly chimpanzee, named Peony, in a captive troop. When her arthritis was so severe that she could hardly walk or climb, unrelated younger chimps would help boost her up or run ahead to draw water from a spigot into their mouths, hurrying back to fill Peony's mouth (de Waal 2009). Bekoff and Pierce (2009) report a similar situation among captive chimpanzees that was documented at a conference on chimpanzee cognition in 2007. "Knuckles" suffered from cerebral palsy. The others, unrelated as well as related, helped the disabled male to survive and treated him very gently, quite unlike the other healthy males in the troop. He was even regularly groomed by the alpha male. Washoe, the first signing chimpanzee, once ran across an electrified fence separating the group from a moat to save a drowning chimpanzee who had accidentally fallen in. Chimpanzees are instinctively afraid of water, but this did not stop Washoe (de Waal 2009). Wild chimpanzees have also been observed repeatedly helping disabled troop members. No reciprocity could be expected and no kinship was required for assistance to be given.

---

we do it. Bonobos, by contrast, are far less aggressive, peaceful primates. Not a single violent attack within Bonobo society has ever been documented (de Waal 1997, Dreifus 2010). Bonobos are our closest relatives, and Chimpanzees are not far behind. De Waal, noting the obvious parallels to both in human society, calls us "the bipolar ape" (2009).

This behavior has not just been observed in apes. It also crosses species lines, not infrequently in favor of our own species. We are well aware of the many instances in which dolphins have saved humans, for no apparent benefit of their own. Just before the Indonesia tsunami of 2004, fishermen by the shore related that dolphins surrounded their boat and pushed it to safer water (Notebook 2006). Sometimes they risk their lives to help: humans have even been protected from sharks by dolphins forming a protective escort around them. One of the most amazing accounts involved three Ethiopian lions rescuing a kidnapped girl. Men abducted the twelve-year-old and held her for days, assaulting her with the intent to force her into marriage. The lions came out of the forest and chased the men away. They then stood guard around the girl, facing outward, until rescuers came. Police Sgt. Wondimu Wedago stated, "They just stood guard until we found her and then they just left her like a gift and went back into the forest" (Police 2005).

Companion animals have also put their lives at risk to help members of their human families. In another case in Colorado, a four-and-a-half pound Chihuahua saved a one-year-old baby from a rattlesnake bite (Chihuahua 2007). Zoey was with the adults on the porch watching the baby play close by in the yard. Suddenly she sprinted from the porch into the grass, between the baby and a rock. The rattler on the rock was in the midst of striking at the child, but Zoey took the bite instead. She nearly died but was saved after quick action by her grateful family. Jet, another black Labrador retriever, also saved his six-year-old friend Kevin Haskell by interjecting himself between the child and a striking rattlesnake. The Haskell family spent thousands of dollars to save Jet, who fortunately did survive (de Waal 2009). These are just two examples among many that could be given.

Nonhuman animals of other species have also been beneficiaries of surprising altruistic action. Several instances of dogs risking their lives by taking actions that resulted in rescuing others from death have been documented. The home of the Gardner family caught fire in 2006 due to faulty Christmas lights. The parents and four children escaped the blazing home, as did Casey, a black Labrador retriever. Casey, however, charged back into the burning house, running from room to room. Firefighters saw Casey discover Cindy, a very large elderly cat, cowering in one of the rooms. Casey nudged Cindy out of the room and into rescuing arms. Mrs. Gardner told reporters, "It was heart-wrenching to lose our home. But Casey is a hero. Thanks to him, we still have Cindy" (Pet Pals 2007).

Accounts of wild nonhuman animals aiding members of other species also abound. An elephant matriarch in KwaZula-Natal rescued a group of captive antelopes by undoing all of the latches on the gate of their pen, permitting them to escape (Bekoff & Pierce 2009). A drowning elderly dog was spontaneously saved by a wild seal, who pushed the dog to safety on the shore (de Waal 2009). In the following account, a different wild seal is the beneficiary of another's aid. On September 3, 2010, Hurricane Earl was raging across Assateague Island, North Carolina. The wild ponies inhabiting the island survived the storm by hunkering down, but there are other species living there as well, including harbor seals and deer. Wildlife writer and biological researcher Robert Gratson, a Pennsylvania State University student, was on the island for a twenty-four-hour study on beach erosion. Trapped by the storm, with gusts up to 60 mph, and forced to spend the night in his battered tent near the woods, he observed a young harbor seal on the wind side of a sand dune, being pummeled by the high winds, sand, and rain, apparently separated from the mother. The waves were as tall as houses as far out as one could see. Out of the woods came a wild Sika buck, who trotted up to the seal and stood by him or her for five minutes. Then, amazingly, Gratson saw the buck bed down besides the small animal, laying his head over the seal's body. The two stayed together until the high winds finally ceased. When the storm abated, the buck got up and walked back to the bush, and the harbor seal moved inland. The Sika deer would have been safer in the bush during the storm's assault, but instead he came out and wrapped himself around the little seal until it was safe to leave his temporary bedmate.[6]

We humans will also rise to the occasion by helping unrelated others who cannot be expected to return the favor, sometimes to the point of death. One famous example is "The Saint of Auschwitz", Father Maximilian Kolbe. The Catholic Priest was imprisoned in 1941 with other Poles in the notorious Nazi death camp. When one man disappeared, the guards selected 10 men at random to be starved to death, presumably to deter other escape attempts. One of the ten begged for mercy, crying out for his family's need for him at home. Father Kolbe volunteered to take his place, and the guards agreed. The men were beaten, starved, and dehydrated,

---

6 | Personal communication with Robert Gratson (14 September 2010).

with only three still living after three weeks. Father Kolbe was one of them. The guards, eager to clear the starvation bunker for future inmates, killed the survivors by injecting carbolic acid into their veins (Kolbe 2010).

So very many other examples could be given, but here is another remarkable account. In January 2005, a man attempting suicide parked his vehicle on train tracks in Glendale, California (Truck Driver 2005). A last minute change of mind led him to hurl himself from the car, but others were not so fortunate. Two commuter trains derailed, trapping several in wrecked cars flaming from spilled diesel fuel. A truck driver on his regular route stopped to help. Dean Jaeschke was the only one willing to aid one badly trapped commuter; the flames were overtaking the railroad car and explosion was imminent. Jaeschke fought to free the man, who begged not to be left to burn alive. He was able to pull him out in time. Although the man's injuries were too severe for survival, he was able to thank his rescuer for being spared a horrible death. Jaeschke could well have joined him in the same death.

Kolbe and Jaeschke are exemplars of human altruism. Dinesh D'Souza explains this and countless other examples of human heroism as "Realm B" action, the God-given possibility of transcending the evolution-driven "Realm A". Richard Dawkins casts such selflessness in a purely secular light, proclaiming that we humans alone are able to rebel against our selfish genes, our superior minds allowing us to rise above their dictates. However, as we know, there is ample evidence that nonhumans can also "rebel"; how can one account for this, when neither kinship nor reciprocity are in play?

Frans de Waal does not find this puzzling at all. Evolution accounts for the perpetuation of individuals who nurture their young and help group members; they tend to be supported by others participating in a network of mutual benefit. However, the result of evolutionary forces—the ability to recognize and respond positively to the needs of others—predisposes these individuals to respond to strangers as well, even when the helpers cannot be expected to benefit from, and may even be harmed by, their own generosity. Presuming that altruism must be limited to kin and reciprocal expectations because that is how the trait has arisen, de Waal writes, is what he calls "the Beethoven error". Beethoven, after all, wrote the most magnificent compositions in an abominably filthy, chaotically cluttered Viennese apartment, proving that "there is not much of a connection between the process of natural selection and its many products" (de Waal

2006, 58). To put it another way, assuming otherwise is, quite simply, committing the genetic fallacy.

We have seen that there is copious evidence that nonhumans sometimes act altruistically, even at great cost to themselves. We have also seen that evolutionary theory is not in conflict with this evidence. Now we must look more closely at the necessary conditions for such behaviors. Dawkins has suggested that well-developed cerebral cortexes enable humans to overrule their selfish genes, as happens in acts of selfless altruism. Not only does this proposal leave nonhuman altruism wholly unaccounted for; it does not square with the experiences of humans who have survived their own altruism. Those experiences, documented in survivor accounts, suggest that reason was not the primary motivator. Empathy, literally "feeling into", the ability to imaginatively project oneself into another's situation, is a necessary and sometimes sufficient condition for altruistic behavior. Dean Jaeschke, the fifty-year-old truck driver who risked his life to pull a man from wreckage about to ignite in flames, explained that he himself was rescued from a burning vehicle at age 17 (Truck Driver 2005). Jaeschke never forgot the rescuer who risked his own life to rescue him. He expressed gratitude for his life, despite the fact that he was so badly burned that forty reconstructive operations were required. Recalling the day of the train derailment, Jaeschke related, "Everybody was saying, 'Get out of there. That thing's going to go up.' I kind of ignored that. I've been through that." He flashed back to the time when he was literally in that same trap as the man he pulled out. He could no more leave the man to burn to death than his own rescuer had. One need not have gone through the same situation as another to empathize with the other, of course, but a clearer case of empathy motivating a heroically altruistic act would be difficult to find.

Empathy, and emotions in general, are keystones of moral behavior, including self-sacrificial altruism. Although, as we shall see, reasoning is also required for full moral agency, it is not the prime factor. There is growing evidence that nonhumans can and do empathize as well. The altruistic nonhuman behaviors documented above are likely grounded in emotional capacities they share with us.

4. EMPATHY OR ANTHROPOMORPHISM?

How can we determine if nonhumans or very young humans are motivated to help others by empathy when they cannot verbally communicate with us? We make inferences on the basis of nonverbal behaviors and physiological (especially neurological) indicators present when we ourselves are motivated by empathy. We are reasoning by analogy, as each one of us does whenever we draw conclusions about another's conscious state.[7] There is no difference in kind between conclusions thus drawn about other humans and those drawn about nonhumans. Making that imperceptible leap from immediate awareness of one's own emotions and thoughts to recognition of another's is not only salvation from solipsism; it is the basis of caring and ultimately of moral agency.

There are two approaches to the scientific study of empathy in nonhumans, and very young humans as well: (1) controlled laboratory experiments and (2) field observations, either in the wild or in semi-confined settings. We will look at three examples from the laboratory and two others from the field, all concerning nonhumans. As will be seen, such examples are open to more than one interpretation.

Many laboratory studies have been done on possible empathy in nonhumans. Some of these experiments are very distressing to those of us who empathize with the subjects. Bekoff and Pierce (2009) comment on one such experiment, published by psychologist Dale Langford (Langford et al. 2006). Adult mice were paired, then one was injected with acetic acid in the presence of the other. In the control group, the injected mouse's lab partner did not witness the former's pain. The mice who watched their

---

7 | The argument from analogy to other minds has been attacked as a very weak inductive argument on the grounds that one has only one's own case to infer from. However, this attack treats two-case inductive analogy as if it were an inductive generalization. Generalizing from but one case is far too small a sample, but this is not what one is doing when one bases a conclusion on a comparison of two cases. When the two cases are highly relevantly similar, the inference can be justified. Behaviorally and physiologically, another human is overwhelmingly similar in these respects to oneself. The same holds for members of many other species, apart from largely cosmetic differences. (It must be noted that the argument from analogy is a logical reconstruction, not a historical account. In infancy, one's experiences quite simply include others. Analysis comes quite a bit later.)

counterparts writhe in burning pain showed much more sensitivity to pain when they themselves were injected than did the mice who did not witness the initial experiment. They writhed far more than the mice in the control group did. In fact, they became more sensitive to pain in other contexts as well. In an earlier set of experiments, this time on rats, psychologist Russell Church (1959) put the animals in neighboring cages. When one rat pressed a lever to obtain food, a severe electrical shock was immediately delivered to the hapless rat in the adjacent cage. Rats who observed their writhing, screaming neighbors soon began to forgo food rather than initiating further shocks.[8] In a third experiment, also involving rats, the animals were taught that a suspended Styrofoam block would be lowered whenever they pressed a lever (Hauser 2007). When neither reward nor punishment followed pressing or not pressing the lever, the rats ceased to press. For half of the rats in the study, the Styrofoam block was then replaced with a live rat in a harness suspended in the air. Predictably, the suspended rat squealed and struggled. The rats at the controls voluntarily pressed the lever to lower the distressed rat to the floor, even though no reward or punishment for them was anticipated.

Let us now turn to two examples of possibly empathetic behavior in nonhumans drawn from narrative ethology in semi-confined settings.

Frans de Waal discusses an event that received worldwide coverage. In 1996 at the Brookfield Zoo in Illinois, a three-year-old child fell over a railing into the gorilla enclosure and knocked himself unconscious. The crowd gasped and the child's mother screamed. One female, Binti Jua, with her own baby clinging to her back, came up to the immobile child, lifting him carefully into her arms. Warning off other approaching gorillas, she carried the small boy to one of the gates through which animal attendants would exit and enter. She handed the boy over to a waiting attendant (de Waal 1996), then quietly returned to her group.

Our second case involves Kuni, a Bonobo captive at the Twycross Zoo in England. Frans de Waal witnessed Kuni apparently trying to save a starling who had flown into a glass wall (de Waal 2009). Kuni went outside her enclosure and picked up the immobile starling, trying to put her on her feet. When the bird did not respond, Kuni tossed her into the air. When

---

8 | An often-cited similar experiment was done on rhesus monkeys (Wechkin et al. 1964). The monkeys starved themselves, one as long as 12 days, rather than shocking monkeys in adjoining cages.

the bird simply fell to the ground, the Bonobo picked her up again and took her to the tallest tree in the enclosure. She then spread the starling's wings and released her, but the bird simply fell to the ground. Following these events, Kuni appeared to stand guard over the starling, preventing other curious young Bonobos from approaching.

Each case above features telling responses to the distress or disability of others. The mice in Langford's study were physiologically changed by witnessing other mice being injected with acetic acid, becoming themselves more sensitive to painful stimuli. The researchers concluded that this was evidence of empathy in those mice: they "felt with" the victims in neighboring cages. The rats who refused food to avoid giving painful shocks to other rats apparently recognized the latter animals' pain and its correlation to their food seeking; they then stopped seeking food. The rats who chose to lower their suspended conspecific to the floor by pressing a lever that brought them no reward at all apparently recognized the latter's distress, responding with helping behavior. Binti Jua treated the unconscious child she rescued with great gentleness, even as she growled at some other gorillas to stay away. Her maternal behavior seemed to reflect her understanding of the vulnerable child's situation. Kuni the Bonobo not only protected a stunned starling; she tried to help the bird to fly by taking her to a tall tree and gently spreading her wings. This appears to be empathy on a high level, as de Waal (2009) points out, given that Bonobos do not fly. Kuni had seen many birds in the zoo and apparently knew what normal behavior for them was. When this attempt failed, Kuni's protection of the fallen starling from other curious Bonobos strongly suggests her recognition of the bird's helplessness.

Not so, say many critics. Social and natural scientists who resist the attribution of empathy to nonhumans have charged those who think otherwise with anthropomorphism. Indeed, many will resist the attribution of any mental or emotional state to nonhumans, arguing that we are simply projecting our own psyches without justification onto the demonstrably nonhuman world. This charge is sometimes grounded by the presumption that a nonhuman animal "mind", if any, is unknowable to us. Bernard Rollin relates the following conversation with an animal researcher: "Talking about whether animals feel pain is like talking about the existence of God." (Rollin 1989, 23) Since one cannot *directly* know that anyone beside oneself has a mind, such a presumption puts one on the fast track to solipsism. The charge of anthropomorphism is nonetheless a serious one. We are obliged to consider competing explanations and to take care that we are not leaping to an all-too-anthropocentric conclusion.

Let us consider alternative explanations for our examples above, taking the laboratory experiments first. The painfully sensitized mice in Langford's study (2006) might have had a purely physiological response to what they witnessed. Do we know that they grasped the pain of the other mice? The rats who refused food to stop the shocking of neighboring rats might have felt discomfort triggered by the sights and sounds next door. Could they have been performing a mechanical action to alleviate their own discomfort without understanding the other rats' plights? Likewise, choosing to lower a screaming, struggling rat to the ground by pressing a lever might be construed as stress alleviation for the lever-presser rather than as an empathetic response.

Note that these alternative explanations do not avoid the attribution of awareness in some form to the nonhumans. Diehard critics of nonhuman animal consciousness might still find them anthropomorphic. Those willing to acknowledge stress or discomfort responses but not empathy could accept these alternative explanations. How do these alternatives compare to the empathy hypothesis? In the case of the Langford mice study, the evidence does seem to fall short of establishing empathy. The physiological changes in the sensitized mice are undeniable, but the psychology that might be involved is speculative. The other two experiments are harder to explain away. Is forgoing food to avoid shocking another rat or lowering a squealing suspended rat to the floor better explained as alleviation of the rat's own stress rather than as an empathetic response? The rats in these experiments acted as young human children would (and, one hopes, at least some adults). We attribute some level of empathy to those children. (We will shortly consider some studies of infant and toddler empathy and further discuss what researchers call "emotional contagion"). Moreover, forcing the choice between the stress alleviation and empathy hypotheses is a false dilemma. Self-reflective adults know that the stress and discomfort we feel when another is hurt results from our recognition of the other's distress. Why should the preverbal children and our rats be any different? Some very small children will run away from another's distress, presumably alleviating their own stress rather than feeling the need to assist, but others will actively seek to comfort and help. The helping babies, like the mice and the rats, may not be able to tell us their feelings, but we do not deny that they are empathizing. (Even the children who just try to escape could be empathizing. Empathy is necessary but not sufficient for sympathy.) It is consistent, not anthropomorphic, to explain the rats' helping behaviors in the same way.[9]

Let us now turn to the two examples from narrative ethology. One of those cases, Binti Jua's rescue of the three-year-old human child, is open to an alternative explanation. Bekoff and Pierce relate the following backstory (2009). The female gorilla was raised by humans in captivity and had to be taught how to care for her own baby. The keepers modeled nurturing behavior to her by, among other means, giving her stuffed toys and training her to treat them gently. They also taught her to bring her stuffed toys to them. Perhaps Binti Jua was doing a learned exercise, confusing the unconscious child for a new toy, when she gently brought him to staff at the gate. Growling at the other gorillas to keep away from the child might have stemmed from proprietary motives. In this particular case, the training explanation is at least as plausible as the empathy hypothesis.

However, it is much more difficult to interpret the Kuni case in a non-empathetic manner. What evidence do we have for anthropomorphism here? Critics going back to the times of psychological behaviorism's founding would reply that one should follow Lloyd Morgan's "Canon": one ought not to invoke a higher faculty to explain behavior when a lower one will do (Morgan 1894). Do not attribute animal behavior to thoughts or emotions when an appeal to instinct or conditioned responses will do. The problem is that Kuni's behavior with the stunned starling cannot reasonably be construed in these ways. The behavior of Binti Jua could possibly be accounted for in terms of conditioning, but Kuni was not responding in terms of any known instinct, nor had she been conditioned to react in the way that she did. Her actions were a surprise to the observer at Kuni's zoo (de Waal himself). The same was true of the mice and rat researchers.

As Rollin (1989) has pointed out, the assumption that anything more than conditioned responses or instincts—mental states—may only be at-

---

9 | This is especially warranted given the abundance of evidence supporting the attribution of significant intelligence to rats (Angier 2007). Laboratory researchers report that the rats apparently dream just as we do, solve complex problems in creative ways, come when called, show affection, play, and even display metacognition (the ability to know when they know or do not know).

tributed to humans[10] flies in the face of evolutionary theory. In terms of physiology and behaviors, we see a continuity of traits; should it not be the same with mental attributes? There is no reason to assume that such attributes appeared without precedent of any kind and every reason to assume otherwise. Moreover, as Rollin notes, the vast amount of research done using nonhumans to model pain, fear, anger, learned helplessness, depression, maternal deprivation, social isolation, etc., obviously presumes that the nonhumans forced to undergo these experiments are similar to us in these respects.[11] It is ironic indeed that many of those who dismiss ethological interpretations attributing thoughts and emotions to nonhumans as "anthropomorphic" are the same ones who engage in invasive, painful psychological research (Rollin 1989).

---

10 | This was itself taboo in the heyday of behaviorism, which regarded appeals to mental states as inherently untestable.

11 | University of Wisconsin psychologist Harry Harlow's two decades of experiments on young rhesus monkeys resulted in numerous publications about maternal deprivation, abuse, and long-term isolation (Harlow & Mears 1979). In these experiments over the years, models for psychosis were created, along with models for abusive mothers. Young rhesus monkeys whose only mother figures were wire models designed to shock them or perforate them with spines when they sought to embrace them predictably displayed frightened and deeply depressed behavior. Female monkeys who were raised in total isolation, then forcibly impregnated, had their babies taken from them. When the mothers were later introduced to their young offspring, they were at best unresponsive and at worst brutally abusive. The experiments were from the beginning justified by Harlow as being highly applicable to human mother-child relationships. The results were of course predictable, given the strong similarity between the species. Philosopher Michael Allen Fox (1986) defended these and other experiments as beneficial to humans, but within months of the publication of his book, he retracted it and became an antivivisectionist. He revealed that his defense of Harlow's research shocked him so much, upon reflection, that he wholeheartedly rejected his earlier views (Fox 1987). I have argued elsewhere (Pluhar 2006) that there is no logical or moral justification for performing experiments on nonhumans that we would deem unethical to perform on humans. The continuity we see between nonhuman and human mental traits, contrary to the charge of anthropomorphism, bids us to be consistent as well as empathetic in our treatment of humans and nonhumans.

Frans de Waal has more recently made the same case against the charge of anthropomorphism. He argues that behavioral science is torn between what he calls "cognitive parsimony" and "evolutionary parsimony" (de Waal 1999, 2006). Morgan's Canon dictates cognitive parsimony: invoke the lower capacity in preference to the higher one. Evolutionary parsimony holds that when genetically close species behave in similar ways, their mental states are probably also similar. Evolutionary parsimony is exactly what Darwin's theory would lead one to expect, and it provides elegant rather than forced interpretations of nonhuman behaviors. de Waal lodges a counter-charge against those who charge ethologists with anthropomorphism: they are guilty of "anthropodenial".

5. From Emotional Contagion to Sympathy and Fairness

Distancing ourselves as best we can from both anthropomorphism and anthropodenial, let us look at the nature of empathy in various species. In humans and nonhumans alike, the origin of empathy is to be found in "emotional contagion": the emotional state of one individual excites a matching state in another (Hatfield et al 1993). When one baby in a roomful of babies begins to cry, he is soon joined by others, for example; the same occurs in a roomful of puppies. We can find the physiological basis of emotional contagion in the recently discovered phenomenon of neural mirroring, pioneered by a group of neurophysiologists led by Giocomo Rizzolatti (1996, 1999). The research has been replicated in both monkeys and human beings; other species will presumably be tested as well. Remarkably, when we watch another person reaching for a glass, the areas in our own brains correlated with that activity are activated. If we are shown a video of another person having a painful experience, the pain mechanisms in our own brain are stimulated. This could well help to explain the physiological sensitization of Langford's mice. As former President of the United States Bill Clinton once famously said, "I feel your pain!".

Frans de Waal explains that emotional contagion is not necessarily sympathetic in nature; instead of being moved to comfort a distressed individual, one might seek to remove oneself from the situation in order to ease one's own distress (2006). A child confronted by another crying child might respond by giving the other child a hug or he might run to his mother for solace and relief from distress. (Adults are no different. Some actively comfort the afflicted while others remove themselves from individuals whose pain causes them to feel uncomfortable.) Psychological researcher Carolyn Zahn-Waxler set out to determine if human children barely over a year old were able to exhibit sympathetic, comforting responses to distress (1992). Family members in households who agreed to participate in the study pretended to cry or choke. The young children in the family were not only themselves distressed; they did what they could to help and comfort the actors. One unanticipated outcome of the study, however, was that household pets showed the same responses as the babies!

Those of us who have enjoyed the companionship of cats or dogs in the household are not surprised by this result. Our nonhuman companions are at least as comforting and concerned as our human family members are when we cry, get hurt, or are sick. Their eyes have the same look of worry as human eyes. (My husband and I routinely tell each other to "Tell her/him it's OK" to reassure them.) Dogs will whine and lick us and stay by our sides; cats will come running, stare, and cuddle beside us. (One of our feline companions, Abby, will come running and lie full length on our chests, which has a remarkably calming effect.) Household companions will do the same for other companion cats or dogs who are in distress.[12]

What is required for one to get beyond mere emotional contagion? The step from emotional contagion to full empathy and sympathy requires a sense that one is separate from the individual whose emotional state is matched by our own. This depends on developing a sense of self, then on recognizing the other as another self (de Waal 2009). How can one determine, first, whether a human or nonhuman has developed a sense of self?

A sufficient condition for self-recognition is the old mirror test. If a child or nonhuman can recognize his or her own reflection, that individual is surely self-aware. This happens in human children from the ages of eighteen to twenty-four months of age, except for some autistic or mental-

---

12 | One famous nursing home cat, Oscar, specializes in identifying dying patients and cuddling with them until they pass on. It is not known how Oscar can tell if a person is dying. He has never made a mistake, and the nursing home staff's first indication of impending death is often a visit by Oscar, who will not exhibit this behavior in any other circumstances. He is not otherwise friendly with the patients. Whatever allows the cat to recognize failing vital signs in strangers, his behavior in these cases appears to be comforting (Dosa 2010).

ly disabled children (Hauser 2007). Others so far known to pass the mirror test are apes (Gallup 1970), elephants (de Waal 2009), dolphins (Reiss and Marino 2001), and magpies (Prior et al 2008). The magpie example is particularly fascinating, since birds lack a cerebral cortex. However, like mammals, they do have basal ganglia, which might help explain their high intelligence (some problem-solving bird behavior is comparable to that of chimpanzees). The basal ganglia in mammals are very specialized from region to region, but undifferentiated in birds: this very lack of differentiation allows them to multitask very efficiently. The result: information processing is possible at a high level (Kluger 2010). This is especially true of corvids (crows, ravens, jays, magpies) and parrots. Prior's conclusions are consistent with evolutionary theory: "Our findings provide the first evidence of mirror self-recognition in a non-mammalian species. They suggest that essential components of human self-recognition have evolved independently in different vertebrate classes with a separate evolutionary history" (Prior et al 2008).

If passing the mirror recognition test is required for self-awareness, and self-awareness is necessary for empathy and thus moral agency, most species would be disqualified from the moral realm. However, we have excellent reason to doubt this consequence. First of all, can we be so sure that a given nonhuman has "flunked" the test? Frans de Waal reports that monkeys, unlike apes, do not pass the standard mirror recognition test. If you mark them with rouge or the like and expose them to a mirror, they do not try to touch it or rub it off. However, there are other signs that monkeys might well be aware that they are seeing their own mirror reflections. An experiment was designed by de Waal in which a Plexiglas barrier is put in front of a monkey. On the other side they placed, in turn, (1) a familiar monkey, (2) a stranger monkey, and (3) a mirror (de Waal et al. 2005). There was a dramatic difference in the reaction of every monkey tested. Since, unlike Harry Harlow, de Waal never separated mothers from infants, mothers cradled their infants tightly and did not allow them to wander when a stranger was on the other side. When they faced their own reflections, they made prolonged eye contact, and let the youngsters wander as they wished. Familiar monkeys were ignored, and they quickly turned their backs to strangers. Perhaps we have not been administering the other mirror recognition tests empathetically enough.

Anyone who has tried "the mirror game" with a kitten heretofore unexposed to a mirror can relate the hilarious results. Kittens are shocked by the apparition in the mirror and treat it aggressively, fluffing out their fur, hopping sideways, hissing, spitting, and checking behind the mirror if they can. This goes on for quite some time. As the kittens grow, however, they seem quite jaded when held in front of a mirror. They are not alarmed, surprised, or upset, and will gaze calmly at the reflection. They also are unconcerned by the human holding them up, apparently recognizing us easily (this is not how they act when confronted with a stranger). They may not try to lick lipstick off their noses, should we have the audacity to put it there surreptitiously, but how can we say they do not recognize themselves? We may not know enough about different species for the mirror test to settle the self-recognition question.

Secondly, as Hauser (2007) points out, there are humans with a rich sense of self-awareness who are unable to recognize themselves in a mirror. Victims of prosopagnosia, or face blindness, have a congenital or acquired brain disorder that prevents them from recognizing other's faces and sometimes their own (NINDS 2007).

Thirdly, there is compelling evidence that a concept of self occurs as early as two months of age in human children (Rochat & Striano 1999). Although the children are not fully self-reflective, as Hauser cautions, they can control their own actions to consistently bring about desired results (2007). When you can distinguish self from non-self and engage in goal-directed behaviors, you are on the road to agency. The developmental psychological literature indicates that human children are incipient agents before their first birthdays (Hauser 2007). This is also true of many nonhumans, most likely at an earlier stage of life. The complex behaviors required for survival depend on one not mistaking oneself for a tree limb, a tasty fruit, a parent, or a stranger. (It also requires one to recognize the intentions of others, as we shall soon see.) Our feline companion Abby will lean up on a closed door and attempt to move the door knob with her paws; she also (unsuccessfully) tries to open the refrigerator door. (We have not trained her to do these things, but Siggi, another cat in our household, did learn this behavior from her.) She is not in the least confused about where her paws end and the door begins, nor about the difference between herself and each of the other members of the household, who in turn give every indication of knowing about who is who.

We are reminded by de Waal (2009) that empathy is multi-layered, beginning with emotional contagion and progressing to concern and targeted helping. Targeted helping requires recognition of others and their motivations, which implies that one can grasp their points of view. This sounds quite sophisticated, but recent and current research in developmental psychology as well as narrative ethology supports the presence of these capacities even in tiny children and nonhuman animals.

Recent research on very young human children supports the hypothesis that consolation and perspective taking develop surprisingly early for them. The capacities that make this possible are also present in the young of other species. A team of psychologists at the Infant Cognition Center at Yale University studied babies from six to ten months old. As the authors put it, "all social animals" need certain skills to survive in communities. In particular they "must be able to assess the actions and intentions" of others and "make accurate decisions about who is friend and who is foe, who is an appropriate social partner and who is not" (Hamlin, Wynn, Bloom 2007, 557). They found that very young babies were able to tell helpful from hindering actions and could distinguish helping and obstructive behaviors from neutral behaviors. The babies had decided preferences for helpful individuals and even sometimes punished the hindering ones. The infants watched a puppet show displaying three puppets playing with a ball. The "neutral" puppet, placed in the center, would slide the ball to the "helpful" puppet on the right, who would obligingly pass the ball back to the center puppet. The ball would then be passed to the "hindering" puppet on the left, who would run away with the ball. The helpful and the obstructive puppets were then placed in front of the babies, each with an equal pile of treats beside it. The babies were asked to take a treat from one of the piles, without the pile being specified. Most of the children immediately took a treat from the hindering puppet. As if that were not enough, some of them actually smacked the "bad" puppet in the head! The authors conclude:

"These findings constitute evidence that preverbal infants assess individuals on the basis of their behavior towards others. This capacity may serve as the foundation for moral thought and action, and its early developmental emergence supports the view that social evaluation is a biological adaptation." (Hamlin, Wynn, Bloom 2007, 557)

Since this experiment, the authors have found similar results when testing even younger babies (Bloom 2010). These findings are fully consistent with the consolation behaviors and targeted helping that we see in the very young as well. It is particularly fascinating to see their emerging sense of fairness and when that fairness is violated.

The findings are also consistent with the ample evidence of nonhuman empathy we have already discussed. This includes perspective taking. Kuni's attempt to revitalize the stunned starling by spreading his or her wings and launching the bird from a tall tree is an outstanding example. "Pointing", as de Waal (2009) notes, is also an indicator of being able to take another's point of view. The concept of pointing is far broader than the iconic outstretched index finger immortalized so beautifully on the Sistine Chapel ceiling. It refers to drawing another's attention to something unnoticed or unseen by that other, by means of a gesture or other behavior. Nikkie the chimpanzee was on one side of a zoo moat and de Waal was taking notes on the other. Tall berry bushes grew behind de Waal and he usually threw a handful across the moat when he was there, but this time was so engrossed in his notes that he forgot. Nikki stared hard at de Waal, then jerked his eyes away to a point over de Waal's shoulder. He then locked eyes again, followed by the same emphatic jerk of the head. The primatologist turned around to see the berry bushes—exactly where Nikkie had indicated.

Such behavior, so clearly implying high-level empathy, is not restricted to primates. Anyone who has ever had a canine family member is familiar with "Please let me out" behavior: running back and forth from you to the door, barking, staring intently at you and then at the door, scratching at the door, more staring, etc. (Of course some dogs will literally point as well!) As long as I can remember, I have shared my home with companion dogs or cats. I cannot count the number of times I have been escorted to the refrigerator. Our feline companion Lindi must feel that she has to work very hard for her meals. Wherever I am, she runs up to me, meows, stares intently into my eyes, then begins to run toward the kitchen. She always stops, looks over her shoulder, catches my glance, and then propels herself forward again at top speed. Often she has to double back to try to get me. (In the old television series "Lassie", the heroic collie had to work just as hard to get little Timmy's mom and dad to follow her to whatever trouble the child had gotten himself into that week.)

"Pointing" can be deceptive too. Apes, monkeys, ravens, crows, and jays, among other species, will deliberately mislead others about where a food stash is stored, or will give false alarm warnings to have food to themselves (Hauser 2007). While such behavior is not morally praiseworthy, it assuredly is empathetic.

Playing with others also presupposes perspective taking and an assessment of the other's intentions. There is a world of difference between fighting and play-fighting, stalking with deadly intent and play-stalking. As Bekoff and Pierce (2009) relate, there are signals and rules that individuals learn to recognize during play. Mammals and birds engage in these behaviors. Monkeys, apes, cetaceans, elephants, canids, felids, rodents, and ungulates join humans in being the most playful of animals. Players also display punishing behavior when their play-partners violate the rules. Could this arise out of recognition that one's partner has misrepresented himself—that he has been acting under false pretenses?

There is evidence to support this interpretation. The nascent sense of fairness, made possible by empathy, that the Yale infant cognition researchers identified in preverbal toddlers has also been seen in nonhumans. Bekoff and Pierce (2009) and de Waal (1989, 1996, 2006, 2009) have documented numerous instances involving different species in captive settings as well as in the wild. Primates and members of other species also (e.g., dogs and cats) will punish those who behave unfairly, as does the child who smacks the errant puppet. This is what one would expect among social animals, humans included: if the rules are not adhered to, order must be restored. One feels this especially keenly when one is the disadvantaged party. Frans de Waal (2009) relates a charming story by Irene Pepperberg, the psychologist who worked with the famous African gray parrot Alex. The full account is in her memoir (Pepperberg 2009). When she would sit down to dinner with Alex and Griffin, another parrot, they literally shared the food on her plate. When green beans, a special favorite, were featured, she had to make sure the piles for each parrot were exactly equal; otherwise there would be a raucous complaint of "Green bean!" from the offended bird.

We have seen that nonhuman animals and even very young humans are agents who possess the basis for moral behavior: empathy and fairness. This accounts for the numerous instances of altruistic behavior observed in many species besides our own. We might call these nonhumans and small children incipient moral agents. Nonetheless, fully blown moral agency is not present in the very young or, as far as we know, in nonhumans of any age. Human children and nonhumans as well tend to be biased toward those most like them, restricting the circle of concern rather closely around them (Bloom 2010). Leaps outside the circle can be made, as we have seen, but there is a pervasive preference for one's "own kind." While, sadly, one must admit that vast numbers of adult humans fail in exactly the same way, they are capable of better. It turns out that reason at a significant level, not just emotion, is required for paradigmatic moral agency.

6. From Agency to Moral Agency: Reason and Rights

I take my departure from a key argument by philosopher Alan Gewirth (1978). In the tradition of Immanuel Kant, he identifies universalizability as a requirement for moral agency. Imagine a young agent who has reached the stage of cognitive development that enables her to reflect on the preconditions of her own agency. Agents have goals they wish to pursue; i.e., they act intentionally. Agents are inherently purposive. Pursuing a goal implies that one values that goal; i.e., that one regards it as good or desirable. Whatever specific goals the reflective agent wishes to achieve, she realizes that she requires two basic goods: freedom and well-being. Indeed, these two goods are the necessary conditions for successful agency. Thus, as an agent, she realizes that she values freedom and well being and that as an agent she believes she must have these goods. (Even the suicidal agent requires freedom to act, and her expectation of well-being at that time is the cessation of life, or in the case of altruistic suicide, the accomplishment of a much desired greater good.) The next step in the argument concerns the agent's realizing she *must* hold that other agents should not interfere with her freedom and well-being. Otherwise, as Gewirth argues, she would contradict herself. She would hold both that "I must have freedom and well-being" and "Others are permitted to deprive me of freedom and well-being." It follows that the reflective agent must, if she is consistent, claim the right to noninterference from other agents. Her very status as an agent is the logical justification of the claim to noninterference: she cannot otherwise be an agent.

Now we come to the final key step in the argument: the move from agency to moral agency. Since it is her agency that justifies her claim of noninterference from other agents, she must also conclude that any other agent has the same claim against her. Consistency requires the extension of the same right the agent claims to every other agent. One universalizes: this is how one transcends the bias that otherwise blinds one to the interests of those outside of one's own circle of similar beings. The argument continues by claiming certain minimal rights of assistance (e.g., the right to be assisted in staying alive, provided others are not unreasonably burdened or endangered by one's claim) and, again, the logical requirement that these rights be extended to others.

It is vital to see that these other agents need not themselves be reflective agents to be accorded rights to freedom and well being. Even agents who do not have our human agent's capacity to universalize need freedom and well being to act. Although Gewirth himself rejects the extension of rights to nonhuman sentient beings, the logic of his argument actually embraces them.[13]

Despite the fact that we humans are, as far as is known, the only moral agents on our planet, it follows that this capacity does not endow us with greater moral significance than the very young or the inherently less reflective. The greater reasoning ability that makes moral agency possible does not endow us with more value than any small child, mentally disadvantaged human, or sentient nonhuman, but, unlike them, we do have duties grounded in our moral agency. Our moral agency is the source of our moral responsibility to all others, especially the vulnerable. As the Bible puts it, "From everyone who has been given much, much will be required; and to whom they entrusted much, of him they will ask all the more" (Luke 12:48, New American Standard Bible).

Of course, as David Hume reminds us, reason alone, "the slave of the passions", cannot compel us to be moral beings: we must *want* to be so (Hume 2007, 266). One can rightly say with Gewirth, however, that the *rational* agent will be logically required to extend rights to others. The rational *and* empathetic agent will also want to do so. She will probably find herself sometimes going beyond the sphere of rights recognition, which is morally obligatory, to altruistic action that is praiseworthy but not morally required. When she does so, she will be in good keeping with many nonhumans and young humans who act out of empathy and sympathy.

---

13 | For a full discussion of Gewirth's argument and its critics as well as my own argument that it justifies the moral rights of all sentient beings, please see Pluhar (1995, ch. 5).

References

Angier, N. (2007), "Smart, Curious, Ticklish. Rats?", The New York Times (26 July 2007), NYTimes.com.
Barrow, J.D., Tipler, F.J. (1986), The Anthropic Cosmological Principle, Oxford: Clarendon Press.
Bekoff, M., Pierce, J. (2009), Wild Justice, Chicago, IL: University of Chicago Press.
Bloom, P. (2010), "The Moral Lives of Babies", The New York Times Magazine (3 May 2010), NYTimes.com.
Church, R. (1959), "Emotional Reactions of Rats to the Pain of Others", Journal of Comparative and Physiological Psychology 52/2, 132-134.
Collins, F. (2006), The Language of God, New York: Free Press.
Chihuahua (2007), "Chihuahua Steps Between Rattler, Toddler", KXAS Dallas, TX (23 July 2007), Nbc51.com
Connor, R.C., Heithaus, M. R., Barre, L.M. (1999), "Superalliance in Bottlenose Dolphins", Nature 371, 571-572.
Darwin, C. (2003), The Origin of Species (150th Anniversary Edition), New York, Signet Classics.
Dawkins, R. (2006), The Selfish Gene (30th Anniversary Edition), New York: Oxford University Press.
de Waal, F. (1989), "Food Sharing and Reciprocal Obligations in Chimpanzees", Journal of Human Evolution 18, 433-459.
de Waal, F. (1996), Good-Natured: The Origins of Right and Wrong in Humans and Other Animals, Cambridge, MA: Harvard University Press.
de Waal, F. (1997), Bonobo: The Forgotten Ape, Berkeley, CA: University of California Press.
de Waal, F. (1999), "Anthropomorphism and Anthropodenial: Consistency in our Thinking About Humans and Other Animals", Philosophical Topics 27/1, 255-280.
de Waal, F., Dindo, M., Freeman, C., Hall, M. (2005), "The Monkey in the Mirror: Hardly a Stranger", Proceedings of the National Academy of Sciences, USA 102/32, 11140-11147.
de Waal, F. (2006), Primates and Philosophers, Princeton, NJ: Princeton University Press.
de Waal, F. (2007), Chimpanzee Politics: 25th Anniversary Edition, Baltimore, MD: The Johns Hopkins University Press.
de Waal, F. (2009), The Age of Empathy, New York: Harmony Books.

Dosa, D. (2010), Making Rounds with Oscar: The Extraordinary Gift of an Ordinary Cat, New York: Hyperion.

Dreifus, C. (2010), "Why Bonobos Don't Kill Each Other", The New York Times (2 July 2010).

D'Souza, D. (2009), Life After Death, Washington, DC: Regnery Publishing.

Dyson, N. D., Goldsmith, D. (2004), Origins, New York: W.W. Norton & Company.

Fox, M.A. (1986), The Case for Animal Experimentation: An Evolutionary and Ethical Perspective, Berkeley, CA: University of California Press.

Fox, M. A. (1987), "Animal Experimentation: A Philosopher's Changing Views", Between the Species 3/2, 55-60.

Gallup, G. (1970), "Chimpanzees: Self-Recognition", Science 167, 86-87.

Gewirth. A. (1978), Reason and Morality, Chicago, IL: University of Chicago Press.

Hamlin, K., Wynn, K., Bloom, P. (2007), "Social Evaluation by Preverbal Infants", Nature 450, 557-559.

Harlow, H., Mears, C. (1979), The Human Model: Primate Perspectives, Washington, D.C.: D.H. Winston.

Hatfield, E., Cacioppo, J., Rapson, R. (1993), "Emotional Contagion", Current Directions in Psychological Science 2, 96-99.

Hauser, M. (2007), Moral Minds, New York: Harper Perenial Edition.

Hawking, S. (1988), A Brief History of Time, New York: Bantam Books.

Hawking, S., Mlodinow, L. (2010), The Grand Design, New York: Bantam Books.

Hume, D. (2007/1739), A Treatise of Human Nature, ed. D. Norton & M. Norton, Oxford: Oxford University Press.

Huxley, T.H. (2004/1894), Evolution and Ethics, Amherst, NY: Prometheus Books.

Jacquet, L. (2005), "March of the Penguins" (documentary film).

Kant, I. (1989/1785), Foundations of the Metaphysics of Morals, ed. L.W. Beck, Englewood Cliffs, NJ: Prentice-Hall.

Kluger, J. (2010), "Inside the Minds of Animals", Time Magazine (16 August 2010).

Langford, D., Crager, S., Shehzad, Z., Smith, S., Sotocinal, S., Levanstadt, J., Chandra, M., Levitan, D., Mogil, J. (2006), "Social Modulation of Pain as Evidence for Empathy in Mice", Science 312, 1967-1970.

Linzey, A. (2009), Creatures of the Same God, Herdon, VA: Lantern Books.

Lynch, J. (2007), "Pithecophobes of the World Unite", Scienceblogs. http://scienceblogs.com/mt/pings/60527

Kolbe (2010), "Maximilian Kolbe", Jewish Virtual Library, American-Israeli Cooperative Enterprise.

Morgan, C.L. (1894), An Introduction to Comparative Psychology, London: Walter Scott.

Ninds (2007), National Institute of Neurological Disorders and Stroke (NINDS), Prosopagnosia Information Page, National Institutes of Health. USA.gov.

Nietzsche, F. (1961/1895), "The Antichrist", in: The Portable Nietzsche, ed. W. Kaufmann, New York: Viking Press.

Notebook (2006), "Notebook" (March 2006), Time Magazine.

Pepperberg, I. (2009), Alex & Me: How a Scientist and a Parrot Discovered a Hidden World of Animal Intelligence—and Formed a Deep Bond in the Process, New York: Harper Paperbacks.

Pet Pals (2007), "Pet Pals" (March 2007), Reader's Digest.

Pluhar, E. (1995), Beyond Prejudice: The Moral Significance of Human and Nonhuman Animals, Durham, NC: Duke University Press.

Pluhar, E. (2006), "Experimentation on Humans and Nonhumans", Theoretical Medicine and Bioethics 27/4, 333-355.

Police: Lions Free Kidnapped Girl (21 June 2005). Addis Ababa, Ethiopia: Associated Press Report, reprinted by CNN.com. http://www.cnn.com/2005/WORLD/africa/06/21/ethiopia.lions.ap/index.html

Prior, H., Schwartz, A., Guentuerkuen, O. (2008). "Mirror-Induced Behavior in the Magpie: Evidence of Self-Recognition", Public Library of Science 6/8, e202.

Reiss, D., Marino, L. (2001), "Mirror Self-Recognition in the Bottlenose Dolphin: A Case of Cognitive Convergence", Proceedings of the National Academy of Sciences, USA 98/10, 5937-5942.

Rizzolatti, G., Fadiga, L., Marelli, M. Bettinardi, V., Perani, D., Fazio, F. (1996), "Localization of Grasp Representation in Humans by Positron Emission Tomography", Experimental Brain Research 111, 246-252.

Rizzolatti, G., Fadiga, L., Fogassi, L., and Gallase, V. (1999). "Resonance Behaviors and Mirror Neurons", Archives Italiennes de Biologie 137: 83-89.

Rochat, P., Striano, T. (1999), "Emerging Self-Exploration by Two Month Old Infants", Developmental Science 2, 206-218.

Rollin, B. (1989),The Unheeded Cry, Oxford: Oxford University Press.

Susskind, L. (2006), The Cosmic Landscape: String Theory and the Illusion of Intelligent Design, New York: Bay Back Books.

Swinburne, R. (2004), The Existence of God, Oxford: Clarendon Press.

Truck Driver (2005), "Truck Driver Rushed to Aid Train Wreck Victims", Associated Press Report (27 January 2005), reprinted by CNN.com. http://www.cnn.com/2005/US/01/27/derailment.rescuer.ap/index.html

Van Biema, D. (2006), "God vs. Science." Time Magazine (13 November 2006).

Wechkin, S., Masserman, J., Terris, W. (1964), "Shock to a Conspecific as an Aversive Stimulus", Psychonomic Science 1/2, 47-48.

Wade, N. (2010), "Harvard Finds Scientist Guilty of Misconduct." The New York Times (21 August 2010), NYTimes.com.

Zahn-Waxler, C., Radke-Yarrow, M., Wagner, E., Chapman, M. (1992), "Development of Concern for Others", Developmental Psychology 28, 126-36.

Part Three
The Diversity of Animal Ethics

9. Animal Rights
A Non-Consequentialist Approach

Uriah Kriegel

1. Introduction

It is a curious fact about mainstream discussions of animal rights that they are dominated by consequentialist defenses thereof, when consequentialism in general has been on the wane in other areas of moral philosophy. In this paper, I describe an alternative, non-consequentialist ethical framework (combining Kantian and virtue-ethical elements) and argue that it grants (conscious) animals more expansive rights than consequentialist proponents of animal rights typically grant. The cornerstone of this non-consequentialist framework is the thought that the virtuous agent is s/he who has the stable and dominating disposition to treat all conscious animals, including non-human conscious animals, as ends and not mere means.

2. The Consequentialist Case for Animal Rights

Perhaps the most influential case for animal rights (see, most notably, Singer 1975) is consequentialist in spirit and relies on two premises. The first is philosophical: the right moral action in every circumstance is that which maximizes pleasure and minimizes pain. The second premise is empirical: that many animals—certainly most animals we have dealings with in our everyday life, including animals used in the food and clothing industries—can experience pleasure and pain. Let us state the relevant consequentialist thesis as follows:

(CT) In deciding what actions to perform, one ought always to attempt to maximize the pleasures and minimize the pains consequent upon one's actions.

For the purposes of a consequentialist defense of animal rights a weaker thesis—taking pain and pleasure to be sufficient conditions for moral relevance, say—may be enough. But (CT) will do for the sake of illustration.

As just formulated, this consequentialist case for animal rights is couched in terms of pain and pleasure. One often finds the case put in those terms, but sometimes it is also put in terms of suffering and joy (or enjoyment). There are two ways to understand the relationship between pain and suffering, pleasure and joy. One construes suffering as a deeper, more involved, perhaps more intellectual kind of pain, and correlatively joy as a deeper and more cognitive form of pleasure. The other focuses not on depth but length: suffering is a prolonged, systematic, and stable exposure to pain, joy a prolonged and stable kind of pleasure. In any case, it appears that suffering and joy can be *analyzed* in one way or another in terms of pain and pleasure. For this reason, I will focus henceforth on the latter. My contention is that the notions of pain and pleasure is ambiguous, and it would follow from this that so are the notions of suffering and joy.

The ambiguity can be appreciated through discussion of David Chalmers' (1996, ch.1) claim that mental terms typically lead a 'double life'—they have a *psychological* life and a *phenomenological* life: they can be taken to denote mental states conceived of in terms of their psychological role, or mental states conceived of in terms of their phenomenal character. To conceive of a mental state in terms of its psychological role is to conceive of it as essentially the kind of state that has a certain functional role within the subject's overall psychology, that is, the kind of state that has certain typical causes and effects. These causes and effects can be restricted to sensory inputs, behavioral outputs, and other mental states, but can also be taken more widely to include distal causes and effects in the subject's environment. To conceive of a mental state in terms of its phenomenal character is to conceive of it as essentially the kind of state that has a certain felt quality, the kind of state there is something it is like for the subject to be in.[1]

---

1 | At the background is a general distinction between two conceptions of mind. The psychological conception of mind characterizes mental phenomena third-personally in terms of their causal relations to each other and to the environment; the phenomenological conception characterizes them first-personally in terms of

The implication for pleasure and pain is clear. Mental states can be classified as pain either because (roughly) they are typically caused by harmful stimulation (e.g., tissue damage) and cause aversive reaction (e.g., cringing), or because they feel that particular unpleasant way—they *hurt*. Correspondingly, the term 'pain' can be used to denote either any mental state that typically is suitably caused by harmful stimulation and causative of aversive reaction or any state that feels that particular unpleasant way.[2]

The upshot is that we need a distinction between *psychological pain*, which is pain conceptualized through its mechanical or functional profile, and phenomenological *pain*, which is pain conceptualized through its experiential or phenomenal profile. Ditto for pleasure: there is *psychological pleasure*, which is a state playing the pleasure role, and *phenomenological pleasure*, which is a state experienced as pleasurable by the subject. The effect of this distinction is to render CT ambiguous. For CT now admits of three different interpretations, calling on us to minimize/maximize either (i) psychological pain/pleasure, (ii) phenomenological pain/pleasure, or (iii) both psychological and phenomenological pain/pleasure.

It seems clear that the second interpretation is greatly preferable to the first. Although the issue is not trivial, it is fairly obvious that, other

---

their phenomenal or subjective feel. The former focuses on the *mechanical* dimension of mental life, the latter on its experiential dimension. Both dimensions are real and central to the nature of mind, so there is no substantive question here of which conception is 'more accurate'—both are important.

2 | These classification criteria not only are distinct, but also do not coextend. Suppose a subject experiences a toothache, but upon noticing a fire in the kitchen starts attending to the fire and is thus too distracted to experience the toothache, which unfortunately reappears as soon as the kitchen drama is over. Should we say that this subject had a single continuous toothache, which went unconscious at some point and was then consciously experienced again, or that the subject had two distinct pains, separated by a painless interval? The answer, of course, is that we should say both, but in different senses of 'pain'. In the *psychological* sense, there is only one pain. This is because there is unconscious pain—a mental state which is not experienced by its subject but which nonetheless plays the pain role in the subject's psychology. In the *phenomenological* sense, by contrast, there are two pains, and there is no such thing as non-experienced pain—as soon as the early pain is phenomenally extinguished, it goes out of existence, and a new one reemerges when the phenomenology of pain reappears later.

things being equal, producing phenomenological pleasure in someone is commendable while producing phenomenological pain is criticizable. (The issue is not trivial because it is not obvious *why* this is the case; but it does seem obvious *that* it is the case.) By contrast, it is hard to see how producing psychological pleasure and pain is supposed to be commendable or criticizable. Suppose that, perhaps *per impossibile*, a race of zombies was discovered or created (and ascertained to be zombies) who were functionally indistinguishable from us, in the sense that the functional organization of their psychology would be identical to ours. These zombies would have internal states with the same functional role as our pleasures and pains, but would never consciously experience pleasure or pain. In other words, they would undergo psychological pleasures and pains but not phenomenological pleasures and pains. On the face of it, there is no reason to think that causing these zombies the internal states corresponding to our pleasure would be worth the effort and investment, or that causing them the internal states corresponding to our pain experiences would be worth the effort of avoiding. If the zombies do not *experience* their pleasures and pains, but simply *host*, so to speak, internal states with the pleasure/pain functional profile, their internal states do not have any moral weight.

The point can be brought out in a different way. Consider that it is only when a pain is experienced that it hurts the person undergoing it—that it is only when a pain is experienced that the person is *pained by* the pain; and likewise, that only when a pleasure is experienced that it *pleases* its subject. If there are internal states that do not pain or please the persons undergoing them, but which deserve the names 'pain' and 'pleasure' for some other reason (e.g., due to their functional role), those states do not carry any moral weight. For it is the pains and pleasures *of persons*, or *subjects*, that interest us.[3] From this perspective, the key moral difference between phenomenal pain/pleasure and psychological pain/pleasure is that only the former are inherently such as to pain/please their subject. A psychological pain is often associated, as a matter of contingent fact, with

---

3 | Sometimes the term 'person' is used to refer to any subject of conscious experience, or any subject of moral worth, whereas on other occasions it is used to refer only to human subjects, or subjects with relatively sophisticated inner life. I use it here in the former sense, and add 'or at least of subjects' for the benefit of those who insist on using it the latter way. This is just a terminological matter.

a phenomenal pain, and may to that extent be said to pain its subject. But only phenomenal pain is such as to pain its subject in and of itself.

Notice now that since we found psychological pains and pleasures to be morally insignificant, it would seem that the second interpretation of CT is preferable not only over the first one, but also over the third one, that which recommends maximizing both phenomenological and psychological pleasure and minimizing both phenomenological and psychological pain. That is, the moral weight of CT is better captured through the following principle:

(CT+) In deciding what actions to perform, one ought always to attempt to maximize the phenomenological pleasures and minimize the phenomenological pains consequent upon one's actions.

I take this point to be in line with the standard consequentialist defense of animal rights, as can be seen by its common appeal to the notion of *sentience* (Singer 1975).[4] The term 'sentience' is hard to associate with merely psychological or functional states; rather, it intimates a phenomenal, experienced state. Animals may indeed have rights insofar as they are sentient, but sentience is probably associated only with the capacity to be in internal states with a phenomenal character, an experiential dimension—not with the capacity to be in internal states with a functional role.

3. A NON-CONSEQUENTIALIST FRAMEWORK

The immediate alternative to consequentialism is of course deontologism, of which the Kantian variety is the best known. For my part, I find the second formulation of the categorical imperative, the 'humanity formula', the most compelling: one should always act in such a way that one treats humanity, whether others' or one's own, as an end in itself and not merely as a means to some other end. Perhaps because this formulation of the categorical imperative, and Kant's moral philosophy as a whole, restrict moral worth to the sphere of humanity, Kantian defenses of animal rights are hard to come by. But it should be straightforward for a proponent of

---

4 | This is not to say that Singer is committed to the entire picture of the nature of pain and pleasure that we have developed thus far.

animal rights with Kantian predilections to modify Kant's dictum to encompass the sphere of the sentient or conscious. Let us call the following the *consciousness formula*:

(CF) One should always act in such a way that one treats conscious creatures as ends in themselves and not merely as means to other ends.

There are complicated questions surrounding whether Kant's own reasons for putting forward the categorical imperative can survive this modification. The answers are probably negative. But regardless of how that turns out, it is clear that (CF) is a coherent position, and can therefore be adopted by a non-consequentialist proponent of animal rights.

The case for (CF) is unlikely to be Kantian, then, but I think it should be clear what kind of case it would be, since it speaks to the combination of deontological and animal-rights sensibilities. This array of sensibilities is well captured in something like the following bit of reasoning: all conscious/sentient creatures have moral worth; one ought to treat creatures with moral worth as ends rather than as mere means; therefore, one ought to treat all conscious/sentient creatures as ends rather than as mere means.

The other commonly discussed alternative to consequentialism is virtue ethics, which focuses not on the moral status of individual acts but on those of agents and their stable dispositions to act. Interestingly, there is no reason this perspective could not be incorporated into the Kantian framework to form a moral dictum that would speak to both Kantian and virtue-ethical sensibilities. The resulting moral principle, upon which I propose to pin animal rights, is thus this:

(CF+) One ought to have the stable, dominating disposition to treat conscious creatures as ends in themselves and not merely as means to other ends.

Call this the *virtue-ethical consciousness formula*. I will not argue for it here—that is the proper target of a much larger project. But it is significant that this principle has never been explicitly articulated (to my knowledge) and yet carries quite a bit of intuitive appeal. What I propose to do in the remainder of this section is two things: first, elucidate and flesh out (CF+); second, point out a couple of ways in which it grants conscious animals more rights than consequentialism.

Start with the notion of a disposition to treat someone a certain way. The metaphysics of dispositions is a contentious area of research, but the first analysis to come to mind is the so-called simple conditional analysis (Quine 1960): *x* has the disposition to exhibit manifestation M in circumstances C iff: if C were the case, *x* would exhibit M. Many philosophers today reject the simple conditional analysis, in favor of either a complicated conditional analysis (Lewis 1997), a non-conditional analysis (Fara 2005), or a primitivist account (Molnar 1999). At the same time, the simple conditional analysis has been defended recently as adequate after all (see, e.g., Choi 2008). We need not enter this fray here. Different accounts of disposition will result in different understandings of the disposition to treat conscious creatures as ends and not mere means. It is easiest, for purposes of exposition, to illustrate matters with the simple conditional analysis. According to it, a person has the disposition to treat conscious creatures as ends and not mere means iff the following conditional is true of her: in most circumstances, she would treat conscious creatures as ends and not mere means. So if we use the simple conditional analysis, what (CF+) demands from us that is that we treat conscious creatures as ends and not mere means in most circumstances.

Note that this conditional requires that the disposition manifest itself in *most* circumstances. This is what the qualifier 'stable and dominating' is supposed to capture: the greater the variety of types of circumstance in which the disposition is manifested, the stabler the disposition, and the greater the number of times the agent manifests the disposition in each type of circumstance, the more dominating the disposition.[5] Clearly, on the whole the more stable and dominating the disposition, the more commendable the agent, given the kind of sensibilities catered to by (CF+). But it is an interesting question whether our ideal should be that the disposition be *totally* stable and dominating, that is, manifests itself in *every* circumstance. On the one hand, the *phronimos*, or the ideally virtuous agent, surely treats conscious creatures as ends in themselves *always and everywhere*. At the same time, it appears to be a psychologically contingent fact about sub-optimal moral agents such as us that absolute adherence to moral dicta tends to make us dour and intolerant: we run the danger, in our puritanism, of becoming deeply disappointed with humanity (for fail-

---

5 | For a related distinction between a trait being broad and a trait being stable, see Tiberius (2008).

ing to live up to the moral standards we live up to) and ultimately adopting a derisive and uncompassionate attitude towards our peers. To avoid these pitfalls, it may be wise for us to demand of ourselves something less than a perfectly stable and dominating disposition.[6]

The last clarification we ought to offer is of the phrase 'ends and not mere means'. Here too, the existing literature is vast and there is no need, nor hope, for us to make an original and plausible contribution to it here. It bears stressing, however, that not treating someone as a *mere* means does not entail not treating them as a means. If A treats B both as a means and as an end, A does not treat B as a mere means, in the sense that A does not treat B merely as a means. This is why asking someone for the time does not *necessarily* involve treating them as mere means, although it may, namely, if the agent does not treat the patient *also* as an end. This raises the thorny issue of what is involved in treating someone as an end (since it cannot be analyzed in terms of not treating them as a means, given that one can treat a person both as an end and as a means). Presumably, it involves the agent's keeping in mind, in her dealings with the patient, the right psychological attitude (respect, empathy, love, or what have you) toward the patient. For my part, I am tempted by the view that there is a *sui generis* phenomenology of treating someone as an end, and that the treating of someone as an end is to be analyzed in terms of the presence of this phenomenology. Another tempting view is that there is a special kind of affective state, which may be called with some qualification love, that is involved in this.[7] Again, different positions on this matter will result in different versions of (CF+).

---

6 | It is an intriguing question what this would imply in practice. One possibility is to force ourselves to treat conscious creatures as mere means on occasion. Just how often 'on occasion' should be ought to be determined by psychological research on the forming of the dour and intolerant attitude of which I spoke. It may well be that such research will discover that my observation is simply wrong (perhaps it is based on the wrong anecdotes), or that it can be avoided by simpler means. Whatever such research turns up would have to be integrated into the Kantian virtue-ethical stance I describe here.

7 | These two views are, moreover, clearly compatible. Unfortunately, and somewhat surprisingly, there is relatively little work on the analysis of treating someone as an end, even among Kant scholars. Moreover, it would seem that Kant himself had little to offer on this matter, so that many interpretations are in principle open

(CF+), so understood, diverges from (CT+) in its practical prescriptions in a number of ways. Perhaps the most striking of these is the fact that, if a conscious animal could be killed without causing pain to it (or anybody else), it is not clear that (CT+) would prohibit the killing. As a matter of fact, conscious animals raised today in the mainstream food industry typically lead miserable lives of ceaseless suffering. However, it is conceivable that some conscious creatures be brought up in quite pleasant circumstances, albeit for the purpose of eventual—but painless—slaughter. (Indeed, it is not implausible that this in fact takes place in some less industrialized parts of the world.) The consequentialist defense of animal rights seems to me not to militate at all against such a practice. A dead animal does not experience pain, so as long as his or her death is painless, the killing of the animal does not contribute to the overall amount of pain in the world and is therefore at worst morally neutral. The virtue-ethical Kantian framework I have presented clearly does militate against this practice, however, since the relevant conscious creatures are treated as mere means, insofar as it is impossible to treat someone also as an end in killing them in order to fulfill one's own gastronomic desires.[8]

Similarly, consider the possibility of raising conscious animals, in a humane and painless way, for the purpose of consuming their products (e.g., milk). Traditional farming without commercial ambition often took this form. Again, it does not seem that (CT+) would militate against such a practice, but (CF+) certainly does.[9] The more general point to appreci-

---

(see Griffin 1986). But the Kantian proponent of animal rights could just suggest here that whenever some consensus emerges regarding the correct analysis of this matter, it could be plugged into (CF+).

8 | At the same time, note that (CF+), like (CT+), does not prohibit eating, say, cows altogether: a cow dead of natural causes, since it is no longer conscious, has no rights, and can be eaten. (This is, by the way, the current practice in Bhutan.)

9 | Thus, if combined with the view that all animals are conscious, (CF+) would prescribe not only vegetarianism but veganism. For reasons explained earlier, I think it should only be combined with the claim that all *mammals* are conscious, and so veganism does not follow: we are most certainly justified in consuming honey, for instance, since bee brains most certainly do not engage in higher-order monitoring (and if I am right, the same holds also for the products of fish and chickens). (A qualification is necessary here, however. My claim is that using the products of these unconscious animals is not intrinsically wrong. But there may

ate here is that (CF+) and (CT+) must diverge, since whether an animal is treated as a mere means and whether it is pained are two different matters. Doubtless they overlap quite often in practice, but they are distinct nonetheless: an animal, even a human animal, can be pained without being treated as a mere means (as when we tell a friend a painful truth because it is the right thing to do), and can be treated as a mere means without being pained (as with the aforementioned well-treated cows). My claim is that in all these cases, it is treating the animal as a mere means, rather than paining the animal, that tracks moral wrongness as such.

These are different facets of the more general fact that (CF+) prohibits treating conscious animals as a resource for and by humans. This general fact, it seems to me, may well capture the moral sensibility that animates the case for animal rights. Yet there is nothing in the consequentialist approach to animal rights that speaks to this concern. By contrast, the virtue-ethical Kantian approach I have adopted, in giving all conscious animals intrinsic moral worth, ensures that conscious animals do not derive their worth from the value they have for humans. Within this approach, accepting the use of conscious animals for our own purposes under the condition that they are well-treated and are not suffering is akin to defending humane slave owners on the grounds that they offered their slaves a comparatively pleasant life. Even if such slaves worked regular hours and were generously compensated, indeed worked less and were better compensated than they would be as free men and women, the very fact that they would be considered the possession of, and a resource for, their owner is what we would find so morally objectionable. By the same token, the very fact that some conscious creatures are treated as a resource for other conscious creatures, I contend, should raise in us moral indignation,

---

be ways in which it is instrumentally wrong. For example, gratuitous torturing of an unconscious animal that elicits in us the intuitive ascription of consciousness is sure to do harm to our character, and therefore such torturing is morally wrong, though only instrumentally. Perhaps the treatment of geese in the context of *foie gras* production is a good example: it is not intrinsically wrong, on my view, since geese are probably unconscious, but it is instrumentally wrong, in that it desensitizes us to what would be cruel treatment if geese were conscious.) At the same time, according to (CF+), commercial products involving the products of mammals are morally tainted one and all: leather jackets, shoes, and belts, fur coats, ivory sculptures, etc. are all to be avoided.

indeed possibly the very same moral indignation. This is the deep motivation for defending animal rights.

4. The Question of Animal Consciousness

The non-consequentialist framework I have articulated leaves open what is perhaps the most important question from the standpoint of *practical* ethics: which animals should be treated as ends and not mere means? The reason this is left open is that the above non-consequentialist framework is silent on the question of which animals are conscious or sentient. The question is of course empirical, and so the role of the philosopher in answering it is limited. One role s/he can adopt, however, is methodological: to offer the general form of a procedure for generating a reliable conjecture concerning the extent of consciousness within the animal kingdom. The procedure I would like to propose is fairly straightforward: we should seek the neural correlates of consciousness/sentience in creatures that are unquestionably conscious, then attempt to establish which other creatures, if any, exhibit neural structures relevantly similar to these. Several clarifications are in order.

First, which animals are 'unquestionably' conscious depends on what we take 'unquestionably' to mean. I suggest that the best understanding of 'unquestionably' is as follows: it is unquestionably the case that p just in case any claim that $\sim p$ would not be taken seriously within the relevant community of inquiry (where this could be operationalized in terms of publications in peer-reviewed journals, presentations in academic gatherings, or some such indicators). In the present case, then, a creature is unquestionably conscious just in case the claim that it is not conscious would not be taken seriously within the cognitive-scientific community. Since as a matter of fact even Daniel Povinelli's claim that chimpanzees are unconscious (see Povinelli et al. 1994) has been taken seriously, but no claim that normal adult humans are unconscious has ever been taken seriously, I suggest that we consider normal adult humans as our paradigmatically unquestionable instance of a conscious creature.[10]

---

10 | The term 'seriously' is problematic, inasmuch being taken seriously comes in degrees. Some philosophers—eliminativists—have argued that *nobody* is conscious, not even humans (Churchland 1984). This has always been a marginal

Secondly, what makes a brain structure 'relevantly similar' to another is also problematic, especially in the context of cross-species comparison. Neuroanatomical comparison, in particular, may be neither reliable nor feasible. Better to focus on comparisons of structures as functionally individuated. Thus, one brain *region* may be different in terms of its spatial location from another and yet qualify as a similar brain *structure*, namely, if the two regions perform the same neural function.

Thirdly, the fact that a brain structure is relevantly similar to one that underlies consciousness does not *guarantee* that it too underlies consciousness, and likewise the fact that it is relevantly *dis*similar to one that underlies consciousness does not guarantee that it does *not* underlie consciousness. However, such relations of relevant similarity and dissimilarity do offer defeasible evidence of underlying consciousness (or lack thereof), by supporting an inference to the best explanation to that effect. Such an inference makes its conclusion *probable*, though it does not guarantee its truth. Thus if brain structure S_1 underlies consciousness in creature C_1, where C_1 is unquestionably conscious, and structure S_2 is relevantly similar to S_1, then it is probable that S_2 underlies consciousness in C_2; and if S_2 is relevantly dissimilar to all brain structures of all unquestionably conscious creatures, then S_2 probably does not underlie consciousness in C_2.[11]

---

view, however, in a way Povinelli's view has not. I recognize, however, that there may be an element of artificiality in deciding what we should take as unquestionable cases of consciousness. Perhaps all apes could be taken as unquestionably conscious.

11 | It might be objected that while the presence of the right brain structure clearly provides evidence for the presence of consciousness, the absence of the former does not provide evidence for the absence of the latter. As it is sometimes put, absence of evidence does not provide evidence of absence. My response to this is twofold. First, for reasons I cannot go into here, and which have to do with Hempel's (1945) diagnosis of the so-called Raven Paradox, I think that absence of evidence is evidence of absence, albeit in some circumstances comparatively weak evidence. Secondly, whether the absence of the right brain structure provides strong evidence for the absence of consciousness is crucially tied up with the question of whether consciousness is multiply realized across the animal kingdom. The question here is not the *philosophical* question of whether consciousness is multiply realiz*able*, but the *empirical* question of whether it is really multiply realized in the actual world. Following a number of philosophers, while I am

Incorporating these clarifications into our understanding of the empirical procedure I described leads to the following methodological principle:

(M1) For any brain structure S of a creature C, if there is a brain structure S* of normal human adults, such that (i) S* underlies consciousness in normal human adults and (ii) S is neurofunctionally similar to S*, then (probably) S underlies consciousness in C; and if there is no brain structure S* that satisfies (i) and (ii), then S probably does not underlie consciousness in C.

With (M) in place, we can generate a list of (probable) conscious animals as soon as we establish two things: first, which brain structure(s) underlie consciousness in normal human adults, and second, which animals have brain structures neurofunctionally similar to those structures in the human brain. These are what we might call *purely empirical* questions.[12]

One final methodological-cum-ethical comment is called for, however. Scientific knowledge, being *a posteriori*, is uncertain: the appropriate credence in a scientific proposition—including regarding the neural correlates of consciousness—is always less than 1. This may inspire a protestation to the effect that even a low probability of consciousness in an animal should suffice to grant it animal rights, because the moral costs of error in this area are gigantic (see Singer 1975 for a similar consideration). This consideration can be cast as an objection to the inference from a claim of the form 'animal A is probably unconscious' to a claim of the form 'animal A should not be granted rights'. According to the objector, as long as there is a non-negligible probability that an animal is conscious, we should grant it the rights of conscious animals, because doing so guarantees that we would not be unwittingly committing moral horrors. In reaction, I want to embrace the spirit of the objection but reject its letter (at least on one reading of what the letter is). (Warning: my discussion will make use of certain toy examples that greatly oversimplify the matter, but

---

sympathetic to the philosophical claim of multiple realizability, I find no evidence whatsoever for the actual multiple realizedness of any mental property including consciousness (see especially Shapiro 2008).

12 | Moreover, they are questions that the scientific community is at present very much unsure about. I have my own speculative views on this (Kriegel 2009, ch.7), but I will not go into them here for want of space.

this will help to see what I think is right about the spirit of the objection and where its letter may go wrong.)

First, however, we should keep in mind a distinction between two ways in which considerations of probability enter the picture. Suppose for the sake of argument that a scientific consensus emerged that only mammals are conscious. Our credence in this scientific proposition would not reach 1 at that point. Suppose further that, being of a critical bent, and keeping in mind all the hidden social, methodological, and philosophical assumptions that go into constructing a consensus, our credence in the scientific consensus being strictly true is .55. It follows that our credence in any implication of the scientific consensus, including for animal rights, cannot exceed .55. This is one way in which a more attenuated picture is forced on us by consideration of probability. However, the objection before us pushes beyond this. The objector claims rather that if we have a credence of .05 that oysters are conscious, we ought to have credence of 1 that oysters ought to be treated as ends and not mere means.

Put this way, I think the objector's claim is too strong to be plausible. According to panexperientialists, everything in the universe has a degree of phenomenal consciousness, if only a very small one. Since their position is coherent, and some of the arguments for it are not altogether ludicrous (Chalmers 1996), I have .01 credence that vegetables are phenomenally conscious as well. Surely, however, I ought not to treat vegetables as ends in themselves on the grounds that panexperientialism is coherent and non-ludicrous. I take this to be a *reductio ad absurdum* of the strong claim that any non-negligible probability of consciousness entails treating as an end: the result of adopting that claim is to treat *everything* as an end.

It would, of course, be entirely arbitrary to declare that although a non-negligible probability of consciousness does not secure rights, a probability of .08, or .12, or some such figure, does. More generally, there is something wrong about the idea that there is a cut-off point beyond which credence in an animal's consciousness should entail a credence of 1 in the animal having the rights of conscious animals. A more sensible model would embrace a non-trivial function from credence in consciousness to credence in rights. The dogmatic model we have worked with thus far matched .12 credence in an animal's being conscious to .12 credence in it deserving the rights of conscious animals. The objector's model matches .12 credence in the animal's being conscious to a credence of 1 in it deserving the rights. Neither is plausible. It is much more reasonable, it seems to me, to adopt a function that, say, matches .12 credence in consciousness to .4 credence in rights. Obviously, we cannot expect that there be objective facts about the 'correct' function. But I hope that this illustration makes clear what I think is correct about the spirit of the objection before us. What is correct about it is that the dogmatic function from credence in consciousness to credence in rights is wrongheaded: the moral cost of making a moral error is such that a more 'proactive' function should be embraced.

One way to think of the 'correct' function issue is in terms of the stability and dominance of one's disposition to treat animals as ends and not mere means. As noted above, the more stable and dominant her disposition, the more morally commendable the agent is (modulo the mentioned worries about puritanism). We can incorporate the considerations we have been discussing in the present section into this framework: *mutatis mutandis*, an agent who treats an animal in whose consciousness she has .12 credence as an end and not mere means 40 % of time is more commendable than an agent who treats such an animal as an end 30 % of the time and less commendable than one who treats it as an end 50 % of the time. Likewise, an agent who treats an animal in whose consciousness she has .12 credence as an end and not mere means 40 % of time is *mutatis mutandis* more commendable than an agent who treats an animal in whose consciousness she has .17 credence as an end and not mere means 40 % of the time, and less commendable than one who treats in such a way an animal in whose consciousness she has .07 credence. This is because of variation in the stability and dominance of the key disposition in these various agents.

As warned above, this discussion makes free use of oversimplifying toy examples. The lived reality of moral conduct is not as clean-cut as the assignment of precise figures in the above discussion suggests. I have adopted this way of discussing the objection merely as an expository device, by way of showing what I think is right about the objection and what I think is wrong. It is right that the mere probability that an animal is conscious should importantly boost its claim to having moral rights. It is wrong that any non-negligible probability secures those rights absolutely.

5. Conclusion

The history of moral progress is the history of widening the circle of recognized moral worth, whereby each group grants more 'others' the same rights they enjoy themselves. Certainly in the West we have witnessed this process in the form of dehumanizing less and less (first with respect to other ethnicities, then other races, and so on and so forth). Currently on the forefront of the Western agenda is the widening of the circle to people of different sexual orientation, and since history has nowhere to march but forward, this issue will most certainly be eventually settled in favor of equal rights across orientations. But where does the process end? Where is the point beyond which there is no need to progress? In short, what is the end of moral history? It seems to me that the circle of the conscious is the widest circle of moral worth, and moral history will come to an end when all conscious creatures will enjoy the equal right to be treated as ends in themselves and not merely as means.[13]

References

Chalmers, D.J. (1996), The Conscious Mind, Oxford, New York: Oxford University Press.
Choi, S. (2008), "Dispositional Properties and Counterfactual Conditionals", Mind 117/468, 795-841.
Churchland, P.S. (1984), Matter and Consciousness, Cambridge MA: MIT Press.
Dretske, F.I. (1995), Naturalizing the Mind, Cambridge MA: MIT Press.
Fara, M. (2005), "Dispositions and Habituals", Noûs 39/1, 43-82.
Griffin, J. (1986), Well-Being, Oxford: Clarendon Press.
Hempel, C.G. (1945), "Studies in the Logic of Confirmation", Mind 54, 1-26.

---

13 | For very helpful comments on a previous draft, I would like to thank Sebastian Leugger and especially Anne Baril and Stephen Biggs. For important conversations, I would like to thank Benji Kozuch, David Rosenthal, and Mark Timmons. I have also benefited from presenting this paper at the 2010 meeting of the Canadian Society for the Study of Practical Ethics, and am grateful to the audience there.

Kriegel, U. (2009), Subjective Consciousness: A Self-Representational Theory, Oxford: Oxford University Press.

Lewis, D.K. (1997), "Finkish Dispositions", Philosophical Quarterly 47, 143-158.

Molnar, G. (1999), "Are Dispositions Reducible?", Philosophical Quarterly 49, 1-17.

Povinelli D.J., Rulf, A.B., Bierschwale, D.T. (1994), "Absence of Knowledge Attribution and Self-recognition in Young Chimpanzees (Pan troglodytes)", Journal of Comparative Psychology 108/1, 74-80.

Quine, W.V.O. (1960), Word and Object, Cambridge MA: MIT Press.

Shapiro, L. (2008), "How to Test for Multiple Realization", Philosophy of Science 75/5, 514-525.

Singer, P. (1975), Animal Liberation, New York: Random House.

Tiberius, V. (2008), The Reflective Life: Living Wisely with Our Limits, Oxford, New York: Oxford University Press.

10. Taking Sentience Seriously

Gary L. Francione

1. Introduction

In 1993, a number of scholars collaborated on a book of essays entitled *The Great Ape Project* (GAP) (Cavalieri & Singer 1993). The book was accompanied by a document, *A Declaration on Great Apes*, to which the editors and contributors subscribed. *The Declaration* stated that the great apes "are the closest relatives of our species" and that these nonhumans "have mental capacities and an emotional life sufficient to justify inclusion within the community of equals" (Cavalieri & Singer 1993, 5). In recent years, reflecting the inquiry and concerns of *GAP* and the organization of the same name that evolved from it, a considerable literature has developed that discusses the extent to which the great apes, dolphins, parrots, and perhaps other animals have certain cognitive characteristics thought to be uniquely human (Hauser 1996, 2000; Hillix & Rumbaugh 2004; Bekoff & Jamieson 1996; Savage-Rumbaugh & Lewin 1994; Wise 2000, 2002). These characteristics include self-awareness, emotions, and the ability to communicate with a symbolic language. This literature poses the question whether we must, therefore, rethink our relationship with nonhumans and accord those who possess these characteristics greater moral consideration and legal protection. *GAP* popularized what I call the "similar-minds theory" of the human/nonhuman relationship (Francione 2005, 51-52).

The similar-minds approach has spawned an industry of cognitive ethologists eager to investigate—ironically often through animal experiments—the extent to which nonhumans have human-like cognitive characteristics. The flipside of the similar-minds theory is that those nonhumans who are merely sentient—capable of experiencing pain and suffering but who lack these other cognitive capacities—are still *things*, entitled to "humane" treatment but not the preferential treatment that we are obligated to accord nonhumans with minds like ours.

I was a contributor to *GAP* and an original signatory to *A Declaration on Great Apes*. Nevertheless, in my 1993 essay in GAP (Francione 1993, 253) and at greater length in my subsequent writing, particularly in *Introduction to Animal Rights: Your Child or the Dog?* (Francione 2000, 116-127) I have expressed the view that sentience alone is sufficient for full membership in the moral community and that no other cognitive characteristic is required.

The similar-minds theory is presented by its proponents as progressive because it appears to allow the inclusion of at least some nonhumans in the community of equals. This characterization is inaccurate in that the opposite is true: similar-minds theory will only facilitate our continuing to exclude virtually all nonhumans from the moral community. The problem lies in the attempt to link cognitive characteristics with moral significance. Although similar-minds theory is ostensibly a recent phenomenon, linking the moral status of nonhumans to cognitive characteristics beyond sentience is not new. Indeed, this idea has, in one form or another, characterized our thinking about the moral status of nonhumans for a long time, and it is responsible for a good deal of mischief.

In this article, I very briefly discuss the history of this idea. I then present several reasons why we should abandon the theory in favor of requiring only sentience for full membership in the moral community.

2. BENTHAM, SENTIENCE, AND ANIMAL USE

Until the nineteenth century, nonhumans were for the most part regarded as things and not as moral persons because we believed that they lacked some supposedly uniquely human characteristic that made us qualitatively different from them and deprived them of any moral significance. From the pre-Socratics through Plato and Aristotle, to the Middle Ages and St. Thomas Aquinas, and through the Enlightenment and Descartes, Locke, and Kant, theorists maintained that animals, unlike humans, were not rational, self-aware, or capable of abstract thought, language use, or reciprocal moral concern for humans.[1]

---

1 | There were, of course, some exceptions to this view. For an excellent discussion of the treatment of nonhumans in Western philosophy, see Steiner (2005).

As a result of these supposed differences, humans could not have any moral obligations that they owed directly to nonhumans and the latter could not be members of the moral community (Francione 2000, 1-3, 103-106, 111-113).[2] To the extent that humans had any obligations that concerned animals, these obligations were actually owed to other humans. A moral obligation not to inflict gratuitous harm on animals was really one owed to other humans to avoid conduct that would lead to the unkind treatment of humans. Similarly, there were virtually no laws before the nineteenth century that established legal obligations that were owed to animals as distinguished from those that concerned animals but that were really owed to humans in their capacity as owners of animals (Francione 2000, 3).

Progressive social movements developed that demanded greater rights for women and the abolition of human slavery and proposed that we have moral obligations to other animals not connected to whether our treatment of them affects other humans. Although there were many theorists and advocates concerned about our treatment of nonhumans, a particularly important and influential one was British lawyer and philosopher Jeremy Bentham (1748-1832). Bentham rejected the view that we could exclude nonhumans from the moral community and treat them as things because they lack certain characteristics that we regard as necessary for moral personhood. According to Bentham,

"a full-grown horse or dog, is beyond comparison a more rational, as well as a more conversible animal, than an infant of a day, or a week, or even a month, old. But suppose the case were otherwise, what would it avail? The question is not, Can they *reason*? nor, Can they *talk*? but, Can they *suffer*?" (Bentham 1970, 282f)

---

2 | There is a sense in which Descartes should be considered separately in that he arguably maintained that animals are not sentient whereas the others acknowledged that animals are sentient and have interests but that we may ignore those interests because animals lack other cognitive characteristics. If animals are not sentient, then they can have no interests and it would make no sense to talk about having any obligations to them (Francione 2000, 2-3, 104). See note 15 (discussing sentience as a necessary and sufficient condition for possessing interests). In addition to having minds that are dissimilar, animals are regarded by some as lacking souls and as being spiritually inferior to humans (Francione 2000, 106-111).

Bentham thereby rejected the link between cognitive characteristics and moral status that had dominated Western thinking about nonhumans for the past several thousand years in favor of the position that only sentience is required for animals to be members of the moral community. Or did he?

Bentham did not conclude from the view that only sentience mattered that we should stop using and killing animals for human purposes. Although he ostensibly argued that rationality or language ability is not required for moral significance, he certainly did not regard cognitive differences between humans and nonhumans as irrelevant. He believed that nonhumans, unlike humans, are not self-aware and do not have a sense of the future. Although this does not mean that we can ignore animal suffering, it does mean that animals do not have an interest in continuing to live and, so, we can continue to use them. Bentham stated:

"If the being eaten were all, there is very good reason why we should be suffered to eat such of them as we like to eat: we are the better for it, and they are never the worse. They have none of those long-protracted anticipations of future misery which we have. ... [and] are never the worse for being dead." (Bentham 1970, 282)[3]

According to Bentham, animals do not care whether we use or kill them for our purposes as long as we do not make them suffer unduly in the process. He did not question the status of animals as property because he did not regard the ownership and use of animals for human purposes as per se objectionable. The primary issue for Bentham was not *whether* we used animals, but *how* we used them.

As I discuss in the following section, the property status of animals meant that Bentham's revolutionary call in favor of sentience turned out to be rather hollow. Although Bentham purported to reject the link between

---

3 | See note 14 below (discussing John Stuart Mill's views on differences between humans and other animals). Animal rights theorist Tom Regan comes close to Bentham's position when he argues that death is a greater harm for humans than for nonhumans, and that if we are faced with a "lifeboat" situation in which we can choose to save four humans or a million dogs, we ought to choose to save the humans because of this qualitative difference. See Regan (1983), 324f; for a discussion of Regan's position, see Francione (2000), 215 n.61.

cognitive characteristics and moral status, he merely reintroduced it in another form.

3. Conventional Wisdom and Animal Welfare

Bentham's view is embodied in the principles of animal welfare that reflect our conventional wisdom about our moral obligations to animals. According to that conventional wisdom, we can use animals for our purposes, but, because animals can suffer, we must take their suffering seriously and not treat them as mere things. Most of us agree that it is morally wrong to inflict "unnecessary" suffering on nonhumans and that we are obligated to treat animals "humanely." This notion is so uncontroversial that we have criminal laws, which originated in nineteenth-century Britain and are now ubiquitous, that purport to impose criminal penalties on those who fail to treat animals "humanely" or who inflict "unnecessary" or "unjustified" suffering on them (Francione 2000, 7-9). In short, it seems that we have accepted Bentham's moral theory about the importance of sentience and implemented it in our law. And that is precisely the problem.

An examination of the conventions of animal welfare reveals confusion. If a prohibition against unnecessary or unjustified suffering of nonhumans is to have any meaningful content, it must preclude the infliction of suffering on nonhumans merely for our pleasure, amusement, or convenience. But the vast majority of the suffering and death that we impose on nonhumans can be justified *only* by our pleasure, amusement, or convenience and cannot, by any stretch, be characterized plausibly as "necessary" (Francione 2000, 9-30).

It is, for instance, not necessary to eat animals or animal products; indeed, animal products are increasingly believed to be detrimental to human health, and animal agriculture is unsound as an ecological matter. The best justification that we have for inflicting pain, suffering, and death on the over ten billion land animals that we kill and eat annually in the United States alone is that we enjoy the taste of meat and dairy. It is certainly not necessary to exploit animals for entertainment purposes or for recreational hunting. There is only one area in which a plausible necessity argument can be made—the use of nonhumans in experiments to find cures for serious human illnesses (Francione 2000, 31-49). Although necessity claims in this context are suspect as well, it is the only use of nonhumans that cannot be summarily dismissed as nothing more than the infliction of suffering and death for trivial reasons.[4]

In sum, we suffer from a sort of "moral schizophrenia" where animals are concerned. On the one hand, we claim to take animal suffering seriously and to regard unnecessary suffering as morally wrong. On the other hand, the overwhelming number of ways in which we use nonhumans—and the resulting suffering—cannot be regarded as necessary in any coherent sense. Many of us who live with nonhumans regard them as members of our families. Nevertheless, we turn around and stick forks into other nonhumans who are not relevantly different in any way from the animals whom we love.

Our moral schizophrenia about animals is related to their status as our property (Francione 2000, 50-80). Although we claim to take animal interests seriously, animals necessarily remain as nothing more than things because they are commodities that we own and that have only the value that we choose to give them. In *Animals, Property, and the Law*, I argued that, although animal welfare laws seem to require that we balance human and nonhuman interests in determining the propriety of animal use or treatment, any supposed balance is meaningless because what we purport to weigh are the interests of property owners against the interests of their animal property. The result of this exercise is predetermined from the outset by the property status of the nonhuman.[5] The animal in question is always a "food animal", "game animal", "rodeo animal", "pet", or some other form of animal property that exists solely for our use and has no value except that which we give it.

Because animals are property, they are considered as having no inherent or intrinsic value, and we are generally permitted to ignore whatever

---

4 | This is not to say that I regard the use of nonhumans in experiments as morally justifiable. I do not (Francione 2000, 156-157, 2006a). I do, however, regard our use of animals for food, entertainment, and hunting (uses that account for the vast majority of the suffering and death that we impose on nonhumans) as transparently trivial.

5 | See Francione (1995) (discussing the failure of animal welfare laws to provide any significant protection to animals because of their status as property and the inability to balance in any meaningful way the interests of property against those of property owners).

interests they may have whenever it benefits us to do so. We may impose on them horrendous pain and suffering, clearly amounting to what would be regarded as torture if inflicted on humans, as long as it is regarded as necessary according to the norms that constitute the particular form of institutionalized exploitation. For instance, cattle have an interest in not being castrated without anesthesia or branded with a hot iron—both very painful procedures—but these are regarded as "necessary" because they are "normal" agricultural practices. The "suffering" of property owners who cannot use their property as they wish counts more than the suffering of nonhumans. The requirement that we treat animals "humanely" and do not inflict "unnecessary" suffering is, in reality, nothing more than an injunction not to impose more pain and suffering than is required to facilitate particular animal uses in an efficient manner, and animal interests have no intrinsic value in our assessments.

Although we could certainly treat nonhuman animals better than we do now, their status as property militates strongly against any significant improvement.[6] Moreover, as I argued in *Rain Without Thunder: The Ideology of the Animal Rights Movement* (Francione 1996), there is no empirical evidence to indicate that animal welfare regulation will lead to the abolition of animal exploitation. Indeed, it appears as though animal welfare regulations do little to reduce actual animal suffering and have as their primary effect making humans feel more comfortable about exploiting nonhumans. We have had animal welfare laws for the better part of two hundred years, and we are exploiting more nonhumans today than at any point in human history.

In sum, although our conventional moral and legal thinking appears to reject the link between cognitive characteristics and moral status and to regard sentience alone as morally significant, the property status of animals rests squarely on the view that animals, unlike humans, do not have an interest in their lives because they are cognitively different from us. So although we reject the link in one sense, we accept it in another sense through the position that supposed cognitive differences justify our using

---

6 | See Francione (1995), 14 (arguing that the status of animals as property makes better treatment difficult but not impossible). In the decade since I wrote *Animals, Property, and the Law*, there have been no significant improvements in animal welfare, at least in the United States, despite there being an extremely active and well-financed animal welfare movement. See also Francione (2007).

animals in ways in which we do not use any humans. The result is that our moral and legal acceptance of the importance of sentience has not resulted in any paradigm shift in our treatment of nonhumans. Indeed, some of the most shocking forms of animal exploitation, including intensive animal agriculture or what is called "factory farming", have developed in the past one hundred years—when we claimed to embrace a more enlightened view of the moral status of nonhumans and of our moral and legal obligations to them.

4. The Problems of Similar-Minds Theory

The primary difference between the recent resurgence of the similar-minds approach represented by *GAP* and similar approaches and the view put forward by Bentham and incorporated into conventional animal welfare theory is that modern ethological research indicates that there may be some nonhumans whose minds may be sufficiently like ours in ways that Bentham and others did not recognize and who may thereby be entitled to greater moral and legal consideration. Perhaps it is time to take a closer look at the entire enterprise of linking the moral significance of nonhumans with cognitive attributes beyond sentience, rather than trying to determine whether some nonhumans have such cognitive attributes or have them in a way that makes them sufficiently similar to humans to merit moral and legal personhood.

As a preliminary matter, there is a sense in which the similar-minds theory is decidedly odd. Is there anyone who has ever lived with a dog or cat who does not recognize that these nonhumans are intelligent, self-aware, or emotional, even though they are more genetically dissimilar to us than are the great apes? My partner and I live with five rescued dogs. If someone were to question whether our canine companions had these mental characteristics, we would find that as odd as an inquiry about whether they had tails. This is not a matter of anthropomorphism, the ascription of human qualities where there is no empirical basis. There is simply no way that we can plausibly and coherently explain the behavior of these nonhumans without relying on concepts of mind. Nonhumans may not have intentional states that are predicative in the same way as are intentional states that involve symbolic communication, but they certainly do have cognitive states that are equivalent to beliefs, desires, etc.

Moreover, 150 years after Darwin, it is astonishing that we are so astonished that other animals may have characteristics thought to be uniquely human. The proposition that humans have mental characteristics wholly absent in nonhumans is inconsistent with the theory of evolution. Darwin maintained that there are no uniquely human characteristics: "[T]he difference in mind between man and the higher animals, great as it is, is certainly one of degree and not of kind" (Darwin 1981, 105; Rachels 1900). That is, Darwin recognized that the differences between human and nonhuman minds are quantitative and not qualitative. He argued that nonhumans are able to think and possess many of the same emotional attributes as humans. This is not to say that there is not a significant difference in cognition between an animal that uses symbolic communication and one that does not; it is only to say that the difference is not qualitative in that one animal has a cognitive characteristic that has no equivalent in the other.

Although I believe that nonhumans do possess the characteristics that we regard as uniquely human, I also realize that there is controversy on this point, and, in any event, there are certainly differences between human minds and the minds of other animals who do not use language. There are, however, at least two reasons to reject the notion that nonhumans must be more than sentient to have full membership in the moral community. One difficulty is primarily practical and concerns whether similar-minds theory will result in any meaningful change even for those nonhumans who have cognitive characteristics very similar to our own. The other difficulty is primarily theoretical and concerns the failure of the theory to address the fundamental moral question of why any characteristic other than sentience is necessary in order to have full membership in the moral community.

4.1 Similar-Minds Theory: A Further Delay of Justice?[7]

It is likely that similar-minds theory will do nothing more than delay our confronting our moral and legal obligations to nonhumans for an indeterminate time while we purport to amass the empirical evidence necessary to conclude that at least some nonhumans have minds similar to those of

---

7 | For a further discussion of the ideas discussed in this section, see Francione (2000), 117-119.

humans. But even when there is absolutely no doubt about this similarity, we ignore the evidence and continue our exploitation. For example, the similarities between humans and chimpanzees are unmistakable. Chimpanzee DNA is 98.5 percent the same as ours, and chimpanzees have a cultural and mental life very similar to our own. We have known about these similarities for a while now; indeed, the whole point of *GAP* was to present the overwhelmingly powerful case that there are no relevant differences between humans and the great apes for purposes of inclusion in the moral community. Nevertheless, we still continue to imprison chimpanzees in zoos and use them in biomedical experiments. Even Jane Goodall, who was described in *GAP* as a "person who has made people appreciate that chimpanzees are individuals with different personalities and complex social relationships" (Cavalieri & Singer 1993, 10), has declined to call for a complete ban on our use of these nonhumans.

A related problem is that the similar-minds theory does not specify the extent to which a nonhuman must possess a particular characteristic before we consider that nonhuman to be sufficiently "like us" for purposes of moral significance. For example, "[a] growing body of evidence seems to show that parrots, like chimps and dolphins, can master complex intellectual concepts that most human children are not capable of mastering until the age of 5" (Mullen 1997, 1; see also Hillix & Rumbaugh 2004). We have historically regarded the ability to have abstract ideas as uniquely human and as indicative of a qualitative difference between humans and nonhumans. We know now that we may have been mistaken about this as parrots and other nonhumans also seem to have some form of abstract thought.[8] We are, however, still selling parrots in pet stores. How intelligent does the parrot have to be before we conclude that the parrot qualifies for membership in the moral community? Does the parrot have to have the conceptual ability of an eight-year-old? A twelve-year-old? Similarly, some chimpanzees have exhibited the ability to use and to manipulate human language; how extensive must their vocabulary and syntactical ability

---

8 | It may, of course, be argued that the parrot (or, indeed, any nonhuman) does not have the ability to engage in abstract generalization but only the ability to form complex associations. See Steiner (2005), 30-31. But the ability to discriminate that is required in order to form complex associations would seem to involve some level of abstract thinking.

be before we conclude that humans and at least nonhuman primates have similar minds?

The problem with this game of special characteristics is that nonhumans can never win. When we determine that parrots have the conceptual ability to understand and manipulate single-digit numbers, we demand that they be able to understand and manipulate double-digit numbers in order to be sufficiently like us. When a chimpanzee indicates beyond doubt that she has an extensive vocabulary, we demand that she exhibit certain levels of syntactical skill in order to demonstrate that her mind is like ours. The irony, of course, is that whatever characteristic we are talking about will be possessed by some nonhumans to a greater degree than some humans, but we would never think it appropriate to exploit those humans in the ways that we do nonhumans.

There is a legitimate concern that the similar-minds theory is really an *identical-minds* theory and that animals will never be regarded as entitled to full membership in the moral community unless their minds are exactly like ours. Even then, there is no guarantee that we will not discriminate against nonhumans. After all, in the nineteenth century, racists relied on phrenology, or the "science" of determining personality traits based on the shape of the head, to declare that people of color, Jews, and others had different minds. Thus, even having an identical mind is not sufficient if there is a reason and desire to discriminate. Given that there probably are differences between the minds of animals who use symbolic communication and those who do not, the similar-minds theory will only be a prescription for the continued oppression of nonhumans as we pursue the endless quest for an identity that may never be realized, particularly if we are motivated by a desire to continue to consume animal products.

4.2 Similar-Minds Theory: Begging the Question[9]

Even if similar-minds theory resulted in our recognizing the personhood of some nonhumans, such as the great apes or dolphins, what about the vast number of animals who will never demonstrate the ability to use human language or the other characteristics that we associate with human minds? Although the similar-minds approach claims that, as an empirical

---

9 | For a further discussion of the ideas discussed in this section, see Francione (2000), 111-127.

matter, we may have been wrong in the past and at least some nonhumans may have some of the aforementioned characteristics, it does not address the underlying—and fundamental—moral question: why is anything more than sentience necessary for nonhumans to have the right not to be treated exclusively as means to human ends?

Similar-minds theory begs the moral question from the outset by assuming that certain characteristics are special and justify differential treatment. For example, we claim that humans are the only animals (apart perhaps from some great apes) who can recognize themselves in mirrors. Even if that is true, what is the moral significance of this supposed fact? My rescued border collie may not be able to recognize herself in a mirror, but she can jump about six feet from a sitting position—something that I certainly cannot do, and, as far as I am aware, no other human can do either. Birds can fly without being in an aircraft; no human can. Fish can breathe underwater without the aid of a snorkel or air tank; no human can. The similar-minds theory begs the moral question from the outset because it assumes that our abilities are morally more valuable than *their* abilities. There is, of course, no justification for this position other than that *we* say so and it is in *our* interest to do so.

Moreover, even if all animals other than humans were to lack a particular cognitive characteristic beyond sentience, or possess that characteristic to a lesser degree or in a different way from humans, such a difference cannot serve to justify our treatment of nonhumans as things. It may be the case that differences between humans and nonhumans are relevant for other purposes. For example, no one maintains that nonhumans ought to drive automobiles or attend universities. However, any such differences have *no* bearing on whether we should eat nonhumans or use them in experiments, nor should they. This is clear in situations in which only humans are involved. Whatever characteristic we identify as uniquely human will be seen to a lesser degree in some humans and not at all in others. Some humans will have the exact same deficiency that we attribute to nonhumans. This deficiency may be relevant for some purposes, but it is not relevant to whether we enslave such humans or otherwise treat them as commodities with no inherent value.

Consider the characteristic of self-awareness. It would seem that *any* sentient being must be self-aware in that to be sentient means to be the sort of being who recognizes that it is *that* being, and not some other, who is experiencing pain or distress. Biologist Donald Griffin has observed that if animals are conscious of anything, "the animal's own body and its own actions must fall within the scope of its perceptual consciousness" (Griffin 2001). We nevertheless deny animals self-awareness because we maintain that they cannot "think such thoughts as 'It is *I* who am running, or climbing this tree, or chasing that moth'" (Griffin 2001). Griffin maintains that

"when an animal consciously perceives the running, climbing, or moth-chasing of another animal, it must also be aware of who is doing these things. And if the animal is perceptually conscious of its own body, it is difficult to rule out similar recognition that it, itself, is doing the running, climbing, or chasing." (Griffin 2001)

He concludes that "[i]f animals are capable of perceptual awareness, denying them some level of self-awareness would seem to be an arbitrary and unjustified restriction" (Griffin 2001). As I have previously stated, "[w]hen a dog experiences pain, the dog necessarily has a mental experience that tells her 'this pain is happening to me'. In order for pain to exist, some consciousness—some*one*—must perceive it as happening to her and must prefer not to experience it." (Francione 2004, 128)

But even if we require self-awareness in the peculiarly humanocentric sense as the ability to have a "conscious experience ... whose existence and content are available to be consciously thought about (that is, available for description in acts of thinking that are themselves made available to further acts of thinking)" (Carruthers 1992), then many humans, such as the severely mentally disabled, lack self-awareness. A lack of the sort of self-awareness that we attribute to normal adult humans may be relevant for some purposes. We may, for instance, not want to allow a severely retarded person to operate a motor vehicle. Nevertheless, lacking this sort of self-awareness has no bearing on whether we should, for instance, use such humans in painful biomedical experiments. For whatever characteristic we choose, there will be some humans who will have the characteristic to a lesser degree than some nonhumans and some humans who will not have it at all. The lack of the characteristic may be relevant for some purposes, but is irrelevant to whether we treat a sentient human as a thing all of whose fundamental interests may be ignored if it benefits us to do so.

As I discussed above, although Bentham ostensibly rejected the view that the moral status of nonhumans depends on their having minds similar to humans, he effectively reincorporated that view through the notion that we may continue to use and kill animals because they do not have an interest in their lives. Peter Singer, co-editor of *GAP*, does the same thing. He argues that although only sentience is needed for moral significance and we ought to take animal suffering seriously, it is permissible to continue to use animals because, with the possible exception of great apes, animals do not have a sense of the future and an interest in their lives.[10] According to Singer, "[a]n animal may struggle against a threat to its life" (Singer 1975, 228), but that does not mean that the animal can "grasp that it has 'a life' in the sense that requires an understanding of what it is to exist over a period of time" (Singer 1975, 229). He concludes that "in the absence of some form of mental continuity it is not easy to explain why the loss to the animal killed is not, from an impartial point of view, made good by the creation of a new animal who will lead an equally pleasant life" (Singer 1975, 229). Like Bentham, Singer maintains that it is not the use per se of nonhumans that raises a moral issue but the suffering of the animals incidental to the use. He argues that it is possible to apply the principle of equal consideration—that we should treat similar interests similarly—to nonhuman interests in suffering and that it is not necessary to abolish the property status of nonhumans in order to do so.

The position of Bentham and Singer that, as an empirical matter, animals do not have an interest in their lives rests on a problematic understanding of self-awareness. Any being that is sentient is necessarily self-aware. Any being that is sentient necessarily has an interest in life because sentience is a means to the end of continued existence. To say that a nonhuman is sentient but does not have an interest in continued existence and does not prefer, want, or desire to live is peculiar (Francione 2000, 137-138).[11]

---

10 | See Singer (1975), 18-21, 228-230 and Francione (2000), 135-146 (discussing Singer's position). The view that animals do not have an interest in continued existence and, therefore, that animal use per se is not problematic is proposed by other theorists as well. See Francione (2006b), discussing the views of Cass R. Sunstein, who accepts the views of Bentham and Singer). See also Nussbaum (2004), 299, 314-315, accepting the utilitarian view that the treatment of animals and not their use raises the primary moral issue in the context of killing animals for food.

11 | Moreover, it is virtually impossible to explain a great deal of animal behavior without positing that animals anticipate the future (Francione 2000, 139-140).

According to the Bentham/Singer view, a being, whether human or nonhuman, has an interest in continued existence only if the being has an autobiographical sense of self and can reflect on his or her life. However, there is no reason to link such a mental state with whether we treat someone as the resource of others. For instance, there are humans who experience transient global amnesia and have no sense of the past or the future but have a very distinct sense of self with respect to present events and objects. They are self-conscious but not in the same way as is a human adult without amnesia. That difference may be relevant for some purposes. We might not, for example, give someone without an autobiographical sense of self a scholarship to a university because such a person will probably not benefit from an education. No one would deny, however, that such humans have an interest in their lives. The characteristic of having transient global amnesia is not relevant to whether we treat such people as commodities whose fundamental interests may be sacrificed if it benefits us to do so.

In sum, the similar-minds approach is fundamentally misguided and, at best, will do nothing more than create new speciesist hierarchies in which we may move some nonhumans, such as the great apes or dolphins, into a preferred group[12] but continue to treat all other nonhumans as things that lack morally significant interests. The theory does not explain why sentience is not a sufficient criterion for moral significance but merely assumes that some supposedly uniquely human characteristic is the ticket for admission to the moral community.

5. HUMAN SLAVERY AND ANIMAL PROPERTY

If we were to abandon similar-minds theory altogether, including the Bentham/Singer version of the doctrine, and require only sentience for full membership in the moral community, we would have to abandon our treatment of nonhumans as our property. As I argue in *Introduction to*

---

[12] | See, e.g., *Project R&R: Release and Restitution for Chimpanzees in U.S. Laboratories*, http://www.releasechimps.org ("No other species holds the unique position of chimpanzees—a species with so much that seems 'human'"). Project R&R is a campaign of the New England Anti-Vivisection Society. [Ed. Note: This sentence has been removed from the website.]

Animal Rights, while we do not protect humans from all suffering, we prohibit inflicting suffering on humans incidental to using them merely as the resources of others. We accord everyone, irrespective of his or her particular characteristics, a basic right not to be treated as the property of others (Francione 2000, 90-96). We regard human slavery—even "humane" slavery—as unacceptable.

Bentham opposed human slavery, and, as I have discussed elsewhere, this arguably rested, at least in part, on his recognition that the principle of equal consideration could not be applied to slaves, who would always count for less than their owners did (Francione 2000, 130-150).[13] Bentham, however, failed to see that the same problem exists with animal property. To the extent that nonhumans have an interest in their lives, our use of them in situations where we would use no humans necessarily denies them equal consideration for this interest.

Moreover, even if it is plausible to maintain that nonhumans do not have an interest in continued existence, application of the principle of equal consideration to animal interests in not suffering—already difficult to do because of the need to make interspecies comparisons (Francione 2000, 143)[14]—becomes even more complicated when animals are viewed as human property. The property status of animals serves as what I have discussed elsewhere as a "two-edged sword wielded against their interests" (Francione 2004, 122). Property status stops us from perceiving animal interests as similar to ours in the first instance and subordinates animal interests to human interests even when human and animal interests are recognized as similar because the property status of animals is always a good reason to refuse them similar treatment.

---

13 | Similarly, Singer argues that we should not treat normal human adults as replaceable resources (Francione 2000, 141). Although both Bentham and Singer, who are utilitarians, eschew moral rights, both appear to be at least rule-utilitarians, as opposed to act-utilitarians, when it comes to treating humans exclusively as resources.

14 | Indeed, such comparisons may be impossible. For example, John Stuart Mill, also a utilitarian, maintained that the pleasures of the human intellect have a much higher value than the sensations of nonhumans. According to Mill, "[i]t is better to be a human being dissatisfied than a pig satisfied" (Mill 2002, 233, 242). This would suggest that there is a qualitative difference between humans and nonhumans that would militate in favor of human interests always prevailing.

There is no non-speciesist reason not to recognize that full membership in the moral community requires that we reject the slavery of nonhumans just as we rejected the slavery of humans. This would require that we abolish—and not merely regulate—our exploitation of nonhumans and that we stop bringing domestic animals into existence to serve as means to human ends (Francione 2000, 153-154).

6. Conclusion

The similar-minds theory is not new. It has been around for a long time in the form of various attempts to link cognitive characteristics with moral personhood and has served as the primary theoretical vehicle to exclude nonhumans from membership in the moral community. We supposedly rejected this link when we accepted the principle that the ability to suffer is the only characteristic required for moral and legal significance. But the theory was reintroduced as the belief that nonhumans, unlike humans, have no interest in continued life, and this explains why we did not reject the property status of animals when we tried to apply the principle in moral and legal contexts. Although we claim to take animal interests seriously, we treat animals as nothing more than things.

Whether nonhumans have minds that are similar or identical to ours may be interesting from a scientific perspective, but it is wholly irrelevant from a moral perspective. If we take nonhuman interests seriously, we have no choice but to acknowledge that only sentience is relevant.[15]

---

15 | Professor Taimie Bryant also rejects the similar-minds approach and does not believe that particular human-like cognitive characteristics are necessary for moral status or legal protection (Bryant 2007). There are, however, significant differences in our approaches. In addition to rejecting cognitive characteristics beyond sentience as necessary for moral significance, as I have, she maintains that linking moral significance with sentience alone, as I do, is similarly problematic. She argues that a theory based on sentience is not sufficient to ensure protection for nonhumans because assessments of sentience are equally susceptible of being manipulated so that humans will inevitably be seen as having a qualitatively different level of sentience than nonhumans. This supposed difference will be used to exclude animals from the moral community just as supposed qualitative differences in other cognitive characteristics have been used. Although this use of

This requires that we go one step beyond Bentham and recognize that the property status of nonhumans means that we necessarily subscribe to a similar-minds theory that will result in our never giving animal interests serious, let alone equal, consideration. We should forget about the similar-minds theory. It is nothing but a prescription for confused thinking about the human/nonhuman relationship and a vehicle that will only serve to perpetuate our speciesist oppression of nonhumans. The efforts of animal advocates ought to be directed at promoting veganism and the incremental eradication of the property status of nonhumans.[16]

REFERENCES

Bekoff, M., Jamieson, D. (eds.) (1996), Readings in Animal Cognition, Cambridge, MA: MIT Press.

Bentham, J. (1970), Introduction to the Principles of Morals and Legislation, London: Athlone Press.

Bryant, T. (2007), "Similarity or Differences as a Basis for Justice: Must Animals Be Like Humans to Be Legally Protected from Humans?", Law and Contemporary Problems 70, 207-254.

---

sentience is surely possible, my theory rejects it from the outset in that I maintain that if a being is sentient at all, that being has interests and, if those interests are to be morally significant, the being must have a right not to be treated exclusively as the resource of humans. Bryant's view assumes that sentience is not necessary because we can create a system of duties that do not depend on whether the objects of those duties are sentient. To the extent that she maintains that such obligations are owed to non-sentient beings and do not merely concern those beings, I do not agree. In my view, we cannot owe a duty to a being that does not have interests, and non-sentient beings do not have interests.

16 | For a discussion of incremental change at both the individual and social levels, see Francione (1996), 147-219. I have long argued that an animal advocate who agrees with the abolitionist or animal rights position ought to adopt a vegan lifestyle. On a social level, I have promoted abolitionist education and consumer boycotts. To the extent that advocates seek legislative or regulatory change as part of social change, they should pursue prohibitions that incrementally diminish property rights in nonhumans.

Carruthers, P. (1992), The Animal Issue: Moral Theory and Practice, Cambridge: Cambridge University Press.
Cavalieri, P., Singer, P. (eds.) (1993), The Great Ape Project: Equality Beyond Humantity, London: Fourth Estate Limited.
Darwin, C. (1981), The Descent of Man, Princeton: Princeton University Press.
Francione, G. L. (1993), "Personhood, Property and Legal Competence", in: P. Cavalieri, P. Singer (eds.), The Great Ape Project: Equality Beyond Humantity, London: Fourth Estate Limited.
Francione, G.L. (1995), Animals, Property, and the Law, Philadelphia: Temple University Press.
Francione, G.L. (1996), Rain Without Thunder: The Ideology of the Animal Rights Movement, Philadelphia: Temple University Press.
Francione, G.L. (2000), Introduction to Animal Rights: Your Child or the Dog?, Philadelphia: Temple University Press.
Francione, G.L. (2004), "Animals—Property or Persons?", in: C.R. Sunstein, M.C. Nussbaum (eds.), Animal Rights: Current Debates and New Directions, Oxford: Oxford University Press, 108-142.
Francione, G.L. (2005), "Our Hypocrisy", New Scientist (June 4-10), 51-52.
Francione, G.L. (2006a), "The Use of Nonhuman Animals in Biomedical Research", Journal of Law, Medicine & Ethics (Summer), 241-48.
Francione, G.L. (2006b), "Equal Consideration and the Interest of Nonhuman Animals in Continued Existence. A Response to Professor Sunstein", The University of Chicago Legal Forum, 231-252.
Francione, G.L. (2007), "Reflections on *Animal, Property, and the Law*, and *Rain Without Thunder*", Law and Contemporary Problems 70, 9-57.
Francione, G.L. (2008), Animals as Persons: Essays on the Abolition of Animal Exploitation, New York: Columbia University Press.
Griffin, D.R. (2001), Animal Minds: Beyond Cognition to Consciousness, Chicago: University of Chicago Press.
Hauser, M. (1996), The Evolution of Communication, Cambridge, MA: MIT Press.
Hauser, M. (2000), Wild Minds: What Animals Really Think, New York: Henry Holt and Co.
Hillix, W.A., Rumbaugh, D. (2004), Animal Bodies, Human Minds: Ape, Dolphin, and Parrot Language Skills, New York: Kluwer.

Mill, J.S. (2002), "Utilitarism", in: The Basic Writing of John Stuart Mill: On Liberty, The Subjection of Women, and Utilitarianism, London: Modern Library.

Mullen, W. (1997), "Parrots Don't Just Talk a Good Game", Chicago Tribune (November 7).

Nussbaum, M.C. (2004) "Beyond 'Compassion and Humantiy': Justice for Nonhuman Animals", in: C. R. Sunstein, M. C. Nussbaum (eds.), Animal Rights: Current Debates and New Directions. Oxford: Oxford University Press, 299-320.

Rachels, J. (1990), Created from Animals: The Moral Implications of Darwinism, Oxford: Oxford University Press.

Regan, T. (1983), The Case for Animal Rights, Berkeley: University of California Press.

Savage-Rumbaugh, S., Lewin, R. (1994), Kanzi: The Ape at the Brink of the Human Mind, New York: Wiley.

Singer, P. (1975), Animal Liberation: A New Ethics for Our Treatment of Animals, New York: The New York Review (2d ed. 1990).

Steiner, G. (2005), Anthropocentrism and Its Discontents: The Moral Status of Animals in the History of Western Philosophy, Pittsburgh: Pittsburgh University Press.

Wise, S.M. (2000), Rattling the Cage: Toward Legal Rights for Animals, Cambridge, MA: Perseus Publishing.

Wise, S.M. (2002), Drawing the Line: Science and the Case for Animal Rights, New York: Basic Books.

11. Two Approaches to Animal Ethics and the Case of Great Apes

Alessandro Blasimme, Constantine Sandis & Lisa Bortolotti

1. Introduction

Bans or restrictions on experimentation on great apes are currently in place in New Zealand, Australia, Japan. In Europe, research on animals is regulated by Directive 2010/63/EU, which contains special provisions for non-human primates and great apes (European Parliament 2010). The European legislation guarantees protection for non-human primates and great apes in particular, and restricts their use to specific kinds of scientific research.

In December 2011 in the United States, the National Institutes of Health (NIH) decided to suspend all funding to projects in biomedical and behavioural research requiring experimentation on chimpanzees (Gorman 2011). Whilst there is no general ban to experimentation involving great apes in the US and in some circumstances it is still possible to use chimpanzees in research (e.g. when not using them would slow down research aimed at treating life threatening and debilitating conditions), the decision made by the NIH was regarded as a significant step forward by those campaigning to extend some moral rights to great apes.

In this paper we focus on the reasons why great apes should be considered as part of our moral community and thus be protected from harm by the sort of legislation described above. There are two main approaches to animal ethics. The first is inspired by the *ethic of justice* and focuses on what humans and other animals have in common, that is, those psychological capacities which form the basis for assigning any moral status or rights. If great apes and humans share capacities that are regarded as morally relevant (e.g. sentience and key aspects of personhood), then, depending on the preferred theory of ethics, we can say that some of their morally relevant preferences should be taken into consideration (as in a utilitarian framework) or that some basic moral rights should be granted to them (as in a deontological framework).

The second approach is inspired by an *ethic of care* which focuses on the relationship between humans and other animals. If great apes are vulnerable in ways which make them subject to harm and exploitation in their relationship with us, they ought to be the object of our moral solicitude. As a result, potentially exploitative practices should be avoided whenever possible.

Evidence for the former approach to legislation on research involving great apes is not hard to find. According to the European legislation, for example, if there is scientific evidence that an animal (or a species) can experience pain, suffering, distress and lasting harm, then this animal (or species) is worth some moral consideration. More specifically to great apes, the European legislator affirms that:

"[T]he use of great apes, *as the closest species to human beings with the most advanced social and behavioural skills*, should be permitted only for the purposes of research aimed at the preservation of those species and where action in relation to a life-threatening, debilitating condition endangering human beings is warranted, and no other species or alternative method would suffice in order to achieve the aims of the procedure." (European Parliament 2010, article 18, our emphasis)

As a result of the above-cited considerations, the European Parliament has adopted a complex regulatory approach. Directive 2010/63/EU restricts the use of non-human primates to basic research, translational and applied research on diseases, testing of drugs, foodstuff and feed-stuff, and research aimed at the preservation of the human species. In all those cases, however, the use of non-human primates is only permitted if no alternative is available. As to great apes, the directive states that their use is generally banned, unless it is authorised by a special Committee at the European Commission. Such Committee may only permit the use of great apes provisionally and in exceptional circumstances, as in the case of an unexpected life-threatening outbreak, and provided that no alternatives exist. Furthermore, all non-human primates used in research in European member states from 2022 on, have to come from self-sustaining colonies—this is a demanding requirement, given the economic and logistic costs of keeping relatively large animals in captivity. Overall, this piece of legislation accounts for the moral standing of non-human primates, and of great apes in particular, as superior to that of other animals, and deserving of special protection.

The justification provided by the NIH for reducing the funding for projects involving experiments on chimpanzees was varied but it also includes a reference to the similarities between humans and great apes. The statement by the director of the Institute included scientific reasons (in most cases the use of chimps is deemed as unnecessary), pragmatic reasons (keeping a large number of chimps in humane lab conditions is very expensive), ecological reasons (wild chimps are an endangered species), and purely ethical reasons (chimps are *special*). These reasons are all also echoed in the mission statement of the Great Ape Project—an organisation which has campaigned for years for the extension of some human rights to great apes.

Whether experiments on chimpanzees and other great apes are necessary or even useful to biomedical science has been a matter of contention for some time. Many have suggested that alternative research methods should be used, given that they are not only more conducive to the development of treatment for debilitating diseases, but also more cost-effective (Knight 2007, 281). A report of the Institute of Medicine, entitled *Chimpanzees in Biomedical and Behavioral Research: Assessing the Necessity* (2011), found that "recent advances in alternate research tools have rendered chimpanzees largely unnecessary as research subjects." Scientific and pragmatic reasons of this sort depend on the objectives of current biomedical research and on the practicalities of keeping great apes in captivity in research facilities. As these variables are subject to change, arguments against the use of great apes in research based on these considerations do not support an outright ban on experiments involving great apes but a stricter regulatory framework.

Why are great apes, and chimpanzees in particular, regarded as *special* among non-human animals? Does this special status justify an outright ban on experimentation involving great apes? As quoted in the *New York Times* article reporting on the new policy, Francis S. Collins, the director of the NIH, said that chimps deserve "special consideration and respect", because they are our closest relatives. In the mission statement of the Great Ape Project (GAP), Pedro A. Ynterian, the founder of GAP

Brazil and Director of GAP International is similarly quoted as stating that "[a chimp] thinks, develops affection, hates, suffers, learns and even transmits knowledge. To sum it up, they are just like us". This approach seems to suggest that we should extend some of the moral consideration that we commonly reserve to fellow humans to great apes (chimpanzees in particular), because they are biologically very similar to humans, and share many of their morally relevant psychological characteristics.

The line adopted by the European Parliament and by the NIH reflects a *psychological approach* to the moral status of great apes, which are regarded as special because closer to humans in their psychological capacities than other animals.

There is also evidence that the other approach to animal ethics, the ethic-of-care approach, is often adopted in this context. In the GAP mission statement, we find the following passage:

"[T]he exploitation of great primates in laboratories, circus, entertainment shows and zoos can be considered a kind of slavery, reminding what man used to do with others of his own kind who were considered to be inferior a little bit more than one century ago."

Considerations about possible exploitation are central here, and the concern is that we use great apes for purposes that do not necessarily benefit them. The key issue identified is not what great apes share with humans, biologically or psychologically, but what type of relationship they have with us. The situation of vulnerability in which great apes are now is compared with that of human groups that have been discriminated against in the past. This is an instance of the *vulnerability approach* to the moral inclusion of great apes.

Psychological similarity and vulnerability to exploitation are thought to be competing considerations and to give rise to independent arguments for or against current human practices involving non-human animals (see Bortolotti et al. 2010). In this paper however we argue that, at least with respect to the debate on the treatment of great apes, the two approaches complement each other. We maintain that the extent to which non-human animals are minded is relevant both to whether they have moral status or moral rights and to whether they are the appropriate object of moral solicitude. Vulnerability to harm and exploitation is not ruled out by the possession of even the most sophisticated psychological capacities. On the contrary, the possession of certain psychological capacities can increase an individual's vulnerabilities to certain forms of harm.

In section 1, we briefly introduce the debate on the differences between the psychological capacities of human and non-human animals and consider the role that advances in cognitive ethology and comparative psychology can play in shaping human attitudes towards non-humans. In section 2, we describe the two approaches to the moral treatment of non-human animals by reference to some examples of influential positions in the literature. In section 3, we suggest that the psychological capacities necessary for mindedness come with both psychological powers and vulnerabilities to harm and exploitation. Both powers and vulnerabilities need to be taken into account when considering what we owe to non-human animals in general, and great apes in particular.

2. TO WHAT EXTENT ARE NON-HUMANS MINDED?

In the traditional philosophical literature, the conditions for mindedness include the possession or the exercise of capacities that are highly sophisticated. An individual is regarded as minded only if it has the concept of itself as minded; if it is rational; if it is self-conscious; or if it has a language (see Davidson 1984, 2004; Dennett 1979, 1995; Carruthers 1989 for influential versions of these views). These theses are all motivated by accounts of mindedness that seem very demanding and thus psychologically unrealistic (Bortolotti 2008; Glock 1999, 2000, 2006; Sandis 2006, 2010). They entail, for example, that a dog cannot believe that the cat is on the oak tree unless the dog has a *concept* of cats, oak trees, physical location, etc., understood further as a linguistic representation of some kind.

The question of animal minds is closely related to questions about language or concept acquisition. To misquote Wittgenstein, a dog may now desire to go for a walk immediately, but it cannot now desire to go for a walk next Tuesday. Be that as it may, it remains generally implausible to suggest that in order to have a property it is necessary to possess the concept of that property, or that it is necessary to do something well in order to do it at all. Yet, the aforementioned theories state that it is necessary to have the concept of belief in order to have a belief, or that it is necessary to be at least largely rational in order to be minded. Keith Frankish (2004) helpfully contrasts a behaviour-based concept of mind with the language-involving concept of 'supermind' and, accordingly, distinguishes between two strands of belief. The first ('basic belief') is typically nonconscious, passive, non-occurrent, and *de re* insofar as it is attributable on purely behavioural grounds. The second ('superbelief') may be held consciously, is *de dicto* in typically requiring linguistic conceptualization, and frequently occurrent. Thus we may say that the dog *believes* the cat is on the oak tree, but does not *superbelieve* it. Frankish defers to Norman Malcolm (1973) who "concludes that there is no single paradigm or prototype of thinking and suggests that it was by treating *having thoughts* as the paradigm form that Descartes was led to deny that animals can think" (Frankish 2004, 16n 6). If Malcolm and Frankish are right then it is premature to deny that animals have beliefs.

The issue of animal mindedness has been the focus of sustained philosophical debates (Blasimme & Bortolotti 2010). Hans-Johann Glock (2010) calls the philosophers who deny or underestimate mindedness in non-human animals 'differentialists', as their crucial claim is that there is a qualitative difference between human and non-human animals with respect to mindedness. The *qualitative difference thesis* (hereafter, QLT) affirms that the distinctive abilities of the human cognitive apparatus (such as the ones listed above) are exclusively human traits, and that non-human species do not possess them at all. Our higher cognitive capacities are not due to a difference in degree, but to a difference in kind, since non-human animals, when confronted with cognitive tasks, use entirely different strategies and cognitive tools than humans (see, e.g. Bermúdez 2003; Carruthers 2002). Defenders of the QLT often stress the specificity of human language as a constitutive element of human cognition, thus maintaining that non-human animals fall short of the cognitive capacities associated with language (see, for instance, Chomsky 1980; Jakendoff 2002; Pinker 1994). Animal minds, whatever they are, are not simplified versions of human minds, but thoroughly different cognitive systems. This approach seems committed to the worrying view that there are just two kinds of cognition, *animal* cognition and *human* cognition: "The profound biological continuity between human and nonhuman animals masks an equally profound discontinuity between human and nonhuman minds." (Penn et al. 2008, 110) Yet there is as great a diversity between the cognitive capacities of different kinds of animals as there is between the cognitive capacities of any particular species and that of humans. Derrida (2008, 34) was right to speak of the 'infinite space' that separates "the lizard from the dog, the protozoon from the dolphin, the shark from the lamb, the parrot from the chimpanzee, the camel from the eagle, the squirrel from the tiger, the elephant from the cat, the ant from the silkworm, or the hedgehog from the echidna".

On the opposite camp, Glock identifies 'assimilationists', authors who regard mindedness as a genuinely graded set of capacities and claim that some non-human animals satisfy the conditions for mindedness to some extent (see, for instance, MacIntyre 1999; Dretske 2006; Bekoff et al. 2002; deWaal & Tyack 2003; Pepperberg 2002, 2005; Smith et al. 2003; Tomasello et al. 2003). Comparative cognitive psychology over the past two or three decades has stressed the continuity between human and non-human minds. This tendency is a heritage of the Darwinian intuition that the difference between human and non-human mind is one of degree and not of kind (Darwin 1871). Thus, the mainstream trend in this field is to corroborate what we can call the *quantitative difference thesis* (hereafter, QNT) about animal minds. The assimilationist or quantitative difference thesis affirms that what were thought to be distinctive abilities of the human cognitive apparatus (such as use of a grammatical language, use of symbols, intentionality, recognition of causal patterns, inductive and deductive reasoning, concept manipulation, mindreading, self-consciousness, and so on) are not exclusively human traits, but ones shared by other non-human species. The true peculiarity of human minds is that, typically, they can express these abilities at a higher level of precision and efficiency than any other species; apart from that, there is nothing unique about the human cognitive system (for further argument see Glock 2012).

From the assimilationist perspective, the welfare of non-human animals, as the welfare of humans, is closely connected to their psychological health. The view is that specific uses of non-human animals for human purposes (breeding, transportation, husbandry, commercial agriculture, animal experimentation, entertainment, sport, arts and crafts, clothing, upholstery, zoo-keeping, space exploration, etc.) affect animal minds in ways that are likely to be morally relevant. How do we know how animal minds are affected by these and other related practices? Although valuable insights can be gained from the behavioural sciences, conceptual, epistemological and methodological issues also arise. Not surprisingly, there is philosophical controversy over the interpretation of the available empirical findings (Finkelstein 2007; Glock 2009, 2012; Steward 2009; Stoecker 2009).

One conceptual question, which we shall return to in the next section, is how to identify criteria for mental ascriptions that are relevant to moral decision-making. A different, epistemological question, is how to formulate scientific hypotheses about animal cognition. On the face of it (quite literally), the emotional life of animals is very public and we should not entertain solipsistic thoughts regarding the mechanisms that underlie their behaviour which we are unwilling to take seriously in analogous human cases.

"Animals display exactly how they feel about what is happening to them. Instead of recognizing this for what it is, scientists especially have argued that we can't "know" what animals think and feel." (Bekoff 2010, 55)

One option is to make mental ascriptions to non-human animals by applying the same tools that we use for mental ascriptions to humans: interpretation of the observed individuals' facial expressions and bodily postures and gestures, empathy-driven mental simulation of their mental states (see, e.g. Gordon 1986, 2004; Goldman 1989), and the use of folk-psychological theories (Baron-Cohen 1992; Fodor 1992; Leslie 1995; Gopnik & Meltzhoff 1997). The attempt to apply these tools for mental ascriptions to non-human animals has been criticised as *naïve anthropomorphism*: it uncritically relies on empathy or intuition, whilst failing to take into due consideration the accumulating scientific knowledge about animal mindedness and the evolutionary origins of human mindreading (Mameli & Bortolotti 2006). Given that our capacity for mental ascriptions has evolved to deal with fellow humans, and given how mental ascriptions happen to work, our unaided intuitions are not a reliable guide to understanding non-human animals. As a result, we are prone to ascribe to non-human animals beliefs that they are unlikely to have and fail to ascribe to them beliefs that they can have, because we either overestimate or underestimate their conceptual discriminatory capacities (Mameli & Bortolotti 2006). Anthropomorphism is pervasive and cuts both ways.

Critics who complain about anthropomorphism fail to notice their own anthropomorphisms. The same zoo officials who accuse activists of being anthropomorphic when they call a captive elephant unhappy turn around and freely describe the same elephant as happy (Bekoff 2010, 77).

A more tempered version of the anthropomorphic strategy has been advanced by Morton (1990), who argues for *critical anthropomorphism*, that is, the view that one should not rely purely on common intuitions about animal minds but also pay attention to the results of scientific studies on animal cognition. Supplementing everyday intuitions with the best available empirical knowledge in order to arrive at attributions of mindedness seems like a sensible strategy. We can reliably (though not infallibly) attribute cognitive capacities to non-human animals when the guidance provided by empathetic intuitions is also supported by rigorous scientific research (see also Bekoff 2007). By and large, the behavioural sciences here work by constructing experimental settings in which non-human animals' cognitive capacities can be tested with respect to specific tasks. The choice of the relevant tasks is made in accordance with an understanding of which basic operations are involved in any given cognitive capacity. These are theoretical choices that can be difficult to ultimately justify. Some reference to human cognition is inevitably present in the initial selection of the tasks, at least at a heuristic level (Bekoff 2010, 57-66). Tests are then performed in a scientifically controlled way, and include not just behavioural tasks, but also brain imaging, and the examination of physiological parameters (heart rate, blood pressure, hormonal levels, and so on). Obviously, the results of these tests cannot determine whether the human-centred heuristic choices made at the initial stages of the experimental setting were right, given that the tests were based on those choices.

Another methodological issue is raised by the use of recapitulation. It is characteristic of some comparative psychology to endorse a considerably old biological idea, the biogenetic rule, usually associated in some way with Étienne Serres (1786-1868) and Ernst Heackel (1834-1919). According to this rule the *morphology* and, more interestingly for us, *behaviour* of children recapitulates the phyletic past of our species. In a simplified version, the biogenetic rule could be taken as stating that the child exhibits behaviours that resemble those of adult members belonging to species with which they share an evolutionary past. Referring to comparative anatomy and evolutionary biology Stephen Jay Gould writes:

"Over and over again, we find an explicit appeal to biological recapitulation: since a human embryo repeats the physical stages of remote ancestors, the child must replay the mental history of more recent forebears." (Gould 1977, 136)

He then proceeds to offer a quotation from Friedrich Engels to testify how widespread the idea was, well beyond the biology community:

"Just as the developmental history of the human embryo in his mother's womb is only an abbreviated repetition of the history extending over millions of years, of the bodily evolution of our animal ancestors, beginning from the worm, so the mental development of the human child is only a still more abbreviated repetition of the intellectual development of these same ancestors, at least of the later ones." (Engels 1876, 241)

As a matter of fact, the interpretation of some experimental evidence in behavioural sciences relies on comparisons between children and primates. This idea is common to both assimilationists (QNT) and differentialists (QLT), both employing such comparisons to respectively stress the continuity or the discontinuity between human and animal cognitive capacities (see Penn et al. 2008). Despite the initial enthusiasm, recapitulation has since been widely rebutted as illusory (see, for instance, Raff & Wray 1989 in anatomy; Lerner 1976 in psychology; Medicus 1992), though it also continued to attract many respected scientists (see, e.g. Gould 1977; Osche 1982; Charlesworth 1992). The controversies that surround recapitulation constitute another example of the sort of biases that could compromise the project of making reliable mental ascriptions to non-human animals based on scientific evidence.

Despite the many difficulties they present, we shall attempt to show that studies of animal minds play an important role in shaping our moral attitudes to non-human animals, for they can help us identify both relevant psychological capacities and potential areas of vulnerability.

3. Psychological Similarity to Humans and Vulnerability to Harm and Exploitation

Philosophers who (either explicitly or implicitly) endorse the psychological approach (e.g. Singer 1989; Regan 1983; DeGrazia 1996; Harris 1990), claim that questions of moral status or rights should be settled on the basis of the possession of psychological capacities of some kind. This involves a number of interrelated tasks for the moral philosopher. First, one needs to identify which psychological capacities are morally significant. Here there is no consensus: some argue that all *sentient* beings have a moral status or moral rights, whilst others believe that only those which qualify as *persons* (itself a contested category) do. Second, one needs to establish which (behavioural and physiological) evidence counts in favour of a non-human animal possessing those morally significant psychological capacities. With respect to this, positions vary widely and the very same observed behaviour may be interpreted either as a sign of conscious thought or as an example of mere conditioning. Third, one needs to determine which (if any) non-human animals satisfy the behavioural and physiological conditions for the morally significant psychological capacities. Empirical sciences can offer a substantial contribution to these tasks, provided that the methodological and epistemological difficulties involved in the study of animal minds are duly taken into account.

A general acceptance of the psychological approach can result in dramatically different positions in animal ethics (Sandis 2006, 2010). If moral decision-making includes treating others as ends in themselves (as opposed to mere means) whenever they have *reason*, then the relevant empirical question will be whether non-human animals have or lack reason. For instance, Kant maintained that the suffering of non-human animals is in itself irrelevant because mere animals are not rational beings and so, unlike human animals, lack the related freedom of the will to act according to (or against) reason—which was required for creatures to be considered as ends-in-themselves (Kant 1900-2009, 27, 1321). Kantian morality thus appears to allow people to use non-human animals as mere means, that is to say they may be treated as means to our own ends with no concern for any harm that may be inflicted upon them (but see Kant 1997, 240 for the argument that we nonetheless have *indirect* duties to animals).

If, by contrast, the core principle of moral decision-making is that one should refrain from unnecessarily frustrating an individual's *preference* (Singer 1989), at least when the satisfaction of such preference contributes significantly to the individual's well-being, then determining whether an individual has preferences and can act on them is paramount to the enterprise of populating the relevant moral community. For utilitarians such as Singer the preference that is central to moral consideration is that of not being in pain. This approach led to the recent movement of animal liberation whose aim is to defend the interests of non-human animals *qua* sentient beings. Singer additionally argues that anybody who favours the well-being of, say, a baby with a serious mental illness over that of an advanced animal like an ape or even a pig is guilty of *speciesism*. The comparison implies that even if suffering is all that matters, levels of cognition remain relevant to moral debate because the intensity, duration, and even the distressing nature of suffering can vary depending on the cognitive capacities of the individual suffering.

In these accounts, and other accounts inspired by the psychological approach, if we owe non-human animals anything at all, we do so because they have a psychological power of some sort or another. The vulnerability approach proposes itself as a radical alternative (Clement 1996; Donovan 1996; Held 2006; Tong & Williams 2009). The fundamental issue is not whether non-human animals possess prerequisites that guarantee their inclusion in the moral community, but whether they are vulnerable to harm and to exploitation in their relationship with humans. In feminist writings and theological ethics (e.g. Warren 2000; Slicer 1995; Plumwood 2000, 2002; Curtin 1991) there is much dissatisfaction with the way in which Singer and other ethicists embracing the psychological approach framed the debate on the treatment of non-human animals.

One common complaint is that arguments for the moral status of non-human animals based on their psychological capacities are anthropocentric, because only those capacities that non-human animals share with humans are taken into account, whereas other morally significant considerations that might stem from needs and interests that are distinctive of non-human animals are neglected. Why should non-human animals be respected only in so far as they resemble humans?

"Can we justify sacrificing beings who are extremely vulnerable to the whims and powers of human beings? [...] We all seem to recognize some fairly stringent moral prohibition against taking advantage of the innocent and the vulnerable, even in cases of self-defence, even in lifeboat cases. In fact, taking such advantage is often seen as especially malign. Do animals fall outside the scope of this prohibition completely, and if so, why?" (Slicer 1991, 117)

Another complaint is that the standard approach to the moral status debate polarises reason and emotion, privileging considerations about rationality over considerations about empathy, compassion, imagination, emotional bonds and caring relationships. The conscious attempts to leave emotional responses out of the philosophical reasoning about the moral status of non-human animals is perceived as a rejection of the role of emotions in moral decision-making and a perpetration of the myth of rationality as the supreme ('male') value of Western culture.

Instead of appealing to emotions, Singer's and Regan's arguments appeal to the purely rational demand for consistency. For instance, they appeal to so-called borderline cases—human beings of severely diminished capacities who we nonetheless count fully in our moral thinking. If these individuals are fully morally considerable, so the argument goes, then consistency demands that we likewise count nonhumans of like capacities as fully morally considerable (Clement 2003).

A third worry is that interests and rights are advocated and defended as properties of an *individual*, and as "enablers of autonomy". In such a perspective, the social dimension of human and non-human animal life is overlooked, and so is the value of relationships of care and of interdependence. Objections to autonomy guiding moral decision-making are motivated by the fact that attributing certain psychological capacities to an individual is never sufficient to make moral decisions about the treatment of that individual (see Clement 2003). This position, which places emphasis on caring relationships, has also been adopted by scientists interested in the welfare of non-human animals:

"Type 1 philosophy emphasized justice for animals, and in some cases respect for animals, but gave little attention to caring for animals. Singer made it clear that his concern about animals arose from a desire to see ethical principles properly applied, not from any particular interest in or attachment to animals themselves. [...]. In contrast, the work of animal welfare scientists was strongly oriented toward animal care in the form of improved housing, disease prevention, analgesia, and so on." (Fraser 1999, 175)

The inspiration for the vulnerability approach as applied to animal ethics comes from feminist philosophy. As women were perceived as weaker than men, non-human animals are perceived as weaker than humans. The more powerful in the relationship controls the weaker, and this gives rise to exploitation. Although it is true that, within the terms of moral status debate, connectedness, emotions, compassion and acceptance of the other are often neglected, many expressions of the vulnerability approach sound excessively polemical and derivative and fail to provide independent bases of a positive account. To us, then, the most attractive option is to move towards a hybrid view. We sketch one in the next section.

4. GREAT APES: VULNERABLE AND POWERFUL

Our aim is to revise the psychological approach to animal ethics in the light of the objections raised by the supporters of the vulnerability approach. According to some versions of the psychological approach, non-human animals deserve direct moral consideration because they share some of the same 'powers' as humans, such as certain psychological traits or mental capacities. The suggestion, then, is that one has moral obligations towards those individuals which are psychologically powerful in morally relevant respects. For instance, having the power to make decisions about one's own life becomes the basis for the right to self-determination in the context of political and moral philosophy.

The vulnerability approach, by contrast, is grounded on the idea that non-human animals are often in a weaker or more vulnerable position than typical humans, and this is a reason to care for them and protect them from potential exploitation. An analogous argumentative strategy applies to other vulnerable groups, for instance children living in developing countries where healthcare is not easily accessible. These children are often in a weaker or more vulnerable position than those in affluent societies, and this entitles them to special attention. This approach suggests that moral solicitude should be directed towards those individuals that are vulnerable in morally relevant respects. For instance, one respect in which one can be vulnerable is lack of access to healthcare, which affects negatively the quality of one's life.

In the context of animal ethics, the case of great apes is especially interesting. According to the psychological approach, they should be in a morally privileged position with respect to other non-human animals, assuming that they share with humans many psychological capacities some of which are morally relevant. (And we saw that some of the justification for banning or restricting the use of chimpanzees and other great apes in biomedical and behavioural research is based exactly on their being especially close to us.) Yet according to the vulnerability approach, great apes may be expected to attract *less* moral solicitude than other non-human animals. As they are closer to humans in their psychological powers, they should be less vulnerable than other animals, and thus less subject to exploitation in their relationship with humans. We believe that this way of presenting the case is misleading for a number of reasons. First, whereas the possession of a psychological capacity primarily concerns the individual, at least one sense of vulnerability, vulnerability to exploitation, can be understood and assessed only in the context of a relationship. One can be more or less psychologically powerful independent of the psychological make-up of other individuals, but one is vulnerable to exploitation only in relation to other individuals. Second, and more important for our purposes here, being powerful and being vulnerable are not contradictory attributes themselves: they can be both predicated at the same time of the same subject.

Let us elaborate this point further. A psychologically powerful animal can be vulnerable, just like a vulnerable animal can be psychologically powerful. According to a popular version of the psychological approach, if non-human animals have preferences for states of affairs that affect their physical or psychological well-being, those preferences should not be frustrated but respected. Animals with additional morally relevant preferences may be subject to harm in more ways and to a greater extent than animals without. When preferences about states of affairs that significantly affect the well-being of individuals with interests can be systematically frustrated, there may be vulnerability to harm and exploitation.

The very fact that great apes are psychologically sophisticated makes them more vulnerable than other non-human animals to certain form of harm. Dying can be harmful to those who die, to start with dying is usually accompanied by acute physical pain. However, some claim that death itself harms those who can make plans for the future to a greater extent than those who cannot, as by dying individuals lose the opportunity to achieve their short-term and long-term objectives. Suppose, for example, that great apes have the capacity to make plans for their own future. This would be a significant psychological power that would allow them to shape their existence rather than just experience it. At the same time, however, it would also be a source of vulnerability, as they would have more to lose from dying than animals unable to make plans for the future. The interests of great apes in seeing their plans fulfilled would be frustrated by death.

Singer (2003) and Regan (1983) argue along such lines, but other philosophers believe that psychological similarity between human and non-human animals is irrelevant to the extent to which death is harmful. Gary Francione (2010), for instance, condemns human practices exploiting non-human animals and maintains that the only psychological capacity that matters to the debate is sentience. Death is equally harmful to all sentient beings, as they all have an interest in continuing to live. On his view, no use of sentient non-human animals as human resources can be justified. This is a disagreement about which psychological capacity is relevant to the question whether death is harmful (whether the sophisticated capacity to make plans for the future or mere sentience). But for our present concerns, the interest of the debate about the harm of dying lies in the fact that considerations about psychological powers and considerations about vulnerability to harm and exploitation are intertwined. For Singer and Regan, death is less harmful for those who live in the present and cannot project themselves into the future; for Francione, death is equally harmful for all sentient beings, and is not harmful at all for insentient beings.

There is no doubt that great apes are psychologically sophisticated:

"Chimpanzees, bonobos, and gorillas have long-term relationships, not only between mothers and children, but also between unrelated apes. When a loved one dies, they grieve for a long time. They can solve complex puzzles that stump most two-year-old humans. They can learn hundreds of signs, and put them together in sentences that obey grammatical rules. They display a sense of justice, resenting others who do not reciprocate a favor." (Singer 2006)

Some of the features listed by Singer are at the same time psychological achievements and liabilities to suffering. For instance, by developing stronger bonds with conspecifics with respect to other non-human animals, great apes are more likely to suffer when they are removed from their natural and social habitat. This way of thinking about psychological capacities, as powers and as sources of vulnerability, can help us understand better the debate about the use of great apes in behavioural and biomedical research. It is precisely because great apes and humans share many psychological capacities that great apes are more likely to be deemed as useful research subjects. They become vulnerable to exploitation in the relationship with human experimenters due to their psychological powers.

We have attempted to show that powers and vulnerabilities do not always give rise to competing considerations. How does this affect our proposal? According to the psychological approach, a vulnerable individual can be the object of direct moral consideration if and only if it is also (minimally) psychologically powerful. According to standard versions of the vulnerability approach, a vulnerable individual can be the recipient of moral solicitude even if it has no psychological powers. For the psychological approach, vulnerability is not a sufficient criterion for moral consideration, but a necessary condition. For the vulnerability approach, powers are not necessary for moral solicitude, but can be sufficient if they entail specific vulnerabilities. Thus, the main difference between the two approaches is that for the psychological approach, vulnerability is not a sufficient criterion for moral consideration, whereas for the vulnerability approach it is. Be that as it may, considerations about vulnerability can still do some conceptual work within a psychological approach, namely that of drawing the attention of moral agents towards the specific vulnerabilities of psychologically powerful moral patients.

In the account we are proposing, the role of vulnerability *pragmatically complements* that of psychological powers. We claim that at least some morally relevant psychological capacities are necessarily accompanied by some vulnerabilities. For instance, the power of deliberation is accompanied by the potential harm that derives from being prevented to make one's own choices. The capacity to engage in romantic relationships is accompanied by the potential harm that derives from unrequited love. This does not mean that an increase in powers necessarily brings about an increase in vulnerabilities, but only that it *may* do so. Once one is minimally psychologically powerful, the addition or increase of a relevant power (e.g. better reasoning as an effect of drugs enhancing concentration) need not be accompanied by any additional vulnerability. Can the inclusion of vulnerability into the set of considerations relevant to moral decision-making help us respond to some of the criticism levelled to the psychological approach? We think so, and it can thereby also vindicate the role of the study of animal minds in animal ethics.

The attempt to establish the extent to which non-human animals have the same capacities as humans is valuable and should not be condemned as anthropocentric. Identifying psychological powers helps moral agents determine how vulnerable non-human animals really are to potentially adverse conditions such as death, removal from their natural and social habitat, confinement, and so on. Knowledge of the psychological capacities of non-human animals contributes to identifying the factors relevant to their wellbeing and thus it is important to the assessment of their vulnerabilities as well as their powers. Moreover, the study of non-human minds helps avoid biases in moral decision-making. For instance, there is a tendency in the layperson to sympathize with companion animals whilst ignoring the ethical implications of many human practices involving farm animals. This is understandable: companion animals share meaningful experiences with people and become part of the family, whereas other animals may be seen as a source of entertainment or food. But if farm animals have psychological capacities which render them powerful as well as vulnerable to harm and exploitation, then they deserve moral status and our solicitude even if they do not arouse our compassion.

Great apes also provide an interesting test for our moral intuitions. We tend not to feel as much compassion for the suffering of wild animals as for the suffering of domesticated animals, in part because wild animals do not interact with humans on a regular basis and do not form long-lasting relationships with humans, and in part because we feel no obligation to intervene in the natural hierarchy in which wild animals live. Rescuing gazelles from hungry lions would make no sense unless we could turn lions into practising vegetarians and thus guarantee their survival. But when animals such as great apes are kept captive, for research or entertainment purposes, their well-being is in the hands of those who keep them and the adverse conditions in which they are found are likely to generate compassion and regret. That is why some of the tragic stories of captive chimpanzees capture our imagination (see the account of Nim Chimpsky's troubled life in Singer 2011). The vulnerability approach can explain this shift in intuitions better than the psychological approach. Captive great apes are not necessarily more psychologically sophisticated than those living in the wild, but we care for them more because there is a relationship between them and us, and we are aware that this relationship is likely to be driven by our interests.

To be fair to the psychological approach, what motivates the alleged prioritization of reason over emotion is the desire to avoid biases and critically examine prior assumptions and practices that are ingrained in our way of living. The message in Singer's writings is that one must go beyond the force of pre-theoretical moral intuitions, not because emotional reactions (such as compassionate feelings for the suffering of another) should play no role in moral decision-making, but because they can be easily manipulated and consequently fail to track genuine harm.

In addition, the capacities which philosophers regard as morally significant and which scientists like to study in non-human animals are not exclusively of the 'cold', rational sort. Cognitive psychologists investigating mindedness in non-human animals are as interested in the range and manifestation of available emotions as they are in problem-solving, tool-using, and theory of mind. Indeed, many have recently paid special attention to the presence of apparently moral behaviours in primates, such as excusing the young, helping the weak, and sharing food with the disabled in hierarchically organized social groups (see, for instance, deWaal 1996).

Only by better understanding the minds of non-human animals can one properly appreciate what a genuinely caring relationship with them might be like. The nature of caring relationships is not independent of the psychological capacities possessed by the individuals engaging in those relationships. Caring for individuals with minds involves first and foremost some understanding of what these individuals need in order to live well and flourish. This is clearest when we are thinking about how their needs may be fulfilled.

5. Conclusions

We have argued that the conflict between ethic of justice and ethic of care approaches to animal ethics is only apparent, and particularly misleading in the context of the debate on whether it is permissible to use great apes in research. Accordingly, we developed a hybrid position which holds that the possession of certain psychological capacities is both necessary and sufficient for attracting direct moral consideration whilst acknowledging that part of the reason why some of these psychological capacities are morally relevant is because they come with additional vulnerability to potential harm and exploitation. On this view, conceptual and empirical studies of mindedness in non-human animals can make an important contribution to moral decision-making, so long as epistemic and methodological concerns are taken into account.

If powers can and typically do give rise to vulnerabilities, then a better understanding of the mindedness of non-humans (both in terms of cognition and affect) can enhance one's capacity for empathy. Human beings tend to empathize with those who share the same circumstances. For instance, people who have lost children to an incurable illness often choose to devote time and energy to promote research on that particular illness, because they understand 'from the inside' what parents in the same situation must be feeling, and genuinely want to improve the chances of survival for those other children. Knowing that the intelligence and emotional life of non-humans is closer to that of humans than it seems, and realizing that non-human animals are able to have many of the experiences humans have (albeit in different circumstances and with different qualities), as well as some that humans lack, can increase both the intensity and the scope of human compassion towards them. The importance of identifying a common ground is even more evident in the ethical debates about human practices involving great apes, which are, in many relevant respects, closer to humans than other animals.

In the literature on the ethic of care, it is openly acknowledged that caring involves skills and competencies, as well as certain moral attitudes. For instance, Maeckelberghe (2004) argues that caring for the vulnerable presumes *attentiveness* and *competence*. The situation in which one assumes the responsibility for providing care but subsequently fails to provide good care due to a poor assessment of the needs of the vulnerable is problematic and should obviously be avoided. The psychological approach, improved by considerations about vulnerability and informed by conceptual and empirical studies of mindedness in non-human animals, can tell us which non-human animals have morally relevant interests and how we can respect such interests.

The case of great apes illustrates how the possession of sophisticated philosophical capacities does not rule out vulnerability to harm and to exploitation in the relationship between humans and non-humans. Quite to the opposite, we have argued. Complex mental traits are themselves the source of specific and morally relevant vulnerabilities. Dedicated legislation, at least in Europe, incorporates both considerations about vulnerability and considerations about sophisticated mindedness as sources of moral concerns for non-human animals, whereas philosophers have tended to see the two sets of considerations as distinct and in competition with one another. In this paper, we have suggested that we should look at how facts about vulnerability and mindedness bear on each other to determine the specific moral worth of vulnerable highly minded non-human animals.

REFERENCES

Baron-Cohen, S. (1992), Mindblindness, Cambridge, MA: MIT Press.
Bekoff, M. (2007), The Emotional Life of Animals, Novato CA: New World Library.
Bekoff, M. (2010), The Animal Manifesto, Novato, CA: New World Library.
Bekoff, M., Allen, C., Burghardt, G. (eds.) (2002), The Cognitive Animal: Empirical and Theoretical Perspectives on Animal Cognition, Cambridge, MA: MIT Press.
Bermúdez, J.-L. (2003), Thinking without Words, Oxford: Oxford University Press.
Blasimme, A., Bortolotti, L. (2010), "Intentionality and the Welfare of Minded Non-Humans", Teorema 29/2, 83-96.
Bortolotti, L. (2008), "What Does Fido Believe?", Think 7/19, 1-9.
Bortolotti, L., Sandis, C., Blasimme, A. (2012), "With Power Comes Vulnerability", paper presented at the conference "Humans and other Animals", Institute of philosophy London, 11-12 June.
Carruthers, P. (1989), "Brute Experience", Journal of Philosophy 86/5, 258-269.
Carruthers, P. (2002), "The Cognitive Functions of Language", Behavioural and Brain Sciences 25/6, 657-726.
Charlesworth, W.R. (1992), "Darwin and Developmental Psychology: Past and Present", Developmental Psychology 28/1, 5-16.
Chomsky, N. (1980), Rules and representations, New York: Columbia University Press.
Clement, G. (1996), Care, Autonomy, and Justice: Feminism and the Ethic of Care, Boulder: Westview.
Clement, G. (2003), "The Ethic of Care and the Problem of Wild Animals", Between the Species III, http://cla.calpoly.edu/bts/issue_03/03clement.htm, accessed April 2010.
Curtin, D. (1991), "Toward an Ecological Ethic of Care", Hypatia 6/1, Ecological Feminism, 60-74
Darwin, C. (1871), The Descent of Man, and Selection in Relation to Sex, London: John Murray.
Davidson, D. (1984), "Thought and Talk", in: D. Davidson, Inquiries into Truth and Interpretation, Oxford: Clarendon Press, 155-170.
Davidson, D. (2004), "What Thought Requires", in: D. Davidson, Problems of Rationality, Oxford Clarendon Press, 135-150.

De Grazia, D. (1996), Taking Animals Seriously, Cambridge: Cambridge University Press
de Waal, F.B.M. (1996), Good Natured, Cambridge, MA, London: Harvard University Press.
Dennett, D. (1995), "Do Animals Have Beliefs?", in: H. Roitblat, J.-A. Meyer (eds.), Comparative Approaches to Cognitive Science, Cambridge, MA: MIT Press: 111-118.
Dennett, D.C. (1979), "Intentional Systems", in: D.C. Dennett, Brainstorms: Philosophical Essays on Mind and Psychology, Montgomery, VT: Bradford Books, 3-22.
Derrida, J. (2008), The Animal That Therefore I Am, New York: Fordham University Press.
Donovan, J. (1996), "Animal Rights and Feminist Theory", in: J. Donovan, C.J. Adams (eds.), Beyond Animal Rights: A Feminist Caring Ethic for the Treatment of Animals, New York: Continuum, 34-59.
Dretske, F. (2006), "Minimal Rationality", in: S. Hurley, M. Nudds (eds.), Rational Animals?, Oxford: Oxford University Press, 107-115.
Engels, F. (1954/1876), "The Part Played by Lbour in the Transition From Ape to Man", in: F. Engels, Dialectics of Nature, Moscow: Foreign Language Publishing House.
European Parliament (2010), Directive 2010/63/EU of the European Parliament and of the Council of 22 September 2010 on the Protection of Animals Used for Scientific Purposes. Official Journal L 276, 20/10/2010 P. 0033-0079.
Finkelstein, D. (2007), "Holism and Animal Minds", in: A. Crary (ed.), Wittgenstein and the Moral Life: Essays in Honour of Cora Diamond, Cambridge, MA: MIT Press, 251-278.
Fodor, J. (1992), "A Theory of the Child's Theory of Mind", Cognition 44/3, 283-96.
Francione, G. (2010), "The Abolition of Animal Exploitation", in: G. Francione, R. Garner (eds.), The Animal Right Debate: Abolition or Regulation? New York: Columbia University Press, 1-102.
Frankish, K. (2004), Mind and Supermind, Cambridge: Cambridge University Press.
Fraser, D. (1999), "Animal Ethics and Animal Welfare Science: Bridging the Two Cultures", Applied Animal Behaviour Science 65/3, 171-189.
Glock, H.-J. (1999), "Animal Minds: Conceptual Problems", Evolution and Cognition 5, 174-188.

Glock, H.-J. (2000), "Animals, Thoughts and Concepts", Synthese 123/1, 35-64.

Glock, H.-J. (2006), "Thought, Language and Animals", in: M. Kober (ed.), Deepening our Understanding of Wittgenstein, Special Issue of Grazer Philosophische Studien 71/1, 139-160.

Glock, H.-J. (2009), "Can Animals Act For Reasons?", Inquiry 52/3, 232-254.

Glock, H.-J. (2010), "Animal Agency", in: T. O'Connor, C. Sandis (eds.), A Companion to the Philosophy of Action, Oxford: Blackwell, 384-392.

Glock, H.-J. (2012), "The Anthropological Difference: What Can Philosophers Do To Identify the Differences Between Human and Non-human Animals?", in: C. Sandis, M.J. Cain (eds.), Human Nature, New York: Cambridge University Press.

Goldman, A. (1989), "Interpretation Psychologized", Mind & Language 4/3, 161-85.

Goodin, R. (1985), Protecting the Vulnerable: A Re-Analysis of Our Social Responsibilities, Chicago: University of Chicago Press.

Gopnik, A., Meltzoff, A. (1997), Words, Thoughts and Theories, Cambridge, MA: MIT Press.

Gordon, R.M. (2004), "Folk Psychology as Mental Simulation", in: E.N. Zalta (ed.), The Stanford Encyclopaedia of Philosophy, Stanford: Stanford University, http://plato.stanford.edu/archives/fall2004/entries/folkpsych-simulation/, accessed January 2012.

Gordon, R. M. (1986), "Folk psychology as simulation", Mind & Language 1/2, 158-171.

Gorman, J. (2011), U.S. suspends use of chimps in new research. New York Times, December 15, http://www.nytimes.com/2011/12/16/science/chimps-in-medical-research.html?_r=1&ref=nationalinstitutesofhealth, accessed 16 January 2012.

Gould, S.J. (1977), Ontogeny and Phylogeny, Cambridge, MA: Harvard University Press.

Harris, J. (1990), The Value of Life, London: Routledge.

Held, V. (2006), The Ethics of Care: Personal, Political, and Global, Oxford: Oxford University Press.

Kant, I. (1900-2009), Gesammelte Schriften (Collected Works), ed. Royal Prussian (subsequently German, then Berlin-Brandenburg) Academy of Sciences. Berlin, Georg Reimer, subsequently Walter de Gruyter, 29 vols, in 34 parts.

Kant, I. (1997), Lectures on Ethics (ed. P. Heath, J.B. Schneewind), Cambridge: Cambridge University Press.

Institute of Medicine Committee on the Use of Chimpanzees in Biomedical and Behavioral Research (2011). Chimpanzees in Biomedical and Behavioral Research: Assessing the Necessity (Consensus Report). Available at http://www.iom.edu/Reports/2011/Chimpanzees-in-Biomedical-and-Behavioral-Research-Assessing-the-Necessity.aspx, accessed January 2012.

Knight, A. (2007), "The Poor Contribution of Chimpanzee Experiments to Biomedical Progress", Journal of Applied Animal Welfare Science 10/4, 281-308.

Lerner, R.M. (1976), Concepts and Theories of Human Development, Reading, MA: Addison-Wesley.

Leslie, A. (1995), "A theory of agency", in: D. Sperber, A. Premack (eds.), Causal cognition, Oxford: Oxford University Press, 121-141.

MacIntyre, A. (1999), Dependent Rational Animals: Why Human Beings Need the Virtues, London: Duckworth.

Maeckelberghe, E. (2004), "Feminist Ethic of Care: A Third Alternative Approach", Health Care Analysis 12/4, 317-327.

Malcolm, N. (1972), "Thoughtless Brutes", Proceedings and Addresses of the American Philosophical Association 46, 5-20.

Mameli, M., Bortolotti, L. (2006), "Animal rights, animal minds and human mindreading", Journal of Medical Ethics 32/2, 84-89.

Morton, D.B., Burghardt, G., Smith, J.A. (1990), "Critical anthropomorphism, animal suffering and the ecological context", Hastings Cent Report 20, 13-19.

Osche, G. (1982), "Rekapitulationsentwicklung und ihre Bedeutung für die Phylogenetik. Wann gilt die 'Biogenetische Grundregel'" [Recapitulation and its implications for phylogeny. When is the biogenetic rule valid?], Verhandlungen des Naturwissenschaftlichen Vereins in Hamburg (NF) 25, 5-31.

Penn, D.C., Holyoak, K.J., Povinelli, D.J., (2008), "Darwin's mistake: Explaining the discontinuity between human and nonhuman minds", Behavioural and Brain Sciences 31/2, 109-178.

Pinker, S. (1994), The Language Instinct, New York: W. Morrow.

Plumwood, V. (2000), "Integrating Ethical Frameworks for Animals, Humans, and Nature: A Critical Feminist Eco-Socialist Analysis", Ethics and the Environment 5/2, 285-322.

Plumwood, V. (2002), Environmental Culture: The Ecological Crisis of Reason, London: Routledge.

Raff, R.A., Wray, G.A. (1989), "Heterochrony: Developmental Mechanisms and Evolutionary Results", Journal of Evolutionary Biology 2, 409-434.

Regan, T. (1983), The Case for Animal Rights, Berkeley, CA: University of California Press.

Sandis, C. (2006), "Animals", in: M. Cohen (ed.), Essentials of Philosophy and Ethics, London, New York: Hodder Education/Oxford University Press.

Sandis, C. (2010), "Animal Ethics", in: R. Corrigan, M.E., Farrell (eds.), Ethics: A University Guide, Gloucester: Progressive Frontiers Press, 21-39.

Singer, P. (1989), "All Animals Are Equal", in: T. Regan, P. Singer (eds.), Animal Rights and Human Obligations, Englewood Cliffs, NJ: Prentice Hall, 6-12.

Singer, P. (2003), Practical Ethics (2nd ed), Cambridge: Cambridge University Press.

Singer, P. (2006), "The Great Ape Debate", URL: http://www.project-syndicate.org/commentary/singer11/English, accessed January 2012.

Singer, P. (2011), "The Troubled Life of Nim Chimpsky", New York Review of Books, August 18th. URL: http://www.nybooks.com/blogs/nyrblog/2011/aug/18/troubled-life-nim-chimpsky/, accessed January 2012.

Slicer, D. (1991), "Your Daughter or your Dog? A Feminist Assessment of the Animal Research Issue. Hypatia 6(1): 108-124. Reprinted in J. Donovan, C. Adams (eds.) The Feminist Care Tradition in Animal Ethics: a Reader, Columbia: Columbia University Press 2007, 107-124.

Slicer, D. (1995), "Obligations to Animals Are Not Necessarily Based on Rights", Journal of Agricultural and Environmental Ethics 8/2, 161-170.

Smith, J.D., Shields, W.E., Washburn, D.A. (2003), "The Comparative Psychology of Uncertainty Monitoring and Metacognition", Behavioural and Brain Sciences 26/3, 317-373.

Steward, H. (2009), "Animal Agency", Inquiry 52/3, 217-231.

Stoecker, R. (2009), "Why Animals Can't Act", Inquiry 52/3, 255-271.

Tomasello, M., Call, J., Hare, B. (2003), "Chimpanzees Understand Psychological States—The question is Which Ones and to What Extent", Trends in Cognitive Sciences 7/4, 153-156.

Tong, R., Williams, N. (2009), "Feminist Ethics", in: E. Zalta (ed.), The Stanford Encyclopaedia of Philosophy, URL: http://plato.stanford.edu/entries/feminism-ethics/, accessed January 2012.

Warren, K. (2000), Ecofeminist Philosophy: A Western Perspective on What It Is and Why It Matters, Lanham, MD: Rowman and Littlefield.

12. Personhood, Interaction and Skepticism

Elisa Aaltola

1. INTRODUCTION

Personhood is often understood to be restricted to all and only human beings. Thus, the term has become synonymous with the membership of *Homo sapiens* (see Goodman 1988). Particularly two lines of justification have been offered for this view.

According to one approach, it is self-evident that human beings are morally more valuable than other creatures. Human specialness is both discernible and indisputable, which again means that no further justification needs to be offered. "Personhood" is seen to mark this specialness, and as such belongs to all and only humans. Historically, this approach has gained prominence from the teleological cosmology advanced by Aristotle and Thomas Aquinas, within which the less perfect beings serve the more perfect. It still resonates today in narratives, which position *Homo sapiens* as the most "advanced" and thus valuable species with natural moral supremacy over other animals (see Midgley 2002). The other approach stipulates that personhood is restricted to human beings because of their cognitive capacities. Hence, it is not human species *per se* that matters, but rather the cognitive capacities manifested by the majority of its members. Rationality, self-awareness, propositional language, intentionality, moral agency—amongst others—are brought forward as capacities that render all and only human beings persons (Cohen 1997).

For decades, animal ethics has pointed toward the difficulties within both of these approaches. In relation to the first, it has been claimed that reference to "self-evidence" is not a moral justification but rather something based on culturally and politically coloured presumptions. We tend to perceive certain things as "self-evident" because of the influence of the surrounding culture or because it suits our self-interest to do so. There is undeniable convenience in believing that only humans can be persons, for it makes living in the contemporary, anthropocentric society much easier, and enables individuals to continue animal consumption. Yet, justification remains lacking, as we are not told *why* human species is linked to special value—only that this link should be blatant for all to see. As the example of intra-human inequalities manifests, the road of non-justification is both ignorant and dangerous. There are various cultural and historical contexts, within which it is or has been self-evident that women are not persons, and the perceptive response to such claims is the demand for justification. According to many in animal ethics, the same demand has to be applied in the context of non-human animals. The second view fairs no better. The notorious "Argument from Marginal Cases" has pointed out that any of the suggested perfectionist capacities that would qualify capable adults to be persons would also disqualify vast numbers of human beings due to the fact that they are not, for instance, rational and moral agents (Dombrowski 1997). Such disqualification appears morally abhorrent on a very elemental level and therefore the criterion must be misplaced.

Now, it has been maintained, contra what is suggested above, that self-evidence may suffice, and that the Argument from Marginal Cases bears no relevance. According to this Wittgensteinian take, language forms the limits of our reality and is thus also the basis of normativity. If meanings central in our language games imply that all and only human beings are persons, we should accept this without "deflection" into further justification and facts (Diamond 2004, 2008). However, there are problems with this take. It remains unclear why the search for justification would lay outside the bounds of what is meaningful—on the contrary, as the case of intra-human inequalities shows, the demand for justification in the context of moral issues is arguably a basic meaning to most of us. That is, in the field of morality, one central meaning states that presumptions alone do not suffice.

Still, this critique points toward a fruitful direction. Besides the Argument from Marginal Cases, there is another reason to abandon perfectionism. It strikes as somewhat clinical and detached to maintain that perfectionist capacities are the requirement of personhood. It would rather seem that personhood is a "thick concept" that cannot be applied merely on the basis of logics and inference. Perhaps it concerns more our *approach* to other beings than the specific capacities of those beings. Moreover, perhaps it is a more dynamic concept than traditionally allowed for.

This is where the paper gains its impetus. The goal is to map out a way of understanding personhood that highlights these two aspects: the approach toward and the dynamics with other beings.

2. PERSONHOOD AND INTERACTION

Following Daniel Dennett, Juan Carlos Gómez has linked personhood to intentionality. However, unlike Dennett, he maintains that intentionality does not require the capacity for conceptualization. Gómez emphasizes that second order beliefs concerning "personhood" are not the necessary criteria for personhood: "Being aware of being a person is a different phenomenon from being a person" (Gómez 1998). In other words, personhood does not depend on conceptualization in the first or third person sense: we do not need to have self-consciousness ("I am a person") or a theory of mind ("she is an intentional being and therefore a person") in order to qualify as persons. Gómez suggests that what suffices is the ability to understand intentionality in the *second person sense*: all that is required is immediate and non-conceptual understanding that there is an intentional "you" in front of oneself.

The intersubjective model Gomez brings forward is this: I engage in interaction with another being, whom I recognize as a somebody, and whom I know to be able to recognize me as a somebody, too. Here recognition is based on second person immediacy rather than concepts, and comes to exist when I behave intentionally towards another, who behaves intentionally towards me. Personhood is built upon this dynamic. Direct or immediate recognition of intentionality plays a significant part, and takes the form of "feeling the subjectivity of others" and "relating to others" in, for instance, "face to face interactions". Gomez claims that: "Others are not understood as persons because we infer from their behaviour that they must have intentions and ideas about other people's intentions, but because we are capable of engaging with them in specific patterns of intersubjective interactions that include emotional and expressive behaviours [...] Persons are capable of representing others as 'second persons', i.e. as creatures capable of engaging in intersubjective encounters" (Gómez 1998). Therefore, personhood springs from a type of *aware interaction*.[1]

But what, exactly, does this aware interaction consist of? Gomez offers broad guidelines rather than a precise criterion. However, we can surmise that a being would have to be 1) intentional, 2) phenomenally conscious, and 3) capable of categorical perception in order to be a person. The crucial point is that all of these capacities would only need to exist on the first-order level. Therefore, a cow would not need to be able to reflect upon her own intentionality or consciousness, and she would not need to have the concept "category". What suffices is that she can direct her behaviour in relation to another being, have *qualia* or felt experiences (the famous Nagelian viewpoint to the world), and be able to categorize her surroundings at least in a rudimentary way that allows her to differentiate the "you" in front of her from other creatures, things and entities.

Gomez concludes that some primates are persons. The conclusion could be extended somewhat: there appears to be no reason why also many other animals would not fulfil the criteria. This extension can be supported by research that shows particularly social animals to manifest highly sophisticated forms of interactive behaviours, which seem to be based on the understanding of the opponent as an intentional creature in the second person sense. Thus, for instance (as Marc Bekoff has shown), dogs' play includes a rich variety of gestures that imply the gesturing dog to perceive the opponent as an intentional being, and to understand that the opponent views herself and her gestures as indications of intention (Bekoff 1999; 2002). Perhaps we need not refer to social animals, for also solitary creatures can manifest sophisticated forms of recognition of the intentionality of other beings and thus, for instance, a predator will anticipate the movements of her prey (and *vice versa*). The conclusion gains at least some support from everyday experience. When acting in relation to a dog or a deer, it in a very immediate sense appears odd or even absurd to insist that the animal has no (at least rudimentary) intentions, awareness, or categories. How we immediately react toward the animal, anticipating

---

[1] | A similar approach has been offered by Mary Midgley, who maintains that personhood is based on "emotional fellowship" (Midgley 2003, 169).

her reactions toward ourselves, gives ground for a dynamic within which denying the animal's existence as a "you" becomes difficult.

Therefore, Gómez brings forward a model of personhood, which renders personhood into an act rather than a quality. It becomes something dynamic and performative instead of a matter reduced to fixed, perfectionist capacities. This, intriguingly, would imply that personhood is not an internal characteristic, but something that exists outside and between beings. Of course, personhood would require the existence of the aforementioned capacities, but it would remain more than their total sum, and emphasis would be on the type of dynamics they enable. This is exemplified in the generic aspect of the approach. Gómez argues that the capacity to recognize intentionality renders both oneself *and* the other a person. That is, the moment of recognition means that both the other creature and myself are persons: "I am a person in so far as I and another perceive and treat each other as persons". (Gómez 1998) Personhood comes to exist via aware interaction, and covers all the beings engaged in that interaction.

Does this mean that I am not a person if nobody treats me as such? What about moments when I am not interacting—do I lose my personhood? Aware interaction is the origin of personhood: it is the element that brings personhood to life. However, one does not have to remain in a constant state of aware interaction to be a person: it is also the capacity, tendency and potentiality toward and not only the actuality of aware interaction that matters. This slight modification of Gomez's model also offers a reply to the first question. It is the potential to be treated as a person that is significant and therefore, even beings, whom nobody has ever related to as a "you", can lay a claim on personhood. Yet what about animals, with whom interaction is very difficult? Although Gomez emphases primates and thus animals, who have the capacity for highly human-like interactions, it is here suggested that the notion of "interaction" needs to be understood in a broad sense that avoids anthropocentric stipulations. Interaction can be manifested in various ways, and at times recognizing it requires an open mind toward inter-species differences (see also Aaltola 2008).

3. Immediacy

Therefore, personhood can be approached via the notion of "aware interaction". However, this approach faces a number of questions and possible problems. The first of these concerns immediacy. Personhood takes place outside mediations (such as propositional language): it is directly experienced. But what, precisely, does this immediacy comprise of?

"Immediacy" is often viewed as something akin to "intuition". Intuition has been the elusive target of much pondering in the history of philosophy. Scotus and Ockham refer to intuition as direct knowledge concerning external objects, but after it emerged that this knowledge can be factually false (perception required for direct knowledge can lead us astray) emphasis was moved on to internal objects and ideas: intuition was a direct form of grasping the truth-value of ideas. Neither setting serves our purposes of understanding the immediacy of interaction. Fortunately, Edmund Husserl offered an alternative account. For him, intuition is a type of givenness, within which things are handed to us directly: intuition is not mere subjective imagination but is offered to us by the external reality. This lends intuition the quality of evidentness: intuitive knowledge is perceived to be evidently true. Because it is not created by us but rather given to us by the outside world, there need not be further justification for accepting it (Hintikka 2003). Visual perception is the most basic form of intuition. However, for Husserl, there is a broad range of "self-evident forms of experience" (Smith 2007, 324). Here, the earlier account of intuition as direct knowledge concerning the external world is transformed into a self-evident givenness, within which falsehood does not appear as a meaningful possibility.

Following this, it can be asserted that immediacy need not be anything unfathomable or mystical. Rather, it goes hand in hand with the perceived evidentness of things, such as when a colour is evident to the eye. One possibility is that the immediacy of interaction gains its basis here. The intentions of the other being are evident: they are given to us. No lingual mediation has to take place. But how, exactly, are they given?

Here embodiment and empathy are relevant. The experience of one's body is an important element in empathy toward other beings, for it permits seeing also other bodies as bodies intertwined with minds—a sense of self is transferred. Together, these two factors support and intertwine with immediacy and intuition, and as a result it seems evident that, for instance, many animals are cognitive creatures. As the Husserl scholar David Woodruff Smith states: "I see this dog, immediately and 'intuitively', as a being that is a body animated with experiences of seeing and willing" (Smith 2007, 228). Crucially, empathy and embodiment are also linked to personhood. They enable one to perceive other beings—not merely as physical bodies—but as fellow subjects. In fact, they form "our primary form of experience of others, as others" (Ibid.). A type of "empathic intuition" ensures the personhood of others: we do not deduct or infer that others are persons, but rather immediately recognize them as such. Husserl states that: "Now, as to the persons we encounter in society, their bodies are naturally given to us in intuition just like the other objects of our environment, and consequently so are they as persons, unified with the bodies. But we do not find two things there, entwined with one another in an external way; bodies and persons. We find unitary human beings, who have dealings with us." (Husserl 1990, 235) Hence, empathy and embodiment are the "structure" that enables immediate knowledge on which interaction and ultimately personhood rest. It is because we are embodied creatures and persons ourselves that we can instantly recognize and relate to also given other embodied creatures as persons.

Also Merleau-Ponty underlines embodied empathy. For him, the body is the commonality we share with others and a factor that enables recognition of mutuality. The body builds an empathetic bond between creatures: "It is precisely my body that perceives the body of the other and discovers there a miraculous extension of my own intentions, a familiar way of dealing with the world." (Carman 2008, 143) The bond created by the body is unarticulated and unthinking. Significantly, Merleau-Ponty argues that this allows one to view others as persons: "Others are always already persons like myself." (Ibid., 141) Therefore, again shared embodiment and empathy permit immediate recognition of mutuality and personhood. The implications from the viewpoint of aware interaction are clear. The immediacy presumed by Gómez's approach can be partly explained by empathy and embodiment.

For Merleau-Ponty an example of embodied empathy are small children, who in an immediate and direct manner, unaffected by language, engage in interaction with others. Whereas contemporary rationality would like us to rid ourselves of this childlike state, Merleau-Ponty argues that adult thinking should remain open to it (Carman 2008). The child feels that others are accessible to her, and that she herself is accessible to others—the notion of mechanical, mindless and valueless beings makes little sense. Hence, Merleau-Ponty positions an unconventional way of looking at things (childlikeness) as a basis for perceiving personhood. A similar move is made by Husserl. Husserl urges us to turn to intuition instead of relying on mathematizing academic jargon, for only the former can offer genuine understanding: "If we would touch on the thing itself, then it is required of us, assuming we wanted to grasp the essence of the thing and determine it conceptually, that we not be content with vague locutions and traditional philosophical preconceptions but instead draw from the very source of clear givenness." (Husserl 1990, 34)

This is perhaps the most fruitful reminder the grand phenomenologists can offer in the present context. In order to recognize personhood in non-human animals, we may need to drop conventional frameworks. Husserl urges us to get rid of cultural preconceptions, and Merleau-Ponty pushes us toward the childlike way of perceiving things.[2] In either case, what is required is the willingness to step outside fixed mediations. Hence, not only embodiment and empathy, but also willingness to clear interfering conceptual clutter, allow for immediacy and recognition of personhood. On the most obvious level, this means that anthropocentric assumptions concerning other animals must be pushed aside. Moreover, it means that instead of rationality and inference, there is a need for non-lingual and even childlike inquisitiveness and open mindedness in our dealings with non-human creatures.

4. Normative Relevance

Husserl argues that others are constituted via "values of love", which in its most rudimentary sense means that they are viewed as significant beings in themselves. Smith describes this as following: "This principle presupposes the 'constitution' of others as other *subjects*, fellow *persons* in our *intersubjective* world." (Smith 2007, 379) The moral dimension appears

---

2 | Of course, to some extent this is already an accepted idea. Those, who perceive animals to be persons, are frequently claimed to be faulty of hopeless naivety, and it is often only children whom are given the right to hold on to such a perception. Whereas childlikeness is usually maintained to be a negative factor, following Merleau-Ponty, it could be argued to be something positive or enabling.

obvious at first sight: the personhood that is recognized in the other being has inherent moral significance. That is, as soon as one notes that another creature is an agent capable of relating to oneself, one views her as morally relevant. Yet, the issue is not as clear-cut.

This is because viewing another being as a "you" or a "somebody" does not require that she be viewed as a being with moral significance. The predator may perceive his prey to be a somebody, without any indication of normative awareness. More worryingly, it is entirely possible to perceive a fellow human being as an intentional creature without any notion of her moral relevance (those who commit acts of genocide are most likely quite aware of the fact that the people they are killing are intentional beings). The crucial question becomes: where, exactly, does normativity enter the picture?

Berkeley famously maintained that to exist is to be perceived (*esse est percipi*) (Berkeley 1998, 104). Although Berkeley referred to material things, one possibility would be to extend this to cover also minds: we exist for others, when they pay attention to us. Yet, Berkeley's original claim related to minds suggests a contrary position. Instead of being seen, perhaps it is being able to see that holds relevance: I exist when I perceive. Following these lines, Sartre argues that: "The other is in principle the one who looks at me." (Sartre 1989) Both aspects are pertinent to the interactive approach: the type of intersubjectivity it rests on consists of being seen, and seeing. Yet, the moral element thus-far missing particularly stems from the former. It is when one suddenly sees the other being in a new light, afresh, that the mist of morality descends upon the situation. More specifically, it is when one recognizes the fragility and vulnerability of the other, and feels care toward her condition, that morality is born. Therefore, it is not so much the capable subject—an omnipotent agent of her own actions—that is the basic unit of morally coloured interaction, but rather the vulnerable individual exposed to the actions of others.

This idea is prominent in the philosophy of Levinas and Derrida. Both emphasize vulnerability as a factor that lends the act of looking its normative dimension. The look of a vulnerable creature disrupts the egoistic existence of the contented, Western subject, and forces her to become aware of the plight of others. Quite simply, this is the moment when the notion of "moral relevance" is born. Levinas maintains that the look has a greater moral power than words, as it "convinces even 'the people who do not wish to listen'" (Levinas 1969, 201). In Derrida's philosophy: "The Other leaves a trace of the shock of encounter within me, and how I respond to that trace—whether I affirm or negate, avow or disavow—constitutes ethics, properly speaking." (Calarco 2008, 126)[3] To see vulnerability in another sparks ethics into existence, for it stirs in us the type of primordial sense of care and concern that can surpass, break through and set aside egoistic intentions and restrictions. In other words, seeing fragility in others can evoke the Humean sense of compassion, and make one realize that just as one devalues and hates one's own suffering, the other being devalues and hates hers.

This would mean that the act of recognizing and caring for the fragility of others introduces the needed moral dimension to the interactive approach. The question that emerges, then, is whether one can recognize other animals as delicate creatures, and feel for their vulnerability. For Levinas (and presumably for Sartre), a non-human animal cannot be an "other"—because of their presumed lack of propositional language, other animals cannot truly "look" at us. Hence, Levinas argues that animals do not have "a face" that could communicate their vulnerability to human beings: in the absence of language, representation of vulnerability and subjectivity becomes impossible. Yet, this account is surely missing the point. It is precisely in the absence of language, and other frameworks with a potential to hinder immediacy, that recognition of vulnerability is easiest. That is, it is outside lingual reports and other conceptual apparatuses that an immediate identification with the other creature and her plight becomes possible.

Derrida supports this conclusion. He discusses a cat, who looks at him and whisks him into a momentous episode of inter-species intersubjectivity that manifests the ridiculous nature of the type of anthropocentric metaphysics Levinas follows. Here, the animal's moral presence is obvious and beyond doubt, as is her agency. Derrida calls this a "moment of madness", and emphasizes how it exists outside of language—it is precisely beyond the reach of propositional ramifications that one can truly notice and pay heed to another being, and where ethics comes to exist. In fact, as soon as language enters the picture, these moments of epiphany are lost (Derrida 2001). Following suit, it can be argued that seeing care-inviting fragility in non-human animals is easy, particularly if one lets go

---

3 | Perhaps it could be said that there is a small distance between "response" and "responsibility".

of preconceptions and expectations of language, and enters into a state of intersubjectivity characterized by immediacy rather than words.[4]

As Husserl warns us, preconceptions can lead to blindness. Anthropocentric frameworks that often go hand in hand with the use of propositional language can render that blindness very concrete: we no longer *see* the animal, only the valueless and mindless creature presupposed by speciesist projections. Because of these projections and preconceptions, it is particularly important to seek moments of interaction outside lingual ramifications—it is only here that the animal can truly be met. Here, seeing animal vulnerability, and particularly having emotive responses and compassion toward that vulnerability begin to nurture moral awareness concerning the animal and her personhood.

Therefore, embodied empathy feeds immediacy, and immediacy feeds the type of intersubjectivity that personhood is based on. Yet, the personhood of others manifests a moral dimension only when one understands their fragility and feels compassion toward them. It is because of this that predators do not save their prey, even when they may relate to them as persons, and why many human and non-human animals remain untouched by the plight of others even when they understand that those others are beings with intentions and experiences. The personhood of other beings gains its moral aura only through one having affective reactions toward their vulnerability.

The claim put forward here is that many animals can view each other as persons, but only those capable of feeling compassion can recognize the moral significance within personhood. This would mean that, not

---

4 | Particularly in the ocular-centric Western culture, the act of looking has reserved a crucial role within ethics. The most obvious example of this is the pot-bellied child of human rights adverts, who looks at the camera and interrupts the daily routine of hedonistic consumers. The act of looking becomes a silent moral tool, vastly more powerful than spoken arguments. Its relevance in the context of non-human animals is equally clear. Encountering a wild animal, who looks at oneself, can be a startling experience. For a brief moment, the animal may break down the preconceptions of mundane, generic and faceless "deer" or "squirrel", and become a creature with both individuality and (at least some) moral significance. Little wonder, then, that the look has been utilised in animal rights advocacy: in leaflets and videos, dogs and pigs stare at the camera, hunched back and helpless, through the bars of their cages.

only can human beings see moral value in other animals, but those non-human animals, who are capable of empathy and compassion, can see moral value in human beings. It is no longer just the human creature that recognizes moral significance in others. It is within intersubjective relations of mutual moral recognition that one perhaps comes closest to another being. To reiterate, this can take place—not only amongst human beings—but also between given non-humans, and between, say, human beings and those primates, pigs, or dogs they have tended to with love. Now, it ought to be emphasized that the moral value or relevance of an animal does not depend on her capacity for moral sentiments—also animals incapable of compassion can be morally valuable persons. Yet, it is important to become aware of how "moral agency" may not be quite as narrow a notion as standardly presupposed. Lingual beings are prone to make sense of their moral sentiments via concepts, and eagerly invoke terms such as "rights" or "duties". However, behind these terms lie the core experiences of recognition and care, and it is not only human beings that are capable of possessing them, but also many non-human animals.[5]

5. Individuality

Personhood, in its standard use, is strongly related to the notion of "an individual", which again implies at least a certain degree of independence from others. Interaction, on the other hand, implies mutuality. What, then, is the relation between individuality and personhood under the interactive approach?

One interesting view comes from Gilles Deleuze and Félix Guattari. Deleuze and Guattari search for an escape from the categories "animal" and "human" via emphasizing a movement or a dynamic between the two. We are to follow the dynamic of "becomings-animal" in order to break free from the standard view that emphasizes fixed identities and categories. Becomings-animal is instigated by the "pack". Deleuze and Guattari emphasize the multiplicity of animals ("Every animal is funda-

---

[5] | Perhaps it can even be said that the undue emphasis placed on lingual analysis of normative terms has hindered understanding of morality—maybe morality, too, can only truly be grasped in the type of "moments of madness" Derrida calls for.

mentally a band, a pack", which has "pack modes, rather than characteristics"—Deleuze & Guattari 2004, 264) and argue that it is precisely this multiplicity that fascinates humans and lays the impetus for becomings-animal. Individuality, defined in a monistic, atomistic manner, looses meaning and this moment of finding the pack is depicted with strongly emotional terms. The packs causes an "affect" in us, which throws us into "upheaval": "Who has not known the violence of these animal sequences, which uproot one from humanity, if only for an instant, making one scrape at one's bread like a rodent or giving one the yellow eyes of a feline? A fearsome involution calling us toward unhear-of becomings." (Deleuze & Guattari 2004, 265)

In the pack animal, both multiplicity and exceptional individuality hold prominence. Firstly, Deleuze and Guattari argue that any animal can be approached via multiplicity, and it is obvious they would prefer us to do so. However, the individual is not completely ignored. Deleuze and Guattari underline the "exceptional" individual found in the pack, with whom we form "an alliance" in order to become-animal; she forms "a borderline" that needs to be encountered before the pack can be reached. This individual is the "coarse and rough" aspect of animality—that is, she is the real, concrete being that renders tangible the otherwise abstract and generic animality. She is neither species nor an individual in a traditional sense: "Human tenderness is as foreign to it as human classifications" (Deleuze & Guattari 2004, 270). Instead, she is an "outsider" and a "phenomenon", an example being the whale in *Moby Dick*.

Therefore, Deleuze and Guattari suggest that "individuality" as a monistic, atomistic notion be abandoned. We are offered the lead of the defiant animal and her pack as means with which to look at other beings and ourselves from a new perspective. But how does this relate to personhood? The anthropocentric framework emphasizes fixed categories "human" and "animal". The exclusivity of personhood is built on this notion: humans are categorically distinct from animals, and personhood is a property exclusive to human beings. However, following the viewpoint of Deleuze and Guattari, there is no distinct humanity or personhood exclusive to it. There simply are no fixed categories, identities or essences to hold on to. Moreover, individuality becomes a dynamic matter rather than a fixed, static quality: it is movement and fluctuation, and takes place in relation to others.

This notion of individuality opens the door away from the standard conceptions that underline independence. Not only do individuals undergo constant change, but they also exist in relation to different types of groups and wholes—they are members of packs. Yet, they do not lose their specificity and become one faceless member of a generic group, but instead they retain their concrete particularity. In other words, one does not have to choose between atomistic seclusion and faceless generics, but rather we can combine specificity with mutuality and interrelations. This, again, holds promise of rendering it clear how each animal person can be so vividly different from all others—"that cat" from Derrida's example—yet gain truest meaning only in relation to others, her pack, and ultimately intersubjectivity.

For Deleuze and Guattari, "becomings" is a political concept. With it, we can question hierarchical notions concerning different groups of people or beings. This is perhaps the most fruitful aspect of the type of individuality they bring forth: it allows one to attack anthropocentrism with vehemence. By reminding us that individuality is tied to relations toward others, the pack mode renders it impossible to hang on to illusions of dualism and human supremacy.

6. Propositional Language and Externalism

The interactive approach renders propositional language somewhat irrelevant. However, can we really talk of personhood in the absence of language?

For both Levinas and Derrida, the interruption that causes one to view another being as morally significant takes place outside language. Levinas maintains that "the other" gains her force precisely because she refuses to be categorized: "The face has turned to me—and this is its very nudity. It *is* by itself and not by reference to a system" (Levinas 1969, 75). As seen, Derrida argues that language cannot explain the moment of the cat's gaze and in fact is antithetical to it, as the moment would be lost immediately if language sought to define it. Derrida states that: "Nothing can ever take away from me the certainty that what we have here is an existence that refuses to be conceptualized." (Derrida 2001, 378) Matthew Calarco, who has studied Derrida's views on animals, states that the encounter is an "event", which "jumbles experience of time, self and being", and exposes "the limitations and shortcomings of our existing philosophical language about animals" (Calarco 2008, 126).[6] Therefore, the claim is that interruption or interaction sparks a moral response precisely because it takes place outside language: it is the defiance of familiar conceptualisations that holds the key. Again, Husserl's call for abandoning pre-existing frameworks is answered.

It would seem that the defiance against language is linked to morality because of *specificity*. Language offers broad categories, under which animals are positioned. We talk of "production animals", "fur animals", "vermin", "laboratory animals", "prey", and so forth instead of specific, individual beings. The use of these broad categories can remain antithetical to moral recognition simply because it emphasizes generality whereas the latter requires that the particularity of the animal herself is noted—for Derrida, even the term "animal" is an act of violence in this regard. Intersubjectivity is crucial from the viewpoint of morally relevant personhood precisely because it can exist outside language and can, thus, stir moral recognition: the other being is no longer a distant category but a real, living, breathing, singular entity right in front of us.

Therefore, instead of viewing non-human animals via pre-existing narratives and categories, which will always superimpose on them given expectations (consider viewing pigs via the notion of ham and pork chops), non-conceptual encounters briefly reveal the animal in her specificity (the pig is, for a moment, a creature that has her own desires and intentions). However, we could suggest—as Levinas does—that although recognition of personhood requires defiance of propositional language, in order to *have* personhood a being must still master such language. Is it far-fetched to argue that also those animals that lack language can be persons?

Sarah Whatmore has presented one interesting possibility. Whatmore underlines the actor or "actant" network theory, as advocated by Bruno Latour. One of the central principles of this theory is that agency does not have to be lingual. Rather, it can be found in non-human agents, ranging from other animals to even mechanical objects and weather events that exist in complex relations with each other. Agency is no longer situated within the individual capable of propositional language, but is rather

---

6 | Cary Wolfe (2003) draws similar lessons from Derrida. He argues that animal subjectivity can only be done justice to via an anti-representationalist stance that abandons language as the only way of understanding animality.

found from the relations between multiple beings. Whatmore uses the term "hybrid geography" and argues that it "recognizes agency as a relational achievement... in the fabrics of everyday living" (Whatmore 2007, 339). Agency is what happens between individuals: "Agency is reconfigured as a relational effect generated by a network of heterogeneous, interacting components whose activity is constituted in the networks of which they form a part" (Whatmore 2007, 341). Here the agency of non-humans is not only possible, but in fact vital, for without it the whole network would collapse: if we do not view animals as agents, we lose the counterparts of our own agency.

Now, the view advocated by Whatmore may go a step too far. The concept "agent" seems to suffer from significant inflation if it is made synonymous with just any form of action or causality between different things and entities. It would appear that for "agency" to retain its meaning, intentionality needs to remain an integral part of it.[7] However, the model remains fruitful none-the-less. Particularly the idea of *externality* is interesting. It supports the interactive approach, in that agency and ultimately personhood concern dynamics with other creatures, rather than second order conceptualization. One reason why propositional language has been linked to agency and personhood is found from its representative nature:

---

7 | Chris Wilbert has suggested that, rather than concentrating on agency as an internal quality (as he maintains animal rights literature does), agency ought to be thought of as something that occurs as a result of the "relation effect of *intra-actions* between people, animals, and other phenomena" (Wilbert 2006, 32). Here "intra-actions" are differentiated from "interaction": whereas the latter refers to activity between two separate beings, the former implies that there is no real separation, as "things are always mixed" (ibid.). Hence, activity and agency are constantly taking place between different beings and phenomena to such an extent that these beings and phenomena cannot be categorically separated from each other. Within this model, the lack of need for propositional language is particularly obvious, for when one being is indistinguishable from another, the two will have nothing to report or communicate to each other. However, again, we may have gone a step too far. The individual creature is melting into one mesh of creatures, events and actions, and the unfortunate consequence may be a type of holistic generalism, within which specificity is lost. Externalism holds promise of clearing the need for propositional language, but it needs to remain in *between* beings, not *within* beings that have become one.

it allows one to report one's agency to others. However, if agency and personhood are understood as partially external events, there no longer is a need for representation. This need is based on internalism: internal agency has to be "reported" for others to witness it. Within externalism, agency is already blatant to others, for it takes place in relation to them. The role of propositional language would, at least in this respect, disappear.

Therefore, the argument would be that the reason why propositional language has been placed as the criterion for personhood is found from internalism and the idea that only those, who can report their personhood, are persons. Within an external stance the need for reporting becomes less obvious. Even without such a stance, it is unclear why personhood would depend upon the capacity to report it. Here, we go back to the skeptical view, according to which any cognitive ability is to be doubted if it is not propositionally expressed. This leads us to the final point of criticism.

7. Skepticism

Perhaps the most poignant problem with the interactive approach concerns its assumptive nature. It approaches non-human animals as intentional beings when from all we know they may be utterly blind to the world. Does the approach not rest on animal characters more akin to Disney's imagination than to reality? To answer this skeptical question, we need to look at skepticism a little closer. Here, we find that interaction is not only the key to personhood, but may also act as the basis for recognizing animal minds.

Traditionally, animal minds have been studied from afar, by adopting a "neutral standpoint". In recent years, however, a more interactive view has begun to emerge. Whereas the traditional approach places humans (the observer) and other animals (the observed) in different categories between which there is no contact, and stipulates that only knowledge gathered via such a differentiation will count as valid, here human-animal interaction is the starting point of enquiry. Thus, the renowned ethologist Marc Bekoff argues that: "There are no substitutes for listening to, and having direct experiences with, other animals"—for him, animals are "a way of knowing" (Bekoff 2000, 869). In a similar vein, Martha Nussbaum states that, "all such [fruitful] scientific accounts must begin with experience of interaction between humans and animals" (Nussbaum 2001, 92). We will struggle to gain an adequate perception of the intentionality, beliefs, consciousness and other mental capacities of non-human animals, unless we enter into some type of interaction with them. The skeptical viewpoint and mechanomorphic explanations (according to which the animal will by necessity remain a biological mechanism) have to be replaced with an interactive approach (according to which we must approach the animal as a being with a mind in order to discover that mind) (Crist 1999).

Now, one possible criticism is that if we presume an animal to have a mind, we will begin to witness that mind regardless of whether it is there or not. Thus, Dennett's "intentional stance", within which we presume others to be intentional creatures, may lead to false recognitions of intentionality. The problem with this criticism is, however, that it ignores two factors.

First, also skepticism sets presumptions, which may affect understandings concerning non-human animals. A crucial feature of skepticism is its in-built bias. It is by no means a neutral ground for knowledge, but rather a specific attitude that presumes animals to not have minds until verified otherwise (and verified beyond doubt). Therefore, it can be maintained that also skepticism involves presumptive thinking (Rollin 2007). Ultimately, one needs to make a choice regarding the type of risk one is willing to take. Skepticism offers us denial of minds, with the risk that tens of billions of other animals are unfairly treated each year. To presume that animals have minds offers us the benefit of a doubt, with the risk that we may treat tens of billions of animals better than strictly warranted. It strikes as obvious that the latter risk ought to be favoured simply because it is fundamentally more benign. Erring on the side of intention will not harm anybody, but erring on the side of doubt will have devastating consequences. The choice is made even easier when considering the plentiful evidence offered by cognitive ethology that suggests many non-human animals are capable of highly advanced forms of cognition.

Second, perhaps the minds of other creatures are not the type of phenomena, in the context of which skepticism is meaningful. It can be argued that the intentional stance is *required* in order for one to recognize minds. Instead of the "inferential stance", which rests on objective, neutral inference, we need to prioritize (to introduce one more term) the "affective stance", which approaches the animal as a being with a mind (Jamieson 2002). Whereas the inferential stance will always ask for more proof and thus forever remain skeptical of non-human minds (for it is, following the

12. Personhood, Interaction and Skepticism 313

problem of falsification, impossible to prove the non-existence of an alternative interpretation: no matter how intentional the behaviour of an animal seems, one may always refer to far-fetched mechanical explanations), the affective stance will enable us to view the animal as a cognitive being. It emerges as a necessary setting, for in order to understand an animal, we need to approach her as a being with a mind, as a somebody rather than a thing. Without it, no amount of evidence will ever be enough to manifest beyond doubt that other animals are cognitive creatures. Thus, Raimond Gaita has claimed that should a person approach non-human animals as beings who are not sensate, "then her [a dog's] howling and the howling of a million dogs could not convince him" (Gaita 2002, 61).

It is important to note that, in intra-human dealings, the affective stance holds obvious prominence. We do not approach other humans as beings, who do not have minds. Here Wittgenstein's famous quote—"My attitude toward him [another human being] is an attitude towards a soul. I am not of the *opinion* that he has a soul." (Wittgenstein 1958, 178)—becomes relevant. We do not infer from other humans that they have minds, but rather approach them as minded creatures. In fact, there is no data that could prove beyond doubt that those, who walk around us, have cognition[8], but yet we give other human beings the benefit of a doubt. We need the affective stance, and it is alive and well in intra-human affairs.

Of course, the skeptical approach has been toyed with in this context, too. Descartes, who remained deeply skeptical of animal minds and who to some extent created the mechanomorphia still so common today, also became famous for his initial questioning of the certainty of the minds of other human beings. "The problem of other minds" contains the haunting question: how can I ever know for sure that there is a mind behind even the most complicated and intelligent seeming behaviour? A stern but fair response is that such skepticism remains absurd. It is theoretically possible but void of meaning in relation to lived experiences. As Raimond Gaita points out, this is because we have the concept of a "mind" precisely due to having interacted with other creatures: they have made it possible for us to perceive what minds are (Gaita 2002). Matilda has formed the

---

8 | Hence, Diamond maintains that the existence of a mind cannot be proven via scientific verification: "The other can present me with no mark or feature on the basis of which I can settle my attitude." Here Diamond quotes Stanley Cavell (Diamond 2008, 71).

notion of a mind via interaction with others: she has responded to others and they have responded to her, and this has introduced Matilda to cognition. This is why it makes no sense to question the minds of other human beings, for such skepticism would assume that the concept of a "mind" is detached from our lived experiences: it would gain the form of an abstract and theoretical entity instead of a matter discovered via and conceptually based on interaction.

A similar approach ought to be adopted with non-human animals, as also they are interactive beings who help us to form the concept of a "mind" in the first place. Human beings have developed in relation to bizarre yet in some respects familiar forms of non-human life, and part of this development (whether it happens on the level of individual experience or cultural concept-formation) is interaction, which gives us the inclination of what "a mind" is. Moreover, it offers us the idea that also other animals are, in a blatant and self-evident manner, creatures with cognitive ability. From this viewpoint, questioning animal subjectivity would become absurd. Thus, Gaita argues that: "If the word 'consciousness' means anything then I have no doubt that Gypsy [a dog] is a conscious being." (Gaita 2002, 62) Here, like in intra-human dealings, "Our certainty is without evidence—*completely* without evidence—and is none the worse for that" (ibid.). It becomes non-sensical to deny animal minds, for such denial would defy both the meaning of "a mind" and lived experience. The suggestion is that the concept of a mind is within and between us, and thus we need no evidence in order to recognize it in others and ourselves (even when those "others" are animals). Gaita is talking from a Wittgensteinian viewpoint, the obvious reference for refuting skepticism. Wittgenstein showed why skepticism makes little sense in relation to meanings and language games, which presume that other beings have minds. This presumption is of such integral relevance that questioning it is pointless and foolish. It is all we have to go by.

Skepticism may yield to a notion of a mind that is dehumanized. This notion has lost the roots of lived phenomenologies, which dig deep into human perception and experience, and has instead become a detached and clinical term that rests on mechanical calculations. It risks dehumanizing its users, as one begins to view others via a detached and calculative perspective. Therefore, when the concept "mind" is separated from its original affective context, it risks losing its humane content and stripping some of our own humanity away. Perhaps it is precisely this that turns many humans into moral monsters in their treatment of non-human animals. Their "perceptions have become shallow and faint; they don't see what is there to be seen because they ignore their emotional and imaginative responses and what these responses should reveal to them" (Fox & McLean 2008, 167). Gomez maintains that our ability to view others as persons is the necessary criterion for our own personhood. Perhaps a similar logic applies to humanity: it is only when we seek to approach others via the affective stance that we can retain our humanness (the potential of what it means to be human).

Therefore, instead of adopting skepticism, a fruitful option is to approach also non-human animals as beings who have minds. An important element within this approach is interaction: it is the dynamic between oneself and the other animal that reveals the existence of her mind. It can even be claimed that the concept "mind" was formed within aware interaction, and will only retain its clarity, or "fit" its object, if it is viewed via the affective stance. That is, we see minds in others, because we have experiences of interaction, of relating to another creature on an affective level, and it is only when we let go of those interactions that skepticism and dehumanization step in, with the eventual result being that we question the existence of even our own minds.

In an interesting manner, interaction thus forms a reference point for the recognition of both minds and personhood. In fact, the two are intertwined: recognizing another creature as a "you" goes hand in hand with recognizing her as a creature with a mind. The implication is that the acceptance of animal personhood relies partly on the denial of skepticism. It requires an affective stance: an ability to approach non-human animals as beings with their own minds and intentions. This is not naivety or anthropomorphism, but perhaps even a necessity if concepts such as "mind", "consciousness", and even "personhood" are to have a meaning that suits our everyday experience.

8. Conclusion

Husserl argues that skepticism fails to pay heed to the direct, immediate knowledge of our "life-world", i.e. the everyday, lived reality. Within this lived reality, the world is not seen as an objective collection of mathematically ordered, generic entities, but rather as something formed of innumerous particular beings and things, which we make sense of with the help of values, emotions, and other phenomenal factors. Skeptical science, in contrast, requires uniformity and detachment: the reality needs to be generic in order for the scientist to create abstract principles concerning it, and no phenomenal factors are to affect this act of creation. For Husserl, science can thus be a form of mathematization, which exists in utter conflict with the life-world. Following it, we begin to lose grasp of our surroundings, our experiences, and ultimately ourselves. Thus, a "crisis" is born. With the loss of sense of self, also loss of empathy will take place, which further deepens the crisis (Husserl 1990). We become unable to relate to our surroundings in any other than robotic manner.

It would seem that the contemporary society has adopted a mathematized view to non-human animals. Animals are seen to lack value, minds, and personhood. They are approached with detached doubt and demand for verification, which lead many to doubt even the existence of their minds—let alone their moral relevance—and most characterizations concerning them greatly emphasize mechanic, generic qualities, with each animal being a faceless, purely instinctual prototype of her species. Making sense of animality via anything other than instrumental, calculative reason is discouraged, as values and emotions are labelled as naïve, anthropomorphic and distorted ways of perceiving other animals. The result is a worldview, within which non-human animals become far away, mathematically ordered and controlled beings without moral value. As the perspective to animals becomes dehumanized and robotic, animal subjectivity and personhood become a near impossibility.

There are various elements that add to the weight of the mathematized view. Philosophy, religion, economics, politics, and other such broad factors tend to include aspects that smother moral concern for non-human animals. The most significant of these is hedonism: many are deeply flattered by the notion of being the pinnacle of evolution or the image of God, and many want to reap the economic and culinary benefits of instrumentalising animals.

With this is mind, perhaps what is needed is exposure to other animals. Animal personhood depends, then, not only on moral analysis, but also the willingness to become open or responsive to non-human animals. We need to stop on our tracks of hedonistic, calculating endeavours, and finally notice the animal, let her agency and vulnerability interrupt us. It is here that interaction becomes so important. It is particularly when we expose ourselves to intersubjectivity and interaction with other animals that it becomes evident that the being in front of me cannot be a mere thing or a tool, but something altogether different: a somebody, or (to use Gomez's terminology) a "you". When we feel compassion toward this you, it also becomes apparent that she is a being of moral value. Hedonistic illusions, mathematical detachment, and the type of selfish disregard they feed no longer have a place.

This need not be away from human beings. The ethologist Barbara Smuts has described this type of aware interspecies interaction beautifully in her accounts of direct experiences of non-human animals. In her deeply perceptive explorations, she has found that the willingness to become open toward other animals, and to enter into states of mutuality and interaction with them, will open up entirely new possibilities for also human beings. Smuts argues that: "Experience suggests that by opening more fully to the presence of 'self' in others, including animals, we further develop that presence in ourselves and thus become more fully alive and awake participants in life" (Smuts 2001, 308). This is because interaction with other animals will show us entirely new perspectives and new modes of being, thus liberating us from the narrow restrictions of the anthropocentric order that has eyes only for humanity. She states that: "My awareness of the individuality of all beings, and of the capacity of at least some beings to respond to the individuality in me, transforms the world into a universe replete with opportunities to develop personal relationships of all kinds" (ibid., 301). Therefore, interspecies interaction may only be the beginning to finding the world anew.

Within the interactive approach advocated here, personhood: 1) is a dynamic concept and 2) exists outside language, in the realm of immediacy. This way of approaching personhood is in stark contrast with the traditional view, according to which personhood is 1) a fixed characteristic, and 2) primarily based on conceptual ability. It is the space between two beings, the responding to another creature, that forms the basis of personhood—of both humans and other animals.

REFERENCES

Aaltola, E. (2008), "Personhood and Animals", Environmental Ethics 30/2, 175-193.
Bekoff, M. (1999), "Social Cognition: Exchanging and Sharing Information on the Run", Erkenntnis 51/1, 617-632.
Bekoff, M. (2000), "Animal Emotions: Exploring Passionate Natures", BioScience 50/10, 861-870.
Berkeley, G. (1998/1710), A treatise concerning the principles of human knowledge / George Berkeley (ed. J. Dancy), Oxford: Oxford University Press.
Calarco, M. (2008), Zoographies: The Question of the Animal, New York: Columbia University Press.
Carman, T. (2008), Merleau-Ponty, London: Routledege.
Cohen, C. (1997), "Do Animals Have Rights?", Ethics & Behavior 7/2, 91-102.
Crist, E. (1999), Images of Animals: Anthropocentrism and Animal Mind, Philadelphia: Temple University Press.
Deleuze, G., Guattari, F. (2004), A Thousand Plateaus: Capitalism and Schizophrenia (transl. by B. Massuoni), London: Continuum.
Derrida, J. (2001), "The Animal That Therefore I Am (More to Follow)", Critical Inquiry 28/2, 369-418.
Dombrowski, D. (1997), Babies and Beasts: The Argument from Marginal Cases, Chicago: University of Illinois Press.
Diamond, C. (2004), "Eating Meat and Eating People", in: C. R. Sunstein & M. C. Nussbaum (eds.), Animal Rights: Current Debates and New Directions, London: Routledge, 93-107.
Diamond, C. (2008), "The Difficulty of Reality and the Difficulty of Philosophy", in: C. Diamond, S. Cavell, et al. (ed.), Philosophy and Animal Life, New York: Columbia University Press, 43-89.
Fox, M.A., McLean, L. (2008), "Animals in Moral Space", in: J. Castricano (ed.), Animal Subjects: An Ethics Reader in a Post-human World, Waterloo, CA: Wilfried Laurier University Press.
Gaita, R. (2002), The Philosopher's Dog, London: Routledge.
Gómez, J.C. (1998), "Are Apes Persons? The Case for Primate Intersubjectivity", Etica and Animali 9, 51-63.
Goodman, M.F. (ed.) (1988), What is a Person? (Contemporary Issues in Biomedicine, Ethics and Society), Clifton, NJ: Humana Press.

Hintikka, J. (2003), "The notion of intuition in Husserl", Revue internationale de philosophie 224, 57-79.
Husserl, E. (1990), Ideas: Pertaining to a pure phenomenology and to a phenomenological philosophy (transl. R. Rojcewicz), Dordrecht: Springer.
Jamieson, D. (2002), "Science, Knowledge, and Animal Minds", in: D. Jamieson, Morality's Progress: Essays on Humans, Other Animals, and the Rest of Nature, Oxford: Oxford University Press, 52-70.
Levinas, E. (1969), Totality and Infinity, Duquesne University Press.
Midgley, M. (2002), Evolution as Religion, London: Routledge.
Midgley, M. (2003), "Is a Dolphin a Person?", in: S.J. Armstrong, R.G. Botzler (ed.), The Animal Ethics Reader, London: Routledge, 166-171.
Nussbaum, M.C. (2001), The Upheavals of Thought: The Intelligence of Emotions, Cambridge: Cambridge University Press.
Rollin, B. (2007), "Animal Mind: Science, Philosophy and Ethics", Journal of Ethics 11/3, 253-274.
Sartre, J.-P. (1989), Being and Nothingness, London: Routledge.
Smith, D.W. (2007), Husserl, London: Routledge.
Smuts, B. (2001), "Encounters with Animal Minds", Journal of Consciousness Studies 8/5–7, 293-309.
Whatmore, S. (2007), "Hybrid Geographies: Rethinking the 'Human' in Human Geography", in: A. Fitzgerald & L. Kalof (ed.), The Animal Reader, New York: Berg, 336-349.
Wilbert, C. (2006), "What is Doing the Killing? Animal Attacks, Man-Eaters, and Shifting Boundaries and Flows of Human-Animal Relations", in: Animal Studies Group (ed.), Killing Animals, Chicago, ILL: University of Illinois Press.
Wittgenstein, L. (1958), Philosophical Investigations, Oxford: Blackwell.
Wolfe, C. (ed.) (2003), Zoontologies: The Question of the Animal, Minneapolis: University of Minnesota Press.

13. Eating and Experimenting on Animals
Two Issues in Ethics

Alice Crary

1. INTRODUCTION

Modern industrial societies are distinguished by an array of historically novel practices with animals. These include the 'factory' or industrial farming of land and sea animals and the mass use of animals in education and research and in the testing of medicines, medical procedures and household products. There is nothing especially contentious about the claim that many of these practices raise serious ethical questions. Consider, for instance, standard methods for the factory farming of land animals. These methods have prompted concerns having to do with, among other things, public health, labor practices and the environment.[1] Yet even once we observe that industrial farming and the experimental use of animals are sources of moral controversy, there is still room to ask whether the practices raise moral questions specifically in virtue of ways in which animals are treated within them. After all, it is not difficult to find skeptics who explicitly deny that animals *matter* in the sense of being vulnerable to harms that are not the mere indirect upshots of harms to human beings.[2] At the same time, the organizing conviction of the contemporary animal

---

[1] | For some influential recent discussion of these issues, see Stull & Broadway (2012); Berry (2009); Nestle (2007); Pollan (2006); Schlosser (2002).

[2] | Any adequate list of the writings of the most influential of these critics of animal protectionism would need to include Carruthers (1992); Leahy (1994, ch. 7); Oderberg (2003); perhaps also Scruton (2000). Scruton sanctions the idea of direct duties to individual animals arising from relationships with them, it makes sense to mention his work here given that he denies that we have any *other* duties

protectionist movement is that animals do matter in just this sense (and that, e.g., using kittens as 'balls' in a game of baseball is an abuse, and not simply on account of any injuries that doing so may indirectly inflict on human beings). There is good reason to think that by itself the mere idea that animals matter equips us to criticize factory farms and many labs that do animal testing. But, if we hope to arrive at a good understanding of what is wrong with these practices, and if we also hope to appreciate the character of the difficulties we confront in trying to respond to them, we need insight into what speaks for this idea.

Clarifying what speaks for the idea that animals matter is a task for philosophical ethics. In claiming that this clarificatory task is important, I am implying that there is an important role for philosophy in discussions about the ethical treatment of animals. To be sure, today many books and articles on the ethical treatment of animals are written in a popular style that doesn't presuppose any willingness on the part of their readers to explore specifically philosophical considerations. It is no part of my ambition to deny that there is a place for such popular writing. Nevertheless I am persuaded that philosophical inquiry can contribute significantly to conversations about animals and ethics. The guiding claim of this chapter is that we need to take seriously, and to investigate, the possibility that certain deeply engrained, and often merely tacit, metaphysical assumptions distort discussions about how animals should be treated. Below I describe how a widely accepted yet contestable metaphysic structures the work of many prominent thinkers who hold that animals directly merit specific forms of respect and attention. I show that if we avail ourselves of a quite different metaphysic we radically transform received views about the nature and difficulty of ethical reflection about animals (section 2). I then illustrate what is at issue by turning specifically to the cases of the industrial farming and experimental use of animals. Following up on the work of generations of animal advocates, I describe what it comes to say that in these settings animals are treated as mere objects or instruments that don't matter (sections 3 and 4). I close by discussing how the philosophically unusual approach to animals and ethics that I here explore obliges us to reshape our image of what is involved in understanding, not only what

---

to animals that aren't indirect functions of duties to ourselves or other human beings (see esp. chs. 7 and 8).

is wrong with such practices, but what kinds of challenges we confront in trying to arrive at appropriate responses to them (section 5 and 6).

2. A Brief Overview of Ongoing Conversations about Animals and Ethics

There is a feature of contemporary conversations about animals and ethics that might well strike us. What I have in mind has to do with the approaches that most animal protectionists adopt in their efforts to show that animals matter in the sense outlined above (i.e., in the sense of being vulnerable to harms that aren't mere indirect upshots of harms to human beings). Animal protectionists are committed to challenging the thought that animals are mere objects whose treatment is ethically indifferent except insofar as it affects human beings. It would not be unreasonable to assume that they would want to contest this thought in the most straightforward way, arguing that, far from being indifferent objects, the worldly beings we call animals are as such of interest to ethics. But this is not the approach that animal protectionists by and large adopt. Although writing about ethics and animals is often not terribly philosophically self-conscious, animal advocates generally at least implicitly draw on metaphysical outlooks that prevent them from representing the kinds of worldly beings animals are as in themselves ethically important.

The metaphysical outlooks animal advocates tend to draw on are versions of a philosophically familiar species of naturalism. This species of naturalism is characterized by the following pair of assumptions, namely, the assumption that the natural world is the world that is real as opposed to merely apparent and the further assumption that membership in this world is limited to the subject matter of the natural sciences, or to some proper subset of these sciences. Strains of naturalistic thought distinguished by these assumptions are enormously influential in philosophy, and for the sake of convenience I will speak in this connection of *traditional naturalism*. Within the context of traditional naturalism, the real world is taken to be the ethically neutral world of the natural sciences. So, within this context, animals, insofar as they are conceived as elements of this world, are seen as mere ethically neutral objects. One thing that is striking about the animal protectionist literature, as we might now put it, is that most contributors to it—most thinkers who set out to show that animals directly merit specific forms of respect and attention—help themselves to some version of a traditional naturalistic metaphysic that bequeaths to us this ethically indifferent image of animals.[3]

Consider in this connection what might well be described as the most influential group of animal protectionists, the group whose members are sometimes collectively referred to as *moral individualists*. The distinguishing claim of different moral individualists is that any treatment a creature merits is a function of its individual capacities. While it is possible for a thinker who qualifies as a moral individualist to focus solely on human beings, the mark of the work of those moral individualists who present themselves as animal protectionists is the following two-fold thought. These moral individualists think that consistency obliges us to treat any capacities that we take to be morally significant in human beings to be likewise morally significant in those animals that possess them, and they also think that there are no morally significant capacities that are such that all humans possess them and no animals do. There is, admittedly, some variation in how animal protectionists who favor forms of moral individualism develop this basic position. Whereas some—such as Peter Singer—who are partial to utilitarianism represent sentience as a morally significant capacity shared by many human beings and animals, others—such as Tom Regan—who are partial to rights-based approaches in ethics represent subject-hood as a morally significant capacity shared by many

---

3 | Having just described the tendency of animal advocates to rely on a traditionally naturalistic metaphysic as striking, I should admit that there is one respect in which this tendency is anything but striking. A traditionally naturalistic metaphysic tends to get taken for granted not only in conversations about animals and ethics but also in conversations about ethics more generally. Given that moral philosophers frequently start their reflections about ethical relations among human beings equipped with a traditionally naturalistic metaphysic that obliges them to represent the worldly fact of being human as by itself ethically indifferent, there is a sense in which it is not surprising that thinkers concerned with ethical relations between human beings and animals frequently help themselves to the same metaphysic and thereby oblige themselves to represent the worldly fact of being an animal as by itself ethically indifferent. That the tendency of animal advocates to draw on a traditionally naturalistic metaphysic is in this sense unsurprising should not, however, keep us from being struck by how unhelpful the metaphysic is in light of animal advocates' aims.

human beings and animals. Yet, without regard to what individual capacities they take to be morally relevant, moral individualists who take an interest in the case of animals by and large agree on this much. They agree in at least tacitly assuming, in accordance with the tenets of traditional naturalism, that in our efforts to understand the worldly lives of animals we are limited to the ethically neutral resources of scientific or scientifically sanctioned disciplines.[4] Starting from this assumption, they claim that, if we are to show that the ethical attitudes toward animals they cherish are warranted, we therefore need to identify grounds for these attitudes. They conclude by declaring that we find such grounds in certain individual capacities. This, very generally, is how these moral individualists seek to show that animals matter, and my main point here is that their strategy clearly respects the constraints of traditional naturalism.[5] There is a familiar litany of complaints about moral individualism. All moral individualists, including those who pay special attention to animals, are committed to grounding the treatment they think human beings merit in particular individual capacities. Some of the most widely discussed worries about different moral individualisms have to do with the image of our ethical relation to other human beings that they thus bequeath to us. Many of these worries have to do with the cases of human beings who are cognitively severely impaired, e.g., human beings such as the congenitally severely impaired or retarded, the very sick, the comatose and the extremely senile. It is a straightforward consequence of the logic of moral individualism that the impairments of these individuals weaken their claims to moral consideration. However plausible this seems to moral individualists and

---

4 | I hasten to acknowledge that it is in principle possible for a moral individualist to champion a metaphysic that does not count as a form of traditional naturalism. If we consult the history of philosophy, we find various figures who might well be described as moral individualists who do not favor traditionally naturalistic outlooks. My point here is about contemporary animal advocates who defend positions that qualify as moral individualisms. These thinkers tend to defend their theoretical postures in ways that, while often not philosophically self-conscious, indicate sympathy for traditional naturalism or something very like it.

5 | A brief bibliography of central works of moral individualism might include McMahan (2005); Singer (1990, ch. 1); Rachels (1990); Regan (1983, 2000). For critiques of moral individualism, see, e.g., Diamond (1991a); Gaita (2002); Crary (2011b).

their sympathizers, there is a sense in which it can seem outrageous. For it flies in the face of the idea that seriously impaired human beings merit special solicitude in virtue of their special susceptibility. It also flies in the face of the closely related idea that there is something particularly hateful about intentionally injuring the seriously impaired, something that the fact that these human beings may be unable to understand the injuries inflicted on them not only doesn't mitigate but aggravates.

Cora Diamond was one of the first philosophers to criticize the work of moral individualists in this basic spirit, and Diamond's essays in ethics contain a rich assortment of illustrations of the criticism's point. In one essay, for instance, she asks us to consider the kind of indignation "we may feel at the rape of a girl lacking speech and understanding, lacking what we think of as moral personality and the capacity for autonomous choice, and incapable of finding the event humiliating and the memory painful as a normal woman might" (Diamond 1991b, 56). In a different passage of the same essay, Diamond invites us to acknowledge that "the conviction by a court of a severely retarded person for a crime that required an intention the retarded person could not form [would be] unjust; the less capable of forming such an intention the person is, the more palpable the injustice" (ibid., 53). One thing that emerges from Diamond's examples is, we might say, that moral individualists' strategies for showing that animals matter oblige us to wrongly devalue specifically human lives (as opposed to the lives of human beings who happen to be endowed with such-and-such qualities).[6]

My point here is not that moral individualists defend a sound image of value in animal life and that their work is problematic only insofar as they arrive at it via a distorted image of value in human life. Moral individualists are indeed committed to a distorted image of value in human life. But there are analogous distortions internal to their image of value in animal life. Just as it is jarring and wrong to say that human beings only matter insofar as they have such-and-such capacities with which to register harms done to them, it is jarring and wrong to suggest that animals only matter insofar as they have such-and-such capacities with which to register harms done to them. According to the logic of moral individualism, there is no such thing as harming animals except when there is a question

---

6 | For a helpful discussion of similar themes that is in part a commentary on Diamond's work, see Anderson (2004).

of, say, causing them pain or interfering with their movements. It would follow that there can be no question of wronging a brain dead puppy by using it as a dartboard. Yet it seems just and appropriate to speak in this connection of a failure of proper respect for a living creature. It seems reasonable to say something similar in reference to the behavior of researchers at the University of Pennsylvania Head Injury Laboratory who, as a secret video revealed, mocked and ridiculed their already injured baboon subjects. Shouldn't we say that these researchers exhibited a form of disrespect that wasn't a function of causing the animals extra pain or distress?[7] And shouldn't we say the same about the conduct of workers in a California factory farm who, as another secret videotape showed, pushed cattle too sick to walk around with a forklift? Weren't these people betraying a callousness to ailing creatures that wasn't merely a function of causing additional suffering?[8] There is, as these examples illustrate, good reason to reject moral individualists' preferred image of value in animal life as no more satisfactory than their preferred image of value in human life.

Let me turn now to members of a group of animal advocates who attempt to overcome the limitations of moral individualism just touched on while nevertheless resembling moral individualists in operating within the framework of traditional naturalism. Here I have in mind members of a somewhat distinctive group of Kantian moral philosophers. A number of Kantian moral philosophers—most prominently, Christine Korsgaard and Allen Wood—undertake to use resources from Kant's thought to combat his own notoriously indifferent attitude toward animals. These Kantians differ from moral individualists insofar as they are happy to claim that the plain fact that a creature is an animal, without regard to which individual capacities it possesses, is morally significant.[9] At first glance it might appear that this claim commits them to departing from the ethically neutral ontology distinctive of traditional naturalism. But any appearance of this sort is misleading. When the Kantians in question represent the recognition that a creature is an animal as by itself giving us reason to treat it

---

7 | See Cora Diamond's discussion of this case in Diamond (2001, 137).

8 | Singer discusses this case in Singer (1990, ix). He uses it to motivate his preferred form of moral individualism. He does not take it, as I do, to speak against such individualism.

9 | See Korsgaard (2004) and Wood (1998). For Kant's view of animals, see esp. Kant (1997, 212-213) and Kant (1996, 192).

in particular ways, they also insist that the relevant act of recognition, instead of being even partly a matter of theoretical cognition, is a matter of the adoption of an exclusively practical attitude.[10] The kind of practical attitude that they have in mind is one they arrive at by modifying the logic of Kant's categorical imperative. Whereas the basic idea of the categorical imperative is that a correct moral judgment must affirm practical principle to which every *rational* being could in some sense consent, the basic idea of the modified strategy adopted by the Kantian moral philosophers I am discussing is that a correct moral judgment must also affirm a practical principle which is acceptable in light of the interests characteristic of different non-rational animals (Korsgaard 2004). Without further commenting on this practical strategy, what I want to emphasize right now is that in adopting it these Kantian thinkers preserve the traditionally naturalistic idea that animals, when regarded as worldly beings, are ethically indifferent things. So, like moral individualists, they effectively respect the restrictions of traditional naturalism.[11]

It would be possible to assess the Kantian approach to questions of animals and ethics that I just described in a manner that leaves these restrictions unquestioned. But this isn't my project. What interests me is considering approaches to questions of animals and ethics that reject traditionally naturalistic restrictions. Why shouldn't we say, in a manner that repudiates the terms of traditional naturalism, that there is an entirely straightforward (i.e., not merely practical) sense in which the recognition that a creature is an animal is by itself morally significant? Why shouldn't we depart from moral individualists as well as some Kantian moral philosophers in rejecting the idea that traditional naturalism is an obligatory framework for thinking about how animals should be treated?

A good way to start here is with a rough description of the sorts of philosophical considerations that are taken to speak in favor of traditional

---

10 | This is the guiding theme of Korsgaard (2004).

11 | This is perhaps the right place to mention that Korsgaard is a partial exception to the rule that traditionally naturalistic animal advocates lack an interest in the metaphysical presuppositions of their work. Korsgaard consistently underlines the fact that she favors the sort of metaphysic that I am placing under the heading of "traditional naturalism", sometimes describing it as a metaphysic on which the world is value-neutral or "hard." But even Korsgaard treats her traditionally naturalistic outlook as too firmly established to require a defense.

naturalism.[12] Philosophical defenses of traditional naturalism by and large turn on two main ideas. The first is the idea that the real world is the world that is there anyway, that is, apart from any reference to our perceptual or affective endowments. The second is the idea that the natural sciences (or some proper subset of these sciences) are distinguished by modes of thought in which the mind has a bearing on the world that is maximally independent of any subjective contribution. Taken together, this pair of ideas appears to lend the natural sciences (or some proper subset of them) a special claim to be concerned with the real furniture of the universe and, by the same token, appears to provide support for traditional naturalism.

Despite being widely accepted among philosophers, this approach to defending traditional naturalism has its detractors. A small but well-known group of contemporary philosophers focus their criticisms on the idea that the real world is the world that is there 'anyway'. Members of the group of philosophers I have in mind attack the suggestion of a standpoint from which we could somehow determine that reality is made up of things independent of any reference to human subjectivity, arguing that in thinking and taking in the way things are we necessarily draw on sensitivities of the sort characteristic of us as concept-users. This maneuver positions these philosophers, not only to question the epistemic and ontological privilege that traditional naturalisms assign to the natural sciences, but also to open the door for other equally authoritative forms of discourse. Moreover, in addition to thus criticizing an understanding of the natural sciences as epistemically and ontologically privileged, some of the philosophers in question go on to advance the following claim, namely, that *ethical* discourse, conceived as discourse that deals in aspects of our lives with ineliminable references to our sensitivities, enjoys equal epistemic and ontological authority. The work of these philosophers is noteworthy because it contains a direct challenge to traditional naturalism. These philosophers represent the realm of the real or natural as containing, not only the objects of the natural sciences (as traditional naturalists maintain), but also irreducibly ethical aspects of our lives. They might accordingly be described rejecting traditional naturalism in favor of an alternative that is

---

12 | I am intentionally setting aside *empirical* defenses of traditional naturalism, i.e., defenses that appeal essentially to the success of the natural sciences in explaining aspects of our lives. I regard such defenses as wrongheaded, but I do not discuss them further here.

in specific respects more capacious or broader. For the remainder of this chapter I speak in this connection of *broad naturalism*.[13]

There are a number of contemporary animal advocates who are aptly described as having broadly naturalistic outlooks. These include, to mention but two of the best known, Diamond and Raimond Gaita. I am not here going to discuss details of the work of these broadly naturalistic thinkers.[14] My goal is simply to bring out how the transition to a broadly naturalistic metaphysic can change the terms of conversations about animals and ethics, and right now I want to start by mentioning two very fundamental respects in which moving to a broad naturalism is significant for these conversations.

One thing that is noteworthy about the introduction of a broad naturalism is that it equips us to contest, in the most direct manner, the contentions of those who deny that animals are vulnerable to any wrongs that aren't mere indirect upshots of wrongs to human beings. Now there are no philosophical obstacles to taking at face value examples, of the sort that I adduced in discussing limitations of moral individualism, that suggest that there is a sense in which the mere fact of being an animal is morally important. Not that it is impossible to represent the mere fact of being an animal as morally important within the context of traditional naturalism. As I mentioned a moment ago, some Kantian animal advocates work within a traditionally naturalistic framework in arguing that there is a strictly practical sense in which the recognition that a creature is an animal is by itself morally interesting. What is notable about the advent of broad naturalism is, we might accordingly say, that it equips us not only to represent the recognition that a creature is an animal as by itself morally important but, moreover, to do so in the most uncomplicated way.

This brings me to a second respect in which the introduction of a broadly naturalistic metaphysic is significant for debates about animals and ethics. At the same time that this metaphysic positions us to treat the worldly fact of being an animal as by itself morally interesting, it transforms our understanding of the nature and difficulty of moral thought about animals. Here it is helpful to recall that, however different from each other traditionally naturalistic approaches to questions about ani-

---

13 | For what is arguably the most influential contemporary defense of a form of broad naturalism, see the writings of John McDowell.
14 | I discuss Diamond's work in detail in Crary (2011a).

mals and ethics are, they agree in assuming that the world is ethically neutral. By the same token, traditionally naturalistic approaches also agree in assuming that bringing into view the kind of worldly thing an animal is not a task for ethics proper. Within the context of these approaches, the sort of understanding of animals that is relevant to ethics is handed down to us from disciplines like biology and metaphysics, where these disciplines are taken to be independent of and external to ethics.[15] The point here is not merely that, in contrast to advocates of traditionally naturalistic approaches, advocates of broadly naturalistic approaches can allow that moral insight and imagination are required to bring the sorts of worldly beings animals are into view in a manner relevant to ethics. What distinguishes the work of broadly naturalistic animal advocates is allegiance to a metaphysic on which some real features of the world qualify as ethical because they are such that they can only be properly understood in reference to attitudes. It follows that these thinkers are committed to holding that, in order to do justice to our ethical relationship to animals, we need to be prepared to do a kind of work on ourselves that involves cultivating new attitudes or modes of responsiveness. They are committed to holding that we need to be prepared to explore new attitudes with an eye to improving our sense of what is significant in animals' lives, where this might involve being open to or seeking experiences that challenge our current ways of seeing animals, and where it might also involve exposing ourselves to different ways of seeing animals through the study of history or literature.[16]

This last remark may seem unfair to traditionally naturalistic animal advocates. It is true that some traditionally naturalistic animal advocates represent historical and literary accounts of animal lives as shaping our at-

---

15 | Notice that this is true not only of moral individualists but also of the Kantian animal advocates whose work I discussed earlier in this section. Within the work of these Kantians, figuring out what kind of moral attention animals merit is a matter of applying a merely practical formula modeled on Kant's categorical imperative. While the correct application of the formula presupposes a good understanding of the kind of worldly thing an animal is, such an understanding is supposed to be something that, in accordance with the tenets of traditional naturalism, we derive from disciplines outside ethics.

16 | That bringing animals into view in a manner relevant to ethics may require a kind of emotionally demanding work on ourselves is an important theme of the writings of both Diamond (2006) and Gaita (2002, esp. ch. 8).

titudes in ways that reinforce what they regard as ethically sound views of animals.[17] But this observation doesn't contradict the point I am making. Even those traditionally naturalistic animal advocates who take an interest in historical and literary treatments of animals' lives are committed denying that texts that engage us emotionally may thereby be capable of making a direct contribution to our understanding of animals' lives. So it is fair to say that the kind of critical exploration of different ways of seeing animals that, for the kinds of broadly naturalistic animal advocates I am discussing, is internal to authoritative ethical thought about animals, for their traditionally naturalistic counterparts, it is necessarily external to such thought.

Now we have before us an initial case for thinking advocates of traditionally naturalistic approaches to questions of animals and ethics ought to take an interest in their own philosophical presuppositions. To the extent that, as I just showed, the move to a broad naturalism holds forth the promise of radically altering our understanding of the difficulty of ethical thought about animals, it follows that there is a substantive moral reason to examine the credentials of the traditionally naturalistic metaphysic that underwrites most contributions to contemporary conversations about animals and ethics. Absent such an examination, we cannot exclude the possibility that, in our efforts to identify what is significant in animals' lives, we are simply looking in the wrong direction.[18] The kind of moral danger that is in question here becomes even clearer if we consider some specific issues of concern to animal advocates. Taking my cue from this observation, I now turn to a discussion of factory farming and animal testing.

---

17 | Thus, for instance, in recent work Peter Singer has discussed literary treatments of animals' lives in this basic, positive spirit (see Leist & Singer 2010).

18 | Although for the purposes of this paper I remain agnostic about the soundness of the sort of broadly naturalistic approach to questions of animals and ethics that interests me, elsewhere I offer a defense of such an approach (Crary 2011b).

3. Factory Farming

Several billion land animals are slaughtered for food in the US each year, and the overwhelming proportion of these animals come from industrial or "factory" farms.[19] The label "factory farm" is sometimes challenged by defenders of the food industry on the ground that animal activists use it as a rhetorical weapon,[20] yet it seems undeniable that it accurately describes certain prominent facts about how the farming and slaughter of animals is practiced today in the US (and also elsewhere). During the twentieth century, starting roughly in the 1920s, animal husbandry was radically transformed by pressures to imitate the industrial methods of and thereby lay claim to the economic efficiency of factories. Today the more conspicuous signs of this transformation include the nearly universal use of animals engineered for the quality, size and growth-rate of their edible tissues, the confinement of animals at great densities and the use of large abattoirs that kill animals on assembly lines at high rates. It is fair to say that, within these and other practices, animals are to a great extent treated as mere objects, the handling of which by itself raises no ethical questions.

To say this is not to deny that in these settings animals are recognized as special kinds of entities requiring expert forms of care and attention. Factory farming is an economic enterprise, and it depends for its success on preserving animals in a sufficiently healthy condition up to the time of slaughter. A sophisticated knowledge of animals' biology and characteristic behaviors is required to answer questions about whether specific proposed adjustments to their treatment will translate into gains in efficiency, and within industrial farms such knowledge generally informs decisions about how to treat animals. While this is true, it is also true that factory farming is to an enormous extent structured by the assumption that, once such knowledge has been brought to bear on various economic questions that are taken to be pertinent to the treatment of animals, there are no further questions about animals' treatment that remain to be addressed.

---

19 | For a calculation of the proportions of land animals slaughtered for meat in the U.S. that come from factory farms, see Foer (2009, 271). Foer also discusses intensive methods of farming of sea animals (see, e.g., Foer 2009, 49-50, 189-193), a topic neglected in many critiques of factory farming.

20 | While some people within the agricultural industry prefer to speak of "agribusiness", it is not unheard of for industry insiders to use the term "factory farm."

A few illustrations should serve to bring this out. Consider, for instance, the typical treatment of chickens raised for meat or, as they are called within the industry, "broilers." These birds are engineered so that they have very high rates of "feed conversion", quickly transforming what they eat into muscles and fat and attaining the weight deemed suitable for slaughter. The birds are placed in sheds by the tens of thousands at densities that allow each creature on average something less than a square foot of floor space. At around seven weeks of age, they are packed tightly in crates for transport to industrial slaughterhouses, and, when they arrive, they are hung by their ankles in shackles and drawn along to a machine that cuts their throats. This is the basic approach to raising broiler chickens characteristic of industrial farming, and it is not difficult to see how it can seem economically advantageous. Housing chickens indoors protects them from predators and bad weather, and keeping them at high densities, using industrial slaughter-houses, and engineering them and manipulating their light and feed in ways that speed up their growth make it possible for one individual to oversee the handling of far more birds than traditional farming methods allowed.

These economic advantages notwithstanding, industrial broiler farming is hellish. The birds' accelerated growth leads to fatal deformities in a small percentage and painful injuries in many others. Cramming tens of thousands densely together produces respiratory disease, fatal as well as non-fatal injuries of various kinds and extremely high rates of different infections (including some like E. coli that are caused by fecal contamination). Many chickens suffer broken bones while being captured and crated for transport to slaughter, and they not only receive no further food or water underway but are slaughtered by a mechanical process that, in cases in which it works correctly, kills them while they are still conscious and, in the small but significant number of cases in which it doesn't, scalds them alive. Moreover, the overwhelming tendency within the industry is to treat these aspects of intensive chicken farming as 'problems' demanding a response only when and to the extent to which they are seen to have a negative impact on economic efficiency. Thus, whereas it is standard practice to try to check the spread of disease (to humans as well as to other chickens) by including antibiotics in the birds' feed and incorporating chlorine baths in the slaughter-process—measures that, as counterintuitive as this may seem, are taken to ensure an edible and hence salable end-product—no meaningful steps are taken to change living-conditions that, even with the interventions just mentioned, still lead to significant rates of injury, disease and death. By the same token, since there is no economic incentive, no meaningful steps are taken to ameliorate what birds undergo on the way to and at the slaughterhouse. This is what it comes to to say that while, within factory farming, chickens are taken to require expert care and attention, their handling is not itself treated as raising any specifically ethical questions.[21]

The situation is in essentials the same with the intensive farming of pigs in the US. Pigs are typically engineered not only for high rates of feed conversion but also for the production of lean meat. They are weaned early, after a few weeks as opposed to after several months in the wild, and thereafter they are mostly kept in crowded pens with bare concrete or slatted floors until, at an age of somewhere between six and ten months, they are packed tightly together on trucks for transport to industrial slaughterhouses. The following economic considerations might seem to recommend pig farming in this manner. The early weaning of piglets makes it possible to quickly re-impregnate sows, thus allowing for the production of more pigs. Further, confining pigs in bare and easily cleanable pens, employing large abattoirs, and starting pigs early on feed that, working in tandem with their genetically engineered propensities for rapid growth, speeds up their weight gain makes it possible to significantly reduce the labor costs of raising each animal.

But these gains in efficiency are not without a nightmarish downside. Housing pigs in barren conditions—conditions that, among other things, deprive sows of materials for building protective nests for their piglets— leads to a significant incidence of cases in which mothers crush and kill their own young, and crowding pigs together not only leads to a significant incidence of cases in which pigs bite off each others' tails, thereby causing nasty infections but also, because it means keeping pigs close to large volumes of their own manure, produces high rates of respiratory diseases and infections of various kinds. Further, while, unlike chickens, pigs are covered by the Humane Methods of Slaughter Act, which stipulates that animals be rendered unconscious before being killed, it is well document-

---

21 | The sources I used in arriving at this description of the treatment of broiler chickens include the following texts, which are here listed in reverse publication order: Foer (2009, 129ff); Markus (2005, 22-23); Stull & Broadway (2012, 36-51); Singer (1990, 98-106).

ed that violations occur and that pigs are sometimes dismembered while still conscious. Within the industry, these aspects of the intensive farming of pigs—like the analogous aspects of the intensive farming of broiler chickens—are for the most part taken to call for concerned attention only insofar as they are seen to have adverse economic consequences. Thus, for instance, while it is routine not only to cut down on piglet-crushing by strapping sows into severely restrictive "farrowing crates" but also to eliminate opportunities for tail-biting by cutting off piglets' tails and to control the spread of disease by including antibiotics in pigs' feed, all of these are expedients that are supposed to make sense in economic terms. There is in general no question of undertaking changes to the treatment of pigs that do not make sense in these terms. Nothing substantial is done to alter the living conditions that originally produce piglet-crushing and tail-biting and that, even with the use of antibiotics, still produce high rates of disease, and nothing substantial is done to eliminate the kinds of (predictable if also unintentional) violations of the Humane Methods of Slaughter Act that current slaughterhouse procedures regularly admit. It is thus fair to say that, within the setting of industrial farming, the handling of pigs—like the handling of broiler chickens—is not by itself taken to raise ethical questions.[22]

The point I want to make at this juncture is that anyone who thinks that animals matter (i.e., anyone who thinks that they are susceptible to wrongs that aren't simply the indirect expressions of wrongs to human beings) has grounds for opposing factory farming.[23] The sorts of ethical

---

22 | The sources I used for this description of the life of pigs includes, among others, the following texts, listed in reverse order of publication: DeGrazia (2009); Pollan (2006, 218); Markus (2005, 27-34); Stull & Broadway (2012, 52-64); Singer (1990, 119-129). For documentation of continued violations of the Humane Methods of Slaughter Act, see, e.g., the 2004 United States General Accounting Office Report, "Humane Methods of Slaughter Act: USDA Has Addressed Some Problems but Still Faces Enforcement Challenges."

23 | The accomplishments of different animal welfare organizations in the U.S. that advocate for improved treatment of animals in factory farms, while real, have mostly been limited to passing state legislation to ban some of the most outrageous practices (such as e.g., the use of restrictive "battery cages" for laying hens). The situation in European Union, where factory farms also dominate meat production, is somewhat different. While the EU has prohibited some of the

questions about animals that any such an individual is committed to taking seriously get no hearing within factory farming. Admittedly, some apologists for factory farming present themselves as sensitive to ethical questions, arguing that considerations for treating animals more gently and humanely just happened to be outweighed by human nutritional needs. This argument rings hollow. There is no good reason to believe that the ability of industrial societies like the US to feed their populations adequately depends on factory farming or even that, all things considered, factory farming represents a particularly cost effect method.[24] So there is no good reason to deny that holding that animals matter by itself makes one a critic of factory farming. Let me add that it does not follow from this that people who deny that animals matter cannot be critical of the industrial farming of animals. It is possible to criticize such farming on grounds other than its utter lack of sensitivity to the ethical dimension of human relationships with animals. There are in fact excellent grounds for thinking that criticisms on other grounds are justified.[25] My object right

---

cruelest practices (e.g., the routine tail-docking of pigs, banned in 2003), there are widespread violations and consequent questions about the effectiveness of enforcement.

24 | See the references in the next note.

25 | Significant additional grounds for objecting to factory farming have to do with the fact that, by crowding huge numbers of animals tightly together, it ensures not only that the land on which animals are housed cannot furnish adequate feed but also that it cannot reabsorb the animals' waste. The result is a two-fold environmental problem: feed needs to be transported to animals, a process requiring substantial amounts of fossil fuels, and animal waste—which often causes respiratory diseases in nearby human populations and leaks into water supplies—needs somehow to disposed of. Wendell Berry, who has been writing about these topics for many decades, sometimes glosses this cluster of interrelated problems by declaring that industrial farming is not "sustainable." See, e.g., the essays collected in Berry (2009). See also Michael Pollan's treatment of similar themes, partly inspired by Berry, in Pollan (2006, 65-84). Yet further grounds for objecting to factory farming have to do with widespread human rights abuses in industrial slaughterhouses. For two discussions of this topic, see Schlosser (2002, 149-190), Stull & Broadway (2012, 65-81.) And there are also grounds for objecting that have to do with a variety public health issues. Factory farming tolerates high rates of certain infections among farmed animals, and infected meat sickens and

now is not to explore these other criticisms but to insist on the soundness of the claim that within factory farming animals are treated as mere objects. Below I return to the different strategies for attacking the objectification of animals that I discussed in section 2, applying my earlier reflections to the case of factory farming in particular. I bring out the difference it makes whether, in attacking the objectification of animals, we adopt a traditionally naturalistic approach or instead help ourselves to broadly naturalistic categories. But before addressing this topic I want to describe how animals are also treated as mere ethically insignificant objects in some experimental settings.

4. Animal Testing

Most animal experiments in the US fall under the headings of basic research, toxicity testing (which includes testing of, e.g., pesticides, household products, cosmetics and food additives) and education. Although it is difficult to determine precisely how many vertebrate animals are used experimentally and killed each year, the number currently runs well into the millions.[26] The experimental use of these animals is in part regulated

---

kills a significant number of consumers, Schlosser (2002,193-222). Moreover, there are reasonable—but not yet fully answered—questions about the role of the constant prophylactic use of antibiotics in huge animal populations in creating antibiotic-resistance "superbugs" as well as about whether packing together genetically relatively homogeneous and frequently sick animals contributes to the development of genetically new virus strains that may then jump to human populations (e.g., the 2009 pandemic A(H1N1) influenza strain). When all of these different concerns about factory farming have been surveyed, many of which represent very real if hidden costs, and when it is also taken into account that the system is kept running by significant government subsidies, then, among other things, it seems clear that there is every reason to wonder whether the industrial farming of animals actually has the one virtue for which it is primarily lauded, viz., economic efficiency.

26 | A precise number is hard to get because there is no legislation that mandates the reporting of the numbers of mice, rats and birds that get used experimentally and because these animals in fact represent a huge proportion—some estimates place the number at over 90 %—of those employed and killed for research.

by a set of interconnected laws and policies that ask researchers to regard animal testing not as a matter of the employment of a class of mere objects but as an endeavor that in itself raises ethical questions. The emergence of this regulatory corpus, which developed gradually over the last sixty years, is a sign of a trend toward conceiving animals in the ethical terms distinctive of the common denominator view. Nevertheless, despite the existence of the trend, it is clear that many experimentally used animals are in fact treated as mere—ethically unimportant—objects. By the same token, it is clear that advocacy of the view that animals matter by itself commits us to being critical of animal testing as it is currently practiced. With an eye to showing these things, I here touch on some of the relevant US laws and policies and then make a few remarks about the practices they are intended to govern.

In 1966—largely in response to exposés of the sufferings of dogs in certain experimental settings—Congress passed the Animal Welfare Act, the first animal welfare legislation in the US concerned with animal experimentation. This law empowered the United States Department of Agriculture (USDA) to regulate the sale, transport and care of a selection of kinds of warm-blooded vertebrate animals used for research purposes. At the same time, it explicitly withheld authorization to establish requirements for how the relevant animals were treated within experiments themselves.[27] So, whereas, after the law's passage, the USDA established minimal requirements for, among other things, the humane housing, feeding, watering, sanitation, ventilation and veterinary care of the targeted animals outside the research context, it offered no guidance on their treatment inside this context. This meant that, if a laboratory satisfied the law's requirements for the handling of animals outside experiments, then there were, as far as the law was concerned, no further questions about whether the relevant use of animals was justified and, in particular, no questions that presupposed that the animals mattered or that their experimental employment was itself an ethically charged enterprise. (There was, e.g., no requirement to explore questions about whether proposed

---

27 | See the sentence of section 13 of Public Law 89-544—Animal Welfare Act of 1966 that reads: "The foregoing [standards for humane handling] shall not be construed as authorizing the Secretary to prescribe standards for the handling, care, or treatment of animals during actual research or experimentation by research facility as determined by such research facility."

procedures could be refined to be less painful for the animals involved or about whether the procedures' potential value justified the use of animals in the first place.) To the extent that the Animal Welfare Act licensed researchers to disregard these sorts of questions, it licensed them to regard the animals they were working with as at bottom nothing more than sophisticated tools or instruments that, while requiring technically correct, 'humane' handling, were in themselves ethically insignifcant.

Three years before the passage of the Animal Welfare Act, the National Institutes of Health (NIH) published what later came to be called its *Guide for the Care and Use of Laboratory Animals*.[28] Compliance with the *Guide* was and—throughout its various successive editions—has remained obligatory only for research facilities that receive federal funding.[29] At the same time, the *Guide* was and has remained significantly broader in scope than the Animal Welfare Act. Whereas from the outset the *Guide* applied to all vertebrates, the Animal Welfare Act, which, as I mentioned a moment ago, originally applied only to a select set of warm-blooded vertebrates, now applies to warm-blooded vertebrates with the exception of rats, mice and birds. This exception is noteworthy given that rats, mice and birds make up by far the larger proportion of all animals that get used experimentally, and I return to this topic below. Right now, however, I want simply to observe that, although, like the Animal Welfare Act, the 1963 NIH *Guide* focused largely on formulating standards for the humane care of animals outside the experimental context, it also established guidelines for experimental surgeries and the experimental use of anesthetics. This incursion into the research arena anticipated the direction that US law and policy concerned with animal testing would take.

With its 1985 amendment—which like the original law was largely a response to activists' efforts to expose the suffering of animals used for experimentation—the Animal Welfare Act itself got into the business of

---

28 | The NIH guide was originally called the *Guide for Laboratory Animal Facilities and Care*. In 1972, the title was changed to the *Guide for the Care and Use of Laboratory Animals* to reflect the fact, discussed below in the text, that the *Guide* had moved from primarily regulating the care of animals outside the research context to also regulating the correct use of animals in that context. For a detailed account of this development, see Carbone (2004, chs. 2, 4).

29 | With the passage of Public Law 99-158—the Health Research Extension Act of 1985, this obligation acquired the force of law.

regulating research, instructing the USDA to require animal researchers to consider alternatives to painful and invasive procedures and formulate standards for minimizing suffering within experiments.[30] The 1985 amendment also described a new enforcement mechanism. It called for the establishment by each research facility of a committee—an "Institutional Animal Care and Use Committee"—to monitor and report on compliance with the law's different specifications. The idea for such self-regulatory committees was taken from the NIH's *Guide*, which first proposed them back in 1972 (Carbone 2004, 36). The most recent edition of the *Guide* goes even further in empowering the committees to oversee the treatment of animals within experiments than does the up-to-date Animal Welfare Act. The *Guide* charges these committees with making judgments not only about refining procedures to be less painful and reducing the numbers of animals used but also about whether specific procedures are justified in light of their relevance to "human or animal health, the advancement of knowledge or the good of society."[31] The *Guide* thus issues a clear mandate for experimental practices in which animals no longer have the status of mere tools for research, and, more specifically, it does so by asking researchers to regard animal experimentation as raising ethical questions that presuppose that animals matter and that it is intelligible to talk about the costs to them of specific experimental procedures.

If animal testing by and large bore the imprint of a serious engagement with these sorts of questions, then acceptance of the view that animals matter wouldn't by itself make a person a critic. There are, however, significant limitations not only in the scope of the USDA and NIH regulations that call on researchers to address such questions but also in the agencies' mechanisms for enforcing them. The NIH's *Guide* is, as I noted, obligatory only for those facilities receiving federal funds, and, as I also noted, the Animal Welfare Act, while binding for all facilities doing animal testing, does not apply to cold-blooded vertebrates or to mice, rats or birds. This means, among other things, that non-federally funded facilities using only these animals are exempt from oversight altogether. While the USDA relies partly on a relatively small staff of veterinarians to do on-

---

30 | See Public Law 99-198—Food Security Act of 1985.

31 | The quote from the "U.S. Government Principles for the Utilization of Vertebrate Animals Used in Testing, Research and Training", which is included as Appendix D in the 1996 edition of the *Guide*.

site inspections of research facilities, it also, like the NIH, relies heavily on internal institutional committees—that is, committees drawn up by the very institutions whose research practices are in question. This emphasis on self-regulation distinguishes US from, for instance, the UK, where proposals for animal experimentation are subject to assessment and approval by external committees.[32] Moreover, although there are guidelines for the composition of the internal US committees that are supposed to ensure some independence, the requirements are weak,[33] and it has been documented that committee members' ties to the institutions they regulate prevent them from offering some criticisms that they would otherwise make (Plous & Herzog 2001).

These regulatory shortcomings would be uninteresting if researchers in fact routinely treated animals as creatures whose experimental use by itself raises ethical questions. But to a great extent things aren't like this. This is something that contemporary animal activists deserve credit for showing. Here I am not in the first instance referring to activists' efforts to bring to light cases in which, in the absence of any even putative scientific cause, researchers neglect, mock or torture animals intended for research purposes.[34] This wanton indifference to animals is shocking, and activists' documentation of it has played a role in the legislative history I have been discussing. But the behavior is also highly unprofessional, and it is characteristic of at most a minority of researchers. What I primarily have in mind here are certain much more pervasive research-oriented abuses

---

32 | For a helpful comparison of the way in which animal experimentation is regulated in the US and the UK, see Monamy (2000, ch. 5).

33 | The USDA guidelines, which differ only slightly from those of the NIH, specify that committees be drawn up by the chief executive officer of the facility in question and contain at least three members, including one veterinarian (who may be on the facility's staff) and one person with no personal affiliation to the facility who can "provide representation for general community interests in the proper care and treatment of animals." The language describing the committees' outside members has not been interpreted to mean an animal welfare activist, and most committees do not include an activist. The only restriction the law places on committees larger than three is that "not more than three members shall be from the same administrative unit" of the facility (see Public Law 99-198—Food Security Act of 1985).

34 | See Singer (1990), 80ff.

that activists have also exposed. These further abuses occur within experiments that are accepted as meeting the highest professional and scientific standards. Activists have pointed out that, in published reports of such experiments, researchers not only often openly describe how they submit animals to great pain and distress but, moreover, often do so without any suggestion of interest in questions about whether their procedures are important enough to warrant what the animals were made to undergo.[35] Accounts of these kinds of cases are significant because they draw attention to the pervasiveness within the research community of the attitude that animals are mere tools for research and that they don't in themselves matter.

The introduction of internal institutional committees has tended to temper this attitude in the research facilities that work with them (i.e., those facilities subject to USDA or NIH regulations), but even in these facilities its traces are still apparent.[36] Nor is it difficult to find unqualified expressions of the idea that animals are nothing more than experimental instruments. Here we need only turn to those laboratories that subject animals to great pain and distress in testing cosmetics and new household products.[37] Additionally, there is now a body of sociological work devoted to revealing how an understanding of animals as mere research tools is inculcated in prospective researchers in schools, universities and laboratories.[38] Insofar as this understanding of animals continues to play a significant role in shaping practices of animal testing, it is clear that advocacy of some version of the view that animals matter cannot help but put a thinker

---

35 | Ibid., pp.25-80.

36 | For a good overview of what kind of oversight the committees provide, see Carbone (2002, 181-184). Although Carbone believes that committees take their work seriously (ibid., 94), he notes that they generally focus on technical standards for reducing animals' suffering and avoid questions about the anticipated value of specific procedures. He writes: "At bottom, however, American IACUSs [i.e. *institutional committees*] are much more technical committees than ethics committees. Their work centers on reducing the costs of animals, largely regardless of any weighing of the potential benefits" (ibid., 184).

37 | Although cosmetic animal testing is now banned across the EU, it is still legal in the US.

38 | For a comprehensive discussion of the literature, see Birke, Arluke & Michael (2007).

in the position of a critic.[39] Bearing these things in mind, I return now to what is at stake in the divergence between the different strategies for defending this view that I considered earlier.

5. Different approaches to showing that animals matter

When, in section 13.2, I discussed the divergence between what I am calling traditionally naturalistic and broadly naturalistic approaches to questions of animals and ethics, my emphasis was on how advocates of the different approaches disagree about whether (as those on the traditionally naturalistic side assume) animals qua worldly beings are in themselves ethically insignificant things, or whether (as some on the broadly naturalistic side maintain) they are instead in themselves ethically significant things that we require moral insight to understand. I was particularly interested in describing a broadly naturalistic approach that obliges us to revise widely held assumptions about the nature of ethical thought about animals. The hallmark of the approach I discussed is the following combination of ideas, namely, the idea that the kind of understanding of animals that is relevant to ethics is essentially informed by our sense of what matters in animals' lives and, in addition, the idea that in order to further develop or deepen our understanding we may therefore need to refine our sensitivities. For the sake of simplicity, in the remainder of this paper, I refer to broadly naturalistic approaches and to questions of animals and ethics that are characterized by these ideas simply as broadly naturalistic approaches.[40] What interests me, to put it in these terms, is the contrast

---

39 | My comments here are consistent with recognition of significant differences among the criticisms of animal testing that animal advocates are inclined to offer. Advocates may have very different beliefs about the kinds of treatment that animals merit, with some believing that we simply need better legislation to regulate animal testing, and others simply calling for its abolition. Moreover, even to the extent that they agree about the kind of treatment animals merit, they may (and often do) still disagree about how to proceed politically.

40 | Although I adopt this way of speaking for the sake of simplicity, I am not overlooking the fact that a thinker who champions a broadly naturalist metaphysic could consistently reject both of these ideas. That is, a thinker might demonstrate

between a broadly naturalistic approach and its traditionally naturalistic competitors specifically insofar as this contrast has a bearing on how we address factory farming and animal testing.

Let me start with factory farming. Consider, to begin with, the kinds of criticisms of such farming implied by different traditionally naturalistic approaches to questions of animals and ethics. The first thing to notice is that there is a real variety here. For instance, the critiques of factory farming suggested by different moral individualists reflect the particular individual capacities that they take to be morally relevant. We might say that moral individualists object to factory farming insofar as it causes animals pain and/or interferes with their natural behaviors (e.g., by confining, crowding or killing them). Or, alternately, we might say that moral individualists are committed to holding that carnivorous practices will count as suitably benign if they don't do any of these things.[41] Turning from the work of moral individualists to the work of members of the second group of traditionally naturalistic animal advocates I discussed earlier—i.e., members of the group of Kantian animal advocates that includes Korsgaard and Wood—we find a significant change in outlook on factory farms. What is wrong with such farms, by the lights of the relevant Kantians, is not a function of any individual capacities that the animals in question possess. What is wrong is simply that animals are treated as mere objects or instruments. Indeed it is an implication of the thought of these Kantian philosophers that no alternative to factory farms will be acceptable unless it counts among its governing principles respecting animals' interests and thus treating them as ends in themselves. This Kantian standard for acceptable carnivorousness is not only different from but stricter than the

---

her commitment to broad naturalism by claiming that some things in the world are such that we cannot adequately describe them apart from reference to particular attitudes, and she might at the same time exclude animals from the class of such things (thereby rejecting both of the ideas that distinguish the sort of broadly naturalistic approach to questions of animals and ethics that I am considering).

41 | See in this connection a passage in the writings of the self-avowed moral individualist Jeffrey McMahan in which McMahan imagines with approval a form of carnivorousness that, insofar as it involves the creation of "a breed of animals genetically programmed to die at a comparatively early age, when their meat would tasted best" (McMahan 2008, 72), allows animals not only to live full and relatively pain-free lives but to die naturally.

standard that moral individualists are committed to.[42] So it is fair to speak of real differences among traditionally naturalistic animals advocates not only on the issue of factory farming but also, more generally, on the issue of eating animals.

This variety among traditionally naturalistic animal advocates, however striking, co-exists with a fundamental uniformity. Although traditionally naturalistic animal advocates appeal to different views of what is important in animals' lives in discussing factory farming and other issues, they nevertheless agree in rejecting the idea that learning what is important in animals' lives is essentially a matter of attending to the kinds of worldly things animals are. This merits emphasis because the idea that gets rejected here is central to broadly naturalistic approaches to questions of animals and ethics. Champions of these approaches maintain that there is no such thing as understanding the kinds of worldly beings that animals are in a sense relevant to ethics apart from recognizing that we have reason to treat them in specific ways.[43] This means that, according to broadly naturalistic animal advocates, the person who does not think that there is, say, any reason not to kick aside a squirrel just as one would kick aside debris is in an important respect deficient in understanding. By the same token, it means that, as broadly naturalistic animal advocates see it,

---

42 | One measure of the relative strictness of the standard implied by the thought of the Kantian animal advocates I am considering is that it excludes the supposedly 'benign' form of carnivorousness that McMahan (2008) extolls. The practice of biologically engineering animals so that they die at times convenient for us is surely a practice that fails to treat animals as ends-in-themselves.

43 | Traditionally naturalistic animal advocates are likely to want to protest that coming to see animals qua worldly beings as meriting certain forms of treatment cannot as such be learning about them. For a protest along these lines, see McMahan (2005). Within the context of traditional naturalism, coming to see a thing as meriting certain forms of treatment is a matter of acquiring attitudes that must in principle be separable from any learned content. However compelling this protest seems within the context of traditional naturalism, it loses its traction once we move to a broad naturalism. A broadly naturalistic metaphysic is a metaphysic that leaves open the possibility that some features of the world are such that it is impossible adequately to conceive them apart from reference to certain attitudes. The types of broadly naturalistic animal advocates I am discussing take this possibility to be realized in the case of animals.

the person who is not deficient in understanding necessarily sees animals as warranting respect and attention of various kinds. Bringing these reflections to bear on the case of factory farming, we can say this. If we are rightly convinced that something is horribly wrong with the treatment of animals in factory farms, then, by the lights of broadly naturalistic animal advocates, the kind of practically significant and world-directed understanding of animals that I have been discussing—and that is uniformly excluded by traditionally naturalistic animal advocates—is what grounds our conviction.

These observations put me in a position to say something about the kinds of interventions in conversations about factory farms that, for broadly naturalistic animal advocates, will count as genuinely convincing. Suppose that we ourselves are people who, despite knowing the sorts of facts about factory farms that I surveyed in section 3, do not regard what goes on there to be all that bad. How might the broadly naturalistic animal advocate convince us to change our minds? Because she believes that we require a sense of animals as ethically significant things if we are to see what is wrong with factory farming, her strategy for engaging us will include inviting us to look upon animals in an ethically non-neutral way. Bearing in mind that there are an indefinite number of ways in which the broadly naturalistic animal advocate might issue such an invitation, here's one possibility. She might give us Leonard Woolf's vivid account of the day in his boyhood on which he was asked to drown a litter of day-old puppies. Woolf tells us that, when he put one of the puppies in a bucket of water, a "terrible thing" happened. He writes:

"This blind, amorphous thing began to fight desperately for its life, struggling, beating the water with its paws. I suddenly saw that it was an individual, that like me it was an "I", that, in its bucket of water it was experiencing what I would experience fighting death, as I would fight death if I were drowning in the multitudinous seas." (Cited in Blakewell 2010, 180)

The power of Woolf's description is a function of its ability to re-create for us his experience. The description asks us to imagine the puppy and to recognize, as Woolf recognized, that a thing that struggles and beats its paws is not a mere object but a being with a life like our own in which things matter. Woolf's text is useful to the broadly naturalistic animal advocate insofar as it thus holds forth the promise of changing the way we look upon the puppy, and insofar as it thereby positions us not only to say, with Woolf, that a "terrible thing" happened to that particular creature but also to generalize our insight about it in a way that helps us to understand the brutality of factory farms.[44] Let me offer one further example of a strategy the broadly naturalistic animal advocate might use to get us to look upon animals in an ethically non-neutral way. She might draw our attention to the passage in Marilynne Robinson's novel *Gilead* in which the narrator, the Reverend John Ames discusses how as a boy he once baptized a litter of kittens. Ames discusses the episode within a letter and, in writing about it, he says that he still remembers "how those warm little brows felt under the palm of [his] hand." Then he goes on to describe how he was affected by his efforts to bless the kittens, talking about, in his words, "the sensation...of really knowing a creature...really feeling its mysterious life and your own life at the same time." (Robinson 2004, 23)[45] This passage from Robinson's novel, like the autobiographical text of Woolf's I just discussed, has a certain experiential power. It effectively invites us to remember what it is like to hold a kitten and to imagine for ourselves the—anything but ethically indifferent—mysteriousness of a kitten's existence. This is why the passage is useful to the broadly naturalistic animal advocate. It puts pressure on the way we look upon kittens and other animals, thereby giving us new resources to recognize the cruelty and callousness of what happens in factory farms.

At this point, the traditionally naturalistic thinker is likely to want to issue the following protest. From the perspective of this thinker, it appears that the broadly naturalistic animal advocate's gestures toward get-

---

44 | J.M. Coetzee's account of how, as a boy, he observed the slaughter of a sheep on his uncle's farm is in significant respects similar to Woolf's account of his experience with the litter of day-old puppies. Coetzee depicts himself as watching while two men on the farm "cut its throat then...hold tight as the animal kicks and struggles and coughs while its life-blood gushes out." Coetzee continues to watch, he tells us, as one of the men "flays the still warm body and hangs the carcass from the seringa tree and splits it open and tugs the insides out into a basin: the great blue stomach full of grass the intestines (from the bowel [the man] squeezes out the last few droppings that the sheep did not have time to drop), the heart, the liver, the kidneys—all the things that a sheep has inside it and that he has inside him too" (Coetzee 1998, 98).

45 | I am indebted to Hunter Robinson for drawing my attention to this passage.

ting us to see animals in a new light are at best accidently related to our understanding of animals. So she is likely to want to protest that these gestures cannot be essential to convincing contributions to a conversation about what is wrong with the treatment of animals in factory farms. Although I don't want to deny that this protest seems justified within the context of a traditionally naturalistic metaphysic, I want to stress that, in light of the concerns of this discussion, the protest is nevertheless misplaced. My topic right now is the broadly naturalistic animal advocate's distinctive view of ethical thought about animals. The broadly naturalistic metaphysic this thinker favors is a metaphysic on which some features of the world are such that we cannot adequately describe them apart from reference to attitudes. Within the context of this metaphysic, there is no philosophical obstacle to allowing that conversational interventions that shape our attitudes may thereby make direct contributions to genuine understanding. So, if for the sake of argument we take seriously the idea of a broad naturalism, we deprive the traditionally naturalistic animal advocate's objections to the broadly naturalistic animal advocate's methods of their apparent force.[46]

Thus far in this section I have focused on the different approaches traditionally naturalistic and broadly naturalistic animal advocates take to criticizing factory farming. But much of what I have said applies with very little alteration to the case of animal testing. There is a contrast between the approaches traditionally naturalistic and broadly naturalistic animal advocates take to criticizing animal testing that is exactly analogous to the contrast between the approaches they take to criticizing factory farms. The approaches different traditionally naturalistic animal advocates take to criticizing animal testing are various, reflecting their different views of what matters in animals' lives.[47] At the same time, these approaches resemble each other in excluding the idea, embraced by broadly naturalistic

---

46 | Foer (2009) makes abundant of emotionally charged, literary techniques in his efforts to get us to recognize the wrongness of the industrial farming of animals. The broadly naturalistic thinker might well try to show that many of these techniques, far from being mere expressive accompaniments to Foer's main line of thought, are internal to the case he makes for condemning certain practices.

47 | Whereas moral individualists are committed to criticizing laboratories that do animal testing insofar as they cause animals pain and/or restricts their natural behaviors, members of the group of Kantian animal advocates are committed to

animal advocates, that learning what matters in animals' lives is essentially a matter of attending to the kinds of worldly things animals are. Traditionally naturalistic approaches also resemble each other in excluding the thought, championed by broadly naturalistic animal advocates, that understanding the kinds of worldly beings that animals are in a sense relevant to ethics is inseparable from recognizing that we have reason to treat them in specific ways. This means that the broadly naturalistic animal advocate will be alone in thinking that if a person is rightly convinced that something is terribly amiss with the treatment of animals in, say, laboratories, then her sense of animals as in themselves ethically important beings is what grounds her conviction. By the same token, it means that she will be alone in her views about the kinds of interventions in conversations about animal testing that will count as genuinely convincing. Imagine that the broadly naturalistic animal advocate is confronted with people who know the things about how animals are used in laboratories that I discussed in section 4 and who nevertheless resist the conclusion that there is something wrong about the treatment animals receive there. Her strategy for trying to get such people to see that they have misjudged things will essentially involve inviting them to regard animal in a different light. In this connection, she might, for instance, try giving them James Marsh's 2011 documentary *Project Nim*, with its poignant portrait of a chimp who was used for language studies, or, alternately, she might try getting them to take an interest some of the pathos-filled descriptions of caged animals in the novels of W.G. Sebald.[48] However the broadly naturalistic animal advocate proceeds here, the kind of interest she takes in changing the way her interlocutors look upon animals will place her at a distance from traditionally naturalistic animal advocates. So it is worth stressing that her preferred methods for criticizing animal testing—like her preferred methods for criticizing factory farming—appear justified in the light of her preferred metaphysic.[49]

---

criticizing laboratories that do animal testing simply insofar as they treat animals as mere instruments or objects.

48 | See, in this connection, esp. the opening pages of Sebald's novel *Austerlitz* (Sebald 2001).

49 | One more comment is in order about this section's contrast between how traditionally naturalistic and broadly naturalistic animal advocates approach factory farming and animal testing. The various traditionally naturalistic approaches

6. Conclusion

This concludes my attempt to show that advocates of the different traditionally naturalistic approaches that dominate conversations about animals and ethics ought to take an interest in the question of whether the metaphysic that informs their ethical theorizing is in fact sound. My remarks about different strategies for criticizing the treatment of animals in factory farms and laboratories that do animal testing bring out how, in accepting this metaphysic, traditionally naturalistic animal advocates adopt a very specific, contestable view of ethical thought about animals. At issue is a view that treats as external to ethical thought about animals the sorts of affectively demanding exercises that broadly naturalistic animal advocates take to be essential to such thought. This is why traditionally naturalistic animal advocates should be concerned with the question of the credentials of their preferred metaphysic. An investigation of this question reveals a perspective from which these animal advocates appear vulnerable to the charge of having obscured the nature and difficulty of ethical thought, not only about factory farms and animal testing, but also about the treatment of animals more generally.

---

to this topic that I considered issue in standards for assessing not just existing factory farms and animal testing but also any other actual or potential practices with animals. It might therefore seem striking that, in discussing an alternative broadly naturalistic approach, I didn't mention any general standards. So I want to stress that it doesn't follow from anything I have said that a broadly naturalistic animal advocate couldn't consistently defend such standards and be just as hardheadedly practical and policy-oriented as her traditionally naturalistic peers. All that follows from what I have said is that, if a properly self-conscious, broadly naturalistic animal advocate did advocate a general standard for acceptable practices of eating animals, she would do so in a distinctive manner. Her posture would be that of a person who believes, not only that her confidence in her standard is grounded in her sense of what matters in human and animal life, but also that it is invariably possible that a new experience will challenge her sense of these things and oblige her to revise it and the standard that she once took it to support.

References

Anderson, E. (2004), "Animal Rights and the Values of Nonhuman Life", in: M.C. Nussbaum & C. Sunstein (ed.), Animal Rights: Current Debates and New Directions, Oxford: Oxford University Press, 277-298.

Berry, W. (2009), Bringing It to the Table: On Farming and Food, Berkeley, CA: Counterpoint.

Birke, L., Arluke, A., Michael, M. (2007), The Sacrifice: How Scientific Experiments Transform Animals and People, West LaFayette, IN: Purdue University.

Blakewell, S. (2010), How to Live, or A Live of Montaigne, New York, NY: Other Press.

Carbone, L. (2004), What Animals Want: Expertise and Advocacy in Laboratory Animal Welfare Policy, Oxford: Oxford University Press.

Carruthers, P. (1992), The Animals Issue: Moral Theory in Practice, Cambridge: Cambridge University Press.

Coetzee, J.M. (1998), Boyhood: Scenes from Provincial Life, New York, NY: Penguin.

Crary, A. (2011a), "A Brilliant Perspective: Diamondian Ethics", Philosophical Investigations 34/4, 331-352.

Crary, A. (2011b), "Minding What Already Matters: A Critique of Moral Individualism", Philosophical Topics 38/1, 17-49.

DeGrazia, D. (2009), "Moral Vegetarianism from a Very Broad Basis", Journal of Moral Philosophy 6/2, 143-165.

Diamond, C. (1991a), "Eating Meat and Eating People", in: C. Diamond, The Realistic Spirit: Wittgenstein, Philosophy, and the Mind, Cambridge, MA: MIT Press, 319-334.

Diamond, C. (1991b), "The Importance of Being Human", in: D. Cockburn (ed.), Human Beings, Cambridge: Cambridge University Press, 35-62.

Diamond, C. (2001), "Injustice and Animals", in: C. Elliott (ed.), Slow Cures and Bad Philosophers: Essays on Wittgenstein, Medicine and Bioethics, Durham, NC: Duke University Press, 118-148.

Diamond, C. (2006), "The Difficulty of Reality and the Difficulty of Philosophy", in: A. Crary, S. Shieh (ed.), Reading Cavell, London: Routledge, 98-118.

Foer, J.S. (2009), Eating Animals, London: Penguin Books Ltd.

Gaita, R. (2002), The Philosopher's Dog, Melbourne: Text Publishing Company.

Kant, I. (1996), Metaphysics of Morals (ed. M. McGregor), Cambridge: Cambridge University Press.

Kant, I. (1997), Lectures on Ethics (ed. J.B. Schneewind), Cambridge: Cambridge University Press.

Korsgaard, C.M. (2004), "Fellow Creatures: Kantian Ethics and Our Duties to Animals", in: G.B. Peterson (ed.), The Tanner Lectures on Human Values, 25/26, Salt Lake City: The University of Utah Press.

Leahy, M. (1994), Against Liberation: Putting Animals in Perspective, London: Routledge (revised ed.).

Leist, A., Singer, P. (eds.) (2010), J.M. Coetzee and Ethics: Philosophical Perspectives on Literature, New York: Columbia University Press.

Markus, E. (2005), Meat Market: Animals, Ethics and Money, Boston, MA: Brio Press.

McMahan, J. (2005), "Our Fellow Creatures", The Journal of Ethics 9/3-4, 353-380.

McMahan, J. (2008), "Eating Animals the Nice Way", Deadalus 137/1, 66-76.

Monamy, V. (2005), Animal Experimentation: A Guide to the Issues, Cambridge: Cambridge University Press.

Nestle M. (2007), Fool Politics: How the Food Industry Influences Nutrition and Health, Berkeley, Los Angeles, CA: University of California Press.

Oderberg, D.S. (2003), "The Illusion of Animal Rights", Human Life Review 26/2-3, 37-45.

Plous, S., Herzog, H. (2001), "Animal Research: Reliability of Protocol Reviews for Animal Research", Science 293/5530, 608-609.

Pollan, M. (2006), The Omnivore's Dilemma: a Natural History of Four Meals, New York, NY: The Penguin Press.

Rachels, J., (1990), Created from Animals: the Moral Implications of Darwinism, Oxford: Oxford University Press.

Regan, T. (1983), The Case for Animal Rights, Berkeley: University of California Press.

Regan, T. (2000), Defending Animal Rights, Urbana-Champaign, IL: University of Illinois Press.

Robinson, M. (2004), Gilead, New York: Picador.

Schlosser, E. (2002), Fast Food Nation, New York, NY: Penguin Books.

Scruton, R. (2000), Animal Rights and Wrongs, London: Metro Books (3rd ed.).

Sebald, W.G. (2001), Austerlitz, New York, NY: Random House.
Singer, P. (1990), Animal Liberation, New York, NY: Avon Book (revised ed.).
Stull, D.D., Broadway, M.J. (2012), Slaughterhouse Blues: The Meat and Poultry Industry in North America, Beverly, MA: Wadsworth Publishing (2nd ed.).
Wood, A. (1998), "Kant on Duties Regarding Nonrational Nature", Proceedings of the Aristotelian Society, Supplement 72/1, 1-30.

Contributors

Elisa Aaltola, PhD, works as a senior lecturer in philosophy in University of Eastern Finland. She is currently interested in themes related to intersubjectivity and representations of non-human suffering. She is the author of *Eläinten moraalinen arvo* (2004) and *Animal Suffering: Philosophy and Culture* (2012).

Colin Allen is Provost Professor of History & Philosophy of Science and Director of the Cognitive Science Program at Indiana University (USA). His work spans philosophy of cognitive science, especially animal cognition, philosophy of biology, artificial intelligence, and the digital humanities. He is the co-author with Marc Bekoff of *Species of Mind: The Philosophy and Biology of Cognitive Ethology* (1998) and with Wendell Wallach of *Moral Machines: Teaching Robots Right from Wrong* (2009), and he currently has several projects in animal cognition and intelligent computing applications for philosophy.

Kristin Andrews is Associate Professor of Philosophy and Director of the Cognitive Science Program at York University (Canada). Her work focuses on the philosophy of psychology, especially comparative and evolutionary approaches to social cognition and folk psychology. Currently Andrews is working on a book *The Animal Mind* contracted with Routledge Press, which will address philosophical issues related to animal cognition. She is the author of *Do Apes Read Minds? Toward a New Folk Psychology* (MIT Press 2012).

Marc Bekoff is Professor emeritus of Ecology and Evolutionary Biology at the University of Colorado, Boulder. He is the author of numerous professional papers and has published 22 books, including *The Emotional Lives* *of Animals* (2007), *Wild Justice: The Moral Lives of Animals* (2009), and *The Animal Manifesto* (2010).

Alessandro Blasimme is a Post-doctoral Research Fellow at the Faculty of Medicine, UMR1027 INSERM—Université Paul Sabatier, Toulouse (France). His work focuses on the moral and political philosophy of science and biomedicine. He is currently working on a project on high-throughput genomics and personalized medicine. He holds a PhD in bioethics from the European School of Molecular Medicine, University of Milan (Italy).

Lisa Bortolotti is Professor in Philosophy at the University of Birmingham (UK) and Honorary Associate at the Macquarie Centre for Cognitive Science (Australia). She specialises in the philosophy of the cognitive sciences and in bioethics. She is the author of *An Introduction to the Philosophy of Science* (Polity 2008) and of *Delusions and Other Irrational Beliefs* (OUP 2009), for which she was awarded the APA Book Prize in 2011.

Alice Crary is Associate Professor of Philosophy at the New School for Social Research, New York. Her research and teaching interests include moral philosophy, animals and ethics, philosophy and literature and also feminism and philosophy. Her recent publications include *Beyond Moral Judgment* (Harvard, 2007), "Minding What Already Matters: A Critique of Moral Individualism" (Philosophical Topics 38, 2011), "A Brilliant Perspective: Diamondian Ethics" (Philosophical Investigations 34, 2011) and "Dogs and Concepts" (Philosophy 87, 2012). She is currently completing a monograph entitled *Inside Ethics: Re-situating Human Beings and Animals*.

Gary L. Francione Board of Governors Professor Distinguished Professor of Law and Nicholas de B. Katzenbach Scholar of Law and Philosophy, Rutgers University School of Law, Newark, New Jersey, U.S.A. His work focuses on animal rights theory and legal issues pertaining to animals. He is the author of numerous books and articles, including *The Animal Rights Debate: Abolition or Regulation?* (2010) and *Animals as Persons: Essays on the Abolition of Animal Exploitation* (2008). With Gary Steiner, he edits a series on animal ethics and related issues for Columbia University Press.

Contributors

Hans-Johann Glock is Professor of Philosophy at the University of Zurich and Visiting Professor at the University of Reading. His research focuses on philosophy of language, philosophy of mind, especially animal minds, analytic philosophy, and the philosophy of Wittgenstein. His publications include *A Wittgenstein Dictionary* (1996), *Quine and Davidson on Language, Thought and Reality* (2003) and *What is Analytic Philosophy?* (2008). He currently works on a book on conceptual problems concerning animal minds.

Uriah Kriegel is an associate professor of philosophy at the University of Arizona. His work focuses on philosophy of mind and metaphysics. He is the author of *Subjective Consciousness: A Self-Representational Theory* (OUP, 2009) and *The Sources of Intentionality* (OUP, 2011).

Robert Lurz is professor of philosophy at Brooklyn College (New York). His work focuses on theory of mind and metacognition in animals. He is currently working on a project on free will in animals. He is editor of *The Philosophy of Animal Minds* (Cambridge University Press, 2009) and author of *Mindreading Animals* (MIT Press, 2011).

Klaus Petrus is Lecturer in Philosophy at the University of Berne (Switzerland). Until 2012, he was SNSF-professor of philosophy and head of the research group *meaning.ch*. He is the author of *Tierrechtsbewegung: Geschichte, Theorie, Aktivismus* (2013), has written several articles on the philosophy of language and has edited, among others, *On Human Persons* (2003), *Meaning and Analysis* (2010) and *Lexikon der Mensch/Tier-Beziehungen* (with A. Ferrari, forthcoming).

Evelyn B. Pluhar is Professor of Philosophy at the Pennsylvania State University, Fayette Campus. Her research specialty is the moral status of nonhuman animals. She is the author of *Beyond Prejudice: The Moral significance of Human and Nonhuman Animals* (1995).

Bernard E. Rollin is University Distinguished Professor at Colorado State University, and Professor of Philosophy, Professor of Biomedical Sciences, and Professor of Animal Sciences. A pioneer in animal ethics and consciousness, he is the author of 17 books and 500+ papers.

Constantinne Sandis is Professor in Philosophy at Oxford Brookes University and a Fellow of the Royal Society of Arts. He is the author of *The Things We Do and Why We Do Them* (2012) and has edited or co-edited numerous volumes including *Human Nature* (2012) and *A Companion to the Philosophy of Action* (2010). He is currently completing an introduction to the philosophy of action and beginning a monograph on action in ethics.

Justin E.H. Smith is Professor of Philosophy at Concordia University in Montreal. He is the author of *Divine Machines: Leibniz and the Sciences of Life* (Princeton University Press, 2011), and is currently finishing another book, *Nature, Human Nature, and Human Difference: Early Modern Philosophy in Global Context* (Princeton University Press, forthcoming).

Gary Steiner is John Howard Harris Professor of Philosophy at Bucknell University. He works in the areas of animal cognition and the moral status of animals. He is the author of *Anthropocentrism and Its Discontents: The Moral Status of Animals in the History of Western Philosophy* (2005), *Animals and the Moral Community: Mental Life, Moral Status, and Kinship* (2008), and *Animals and the Limits of Postmodernism* (2013).

Markus Wild is SNSF-professor of philosophy at the University of Fribourg (Switzerland). His work focuses on the philosophy of mind, especially the philosophy of animal minds. He is currently working on a project on teleosemantics. He is the author of *Die anthropologische Differenz* (2006) and *Tierphilosophie* (2008).